WITHDRAWN

The Challenges of Global Business Authority

THE CHALLENGES OF GLOBAL BUSINESS AUTHORITY

DEMOCRATIC RENEWAL, STALEMATE, OR DECAY?

Edited by
Tony Porter
and
Karsten Ronit

Published by State University of New York Press, Albany

For information, contact State University of New York Press, Albany, NY
www.sunypress.edu

Production by Robert Puchalik
Marketing by Michael Campochiaro

Library of Congress Cataloging-in-Publication Data

The challenges of global business authority : democratic renewal, stalemate, or decay? / edited by Tony Porter and Karsten Ronit.
     p. cm.
  Includes bibliographical references and index.
  ISBN 978-1-4384-3156-7 (paperback : alk. paper)
  ISBN 978-1-4384-3157-4 (hardcover : alk. paper)
  1. International business enterprises—Management. 2. International finance. 3. International cooperation. 4. Democracy. I. Porter, Tony, 1953– II. Ronit, Karsten.
  HD62.4.C433 2010
  338.8'8—dc22
                                                        2009034302

10 9 8 7 6 5 4 3 2 1

CONTENTS

FIGURES AND TABLES

PREFACE

The globalization of the economy is moving fast. Can politics catch up? Can some of the democratic practices that we, in one way or another, are familiar with in domestic politics be installed at the global level, or are new devices needed in times of change? Can we observe some mechanisms of participation, accountability, and transparency that will secure democratic input into global policy processes, or is global business authority more or less immune from such developments? Can markets still thrive under the weight of new demands propounded by governments and civic groups? And is new and global regulation simply necessary for markets to function properly? These intriguing problems are studied in this volume in which different institutional arrangements and policy fields are scrutinized.

Although these questions are highly pertinent in an era of economic, societal, and political globalization, they are particularly highlighted by the current crisis in the financial sector, the proper handling of which is relevant not only to this particular industry but also to society at large. As finance globalized, many governments enthusiastically promoted reliance on transnational business authority and self-regulation, and as these governance arrangements have so catastrophically failed there has been an unprecedented democratic debate about business authority and public accountability. The coinciding of the crisis with an American presidential election and with failures in other regulatory areas, such as food safety, further contributed to the vigor of the debate. These questions, therefore, must be attended to in the world of business, among decision makers in the public sector and by affected interests in civil society, not just in addressing current crises, but in fundamentally rethinking the relationship between global business authority and democracy.

Our ambition is to investigate the kaleidoscopic forms of business authority and examine if, how, and when these can be aligned with core democratic practices and norms, something that is neither self-evident, nor can be ruled out beforehand, and which consequently must be carefully studied. We have addressed aspects of these challenges in our previous work, as have all the contributors, and this book project is a natural continuation of our research on business and politics, and private authority, research interests that originally brought us together.

The project leading to this book started life in 2005 when we were preparing a panel sponsored by the research committee on Politics and Business at the congress of the International Political Science Association in Fukuoka, Japan, in the summer of 2006. Panels at the convention of the International Studies Association held in San Francisco, USA, in Spring 2008 gave contributors a further opportunity to discuss the role of globalization and business authority. Meanwhile electronic exchanges with each of the contributors took place to address our shared set of core problems and issues.

As editors we have also had further opportunities to meet in Chicago, Copenhagen, and Hamilton to organize our thoughts and edit the volume. We would like to thank all the contributors who have proved to be a wonderful team. Not only did they all agree to participate but they were very enthusiastic about this project, they displayed great intellectual flexibility, delivered chapters on schedule, and in the final round they were keen to address our core issues more profoundly, essential to producing a coherent volume. We have enjoyed conversations and correspondence with the contributors in ways that have not only benefited this volume, but also have inspired us to formulate new research initiatives.

Our thanks go to two anonymous reviewers who gave us some very useful suggestions for where arguments could be sharpened. Our final thanks go to the people at SUNY. We have benefited from a welcoming and positive attitude at SUNY right from the beginning and its editors have been very helpful in moving the project forward.

Tony Porter
Karsten Ronit
Winter 2009

ACKNOWLEDGMENTS

Two chapters of the book include material that appeared elsewhere and we are grateful for the permissions to include them. Chapter 2 is a revised version of Aseem Prakash and Matt Potoski, "Collective Action through Voluntary Environmental Programs: A Club Theory Perspective," *Policy Studies Journal* 35, no. 4 (2007): 773–92, reproduced with permission of Blackwell Publishing Ltd. Chapter 5 is an abridged and revised version of the article "Setting the Rules: Private Power, Political Underpinnings, and Legitimacy in Global Monetary and Financial Governance," first published in *International Affairs* 84, no. 3 (May 2008), 535–54.

1

GLOBALIZATION AND BUSINESS AUTHORITY

New Modes of Democratic Policymaking?

TONY PORTER AND KARSTEN RONIT

INTRODUCTION

There is a very long tradition of worrying about the relationship of big business to democracy. Big business has often been seen as damaging democracy by manipulating politicians and policy processes in a way that promotes its interests at the expense of the interests of citizens. Concerns about the negative impacts of international business on democracy date back a long time, for instance in discussions of the negative consequences of economic imperialism for the ability of citizens in the global south to determine their own political destinies. Today these worries are tangled up with concerns about globalization. Today the complexity of both business and democracy have increased dramatically, and the problems in their relationship to one another are challenging to diagnose and even harder to solve.

There are several possible—and very different—reactions to worries about the relationship of democracy to global business. In one way or another they all address the overarching question: Will economic globalization lead to a renewal of democratic policymaking, stalemate or decay? One reaction is to reinvigorate the state, the traditional locus of democracy, and to reverse globalization. In cases where the capacities of individual states are exhausted, intergovernmental organizations may step in, bundle resources and control business activity. Another is to deny that business has or should have anything to do with democracy and to argue that commercial activities are quite separate from political ones. A further reaction is to see global business as a general modernizing force that will wear down economic backwardness and have some positive consequences for democracy in many countries and bring these into the world economy. A final reaction is to see business as so overwhelmingly powerful that democracy is likely to be nothing more than a distant ideal for the foreseeable future.

Contrary to these, we argue that it is important to bind business to global policy processes in such a way that the interests of business and citizens more generally are aligned to the maximum extent possible. Put differently, we think that the mechanisms that have been used to try to reconcile business interests and democracy at the nation-state level need to be extended through the much more decentralized and often trans-border networks of public/private interaction that are common today. Contrary to those who see the involvement of business in exchanges with public institutions or self-regulatory arrangements as always leading to "capture" of those policymaking institutions by business, or to an increased ability of business to escape enforcement when it has distanced itself from traditional laws closely managed by the state, we see considerable potential for business to be held accountable. However since this accountability is contingent on the particular nature of the relationship between business and other actors in these decentralized arrangements, it is especially important to specify the conditions under which such accountability will likely occur, and when it will not. Contrary to those who see global business as a harbinger of democracy that will almost automatically bring democracy to countries stuck in economic and political turmoil, we emphasize that globalization will not necessarily lead to such changes. Patience may be a good thing, but efforts are needed on the side of business, civil society, and states to develop a variety of democratic practices. Contrary to those who see politics as controlled by business and see a strong alternative in the concerted efforts of civil society in the marketplace to boycott or chose particular products or corporations, we believe that government, business, and countervailing forces will create better, more durable and encompassing arrangements through negotiating institutionalized arrangements.

We need to improve on the ways we think about both democracy and business at the global level if our concepts are to be equal to this task. Today many new modes of democratic policymaking are being tested, new experiences are gained and analyses capturing these emerging features, their potentials and shortcomings, are needed. We therefore need to expand our notion of democracy beyond traditional institutions of democracy. Approaches that treat democracy as mainly about voting in competitive elections cannot deal with the vast number of ways that important policy decisions are made and implemented in places and processes. Likewise, approaches that treat business as only engaged in lobbying to leverage political decision makers tend to side-step the role of other actors and cannot give a satisfactory description of the forces behind public policy. Finally, theories on business as only exercising its influence through its abstract structural power in market and social relations are not adequate, because such political "undercurrents" fail to identify the strengths and weaknesses of particular deliberate actions of business and it is hard to identify where business poses a barrier to democratic practices, and where this is not the case.[1]

In this chapter we begin to take on these challenges. We start by discussing how our conceptions of democracy can be enriched, especially by adding key dimensions of participation, transparency, and accountability to more traditional properties of democracy. We then emphasize the importance of the three analytical levels at which global business is organized: the firm, industry, and general business levels. The chapter concludes by highlighting the major themes that run through the book, and by providing a roadmap to the rest of the chapters.

ENRICHING CONCEPTIONS OF DEMOCRACY AND GLOBAL POLICYMAKING

Democracy in any language is inevitably one of our most contested, mutable, and polysemic words and in discussing it the challenge is not to define its true or essential character. Doing that would contradict the very notion of democracy, which cannot be defined by fiat, but instead is constituted or performed in continually evolving practices. Instead, our task is to identify openings and potentials that can help these practices evolve further despite the challenges associated with the globalization of powerful business actors.

In enriching our conceptions of democracy in this section we start by setting out essential premises that indicate some ways that the range of actors, institutions, and settings that are to be considered relevant to democracy need to be expanded. After examining current thinking about globalization, business, and democracy we then argue that

democracy is best conceived as having three key dimensions of participation, transparency, and accountability, since these dimensions are
more generalizable than alternatives strongly associated with the classical plebiscitary sides of democratic practices.

Expanding the Applicability of Democracy: Some Premises

An important premise that expands the applicability of democracy is to
move beyond the national level to highlight global policymaking in the
processes that should be integrated into the practice of democracy. This
is a point made by theorists of cosmopolitan democracy such as Held
and Archibugi who have argued that the traditional focus of democratic
theory on the nation-state needs to be rethought as a result of globalization (see for instance Held 1995; Archibugi 2004). While the work of
cosmopolitan theorists is valuable, its treatment of business is lacking
because it tends to move too quickly to political "engineering" without
building upon the many and varied experiences won in and around the
business world. Nevertheless, they usefully draw our attention to the
potential of constructing new institutions and practices at the global or
transnational levels. Relatedly, other public policy literatures have
invested much energy in understanding the challenges posed to the fate
of states, their sovereignty, and national forms of policymaking. A further group of contributions grapple with the nature of international
organizations, and how difficult and problematic it is to establish democratic norms and practices, the core ones known from domestic politics,
at this level and which measures are needed to govern international
organizations (Dahl 1999; Zweifel 2006). Mindful of these challenges to
democratic practices we also need to identify emerging policy
processes and institutions unfolding at global levels rather than just
examining the impact of globalization on national policies, and recognize new processes in and around formal international organizations.

   Another premise that expands the applicability of democracy is to
expand the range of actors that are considered as involved in democratic decision making. Traditionally, citizens were seen as involved primarily by exercising their vote and electing governments. Business and
citizens also each could band together and engage in leveraging political institutions. This provided at most opportunities for an indirect
involvement in deciding on the content of laws, since this latter more
important part of rulemaking was directly controlled by elected
officials. This traditional view has already been widely challenged in
regulation and collective action theories that see business as an advan-

tageous group and that highlight the more direct role that business and other actors can play in rule making, and by political economy theories that trace more direct connections between, on the one hand, multinationals and interest groups and, on the other hand, state officials. With the ongoing globalization of business and policy making this expansive conceptualization of the range of actors involved in rule making needs to be taken even more seriously and future forms of more concerted efforts can be envisaged. As Lavelle (this volume) illustrates, for example, where previously negotiations over sovereign debt were conducted between well-defined blocs, now they involve a much more complex set of private and public actors. At the national level many mechanisms have been used successfully to involve nonbusiness actors such as labor or public interest groups to offset excessive business influence, including more traditional and more contemporary corporatist arrangements, and it is useful to explore the applicability of these at the international level (Ayres and Braithwaite 1992; Cerny 2001; Ronit 2007; Levi-Faur, this volume).

Relatedly, we also need to move beyond the traditional focus on the creation of formal law. Today there are a great many types of rules that carry out similar functions to formal law and that therefore need to be considered in discussions of democracy. Sometimes these can be quite formal and organized, even if they do not take the form of formal *law*, as is the case with many business self-regulatory arrangements. More informal rules can also be important, such as scientific models, social norms, technological protocols, voluntary standards and codes, and belief systems.

A tenor in democratic theory is the control of power, and so it is also important in analyzing democracy under contemporary conditions to move beyond traditional assumptions that power only involves the deliberate deployment of resources by one actor to modify the behavior of another actor. Notions such as other dimensions of power (Lukes 1974) that can prevent certain courses of action getting on the agenda or even being conceived, or "structural power," which relies on systemic inequalities rather than a deliberate deployment of resources, are well developed today in the analysis of power. A very useful analysis of different forms of power in global governance is provided by Barnett and Duvall (2005). However, how one democratizes structural power, or the relationship between structural power and the types of power more traditionally associated with democratic policy and legislative processes, remain very open questions that have not received enough attention. Especially considering the structural power of business we assume structural power should be considered in any analysis of business and democracy.

Current Thinking about Globalization, Business Authority, and Democracy

Many theorists have engaged in full-scale reconceptualizations of democracy that move away from traditional democratic mechanisms and sketch out a set of alternative concrete practices that are linked to particular political or social theories. "Cosmopolitan democracy" (Held 1995), "discursive democracy" (Dryzek 2006), "Empire and multitude" (Hardt and Negri 2004), and "radical democracy" (Laclau and Mouffe 1985) are examples. While some of these efforts can provide valuable inspirations and insights they are not well suited to our task because they are too philosophical to identify the significance of concrete challenges, accomplishments, and opportunities across a range of quite different intersections of global business and democracy, as represented for instance in the variety displayed in the cases explored by contributors to this volume. Similar points can be made about very broad criticisms of the negative consequences for democracy of globalization, capitalism, or the current world order (Hertz 2001; Shutt 2001; Sklair 2002).

There have also been useful efforts to specify institutional mechanisms that implicitly or explicitly address the problem of democratic deficits in global governance. For instance, Grant and Keohane (2005) point to the tension between "participation" models of global accountability in which accountability should be to those affected by institutions and rules, and "delegation models" in which accountability should be to those who create institutions and rules, and they set out seven mechanisms of accountability, some of which can be applied to corporations.[2] However, to get a better understanding of business authority and accountability we must also study how various public actors and civil society actors influence corporate decisions and how business leverages and perhaps even captures public policy (Ebrahim and Weisband 2007).

Patomäki and Teivainen (2004) present a series of concrete proposals for making global institutions more democratic, such as reforming the Bretton Woods institutions, creating a global parliament, and creating better mechanisms for global taxation and sovereign debt management. Koenig-Archibugi (2004) provides a very useful analysis of accountability mechanisms for transnational corporations. However these and other such efforts generally do not directly address the specific role of business in relationship to democracy. Either business is not the focus, or concepts such as accountability or legitimacy do not embrace sufficiently the many ways democracy is or can be evolving.

However, some thinking has already been done that is helpful in understanding specific existing and potential mechanisms to make business and democracy more compatible with one another under conditions of globalization. In this work it is useful to distinguish a range of perspectives on the role of the state that are not always compatible. Work at one end of this range stresses the unique importance of government and formal law while at the other end alternative governance mechanisms such as business self-regulation, reputation, informal norms, and discourses are also seen as very relevant. Argued very broadly, the first end of this continuum tends to be associated with more instrumental perspectives on power, law, and democracy in which citizens and other actors know their interests and tell government to make rules that promote these interests. Those at the other end tend to have a more discursive approach in which the identification and framing of interests crucially involves intersubjective interaction at all stages of the development and implementation of rules.[3]

The first perspective has, for instance, been strongly articulated by Reich in *Supercapitalism: The Transformation of Business, Democracy, and Everyday Life* (2007). Reich argues that while capitalism greatly empowers and enriches individuals in their roles as consumers, democracy and individuals' roles as citizens have been severely weakened by huge infusions of corporate campaign contributions and lobbying as firms try to gain commercial advantage by manipulating regulations and laws. He is harshly critical of efforts to get corporations to be socially responsible since he sees such efforts as distractions from obtaining the only changes that count: democratically chosen rules with the force of law. He opposes expecting corporations to be about anything but maximizing shareholder value. Slaughter (2004), while strongly welcoming the emergence of disaggregated transnational policy networks, stresses the unique role of governments and law in these and calls for this role to be strengthened to address concerns about justice and accountability. Legal scholars such as Aman (2003) have argued that administrative law, which has aimed to reconcile democracy and business regulation through the legal control of independent regulatory agencies, must be extended to the global level. In this volume May's and Smith's contributions are especially consistent with this perspective's emphasis on the need for democracy to build on citizens' relationship with the state and not to treat corporations as citizens.

A more hybrid perspective has been forcefully advocated by Braithwaite and his coauthors. Ayres and Braithwaite (1992) argue that the most effective regulation takes the form of a pyramid with the bottom representing a heavy routine reliance on self-regulation and persuasion that escalates up to a rarer command regulation with nondiscretionary punishment for particular cases where less coercive governance mechanisms fail. Tripartite arrangements with government, business, and public interest groups maximize the efficiency and public benefits of regulation. Braithwaite and Drahos (2000) stress the unique capacity of nongovernmental organizations to promote the sovereignty of citizens with regard to global business regulation, largely because of the importance the authors place on discursive factors, such as principles and models—webs of dialogue are more important than webs of reward and coercion. Similarly, Braithwaite (2006, 884) suggests that developing countries usefully address their governance capacity difficulties by developing "a 'regulatory society' model, bypassing the regulatory state," for instance by using "private bounty hunting" in which nongovernmental actors are offered rewards for detecting regulatory violations. In a different variant of this type of hybrid perspective Benner, Reinicke, and Witte (2004) argue that public and private multisector networks in global governance are best held accountable by a system that involves a mix of public and private mechanisms, including law and markets. In this volume Levi-Faur emphasizes the complementarity of private and public regulation and develops an approach that is also midway along this continuum.

Some perspectives stress the degree to which business arrangements themselves can generate meaningful enforcement pressures. Reputations and market pressures are especially important in rational choice approaches, as is explained in detail by Prakash and Potoski (this volume). If consumers are heavily involved as agents in creating value in brands, for instance with so-called Lovemarks, which "signal an emotional connection and attachment to a brand that goes beyond reason" (Foster 2007, 708), then even voluntary codes that make visible the relationship between a product and a social good to which consumers are emotionally attracted can be an effective enforcement mechanism. Also, other contributions in this volume address the role of private voluntary schemes, how useful such business initiatives can be, and how various factors impose constraints on them. Over the last years a rich literature on such arrangements has developed and their mechanisms have been studied (Ronit 2007), but only to a limited extent have their democratic qualities been thoroughly investigated.

While these differing perspectives can be identified, it must be emphasized that work on globalization, business authority, and democracy is only just beginning. This book adds to and enriches this existing valuable but relatively scarce work in several new and important ways. It pays particular attention to the significance of multiple forms of business authority, analyzing not just institutionalized levels—firm, industry, and trans-industry—but also including the structural power of business. The variation in cases and perspectives of the contributors also provide a richer opportunity to identify the complex mix of opportunities and constraints that are evident in the practical experience of the relationship between globalization, business, and democracy.

Expanding Democratic Practices: Participation, Transparency, and Accountability

In considering democracy in relationship to contemporary conditions, including the globalization of business, it is important that it be defined in a way that allows the concept to be applied in theory and practice across the range of actors, institutions, and settings that were identified above. We could define democracy very broadly, as government *by* the people, *for* the people, and *through* the people.[4] However, this is too broad and abstract for us to identify variation in particular institutional settings. For instance, supporters of international institutions such as the International Monetary Fund could argue that if those institutions exercise decision-making powers that are delegated by democratically elected governments this is consistent with democracy defined as government by the people, but this would obscure ways in which the gap between such decision making and citizens can vary in significant ways across institutions.

We adopt as an alternative the idea of democracy possessing three key defining dimensions: participation, transparency, and accountability. We define participation broadly to include all sorts of involvement in policy processes, the willingness of business and public institutions to exchange with citizens and the efforts of citizens to take part in such policy processes. Transparency refers to the ability of business and public institutions to provide relevant, reliable, and timely information and the ability of citizens to obtain accurate, relevant, and comprehensible information about policy processes. Accountability refers to the ability of business and public institutions to integrate societal concerns into their various practices and the ability of citizens to impose sanctions against conduct that fails to live up to recognized standards. These three labels have been used individually or jointly by a very wide variety of actors, including, for instance, the United Nations and various special agencies, to signal a desire to move a field of activity in the direction of democracy conceived broadly as governance by the people. These dimensions are well suited to the highly complex environments that are associated with the globalization of business, and to many new modes of democratic policymaking evolving alongside traditional institutions.[5]

Individually and together these three labels can be criticized. For instance, transparency has been fiercely criticized as excessively emphasizing the provision of information to market actors at the expense of more subtle social values such as ambiguity (Best 2005) or meaningful regulation. Accountability can be interpreted as a substitution of measurement, calculation, and technologies of control (Power 1994) at the expense of more spontaneous forms of sociality. Participation could be contrasted unfavorably to refusal or resistance by some critics.[6] Such controversies are inevitable in any discussion of democracy. Nevertheless, especially when considered together, participation, transparency, and accountability offer strong analytical advantages in their widespread positive recognition as values, in being sufficiently generic to facilitate comparison across institutional settings, and in being sufficiently concrete to support meaningful assessments of different degrees of democracy in those settings.

We do not, however, argue that these key dimensions are always intrinsically connected. Such features of democracy do not follow a simple evolutionary path where all dimensions mature in a simultaneous fashion, but we see these dimensions as cross-fertilizing each other in a variety of interesting ways—ways that must be analyzed carefully at the global level. Furthermore, the development of these dimensions does not straightforwardly lead to policy outcomes that are held as legitimate by various stakeholder groups and the general public, or provide recognized solutions to issues associated with the current globalization of business. The installment of new democratic practices is not an overall cure that necessarily leads to economic prosperity and improved policy efficiency or effectiveness. We see these new democratic practices as having an intrinsic value related to human autonomy and freedom that is more than instrumental. At the same time, each in their way can provide important building blocks in economic and social problem solving and improve the effectiveness and efficiency of governance, even if they do not always and automatically lead to the desired outcomes. This analysis of participation, transparency, and accountability should be linked to studies on regulation and global public goods (Kaul et al. 2003; de Senarclens and Kazancogli 2007) and the ambition to solve real-world problems, and consequently, it is also our task to identify where these mechanisms prove inadequate for the desired policy outcomes.

ENRICHING OUR CONCEPTIONS OF BUSINESS AUTHORITY

The Firm Level: Individual Political Actions and Voluntary Arrangements

Business is driven by particularistic economic concerns and such motivations are generally at odds with democratic principles. However, business operates according to many norms and rules produced at the level of individual corporations: Some are illegal, as for instance practices that back cartels which undermine a free market, and some are obviously detrimental to democracy, because they aim at toppling democratically elected governments. These actions are difficult to pursue due to the strengthening of normative and legal rules against them and we do not address them in this chapter, but they do exist, are occasionally reawakened, and should not be underestimated. In this book we mainly focus on those norms and rules that are widely used or are seen as legal, and are therefore potentially relevant to the development of democracy. Some may be seen as actively promoting democratic standards. The subject of these norms and rules varies enormously—from labor conditions and marketing practices to investment strategies, etc. (see, e.g., Jenkins, Pearson, and Seyfang 2002).

Some corporate practices are so informal that they are hardly recordable in any systematic fashion; such as a tolerance for internal dissent that may spill out into public debates. Others, such as human resource policies, are installed internally without informing the wider public and thus difficult to identify, and some, like codes of conduct, are made public to relevant players in the business community and other relevant interested parties or the society at large. Transparency is here recognized as an important dimension in democratic policymaking when corporations find new ways to communicate with their complex environment but the proper quality of this transparency also hinges on an enlightened and concerned public.

Analytically, we may distinguish between those norms and rules that solely emerge in the corporations (from within)—or in the industry, as will be dealt with later—those that are imposed or prompted by public institutions (from above), and those that are formulated or created through cooperation between corporations and various stakeholder groups (from below).

First, corporations have authority and discretionary rights to adopt many individual norms and rules and therefore also have a responsibility to promote democratic values (Parker 2002), but these values must be weighed against the profitability motives of corporations. They are also profoundly affected by the societies in which they operate—although a harsh reality is that some corporations seem to ignore this, and some societies are unable to seriously challenge business, in particular in developing countries. This undercurrent of societal soft-power, however, can be an important democratic mechanism influencing business and should be accounted for in a study of globalization. However, this does not suggest that social forces are always taking actively part in the formulation and implementation of private sector–based authority. Fairly often these forces are written off because they interfere with the traditional discretionary rights of corporations.

Recent years have witnessed a growing interest in these forms of corporate rule making. Corporations that were concerned about social and environmental responsibility in the past have become increasingly prolific, and corporations without prior commitments have adopted new strategies to highlight ethical aspects of their behavior. BP's rebranding of itself, as Beyond Petroleum is a well-known example, but the parading of new and social goals must be critically examined. Many initiatives have come from the corporate level but here we must distinguish between initiatives that have a distinct political dimension and are meant to forestall public regulation and initiatives that are taken independent of any public strategy.

Second, major demands and encouragements to beef up corporate responsibility toward society emerge from political institutions, showing that authority making is not merely a business-driven process and that business in some cases pays serious attention to broader accountability issues. The OECD, for instance, has taken an interest in the behavior of transnational corporations and issued guidelines to guide their global operations. In an effort to develop new forms of global governance, the much debated Global Compact has been launched by the UN General Secretary and international agencies have further developed the compact in relation to their concrete policy fields. Many corporations have taken up the challenge and now belong to the program, and the many concrete projects unfold that address labor, environmental, or human rights issues (Kell 2005; Smith, this volume).

On the one hand, this shows the professed willingness of single corporations to adopt and comply with principles that are hammered out in the public realm but at the same time require voluntary action by corporations. On the other hand, this engagement demonstrates corporate responsibility, which can be a vital asset in dealing with other firms in the production chain or with consumers or other interested parties, or to forestall stronger regulation by the state. In other words, responsible corporate performance is an important parameter in competition.

Third, initiatives emerge outside of business and outside of public institutions. Again, various mechanisms are available. Some private authority functions in business are exercised with the clear assistance of countervailing forces such as consumer groups that are invited by corporations to develop and monitor rules. This outside participation provides rule making with a much higher degree of accountability, and from a democratic perspective it is usually seen as superior to independent corporate rule making. Indeed, isolated corporate initiatives are rather viewed as guided by pure economic calculations and rarely catering to wider societal interests, although this is not necessarily a correct interpretation of all corporate strategies.

There are a number of ways that the interaction of firms with various public/private hybrids has consequences for democracy. Many corporate moves have been inspired by the UN Global Compact and similar international initiatives and have taken the form of "partnerships" involving groups with an interest in the environment, labor conditions, human rights, development, and so forth. Another mechanism of private sector authority is related to various types of standardizing, certification, and accreditation (Bernstein and Cashore 2007; Prakash and Potoski 2006), schemes—in which, however, public sector and civil society organizations can be involved and are in some cases even the driving force behind schemes. Again, corporations join these arrangements on a voluntary basis, which means that not all firms are necessarily covered in a given industry, and under these circumstances "membership" also becomes part of the competition between firms. In some legal systems, especially in the United States, private litigation is an important way that citizens use the courts to try to ensure that corporations operate in a way that is consistent with democracy (Kagan 2001). Insurance companies can constrain the antisocial behavior of firms by refusing to cover problematic activities, and auditors and ratings agencies may feel compelled to report not just activities that are illegal, but also ones that if not addressed will destroy a firm's reputational capital.

At the same time that these different practices are unfolding at the level of individual corporations, they have also been explored in scholarly work. Indeed, the study of private norm and rule making has today become a multidiscipline drawing on insights from such diverse areas as business administration, economics, law, sociology, and political science (Porter and Ronit 2006). Admittedly, these disciplines are not equally occupied with the role of corporate behavior, and not all depart from "the corporation" as their basic unit of analysis.

Especially in business administration, but also in law and economics, we find studies concerned with problems of private authority in the context of single corporations. By tradition, sociology and political science, however, are less focused on the role of individual corporations and especially their potential as rule makers, and more emphasis is on the compliance or noncompliance with public regulation, which business must respect just like any other actor. In these disciplines, as will be discussed later, greater emphasis is put on collective action, but changes are taking place leading to the scrutiny of corporate behavior. These different emphases, no doubt, have consequences for the evaluation of single corporations as rule makers. Whereas corporations are more readily accepted as authority builders in, for instance the discipline of business administration where there is a strong tradition of analyzing corporate strategy in the marketplace, we find a great deal of skepticism in the branches of political science, including international affairs, where a key concern instead lies with the conditions of democracy. In the latter traditions the alternatives of private sector authority have been juxtaposed to public sector authority and, accordingly, been regarded as weak, fragile, or even irrelevant (Lipschutz and Rowe 2005) but there are also voices that see the corporations as relevant contributors to global democracy (Haufler 2001). Some of these discussions will be returned to in the next sections.

In general, motivations for socially responsible behavior that is consistent with democratic practices include concerns about a firm's reputation and brand, legal sanctions for misbehavior, the impact on the morale and productivity of a firm's employees, the willingness of suppliers of parts and finance to deal with the firm, and the values of the managers and shareholders of the firm.

In sum, the behavior of single corporations and their role in private sector authority has received growing attention. New links between "business and politics" have thus been forged. Although corporations can play a key role in devising rules and can respond to challenges from public authority and civil society in the process of globalization, their achievements are interpreted quite differently. Some appreciate private authority at the corporate level, and see their practices as a necessary and useful innovation in global governance; others are skeptical and discount this kind of private authority, because they see such initiatives as penetrated by narrow corporate interests and because relevant civil society actors are not sufficiently powerful to control business. Therefore, individual private rule making is not considered a suitable alternative to traditional public regulation.

This does not suggest that arrangements with and without outside participation are seen in the same way. Indeed, arrangements including civic actors are generally held to be more democratic, although these are not necessarily praised as the very formula for democratic policy-making. Negotiations between single corporations and civil society actors and their participation in arrangements definitely have a democratic value but participation is only one aspect of democracy, and participation does not necessarily guarantee real influence. If corporations only exchange with weak groups in civil society without a capacity to put a sustained pressure on corporations, if groups are only involved in the early dialogue with corporations, and if obligations are few and vaguely defined, democracy is also underdeveloped. Therefore, criticism is at its strongest when private authority is unilaterally initiated, run by corporations, and outside of any public control, and weaker when civic groups are involved in more phases and issues of rule making.

Indeed, private authority in business is also established at levels above the individual corporation and it is time to turn to the industry level where rules are more encompassing and more directly embedded in other political processes. In this context, however, also single firms have a role to play—either by pioneering regulation that can eventually be extended to other firms and a whole industry or by implementing and monitoring rules that have been adopted by business associations or other collective entities.

The Industry Level: The Organizing Capacities of Industries and their Regulation

In considering the relevance of the industry level for democracy it is useful to distinguish factors that are primarily linked to the character of the industry itself, including its capacity for self-regulation, but then to also consider the relationship of the industry to the public sector and to other actors, especially civil society. In this section we look at each of these in turn.

There are several very important ways in which the self-regulation of industries has consequences that extend beyond the industry and across borders and that are therefore significant for global democracy. Industry self-regulation may be promoted as an alternative to public sector regulatory protection for citizens, and its adequacy for doing this therefore becomes a major concern. A well-known example is the Responsible Care program of the chemical industry, which, however, has been criticized for its weak implementation (King and Lenox 2000), a problem often facing many industries. Increasingly, governments are urged, for instance by the OECD, to compare the cost effectiveness of regulatory instruments, including self-regulation (OECD 1997), but often the risks that regulation seeks to mitigate are hard to measure or involve value conflicts that are best resolved through political processes rather than budgetary comparisons. Industry is often accused of wanting to regulate its own affairs to avoid public accountability. On the other hand if the same effect can be achieved by self-regulation at lower cost then it may be the best choice. In some cases self-regulation is likely to be more effective than public regulation if firms have an incentive to comply with and enforce rules (for instance to rein in rogue firms that are destroying the reputation and the viability of an industry that relies on trust) since firms may have a much more detailed knowledge of market practices than do governments, or any countervailing power. Under these circumstances a rich variety of institutions are created (Greif 2005).

At the international level where public sector capacity is especially weak self-regulation may play a larger role than at the domestic level. An example is the Equator Principles of leading banks that aspire to govern their project financing activities, a function that would typically be carried out by governments domestically (Martin 2005). Self-regulation may enhance the power of an industry in ways that allow it to promote its own interest at the expense of democratic processes, or that create threats to the well-being of citizens that are best offset by democratic initiatives. The role of the private sector Intellectual Property Committee, led by large pharmaceutical firms, in aggressively promoting the linking of intellectual property rules to trade agreements, is an example (Sell 1999).

International industries vary tremendously in their economic and social character (Hollingsworth et al. 1994; Braithwaite and Drahos 2000; Porter 2002; Porter 1985), and this has political implications that are relevant for democracy. One variation is industry structure. An industry with large numbers of small and highly competitive firms is likely to face collective action problems because of the sheer number of firms to organize and the intensity of the competition felt. At the same time, however, there is also a strong need to organize such fragmented industries. These patterns and challenges will have an impact on the way the industries seek to influence government and their capacity for self-regulation. On the other hand, industries hosting large corporations must cope with different challenges. They may benefit from the relative easiness which small groups are supposed to face in fostering collective action. However, each corporation has sufficient resources to develop and implement political strategies—sometimes their resources are superior to those of public regulators, and they are visible as market players to formulate their own codes of conduct regulating their behavior. In other words, small groups may enjoy a number of advantages in developing collective action (Olson 1965), but also the structure of regulation may typically benefit business and lead to the capture of relevant agencies (Wilson 1980). However, other factors must be accounted for as well.

The retail/wholesale distinction also has relevance for democracy, and different patterns exist across industries (Vogel 2006). For instance incentives for compliance with corporate codes of conduct are more easily produced in retail industries such as cafés or apparel, in which business meets end consumers, when there is concerted action on the consumer side. At the same time this collective action on the consumer side is not facilitated just against the backdrop of the character of the purchased goods. It is also important whether the relevant goods have such a strategic character, for instance the money spent relative to the overall consumption, that it is really worthwhile to engage in concerted action.

Industries with high negative externalities (the degree to which the effects of an industry's activities are not reflected in the prices of its products but instead are imposed without compensation on citizens), such as chemicals, are likely to have democratically inspired regulation, unlike others with low externalities, such as bicycles. At the same time it may be much more complicated to countervail the powers of the chemical industry, which has a strong tradition of associability and superior resources.

Some industries have very particular significance for democratic processes. The news media business has long been recognized as such an industry. Developments in other industries, such as hand-held video cameras and Internet technologies that support alternative media, have fostered democracy, while the cooperation of Yahoo and other search engine firms with China has provoked concern. The roles of large firms in providing electronic voting systems based on proprietary technologies that are not transparent to the public are another more recent and highly controversial example. Diebold's systems, for instance, have been seen by many as vulnerable to manipulation. Diebold provides election systems throughout the United States and elsewhere, including for 109 million voters in Brazil's 2000 election.[7] Industries producing surveillance and military technologies that can be used to suppress dissent are also especially relevant to democracy.

The relationship between industries and public sector actors can vary tremendously across the different stages of the rule-making process. It is recognized that public agencies can be attributed a formal role in private authority, from establishing rules to policing arrangements. Various conflicts arise over how the public sector can best make business arrangements accountable to wider interests outside of business.

For instance, in air traffic, the International Civil Aviation Organization (ICAO), as an intergovernmental organization, has for obvious reasons always been concerned with safety matters, a focus that has grown even stronger since terrorism has become a top priority issue. However, public regulation has here been assisted by private regulation in the stages of implementation where the International Air Transport Association (IATA), as the organization of airline companies, has followed up those of ICAO at the same time that it has devised its own rules. In other words, we find a division of labor between public and private organizations in the global realm (Ronit 2005). As mentioned above, however, the coordination is not always fine-tuned, and disagreement occurs. Conflicts between public and private bodies can, for instance, also be found in the regulation of drugs. Between the World Health Organization (WHO) and the drug producers represented through the International Federation of Pharmaceutical Manufacturers and Associations (IFPMA) there has been disagreement as to who should work out rules. Consequently, in the relations between pharmaceutical companies and health professionals, two sets of regulations apply. In some ways they complement each other, and in other ways they compete with each other.

In a somewhat similar vein, different rule systems have emerged to combat doping in sports. As a private organization, the IOC has for decades enforced a medical code, and a huge system including national committees and accredited laboratories has been installed for its implementation. Doping has become a growing problem, and not every effort launched to combat it by the International Olympic Committee (IOC) has been crowned with success. Accordingly, a number of governments and intergovernmental organizations have seen a need for a new arrangement, and through negotiations with the IOC they have contributed to setting up a new independent agency, the World Anti-Doping Agency (WADA), replacing the old organization and code, and working outside the domain of traditional public agencies but with a clear public input and with new rules of operational transparency.

These cases illustrate the intervening role of public agencies in the processes of private authority building. Yet, public actions vary considerably, and an important factor is the degree to which public institutions act independently or to some extent support business interests or function as a kind of proxy representing civil society. Indeed, civil society interests can sometimes be much more forcefully voiced through public institutions; on the other hand, there is the possibility that civil society organizations and social movements may become formally involved in private authority.

Spontaneous initiatives, social movements, and more established civil society organizations use their leverage to put pressure on governments and international organizations to influence private behavior and rule making at the industry level. (Doh and Teegen 2003). Most interestingly, many civil society actors tend to distinguish between two governance structures: on the one hand "markets" where individual corporations rule, and on the other hand public authority where states and intergovernmental organizations are decisive. In this context, the activation of public authority is viewed as the appropriate means to rebut corporate power and establish a more just global economy. Nevertheless, if civil society actors become involved in holding industries accountable and helping disseminate information then this can enhance participation, transparency, and accountability.

However, we must distinguish between two sorts of non-industry involvement that more authentically bring interests into the very administration of industries. First, to make the many different forms of industry organization viable the participation of professional expertise is relevant. Experts often represent other branches of business, whose primary job it is to provide services and function as a kind of auxiliary to the regulated industry, although the regulation of a profession can be an independent goal (Dezalay and Sugarman 1995). Second, to provide private authority with a sufficient degree of legitimacy, the participation of civil society actors becomes relevant. This participation acknowledges the role played by major stakeholder groups whose interests are affected by private authority. Usually these actors have a qualitatively different role than the experts because they provide stronger criticism and because they are seen as representing major societal interests, and it is exactly in this capacity that they can solidify private authority. In the evolution of private authority it is also likely that civil society actors will become more professionalized. Under these conditions private authority can become an effective democratic complement to public regulation and not merely a sub-optimal solution with fewer democratic qualities.

The General Level: Trans-industry Business Action and Policy Processes

Scholarly work has often sidestepped issues of concerted business action at the global level. Part of the discussion has been phrased in terms of "capitalism" or social class, which are to some degree faceless actors. One avenue of research has investigated the existence of different capitalisms, for instance, models that have evolved at national levels (Levi-Faur and Jordana 2005; Crouch and Streeck 1997), and many different experiences in business, state, and society are synthesized under these "capitalisms." Some studies take a particular interest in the capitalisms of big states and are thus linked with the approach briefly sketched above, but a range of other national models can be analyzed from this perspective, in which the key challenge is to analyze capitalisms comparatively. In the context of our study, however, it would be problematic to neglect the internal and global superstructure of business, and helpful to investigate how these capitalisms may feed into the coordination of business beyond nation-states.

Another line of analysis scrutinizes the role of powerful states, historically the major powers and today the United States, which have been seen as proxies and alternative vehicles for international business and the private character of business action has been obscured. Efforts to analyze the general behavior of business in global politics could be significantly strengthened, although global business is characterized by considerable fragmentation. Considering the huge influence that business is assumed to exercise over our contemporary world it is surprising how few associations claim to speak for global business as a whole. Although different forms of coordination exist through trade associations and informal networks, the existence of only relatively few predominant business associations has been seen as a weakness of business (Kellow 2002).

These associational features, of course, also shape the conditions for business to enter into dialogue with various stakeholder groups and to negotiate arrangements in which democratic assets such as participation, transparency, and accountability are attended to. Indeed, the lack or weakness of countervailing representation is also a major barrier for institutional innovation.

The association that could reasonably be said to make good on the claim of being a general business association is the International Chamber of Commerce (ICC). According to the ICC's self-portrayal, it is "the world's only truly global business organization." The ICC does play an important role, for instance in issuing general policy briefs to promote business interests in the Doha Round of trade negotiations, or resolving business disputes under the ICC International Court of Arbitration. It works in sixteen policy areas, ranging alphabetically from anticorruption to transport and logistics. As a careful examination will reveal, its work is surprisingly limited relative to the huge and ever-increasing visibility of international business activities, but in those areas where it is actually active it has a strong tradition of rule making. This activity, however, is not something that includes civil society participation, and there are risks that business develops rules that are kept in isolation from public scrutiny and still seeks to present these as serving the public good (Underhill 1995).

While none matches the ICC in its aspiration to be "the voice of world business" there are other types of business association that—with declining encompassingness— operate at the peak level, although each is limited in certain respects. Ad hoc high-level trans-industry groups oriented toward particular policy goals exist, for instance, in the financial sector. This sector is a cluster of industries that can be analyzed in their own right, but they also underpin many other industries and provide an essential infrastructure for the operation of business across industries. Hence, it is no surprise that the financial sector has been thoroughly investigated, and that it has generally been concluded that such democratic qualities as participation, transparency, and accountability have been weakly developed in relation to finance and in relation to those international agencies that regulate this part of business (Porter 2005, ch. 9).

Another form of trans-industry organization relates to patent issues. The Intellectual Property Committee was instrumental in getting the Trade Related Intellectual Property provisions of established in the Uruguay Round (May and Sell 2005). This can take a form that is more network than formalized, such as the collaboration between the U.S. Coalition of Service Industries and the European Services Forum or the Services World Forum and the World Business Council for Sustainable Development.[8]

General, informal high-level meetings about the future of the world dominated by business interests, such as those held under the auspices of the World Economic Forum or the Trilateral Commission, are also important. These organizations are not merely social gatherings but also have a part to play in formulating major political strategies, and they bring together political decision makers and representatives of civil society. How much such exchanges lead to the creation of new modes of democratic policymaking is still uncertain, however.

Also relevant are private global standard-setting bodies influenced by business interests, such as the International Organization for Standardization (ISO), which has been concerned with the necessity for accountability, not only to the business world but to society more generally, and which formally involves consumer participation, or the International Accounting Standards Board. Business associations can also represent "coordination services firms" that by virtue of the role they play in organizing and controlling business activities can be said to influence business as a whole, for instance, the International Federation of Accountants and Transparency International. Business-oriented multi-issue think tanks such as the Group of Thirty (Stone 2004; Tsingou 2006) have an impact on policy.

National business associations can exercise a global influence because they are headquartered in a powerful state—for example, the U.S.-based Business Roundtable—and represent significant economic interests. Some regional bodies also have international and global relevance when they coordinate policies. The Transatlantic Business Dialogue, bringing together European and North American business interests in one forum, is also important and has political significance beyond the two originating regions. This initiative has also led to the creation of another organization, The Transatlantic Consumer Dialogue, representing consumers, which has become involved in a number of new policymaking forums.

There are some indications that these peak international business groups have increased in significance over the past decades, as one might expect given the prominence of business in globalization. For instance, a number of the organizations are not especially old: the World Economic Forum was formed in 1971, the Trilateral Commission in 1973, the Group of Thirty in 1978, the Coalition of Services Industries in 1982, the European Roundtable in 1983, the Services World Forum in 1986, and the Transatlantic Business Dialogue in 1995. This suggests that these associations are increasing in number over time and also that they enjoy an increasingly public profile. There are signs that individual peak associations have grown in organizational capacity over time as well. Some have expanded their membership (Carroll and Carson 2003, 54).

General business associations and other formats of business collective action at the global level show different dispositions toward engaging with interested parties in civil society and toward developing new democratic practices. Some are of a genuine elite character, while others are open to dialogue and negotiation, and we seek to answer how these variations can be explained.

However, at the most general level a key concern about business and democracy is its structural power. Although general globally oriented business associations, which can be labeled as expressing "behavioral power," are surprisingly few, business can enjoy other forms of structural power in ways that underpin political action or make this redundant. This also has some consequences for democracy.[9]

One is the dependence of governments and society on business to generate economic growth, which leads to deference to the interests of business, a view found in Marxist-inspired research and beyond. The key role and "privileged" position of business are seen from various angles but a major tenet is that government agendas are linked to the economic resources of corporations, which provide society with prosperity (Lindblom 1977). Developed primarily to explain domestic policy processes, this perspective can also be extended to the international realm. In a somewhat similar vein it can be argued that the world economy depends on corporate initiative and growth, and especially that the major international organizations in finance and trade are generally seen as privileging business interests.

A second form of structural power is the tendency of business to play one jurisdiction off against another by leaving if government policies do not suit business interests (Gill and Law 1989). This may involve an intentional exercise of power by a particular multinational corporation, or it may involve business decisions that are triggered by considerations of profitability with no conscious political intent, but in either case the capacity of business to exit is based on available structural features of their operating environment, such as legal and technical systems that facilitate capital mobility. At that moment in time these structural features do not require deliberate general business political action to bring them into being. Under these circumstances transparency may be very limited, and hence it is difficult to mobilize and coordinate other interests against business at the global level.

A third form of structural, albeit quite elusive, power is the compatibility of strong business-friendly cultural and institutional tendencies. These tendencies include individualism, consumerism, an orientation toward growth, the personal accumulation of wealth, and hostility to the public sector. These cultural tendencies are in part fostered by business across different industries, for instance, with the capacity to exit; they are structural in the degree to which they carry on without the deliberate intervention of business. These features vary enormously across territory and are discussed in the "varieties of capitalism" literature (Hall and Soskice 2001), but they also impact on the global actions of business and consequences for democratic policymaking.

The direct action and symbolic reframing of social movements, which like the structural power of business fall outside the policy processes that we most typically associate with democracy, represent one way that the structural power of business and markets can be countered. Direct action and reframing can challenge structures of practice or thought that otherwise might arbitrarily limit democratic options because they are so routinely handled they are assumed to be necessary.

Public institutions can sometimes be very business friendly, or at least structurally favor business interests as discussed earlier, but there is also the possibility, that some institutions or concrete initiatives are heavily backed by civil society actors. Civil society actors do not always have the power themselves to pressure industries and therefore need alliances with governments and intergovernmental organizations to boost their countervailing force. Elsewhere in the literature it has been argued that advocacy groups can form epistemic communities with public institutions (Haas 1992), and in the context of business authority and democratic policymaking these communities can become an effective counterweight to business power, voluntary corporate schemes, and the private regulation adopted by industry associations.

Although the structural dimension is important, it is crucial not to limit any analysis of business to the dimension of structural power because it cannot supplant manifest business action. First, industry is often divided or constrained by competitive pressures but also by different challenges that make political action more or less relevant, and coordination more or less required. This gives rise to action at different levels of business, as illustrated above. Thus, business political action can both be interpreted as a choice between different models, and something that produces conflicts, and as an appropriate division of labor. Second, structural forms of power are not all-pervasive. Public institutions must also cater to the public good, and we should not ignore the many experiences we already have with the institutions of private sector authority where corporate behavior is coordinated and to varying degrees is inspired by societal values or by effective public regulation. Indeed, this coordination has become a widespread and important practice in many policy fields and in many areas of business activity, and, in turn, these new modes of policymaking and their implications for democratic policymaking must be analyzed. When opening up the box of private authority, we see that many forms are influenced by public institutions, and combinations of private and public institutions and resources occur (Koenig-Archibugi 2002).

CONCEPTUALIZING DEMOCRACY AND GLOBAL BUSINESS: AN OVERVIEW OF CHAPTERS

In this chapter we have suggested areas in which to expand our conceptions of democracy and global business in order to facilitate analysis of their relationship to one another. Traditional conceptions of democracy that focus on classical national institutions and procedures can inspire us but they are far too restricted to be able to address the complex challenges that global business poses for democracy. We need to expand the range of actors, institutions, and settings that we consider in analyzing democracy. We have argued for a focus on participation, transparency, and accountability as a way to identify key properties of democracy that facilitate comparative analysis and political practice across the complex and diverse spaces where global business and issues relevant to democracy overlap. We have argued for the importance of looking concretely at the way that business organizes itself at the firm, industry, and trans-industry levels, and how these may be linked to the structural power of business. In contrast to approaches that treat business more abstractly or in a less differentiated fashion, this disaggregation is important in identifying specific challenges and opportunities for bringing global business and democracy into closer alignment.

Our task in the remainder of the book is to see if the promise of this richer and more differentiated conceptualization of democracy and business can be fulfilled, and consequently whether these processes will lead to democratic renewal, stalemate, or decay. Our discussion so far has provided many examples of ways that the concord and conflict between democracy and global business may vary widely, and we have provided tools to analyze this variation systematically, recognizing that the advancement of democratic principles and practices is very uneven, piecemeal, and without a straight course. However, our examples have only hinted at the many insights that the remaining chapters will provide. Throughout this book this variation will be identified and diagnosed, and new insights, criticisms, and solutions to the problem of democracy and global business will be set out. The book is divided into three sections, although the chapters also address issues that cut across the three sections.

The first section addresses the role of single firm actions and pays special attention to voluntary arrangements. In their various forms, including self-regulation, private standards, codes of conduct, and the idea of corporate social responsibility in general, these have been very controversial, and this is reflected in the different perspectives that our contributors present. Aseem Prakash and Matthew Potoski draw on club theory, a rational choice approach, to show why private authority certification regimes such as ISO 9000 and ISO14000 or the Forest Stewardship Council can meaningfully alter the behavior of firms to serve social purposes. As the authors argue, some forms of business authority may further global accountability. Voluntary clubs can create mechanisms that allow markets to identify and differentiate between firms' compliance with social standards, and since firms value positive brand reputation this can very effectively pressure firms to align their interests and practices with the types of public interests that democracy is intended to promote. This confluence of the inclusion of noncommercial public interests, enhanced information flow, and sanctioning capacity resonates with participation, transparency, and accountability, the three dimensions of democracy identified by this book.

The chapter by Doris Fuchs and Agni Kalfagianni points to concerns about voluntary arrangements in their examination of private rules that have been created by food retail corporations to govern food quality in the global food system. With the help of the criteria of participation, accountability, and transparency the chapter evaluates three frequently discussed concepts of democratic legitimacy: input legitimacy, output legitimacy, and deliberative democracy. In developing and applying these concepts to global food governance, the chapter finds that private standards are deficient and need to be more strongly linked to public forms of authority if democratic legitimacy in this issue area is to be ensured. Fuchs and Kalfagianni highlight the problem of structurally powerful firms using rules effectively to enforce compliance in ways that have not been democratically legitimated.

In contrast Jackie Smith's chapter is critical of the ineffectiveness of one of the highest profile examples of a voluntary arrangement, the United Nations Global Compact. Architects of the United Nations Global Compact argue that this "learning network" will encourage transnational corporations to adhere to international norms. She argues that the failure of the Global Compact to address power imbalances among global actors limits its ability to bring corporate practices in line with global human rights and other norms. More importantly, the Global Compact marginalizes civil society actors in ways that undermine the legitimacy of the global institutional order. Her chapter highlights the importance of bringing the structural power of business into assessments of voluntary arrangements and of examining the specific relationships between business and other actors in any voluntary arrangement.

The second section examines the implications for democracy of the relationship between business and public sector rules at the level of industries. These include rules that constitute firms such as corporation law, rules that regulate the commercially relevant conduct of firms and others, such as intellectual property rights and rules that regulate firms in a particular industry. These various public sector rules do not target specific firms but instead interact with business at more encompassing levels. The industry has often been the most important of these levels, but certain issues, such as intellectual property or corporation law can involve a subset of all industries or cut across all industries.

Geoffrey R. D. Underhill and Xiaoke Zhang analyze the financial industry. Their chapter argues that the failure of the debate over the global financial and monetary governance to address directly its political underpinnings has led to crucial deficiencies. They devote specific attention to international banking and securities regulation. The external constraints of the global financial system are in tension with a range of potential domestic, particularly democratic, political imperatives. Global financial integration encouraged by developed states has strengthened the hand of private interests in the policy process, further constraining the definition of the public interest in a democratic context. As well as identifying problems with participation, transparency, and accountability, developing these conceptually, and linking these to legitimacy, the chapter also advances prerequisites for righting these problems.

Susan K. Sell's chapter studies the pharmaceutical industry and shows that it engages with practices relevant to democracy across multiple levels and jurisdictions. Often this has resulted in outcomes that primarily favor pharmaceutical corporations at the expense of other actors, including citizens in general, but these multiple-level contestations have also asserted the interests of these other actors in ways that are consistent with democracy. Corporations such as Pfizer, Merck, and Bristol-Myers Squibb, sometimes working individually and sometimes collectively, played a major role in promoting intellectual property protection through the United States Trade Representative's office, through horizontal forum shifting (e.g., from the World Trade Organization (WTO) to the World Intellectual Property Organization to the World Health Organization), but also in vertical forum shifting, from multilateral to regional and bilateral negotiations. Recently this vertical approach has included directly suing developing country regulatory authorities in their personal capacity, and even making direct appeals to patients on pricing controversies. However, a variety of actors have also successfully resisted these corporate initiatives.

Christopher May examines the political narratives that corporations rely on to justify their ownership of knowledge on the basis of the encouragement of (individualized) human intellectual enterprise. The corporation's legal personality is a form of structural power with important implications for democracy. He argues that corporations should not be treated like individual citizens with inviolable rights. Instead, if business interests and democracy are to be brought into alignment we need to reassert the original logic of the corporate legal form, namely a grant of authority by the state to carry out certain public purposes. He examines these issues with reference to intellectual property rules where a Janus-faced myth of rights holding and legal corporate personality distorts the intended policy outcomes of those rules.

The third section focuses on business in more encompassing and trans-industry contexts and on public policy processes occurring at the global level. On the public sector side these processes involve a mix of formal intergovernmental organizations, interstate negotiations, and complex new regulatory arrangements. In each of these, private actors are active, also in different levels and forms, and we gain insights into how business interests more broadly are advanced at global levels.

David Levi-Faur explores the significance for democracy of the emergence of new forms of governance where regulation represents the expanding part of government, and where the various modes of governance compete and sometimes are synthesized into global forms of regulation, best described as "regulatory capitalism." State and civil regulation are becoming increasingly important, and different varieties of regulatory capitalism are produced by the interaction of these two types of regulation and variations in the composition of the networks that serve as the backbone and that transform autonomous jurisdictions to interdependent ones. He argues that regulatory corporatism offers the most promise for reconciling globalization, business authority, and democracy.

The chapter by Aynsley Kellow and Hannah Murphy explores the manner in which the character of intergovernmental organizations affects which types and configurations of actors participate and the formation of cooperative or antagonistic relations between nation-states and representatives of business and civil society. In doing so, the chapter seeks to improve our understanding of how these characteristics translate into incentives and constraints that affect the constitution and participation of groups in global governance, which, in turn, has important consequences for transparency and accountability in global governance. They compare four organizations that have been lightning rods for those concerned about democracy and globalization: the World Bank, the International Monetary Fund (IMF), the World Trade Organization, and the Organization for Economic Cooperation and Development.

Kathryn C. Lavelle's chapter compares the way developing states have expressed their interests in shaping the management of sovereign debt in two historical periods. The participation of developing states in shaping their interactions with global financial markets in a setting characterized by power asymmetries is a crucial issue for reconciling globalization, business, and democracy. In the first period, in the late 1970s, governments negotiated among themselves in blocs within the United Nations Conference on Trade and Development framework. In the second period the IMF's statutory proposal for a Sovereign Debt Restructuring Mechanism was debated among states, the New York financial community, the IMF, and NGOs. Lavelle shows how the participation of developing states in this issue area has become more complex and has involved more actors, without necessarily becoming more democratic.

Finally, in the concluding chapter, Tony Porter and Karsten Ronit sum up the findings of the nine chapters and discuss where business creates, conserves, or blocks new forms of democratic policymaking. Why are some corporations and some industries more inclined to engage in such activity than others, and in which areas does business develop new institutions, conserve existing ones, or avoid change? By answering this question we will get a picture of globalization that recognizes the extremely complex character of business and that moves beyond seeing business as a uniform category. By differentiating between various aspects of democracy we also recognize that democracy can develop in different ways and degrees in different business settings. These new global mechanisms, in turn, can be more or less connected with traditional democratic politics. In other words, the introduction of democratic practices of participation, transparency, and accountability is neither wholeheartedly implemented nor rejected. This variation can best be understood if a range of theories of globalization, business, and democracy are integrated. Thus, our synthesis builds upon theories that seek to operationalize democracy and business.

NOTES

1. In this book we emphasize the importance of the structural power of business, but we also wish to understand the agency and contingency of business actors and others. Therefore, here we are noting the failure of some approaches to handle the structure-agent problem adequately.
2. They see market, peer, and reputational mechanisms as especially relevant to firms although where business is involved in hybrid public/private arrangements the other four (hierarchical, supervisory, fiscal, and legal) may also be relevant to business accountability.
3. Risse (2004) usefully applies his distinction between rational choice-based logics of consequences, sociological logics of appropriateness, and a third logic of arguing—a strategic proffering and

evaluation of justifications for action—a tool of "soft steering" to the
issue of democracy and global governance.

4. It should be noted that our interest is in both the "input" side of
   rule making, also sometimes called the procedural dimension, and
   the "output" side, sometimes called the substantive dimension. The
   first primarily concerns the question of whether public and private
   rule makers listen to business to an extent that is harmful for their
   attentiveness to the needs of citizens. The second primarily concerns the effects of rules once they are implemented: Is business
   regulated in such a way as to ensure that its activities are not
   unduly harmful to the public or private interests of citizens, and are
   rules imposed on citizens too focused on the interests of business?
   "Input" and "output" are obviously closely related, especially in
   global public and private policy arrangements in which the same
   actors, in promoting best practices, are simultaneously creating and
   implementing rules. On the procedural/substantive distinction see
   Franck (1995).

5. For other useful approaches to operationalizing democracy beyond
   the state level in a way that allows it to be addressed and compared across multiple levels and settings, see Benz and Papadopoulos (2006) and Dingwerth (2004). The three criteria we have set out
   are more parsimonious than those set out by Benz and Papadopoulos and therefore better suited to the type of comparative analysis
   this book undertakes. Dingwerth's emphasis on participation, democratic control, and legitimacy through discursive practice is close
   to our emphasis on participation, accountability, and transparency.

6. On resistance see Amoore (2005). In his discussion of global civil
   society Scholte distinguishes between *conformists* and *reformists*,
   who are willing to participate along with officials in policy networks and *radicals* who are not. In this book we are defining
   participation widely to include resistance, but nevertheless participation might be seen from the radical perspective as overemphasiz-
   ing the possibility of compromise.

7. See http://www.diebold.com/dieboldes/solutions2.htm. For Diebold's response to criticisms on the internet of its voting system see
   http://www.diebold.com/dieboldes/pdf/rebuttal.pdf. For commen-
   tary on electronic voting in Venezuela, India, and Australia see
   Robert Lemos, "Global Lessons in E-Voting," *CNET News.com,* 30
   September 2004.

8. See for instance the letter signed by these two organizations promoting their view on services in the Doha round of trade negotiations, at www.esf.be/pdfs/ESF%20CSI%20joint%20letter%20to%20

Lamy.pdf. For information on the Services World Forum see www.ucd.ie/sirc/swfintro.html.

9. Agenda setting, or what Bacharach and Baratz (1970) called the "second face of power" blends elements of behavioral and structural power. Barnett and Duvall (2005) distinguish four types of power. In addition to the traditional Weberian "compulsory" power they also identify institutional power, structural power, and productive power. This last is close to the notion of discursive power as used by Fuchs and Kalfagianni (this volume). For present purposes it is sufficient to just distinguish between intentional and structural power while being clear that these interact with one another. We use structural power in its broadest sense to include the institutional and productive variants distinguished by Barnett and Duvall.

REFERENCES

Aman, A. C. Jr. 2003. Globalization, democracy and the need for a new administrative law. *Indiana Journal of Global Legal Studies* 10: 125–55.

Amoore, L. 2005. Introduction: Global resistance—global politics. In *The global resistance reader,* ed. Louise Amoore, 1–11. London: Routledge.

Archibugi, D. 2004. Cosmopolitan democracy and its critics: A review. *European Journal of International Relations* 10, no. 3: 437–73.

Ayres, I., and J. Braithwaite. 1992. *Responsive regulation: Transcending the deregulation debate.* New York: Oxford University Press.

Bacharach, P., and M. Baratz. 1970. *Power and poverty: Theory and practice.* New York: Oxford University Press.

Barnett, M., and R. Duvall, eds. 2005. *Power in global governance.* Cambridge: Cambridge University Press.

Benner, T., W. H. Reinicke, and J. M. Witte. 2004. Multisectoral networks in global governance: Towards a pluralistic system of accountability. *Government and Opposition* 39, no. 2 (Spring): 191–210.

Benz, A., and Y. Papadopoulos, eds. 2006. *Governance and democracy: Comparing national, European, and international experiences.* London: Routledge.

Bernstein, S., and B. Cashore. 2007. Can non-state global governance be legitimate? An analytical framework. *Regulation & Governance* 1, no. 4: 347–71.

Best, J. 2005. *The limits of transparency: Ambiguity and the history of international finance.* Ithaca: Cornell University Press, 2005.

Braithwaite, J. 2006. Responsive regulation and developing countries. *World Development* 34, no. 5: 884–98.

———, and P. Drahos. 2000. *Global business regulation.* Cambridge: Cambridge University Press.

Carroll, W. K., and C. Carson. 2003. The network of global corporations and elite policy groups: A structure for transnational capitalist class formation? *Global Networks* 3, no. 1: 29–57.

Cerny, P. G. 2001. From "iron triangles" to "golden pentangles?" Globalizing the Policy Process. *Global Governance* 7: 397–410.

Crouch, C., and W. Streeck, eds. 1997. *Political economy of modern capitalism: Mapping convergence and diversity.* London: Sage.

Dahl, R. 1999. Can international organizations be democratic: A skeptic's view? In *Democracy's edges,* ed. Ian Shapiro and Casiano Hacker-Cordon, 19–36. Cambridge: Cambridge University Press.

Dezalay, Y., and D. Sugarman, eds. 1995. *Professional competition and professional power. Lawyers, accountants, and the social construction of markets.* London and New York: Routledge.

Dingwerth, K. 2004. Democratic governance beyond the state: Operationalising an idea. Global Governance Working Paper No. 14, December. Global Governance Project.

Doh, J. P., and H. Teegen, eds. 2003. *Globalization and NGOs: Transforming business, government, and society.* Westport and London: Praeger.

Dryzek. J. S. 2006. Transnational democracy in an insecure world. *International Political Science Review* 27, no. 2 (April): 101–19.

Ebrahim, A., and E. Weisband, eds. 2007. *Global accountabilities. Participation, pluralism, and public ethics.* Cambridge: Cambridge University Press.

Foster, R. J. 2007. The work of the new economy: Consumers, brands, and value Creation. *Cultural Anthropology* 22, no. 4: 707–31.

Franck, T. M. 1995. *Fairness in international law and institutions.* Oxford: Clarendon.

Gill, S., and D. Law. 1989. Global hegemony and the structural power of capital. *International Studies Quarterly* 33 (December): 475–99.

Grant, R. W., and R. O Keohane. 2005. Accountability and abuses of power in world politics. *American Political Science Review* 99, no. 1 (February): 29–43.

Greif, A. 2005. Commitment, coercion, and markets: The nature and dynamics of institutions supporting exchange. In *Handbook of new institutional economics,* ed. C. Ménard and M. M. Shirley, 727–86. Dordrecht: Springer.

Haas, P. 1992. Introduction: Epistemic communities and international policy coordination. *International Organization* 46 (Winter): 1–35.

Hall, P. A., and D. Soskice, eds. 2001. *Varieties of capitalism: The institutional foundations of comparative advantage*. Oxford: Oxford University Press.

Hardt, M., and A. Negri. 2004. *Multitude: War and democracy in the age of empire*. New York: Penguin.

Haufler, V. 2002. *A public role for the private sector: Industry self-regulation in a global economy*. Washington, DC: Carnegie Endowment for International Peace.

Held, D. 1995. *Democracy and the global order: From the modern state to cosmopolitan governance*. Cambridge: Polity.

Hertz, N. 2001. *The silent takeover: Global capitalism and the death of democracy*. New York: Free Press.

Hollingsworth, J. R. 1994. *Governing capitalist economies. Performance and control of economic sectors*. Oxford and New York: Oxford University Press.

Jenkins, R., R. Pearson, and J. Seyfang, eds. 2002. *Corporate responsibility and labour rights: Codes of conduct in the global economy*. London: Earthscan. Kline.

Kagan, R. A. 2001. *Adversarial legalism: The American way of law*. Cambridge: Harvard University Press.

Kaul, I., P. Conçeição, K. Le Goulven, and R. U. Mendoza, eds. 2003. *Providing global public goods; Managing globalization*. New York: Oxford University Press.

Kell, G. 2005. The global compact: Selected experiences and reflections. *Journal of Business Ethics* 59, no. 1–2: 69–79.

Kellow, A. 2002. Comparing business and public interest associability at the international level. *International Political Science Review* 23, no. 2: 175–86.

King, A. A., and M. J. Lenox. 2000. Industry self-regulation without sanctions: The chemical industry's responsible care program. *Academy of Management Journal* 43: 698–716.

Koenig-Archibugi, M. 2002. Mapping global governance. In *Governing globalization: Power, authority, and global governance*, ed. David Held and Anthony McGrew, 46–69. Cambridge: Polity.

———. 2004. Transnational corporations and public accountability. *Government and Opposition* 39, no. 2 (Spring): 234–59.

Laclau, E., and C. Mouffe. 1985. *Hegemony and socialist strategy: Towards a radical democratic politics*. Verso: London.

Levi-Faur, D., and J. Jordana, eds. 2005. The rise of regulatory capitalism: The global diffusion of a new order. *The Annals of the American Academy of Political and Social Science* 598 (March).

Lindblom, C. E. 1977. *Politics and markets. The world's political-economic systems*. New York: Basic Books.

Lipschutz, R., with J. K. Rowe. 2005. *Globalization, governmentality and global politics. Regulation for the rest of us?* London and New York: Routledge.

Lukes, S. 1974. *Power: A radical view.* London: Macmillan.

Martin, P. L. 2005. Democracy in the marketplace? The equator principles, global project finance, and new frontiers in global governance. Paper prepared for the International Studies Association Workshop "Finance as Power: The Second Wave," Philadelphia, PA, 17 November.

May, C., and S. Sell. 2005. *Intellectual property rights: A critical history.* Boulder: Lynne Rienner.

OECD. 1997. *Co-operative approaches to regulation.* Public Management Occasional Papers 18. Paris: OECD.

Olson, M. 1965. *The logic of collective action. Public goods and the theory of groups.* Cambridge: Harvard University Press.

Parker, C. 2002. *The open corporation: Effective self-regulation and democracy.* Cambridge: Cambridge University Press.

Patomäki, H., and T. Teivainen. 2004. *A possible world: Democratic transformation of global institutions.* London: Zed.

Porter, M. 1985. *Competitive advantage: Creating and sustaining superior performance.* New York: Free Press.

Porter, T. 2005. *Globalization and finance.* Cambridge: Polity.

————. 2002. *Technology, governance, and political conflict in international industries.* London: Routledge.

————, and K. Ronit. 2006. Self-regulation as policy process: The multiple and criss-crossing stages of private rule-making. *Policy Sciences* 39: 41–72.

Power, M. 1994. The audit society. In *Accounting as social and institutional practice,* ed. Anthony G. Hopwood and Peter Miller, 299–316. Cambridge: Cambridge University Press.

Prakash, A., and M. Potoski. 2006. *The voluntary environmentalist? Green clubs and ISO 14001, and voluntary environmental regulations.* Cambridge University Press.

Reich, R. 2007. *Supercapitalism: The transformation of business, democracy, and everyday life.* New York: Alfred A. Knopf.

Risse, T. 2004. Global governance and communicative action. *Government and Opposition* 39, no. 2 (Spring): 288–313.

Ronit, K. 2005. International governance by organized business—The shifting roles of firms, associations, and intergovernmental organizations in self-regulation. In *Governing interests: Business associations facing internationalization,* ed. Wolfgang Streeck et al., 219–41. London and New York: Routledge.

————. 2007. Introduction: Global public policy—The new policy arrangements of business and countervailing groups. In *Global public policy. Business and the countervailing powers of civil society*, ed. Karsten Ronit, 1–42. London and New York: Routledge.

Scholte, J. A.. 2000. Global civil society. In *The political economy of globalization*, ed. Ngaire Woods, 173–201. London: Macmillan.

de Senarclens, Pierre, and Ali Kazancigil, eds. 2007. *Regulating globalization: Critical approaches to global governance*. Tokyo: United Nations University Press.

Shutt, H. 2001. *A new democracy: Alternatives to a bankrupt world order*. London: Zed.

Sklair, L. 2001. *The transnational capitalist class*. Oxford: Blackwell.

————. 2002. Democracy and the transnational capitalist class. *Annals of the American Academy of Political and Social Science* 581: 144–57.

Slaughter, A-M. 2004. *A new world order*. Princeton: Princeton University Press.

Stone, D. 2004. Think tanks beyond nation-states. In *Think tank traditions: Policy research and the politics of ideas,* ed. Diane Stone and Andrew Denham, 34–51. Manchester, Manchester University Press.

Tsingou, E. 2006. The governance of over-the-counter derivatives markets. In *The political economy of financial market regulation: The dynamics of inclusion and exclusion*, ed. Peter Mooslechner, Helen Schuberth, and Beat Weber, 168–90. Aldershot: Edward Elgar.

Underhill, G. 1995. Keeping governments out of politics: Transnational securities markets, regulatory co-operation, and political legitimacy. *Review of International Studies* 21, no. 3 (July): 251–78.

Vogel, D. 2005. *The market for virtue: The potential and limits of corporate social responsibility*. Washington, DC: Brookings Institution Press.

Wilson, J. Q. 1980. The politics of regulation. In *The politics of regulation*, ed. James Q. Wilson, 357–94. New York: Basic Books.

Zweifel, T. 2006. *International organizations and democracy*. Boulder: Lynne Rienner.

SECTION 1

THE FIRM LEVEL

Individual Political Actions and Voluntary Arrangements

2

PRIVATE AUTHORITY CERTIFICATION REGIMES

A Club Theory Perspective

ASEEM PRAKASH AND MATTHEW POTOSKI

INTRODUCTION

While much of the traditional international relations scholarship privileges states as key actors in world politics and intergovernmental regimes as key mechanisms of global governance, recent scholarship recognizes the important role of non-state actors in politics and private authority regimes as global public policy instruments. This chapter outlines a novel theoretical perspective to study private authority certification regimes (Cutler et al. 1999) by employing the theory of clubs. Private authority certification regimes, or voluntary clubs as we call them here, have sprouted across continents and policy domains. Some voluntary clubs such as ISO 9000 and ISO 14000 are truly global in nature and have been adopted by several thousand firms across a large number of countries. These regimes are typically sponsored by non-state actors, although states can also create such nonbinding or voluntary regimes. They offer some sort of certification or branding in order to help outside stakeholders differentiate regime participants from the nonparticipants.

An important question confronting international relations scholars, and for that matter any scholar interested in the study of governance, pertains to the efficacy of voluntary clubs: under what conditions do they shape the behaviors of the participation actors toward social purposes? Indeed, some research suggests that even public regulation, which is supposed to epitomize transparency, accountability, and legitimacy, might not serve public purposes due to government "capture" by big business (Stigler 1971). If big businesses are able to capture governments, then why would they not also capture voluntary clubs? Such clubs captured by industry would become a mere tool for businesses to appear to be socially responsible without actually having to do anything that promoted social good. These are important issues for everyone who cares about accountability and democracy.

The more technical literature on voluntary clubs has examined the following questions: Under what conditions do voluntary clubs alter the behaviors of the participating actors in ways that serve social purposes? In other words, under what conditions do voluntary clubs induce participating actors to behave in socially useful ways *beyond* what is required by public regulations in the specific jurisdiction in which the actors function? Public regulations require actors to create positive externalities. For example, regulations (with all their imperfections) often require firms to abate pollution. If clubs can induce firms to abate pollution beyond the requirements of public law, then they have served as a useful purpose. As the reader will notice, we are not advocating the replacement of public regulation by private regimes. Instead, with public regulation as the baseline, we are exploring what types of clubs, and under what conditions, can induce firms to create social externalities beyond the legal requirements. Conceptualized in this way, private regimes are not necessarily institutions that replace governments. Rather, we view them as supplementing and enhancing public institutions.

There is a well-developed literature on club efficacy. Scholars have studied conditions under which firms join a specific club and the factors that influence the club's efficacy. We now have a sense that while some clubs are shams and do little to induce firms to improve their social performance, others require participants to take progressive action they would not have taken in the absence of the club, leading them to improve their superior social performance. In sum, while there are several useful studies about the effectiveness of individual clubs, scholars have yet to systematically tie these studies and their findings together. For voluntary programs we need to understand what works and why. Furthermore, we need to understand how the issues of transparency and accountability bear upon the subject of efficacy.

Scholars have responded to these challenges in two ways. First, sensing the absence of theory, some have developed inductive approaches to study voluntary clubs, an "area studies approach"[1] that can go only so far because the theories are tailored and ultimately limited to the individual clubs from which they have been generated. Furthermore, these studies suffer from obvious selection bias because they tend to examine "successful" clubs only. Eventually, strong theory must help to explain both success and failure—which inductive approaches typically fail to do so. The second response has been comparative analyses of voluntary clubs (Lenox and Nash 2003; Darnall and Carmin 2005). While such cross-club studies can shed light on why some clubs are successful and others are not, advancing research and practice requires an encompassing theoretical and analytic framework that identifies voluntary clubs' important features and ties them to club efficacy, thereby leading to better understanding of what types of voluntary clubs work, where, and why. Such a theoretical framework should facilitate comparisons not only among voluntary clubs but also with other policy instruments. Eventually, it will help scholars to explore the phenomenon of private authority and identify conditions under which it can be marshaled to serve public purpose.

Drawing on the economic theory of clubs, we outline a deductive framework for the study of private authority, focusing on specific institutional features and analytic dimensions. We highlight the diversity in voluntary club design, the key variable that policymakers and club sponsors can influence most directly, and relate club design to specific collective action issues that influence club efficacy. After modeling club design as an exogenous determinant of club efficacy, we investigate how the club design itself might be endogenous to institutional and stakeholder context in which the club is established and functions, including stakeholders in other countries.[2] This is important because, as the editors note in the introductory chapter, the idea of democracy should be extended beyond competitive elections to include a broader sense of popular accountability. It follows that in democratic polities firms should have incentives to respond to their stakeholders. While this chapter focuses on club design as a driver of club efficacy, we wish to emphasize that voluntary clubs might induce accountability not only to publics in the country in which participating firms function, but to the relevant publics across the world. The important issue to specify is who counts in the benefit-cost calculations as well as normative assessments of the participating firms. This presents an opportunity for nongovernmental organizations to ensure that a broad range of interests counts in firms' decision making, especially those interests that are not privileged in the normal electoral processes. In some ways, appropriately marshaled private authority can further global accountability. Nevertheless, it needs to be emphasized that democratic decision making and the involvement of a large roster of stakeholders may not lead to efficacious clubs. Indeed, some effective clubs might work simply on the basis of their sound institutional design that focuses on monitoring and accountability, instead of stakeholder involvements, in the shaping of institutional design. Thus, our chapter, hopefully, problematizes the simplistic relationships between democracy and institutional efficacy. Theoretically, our perspective can help private authority scholars place their work within the global governance literature and therefore contribute to broaden the dialogue on institutions and governance. This is because the club perspective can be employed to study governmental as well as intergovernmental arrangements; after all, the issues of institutional efficacy, transparency, and accountability are common to all governance types.

Our essay is structured in the following way. In the first part, expanding on our previous work (Prakash and Potoski 2006a), we outline a generalizable framework for the study of voluntary clubs, based on an economic club model. We conceptualize private authority certification regimes as voluntary clubs that require firms to incur costs not required by law that lead to the production of positive externalities. In return, voluntary clubs provide branding benefits[3] such as shared reputation and goodwill, to participating firms that emanate from their association with the voluntary club brand. In the second part of the chapter, we discuss important issues for the study of voluntary clubs and illustrate how our club approach can help policymakers design superior voluntary clubs.

COLLECTIVE ACTION AND THE CLUB FRAMEWORK

Rational actors are generally unwilling to pay private costs to produce positive social externalities. An externality implies that actors do not fully internalize the costs and benefits of their actions. Consequently, goods with negative externalities are overproduced and goods with positive externalities are underproduced. Pollution is a classic negative externality (but see Coase 1960), and from the other side of the coin, decreasing pollution is a positive externality. A firm might reduce pollution by improving production processes or by adopting new technologies or management systems. In many cases, these are expensive actions for which firms would want some offsetting payoff. The policy challenge is to design institutions that create incentives for actors to incur the costs of internalizing their negative externalities.

Ever since Pigou (1960), government regulations have been viewed as the primary mechanism for compelling firms to internalize costs they would otherwise externalize. Regulations change firms' cost calculus by mandating that firms behave in specific ways, and some regulations stipulate the means for doing so. The case for governmental regulations solving externalities rests on three assumptions. First, public regulations are democratic and fair because governments respond to public concerns (not private interests). Second, governments have the capacities to correctly estimate the cost of externalities and then design regulations to compel firms to internalize them. Third, the state has the capacity to enforce regulations, and firms tend to adhere to the law.[4]

These assumptions are all too often problematic (Fiorino 1999; Coglianese and Nash 2001), particularly in the context of developing countries. Many countries are not fully functioning democracies,[5] and even in established democracies, governments might be unduly influenced, if not captured, by interest groups. In most developing countries, governments have little power to enforce regulations, or even maintain internal order and protect property rights. For reference, of the 177 countries examined in the 2007 Foreign Policy Failed State Index, 32 are listed as failed (Alert category), and another 97 in the danger of failing (Warning category).[6] Thus, well-functioning states are certainly not the norm when one surveys the state of governance across the countries.

Some effective voluntary clubs can be a corrective for government failure. In Mexico, which ranked well in the bottom half of the failed state indexes, Dasgupta et al. (2000) report that adopting environmental management practices along the lines prescribed by ISO 14001 significantly improved Mexican facilities' self-reported compliance with public law. Haufler (2009) shows how the international diamond industry has developed a voluntary club (Kimberley Process) to curb the flow of "blood diamonds" mined illegally in failed African states and used to fund the internal wars.

The upshot of this discussion is that governance mechanisms should be carefully scrutinized for their strengths *and* deficiencies: one should not compare "imperfect" voluntary clubs with a "perfect" governmental regulation or vice-versa. If we accept that all institutions can fail, the scholarly and policy challenge is to identify the conditions and institutions that lead to success and failure.

Voluntary clubs are an important policy instrument in this regard because they can induce participating firms to produce positive externalities not only in response to legal mandates but to exceed them. They implicitly respond to the externality problems resulting from governments' failure to adequately supply or enforce regulations. But how

do these clubs induce firms to pay the costs of solving externality problems? Below we explain how voluntary clubs mitigate collective action
problems inherent in the voluntary provision of such externalities.

Buchanan Clubs and Voluntary Clubs

Clubs are institutions that supply impure public goods. The club literature is well established in public finance and dates back to at least the
1950s (Pigou 1960; Tiebout 1956; and Wiseman 1957). James Buchanan
(1965) is generally credited with introducing the theoretical concept of
clubs. In the Buchanan theory, clubs are institutions for producing and
allocating goods that are neither fully private (rivalrous and excludable), nor fully public (nonrivalrous, nonexcludable). Unlike pure
public goods where the benefits one recipient receives are made available to all, club goods provide excludable benefits that are given only
to those who join (and pay for) the club and withheld from all others.
Club goods are nonrivalrous in that what one individual consumes is
still available for others to consume as well. A good example of a club
in this traditional sense is a movie theatre: the excludable benefit club
members receive is the opportunity to watch a movie on a big screen
with excellent acoustics. Purchased tickets offset the cost of the movie
and facilities. If you do not purchase the ticket, you are excluded from
watching the movie (excludable benefit) and several patrons can watch
a movie at a time (nonrival benefit). Club membership can be allocated
efficiently because if there are persistent, long lines for tickets, the the-
ater owner can hike ticket prices while entrepreneurs can construct
new theatres.

Unlike traditional "Buchanan" clubs whose central purpose is the
production of club goods, the central purpose of voluntary clubs is to
produce positive social externalities. Voluntary clubs provide club
goods to firms that produce positive externalities beyond what government regulations require. Unlike in traditional economic clubs, membership costs in voluntary clubs are not direct payments to sponsors.
Rather, they are the monetary and nonmonetary costs of adopting and
adhering to the club's membership requirements.

From the perspective of (potential) members, voluntary clubs can
generate three kinds of benefits:

- *Social externalities*, which constitute the policy payoff of voluntary clubs;
- *Private* benefits that accrue to a single member firm only;[7]

• *Club goods* that accrue to club members only and are the central motivation for members to join the club.

The production of positive social externalities is the important welfare gain to society and the central justification for voluntary clubs. The positive social externalities voluntary club members produce can have the attributes of private goods (a voluntary club obligating participating firms to pay higher wages to indigenous coffee growers), public goods (a voluntary club obligating participating firms to lower air pollution), common property resources (protecting a fishery) or even club goods (a voluntary club obligating participating forestry firms not to cut trees that are revered by an aboriginal group).

The private benefits of voluntary club membership accrue only to individual club members, not to other club members, and certainly not to nonmembers. For example, a voluntary club designed to protect the environment might require firms to uncover waste in their production process, and thereby increasing profits as Porter and Linde (1995) suggest in the context of governmental regulations. Such private benefits, however, have limited analytical utility for evaluating voluntary clubs because an instrumental actor (such as a profit-oriented firm) is likely to take these actions unilaterally, without joining the club, in order to enjoy the private benefits such actions produce. If the private gain from unilaterally taking such action were sufficient to induce the firm to produce enough positive social externalities, then voluntary clubs would not be necessary.

The central, analytically salient benefit that the members receive for producing the voluntary club's positive externalities is the affiliation with the club's positive brand reputation, a nonrival but excludable benefit as we discuss below. In its broadest sense, voluntary club membership signals to firms' stakeholders about members' clubs, policies, and performance, which can be quite valuable to stakeholders because so much of firms' activities are unobservable (though different stakeholders may have different information about firms' activities). In other words, because outside stakeholders—such as consumers, regulators, investors, and suppliers—are unable to monitor firms' clubs and verify firms' claims, voluntary club membership can solve information asymmetries between firms and their stakeholders. Affiliation with a voluntary club and its reputation thus helps build firms' reputations, which in turn shapes their relations and interactions with stakeholders (Carpenter 2001).

While the voluntary club brand reduces information costs for stakeholders to differentiate socially progressive firms from laggards, stakeholders vary in their abilities to interpret such brand signals, their preferences for the social externalities the firms produce as club members, and their capacities to translate these preferences into rewards or sanctions for firms. Thus, while we focus on voluntary club design as the driver of branding benefits, we recognize that other factors shape the value of a club's brand benefit, such as the stakeholder and institutional context, firm characteristics, and sponsors' attributes. Indeed, our own research on the cross-country ISO 14001 diffusion suggests that that ISO 14001 adoption levels in importing countries influence ISO 14001 adoption levels in exporting countries (Prakash and Potoski 2006b). Further, the commitment to ISO 14001 in the home countries of multinational corporations influences ISO 14001 uptake in the host countries of their subsidiaries (Prakash and Potoski 2007).

Mitigating Collective Action Dilemmas through Institutional Design

All institutions can fail: governments and market failures have been well documented, and voluntary clubs have been shown to fail as well. From a policy perspective, the objective is to understand the conditions under which voluntary clubs fail and how their institutional design, as the key independent variable in their efficacy, can mitigate their failure.[8] The roots of voluntary club failure are collective action problems associated with free riding and shirking. Firms may want to enjoy a reputation for social responsibility without having to actually pay the costs of being socially responsible. Firms hope that the goodwill created by socially responsible firms will spill over to them because the stakeholders, who can not always identify which firms are doing the good deeds, will spread their rewards broadly. Effective voluntary clubs seek to solve such free riding because they make excludable the benefits from producing positive externalities: stakeholders can target their rewards only to firms that have joined the club. Thus, the club's brand curbs free riding; the more credible the brand is, the more attractive it is for firms to join the club and produce the positive externalities it requires.[9]

Another type of free riding pertains to shirking: firms can join a voluntary club and claim to produce positive social externalities but fail to live up to their promises. The club therefore needs to establish mechanisms to compel participants to adhere to club obligations. Widespread shirking undermines the production of externalities and thereby dilutes its credibility. Willful shirking occurs because: (1) the goals of participants and voluntary club sponsors diverge, and (2) participants are able to exploit information asymmetries (regarding their adherence to club standards) between themselves and sponsors and stakeholders. Information asymmetries prevent stakeholders from differentiating club shirkers from nonshirkers.

Voluntary clubs can mitigate shirking by establishing monitoring and sanctioning mechanisms. A voluntary club with a reputation for effectively policing and sanctioning its participants is likely to have a stronger standing among its stakeholders and therefore have a stronger brand reputation among its firms' stakeholders.

The Olsonian Dilemma, Brand Benefits and Club Standards

With public regulations as the baseline, club standards specify what beyond-compliance actions are required for firms to join the voluntary club and remain members in good standing. Some standards specify performance requirements (sometimes called outcome standards) while other standards may be more process oriented, such as requirements that members adopt a management system, or that members regularly consult with community groups. Finally, club standards may limit membership to those that have already established high standards of social performance. In effect, club standards are signals to members' stakeholders regarding what the voluntary club wants members to accomplish, particularly their production of externalities. The standards' stringency serves as a proxy signal for the level of externalities members generate (per capita) and therefore affects the branding benefits members can expect to receive from stakeholders.

While voluntary clubs establish regulations outside the scope of mandatory government law, it is through reference to the requirements of mandatory government regulations that we can observe the "voluntary" component of voluntary clubs and assess the levels of externalities the clubs produce. The voluntary nature of these clubs stems from firms' behavior that produces "positive" social outcomes—positive social externalities—beyond what public law requires. This means of course that the same action that is voluntary in a jurisdiction with less stringent public law could be mandatory in a jurisdiction with stringent public law.

Public law also is the analytic referent for measuring the policy contribution of a club to social welfare: How much more positive social externality does a voluntary club compel its members to produce than they would produce in the absence of the club? The marginal contribution to public welfare from a voluntary club is the value added from its participants' activities that are beyond the applicable legal requirements.

Again, this means that a voluntary club may contribute to public welfare in a jurisdiction with less stringent public law but may offer little or no contribution in a jurisdiction with stringent public law.

To simplify our discussion, we identify two types of club standards. Lenient club standards require little social externality production from members beyond what government regulations require. These are low-cost voluntary clubs for the members but create marginal levels of social externalities, and therefore the value of their brand among stakeholders is relatively low. Of course, even lenient club standards must mandate that members produce some positive social externality, or else the voluntary club would be a mere empty gesture (as some voluntary clubs indeed are).

Stringent club standards require members to produce high levels of positive social externalities, well beyond what government regulations require. For potential participants, these can be high-cost clubs. The advantage of stringent standards is that the club's brand would be more credible and serve as a low-cost tool for signaling voluntary club members' commitment to the club's social objective. Stakeholders would easily and confidently distinguish leaders (members) from laggards (nonmembers) among firms. Armed with this information, stakeholders could reward and punish firms accordingly.

Shirking Dilemma: Monitoring and Enforcement Rules

Shirking is the second source of institutional failure for voluntary clubs. Shirking implies that some participants formally join the club but do not implement and practice the club standards. In doing so, shirkers seek to free ride on the efforts of other members who build the voluntary club's reputation. While nonmembers are excluded from enjoying the benefits of club membership, shirkers enjoy club benefits unless they are discovered and expelled from the voluntary club. As word spreads about large-scale shirking, the club's reputation is likely to diminish and the brand reputation to be undermined.

Willful shirking is facilitated by information asymmetries between voluntary club participants and club sponsors and/or between participants and club stakeholders. By information asymmetries we mean that voluntary club sponsors and stakeholders cannot observe the levels to which an individual participant is adhering to club standards because such activities are inherently difficult to observe or are observable only at significant cost. The net effect is that information asymmetries impose costs on sponsors and stakeholders seeking to differentiate club shirkers from non-shirkers.

Shirking violates appropriate behavior norms (March and Olson 1989), which suggests that shirking can be curbed by sociological pressures (normative, mimetic, and coercive) from other participating firms or even stakeholders. It would be important to understand the general conditions under which such sociological pressures would persuade instrumental firms not to shirk.[10] As scholars interested in studying the consequences of institutional design on collective action, we are more interested in studying how institutional design can address the issue of shirking.

Instead of relying on sociological pressures alone, a voluntary club might seek to mitigate shirking through its institutional design. Monitoring and enforcement mechanisms can compel members to adhere to club standards, particularly if they contain three central components: third-party monitoring, public disclosure of audit information, and sanctioning by club sponsors.[11] It should be noted, however, that some voluntary clubs have none of these components—the Sustainable Slopes Club (Rivera and deLeon 2004) is an example. Based on the design features, we expect such clubs to exhibit high levels of shirking and therefore generate very small amounts of positive externalities, if any. Indeed, Rivera and DeLeon (2002) report that club Sustainable Slopes participants were no greener than nonparticipants. Our framework suggests that policymaker and stakeholders should be skeptical of clubs without any monitoring and enforcement rules.

Voluntary clubs begin to have some credibility regarding their capacity to curb shirking if they exhibit at least one of the three features. Third-party monitoring means that firms are required by the club sponsor to have their policies audited by accredited, external auditors. Thus, the club might stipulate that a periodic approval granted by a third-party auditor is necessary to retain club membership. In some cases, club sponsors may require public disclosure of audit information (as in the European Union's Eco-Management and Audit Scheme). The idea is that by such disclosure, the stakeholders can reward and punish as they deem fit. Finally, the sponsoring organization may itself act upon the audit information and sanction the shirkers.

With a nod toward Hobbes (1651) for his astute observation in chapter 17 of the *Leviathan* that "covenants without swords are but words, and of no strength to secure a man at all," we characterize a club's monitoring and enforcement clubs as "swords." Strong sword clubs have all three components—audits, disclosure and sanctioning mechanisms—and are most likely to curb shirking because they provide for a monitoring mechanism, mitigate information asymmetries between participants and club sponsors/stakeholders and create mechanism for sponsors to sanction shirkers. In extreme cases, sponsors may expel participants from the club, an undesirable outcome for firms if they value the benefits of voluntary club membership. While strong sword clubs should experience less shirking, they can impose more costs on members. Thus, in thinking about club design, policymakers need to examine the marginal addition to overall branding benefits by strengthening club's swords.

Medium sword clubs require third-party audits and public disclosure of the audit findings. Although they do not provide for sanctioning by the sponsoring organization, they are likely to curb shirking because, with public disclosure of audit information, external stakeholders can punish the shirkers for failing to live up to their commitments as club members. The EPA's 33/50 club and the European Union's Eco-Management and Audit Scheme (EMAS) are examples of medium sword clubs. In both these voluntary clubs, firms are subjected to third-party audits and the information on their social performance is available to the public. Because it is not clear whether stakeholders have the willingness and resources to sanction shirkers, we place them in the medium sword category.

Weak sword clubs require only third-party audits. ISO 14001 is an example of a "weak sword" club. The International Organization for Standardization, the sponsoring organization, is not known to aggressively sanction the shirkers. Importantly, the absence of public disclosure of audit information weakens stakeholders' ability to sanction shirking. However, these are also low-cost voluntary clubs and therefore within the financial means of a larger number of firms, as witnessed by the more than 110,000 facilities across 138 countries that had joined the ISO 14001 club as of December 2005.

Based on the above discussion, we identify six voluntary club types (Table 2.1). Important arenas for future research include: How does the institutional-stakeholder environment along with firm characteristics (the relative salience of leaders versus laggards in the population) influence the emergence of various voluntary club types; what is the aggregate impact of a voluntary club in terms of the production of positive externalities, defined as the product of externalities produced by each firm and the total number of club participants? In some instances, policy makers might favor lenient-standard clubs to attract a large roster as opposed to stringent-standard clubs with limited membership. In other instances, lenient-standard clubs might be labeled as

Table 2.1. Analytical Typology of Voluntary Clubs

		Enforcement and Monitoring Rules		
Club *Standards*		*Weak* *Sword*	*Medium* *Sword*	*Strong* *Sword*
Lenient	Social externalities :	low	low-moderate	moderate
	Shirking :	high	moderate	low
	Branding benefits :	marginal	low-moderate	low-moderate
	Cost :	low	low-moderate	low-moderate
Stringent	Social externalities :	low	moderate	high
	Shirking :	high	moderate	low
	Branding benefits :	marginal	moderate	high
	Cost :	moderate-high	moderate	high

greenwashes and attract few members simply because they cannot generate significant branding benefits. Thus, instead of one-type-fits-all, policymakers should recognize that different voluntary club types are likely to best fit different policy contexts for different types of firms. While stringent standard clubs with strong swords might seem the best from an externality generation perspective, these are high-cost clubs that most firms might not find worth their while. On the other hand, weak-sword clubs with lenient standards might generate low levels of externalities per capita, but by attracting a large roster of firm, might lead to the generation of high levels of externalities in the aggregate.

Voluntary Club Size and Crowding

The size of a voluntary club's membership roster affects the strength and value of its brand. More members create opportunities to capture economies of scale in building the club's reputation (McGuire 1972), a dynamic akin to network effects (Bessen and Saloner 1988). Network effects are the changes in the benefit that an actor derives from a good when the number of other actors consuming the same good changes. Positive network effects create increasing returns to scale: with every additional unit, the marginal cost of production decreases. Language groups can be thought of as voluntary clubs amenable to network effects: the more people speak a given language, the higher are the benefits from learning it. Having more members helps advertise a voluntary club broadly among stakeholders as one member's socially desirable activities generates positive reputational and goodwill externalities for other members, so that the value a member derives increases as others join.

The benefits of voluntary club membership are nonrival because the positive branding benefits one member enjoys can be simultaneously enjoyed by other members. However, at some point, crowding may set in—a question that has so far not been systematically examined in the voluntary club literature.[12] While a voluntary club with universal membership would do little to identify which firms were producing desirable social goods, industry-sponsored clubs might desire universal membership of the firms operating in their industry, as is the case with the American Chemistry Council's Responsible Care club, and the American Forestry and Paper Association's Sustainable Forestry Initiative. Thus, similar to the traditional club literature on optimal club size (Cornes and Sandler 1996), there are significant opportunities to examine this issue in the context of voluntary clubs.

Firms within an industry benefit asymmetrically from affiliating with a voluntary club brand. Large or more profitable firms might benefit more from the club because they are more vulnerable to the negative reputational externalities generated by others in the industry. Firms in a "privileged group" (Olson 1965) that disproportionately benefit from a shared reputation (or are disproportionately hurt by its degradation) are likely to take the lead in establishing an industry club. Indeed, this is the story of Responsible Care in the chemical industry (Prakash 2000) and the Sustainable Forestry Initiative in the forestry industry (Cashore et al. 2003).[13] The optimal club size from firms' perspective might vary across firms, even for firms within the same industry.

VOLUNTARY CLUB GOVERNANCE AND CREDIBLE COMMITMENT

Firms constantly look to improve their standing with stakeholders. One might wonder as to what is the point of joining a voluntary club if firms can act on their own to boost their standing with stakeholders. Indeed, it is not hard to think of companies with well-earned reputations for social leadership. Club membership offers several advantages over unilateral action for enhancing firms' reputations among stakeholders. Unilateral commitments to desirable social action may be less credible because they are less institutionalized. When individual firms make their own rules, they can easily change them as well. Of course, a firm may devise some measure to credibly commit to a rule system and not opportunistically change them—as the "credible commitment" literature suggests (North and Weingast 1989).

As institutionalized systems, voluntary clubs enjoy a degree of legitimacy that a firm alone may find difficult to acquire. By joining voluntary clubs whose rules they cannot change in the short run, firms signal their willingness to incur private costs to create positive externalities. However, to capitalize on this legitimacy, clubs themselves must solve two credible commitment problems, one toward firms' stakeholders and a second toward its own members. Failure to solve these problems can undermine the club's standing among firms and stakeholders.

The credible commitment problem toward firms' stakeholders is that after gaining a reputation for strong club, the sponsors may then surreptitiously dilute the standards—capitalizing on reputations' sticky nature (Weigel and Camerer 1988; Schultz, Mouritsen, and Gabrielsen 2001). Anticipating this possibility, stakeholders may withhold the benefits from members until they are confident that sponsors are committed to maintaining the stringency of club standards. Voluntary clubs established by industry associations may be especially vulnerable to such credible commitment problems.

The credible commitment problem toward potential participants is that the voluntary club may tighten its standards after firms have joined, opportunistically exploiting the fact that exiting the club might be costly for firms. Club membership might require investments in infrastructure, technology, or competency assets that are specific to the club and are difficult to apply to alternative uses (Williamson 1986). Firms may be reluctant to join a club that requires asset specific investments that would leave them vulnerable to opportunistic exploitation by sponsors. Retribution costs may also impede firms' ability to leave a club, as stakeholders are likely to punish firms for exiting the club. Because the exit option is costly, voluntary clubs, particularly those sponsored by NGOs, need to signal to potential members that they will not opportunistically tighten the club standards.

We can identify three institutional features voluntary clubs can adopt to counter credible commitment problems. First, voluntary clubs grant external stakeholders—including participating firms and NGOs—political authority in any future changes of their rules, such as the procedures such as the notice and comment provisions of the United States under the Administrative Procedures Act. Voluntary clubs can therefore stipulate "rules for making rules," or "collective choice rules" as Ostrom (1990) terms them, in ways that assure stakeholders that club requirements will not be diluted or changed surreptitiously. The industry-sponsored Sustainable Forestry Initiative is an interesting example of a voluntary club that has designed collective choice rules to mitigate its credible commitment problem. The club sponsors have sought to tie their own hands by creating an External Review Board comprising of "18 independent experts representing conservation, environmental, professional, academic, and public organizations. . . . The volunteer Panel provides external oversight with their independent review of the current SFI club while seeking steady improvements in sustainable forestry practices."[14]

The second credible commitment mechanism is stipulating supermajority voting rules for changing club standards. Consider the case of the International Organization for Standardization which requires that new standards it develops as well as changes in existing standards need to be approved by two-thirds of the members that have participated in the standards development process, and by three-fourths of all voting members of the club.[15] Thus, supermajority voting rules mean the standards cannot be changed easily. In any case, the process of standard development is reasonably transparent and outside observers, even when not represented on technical committees, have a fair amount of information about the deliberations.

A third institutional feature for addressing the credible commitment problem is to submit the voluntary club to an external certification standard specifying how the club is managed. Indeed, we can see the beginnings of an interesting example of a supra voluntary club for certifying quality of other voluntary clubs. The International Social and Environmental Accreditation and Labeling (ISEAL) Alliance is an international NGO made up of international standards-setting organizations.[16] ISEAL's Code of Good Practice for Social and Environmental Standard Setting, launched in 2004, is a set of club standards to guide the development, implementation, and oversight of voluntary social and environmental clubs. The Code's standards specify processes for developing a club's standards, such as extensive stakeholder participation, and procedures for handling disputes. The Code's monitoring and enforcement mechanisms are being refined: there is currently a peer review procedure in place and ISEAL is in the process of developing tools and processes to assess compliance. The goal is to help sponsors develop their clubs by providing best practices benchmarks, and provide governments, NGOs, citizens, and other stakeholders a way to evaluate the quality of different voluntary clubs.

Reputational Commons or Reputations Held in Common?

Voluntary clubs are sometimes tailored for firms in a single industry, such as the chemical industry's Responsible Care club or the forestry industry's Sustainable Forestry Initiative, and at other times for firms across industries, such as ISO 14001 and the Performance Track. Industry clubs raise important theoretical issues about the nature of the branding benefits. It is clear that an industry can acquire a reputation of its own. The tobacco industry, for example, has a reputation for misleading advertising, stifling research about the health consequences of smoking, and so on, even if individual tobacco companies engage in such skullduggery to varying degrees and perhaps some not at all. Yet, an industry's reputation reflects on its individual firms in that people make inferences about a firm based on the reputation of the industry in which it operates.[17] It is therefore fair to say that firms operating in a given industry share a common reputation, or to put it differently, the industry reputation is held in common by firms. Below we conduct a theoretical analysis of industry reputations, and the nature of the policy problem underlying them.

Some scholars characterize industry reputations and industry clubs as "reputational commons" and relate their production and appropriation to the broader literature on common-pool resources (Barnett and King 2006). We believe a more appropriate characterization would be to say industry reputations are "held in common" by members of the industry. As we show below, a *reputation held in common* by firms operating together in an industry (or as part of the same cross-industry voluntary club) is not equivalent to a *reputational commons*, in a common-pool resource sense (Ostrom 1990; Dolsak and Ostrom 2003). The distinction between the two is not about semantics because the collective action dilemmas—and the institutional means to solving them—are quite different for each.

The reputational commons concept can indeed be confusing, so we begin with some conceptual clarifications. The word *commons* has a specific connotation in political economy and public policy. Where a club good is nonrival and excludable, a common-pool resource (often simply called a "common") is rival and nonexcludable.

To illustrate the difference between a good held in common and a common-pool resource, it is useful to return to Garrett Hardin's (1968) pasture, a celebrated example of a common-pool resource. For Hardin, the tragedy of the commons arises because one herdsman cannot exclude others from increasing the flock size, dictated by the nonexcludability dimension in the Ostrom (1990) framework. Because the pasture can support only up to a certain number of sheep (rivalry dimension), adding additional sheep decreases the availability of the good for other herdsmen, leaving each herdsman with the incentives to increase the size of their own herd because s/he expects others to do so in short order. The herdsman wants to be the first-mover—the first to put more sheep on the common—lest s/he lose out on gains from the commons. The herdsman realizes that by adding a sheep to his/her herd s/he enjoys the benefit of raising an extra sheep but bears only a small portion of the incremental cost associated with degrading the pasture. Thus, it is rational for the herdsman to add sheep to his herd without limit. As all herdsmen seek to appropriate the resource before others do, the commons are degraded. Note that the rivalry dimension is accentuated by the nonexcludability dimension because the first-mover advantage associated with overconsumption compels participants to move quickly.

Hardin's pastures are open access resources: anybody can appropriate them and to any extent they want. To avert the commons tragedy, the access to the resource needs to limited only to a given group of herdsmen. That is, rules are required to create excludability. Addressing the rivalry dimension also reduces the commons tragedy. If rules limit herd size, then every herdsman will be prohibited from increasing the herd size indefinitely and will also have the assurance that others face the same constraint. With diminished possibility of facing a "sucker's payoff," the herdsman is less likely to overconsume the pasture. In sum, the solution to the commons problem is to establish property rights that limit the size of the group allowed to appropriate the commons (excludability) *and* the amount each group member is allowed to appropriate (rivalry).

Applying the herding analogy to industry reputations suggests focusing on whether a given industry's reputation is rivalrous (as in common-pool resources) or not rivalrous (as in clubs goods). We suggest that an industry's (or voluntary club's) reputation is a nonrivalrous good held in common by firms of the industry (or club). A firm "consumes" a positive (or negative) industry reputation by enjoying goodwill (or suffering ill will) from stakeholders that see the industry—and consequently the firm—in a positive (or negative) light. While a firm has "consumed" the reputation in this way, this reputation is still available for other firms to "consume": they too can receive good will (ill will) from stakeholders as a consequence of the industry's reputation. If the reputation were rivalrous, once the first firm had "consumed" the reputation, it would no longer be available for the second firm to consume, and firms would consequently race to lower their own standards to exploit the limited and dwindling stock of industry reputation—a dynamic similar to Hardin's herdsmen racing to add sheep to their herd before the pasture is completely overgrazed by sheep of other herdsmen. Since the industry reputation is nonrivalrous, it is not a common-pool resource.

Actions of one firm in an industry have positive or negative consequences for the other industry firms, which is what we mean when we say that the industry reputation is "held in common" by firms. Environmental mishaps by one firm impose negative reputational externalities on other firms in the industry, thereby diminishing the industry's reputation. Firms in an industry realize they all sink or swim together: one firm cannot externalize the costs of the diminished industry reputation on to others. While Hardin's herdsman bears only 1/nth of the incremental cost of his commons consumption, firms all bear the full brunt of the declining industry reputation simply because all firms get tarred by the same negative brush.

The upshot of this discussion is that industry reputations are a shared, nonrivalrous resource. Actions that enhance an industry's reputation, such as by creating an industry-level club, create nonrivalrous benefits for all and actions that diminish an industry's reputations impose nonrivalrous costs for all. The implication for institutional design is that clubs rules should focus on the excludability dimension so that the reputational gains of taking beyond-compliance social actions are appropriated only by members of the club. Because free-rider incentives are strong—firms in an industry cannot be excluded from enjoying the benefits of a positive industry reputation—industry clubs need to ensure that all firms in the industry join the club. This explains why industry associations such as the American Chemistry Council and the American Forest and Paper Association *require* their members to join their own voluntary clubs.

In contrast, solving the commons problems requires not only an exclusion mechanism, but also a partitioning mechanism for solving the rivalry problem. A partitioning mechanism would enable the division of the reputation among industry members. In the herdsman example, an exclusion mechanism would limit the number of herdsman allowed to use the pasture while a partitioning mechanism would limit the number of sheep any herdsman can place into the common pasture. The partitioning mechanism would counter herdsmen's incentives to move first and quickly consume the commons before other herdsmen did the same. We do not think any industry-level club has mechanisms to partition its shared reputation among its members, most likely because the industry reputation is a nonrivalrous good that is quite difficult to partition.

CONCLUSION

The editors of this volume focus on an important issue in the study and practice of international relations: the relationship between globalization, democracy, and big business. Our chapter makes a contribution to this subject by highlighting that private authority certification regimes can be designed to serve broader social purposes. In fact, private regimes, or voluntary clubs as we call them, are in all likelihood more important for failed states because they can create incentives for local actors to adhere to rule systems established by non-state actors. Most importantly, if globalization is enhancing the structural power of big business while weakening governments, voluntary clubs cam potentially reopen the policy space by allowing nongovernmental actors to create new governance structures and create incentives for businesses to join them—as has already taken place in several industries, such as apparel (Bartley 2009), forestry (Cashore et al. 2003), and chemicals (Prakash 2000).

Our framework identified key dimensions that can help both scholars and policymakers identify ex ante the features for effective voluntary clubs. Further, we highlight that such regimes can further global democracy because they might enable stakeholders located aboard to influence participating firms' practices. Yet, we wish to emphasize that voluntary clubs offer no magic bullet to respond to social challenges, especially to the issues of regulation and democracy. Indeed, the persistent and enduring social problems can probably be solved by employing public, and encompassing regulatory, institutions. Furthermore, highly undemocractic clubs that discourage public input might be very effective in terms of changing the behaviors of their participants while open and democractic clubs might be ineffective. Policymakers and stakeholders alike need to assess the situations under which such clubs can usefully supplement public regulation and how they cohere with the broader goals of democracy and accountability. Stakeholders in particular need to assess which clubs are captured by big business and which are not and decide on design principles should they choose to develop their own voluntary clubs.

Our chapter also points to the dilemmas confronting global governors. Designing voluntary clubs requires balancing competing imperatives. On the one hand, to enhance the club's credibility with external stakeholders, sponsors may prefer stringent standards. On the other hand, such standards may lead to low membership—and smaller network effects and scale economies in building the voluntary club brand—as few firms are able to meet demanding membership requirements. Further, with a roster of firms with established superior social credentials, club membership might not increase social externalities simply because the firms becoming members are already at the top of the performance continuum. From a policy perspective, while such voluntary clubs might serve as a useful signaling tool and help stakeholders to differentiate leaders from laggards, the overall welfare gains associated may be marginal. Thus, voluntary club sponsors might instead pitch club standards at a level appropriate for potential participants and acceptable to key stakeholders. Higher levels of heterogeneity in the pool of potential participants and among stakeholders are therefore likely to be associated with higher variations in standards adopted by voluntary clubs operating in the same policy context.

This edited volume is being published at an opportune time. While much has been written about private authority regimes and voluntary clubs, it is time now to take stock of this research and carefully identify concepts that would transform this multidisciplinary research into a theoretically grounded and coherent research club. We hope our chapter makes a contribution toward this end.

Our central contribution is to provide a deductive framework for analyzing voluntary clubs and tying together the findings generated from previous research. Our framework should help future scholars by identifying voluntary clubs' important institutional design features and the collective action problems clubs must solve to be effective. Future research can draw on this paper as a unifying framework to study how the interplay among varying sponsors' attributes, stakeholder and institutional contexts, and firm characteristics influence clubs' efficacy. Future research we hope, will consider not only specific clubs but systematically compare various clubs, and, hopefully, compare voluntary clubs with other policy instruments.

NOTES

This chapter is a revised version of Aseem Prakash and Matt Potoski. 2007, Collective action through voluntary environmental programs: A club theory perspective, *Policy Studies Journal* 35, no. 4: 773–92. Reproduced with permission of Blackwell Publishing Ltd.

1. We owe this point to Tim Büthe.
2. We owe this point to David Baron.
3. This could also be viewed as the "social license" to operate (Gunningham et al. 2003).

4. We recognize that there is a well-established literature examining how factors such enforcement frequency, sanctioning, actor preferences, sociological factors, and procedural fairness influence regulatees' propensities to obey laws (Hoffman, 1997; Winter and May 2001). Space considerations do not allow us to elaborate on these issues.

5. The *Economist* (2007) labels only 28 out of 167 countries as full democracies.

6. http://www.fundforpeace.org/web/index.php?option=com_content&task=view&id=99&Itemid=140; accessed 08/08/07.

7. It is analytically important to differentiate benefits that have characteristics of private goods (rival and excludable) from ones that have characteristics of club goods (nonrival excludable). There is a tendency to subsume clubs benefits under private benefits (see, for example, Delmas and Keller 2005).

8. In his Nobel Prize acceptance speech, Coase (1991) points to the tendency of his critics to benchmark imperfect markets against perfect governments. He calls for recognizing that all institutions fail and for undertaking comparative analysis of how various imperfect institutions fare in the context of a given objective. This important caution needs to be exercised by detractors (who tend to focus on club failures and ignore governmental failures) and supporters (who tend to focus on government failures and overlook club failures) of voluntary clubs.

9. If stakeholders are unable to distinguish between effective voluntary clubs and greenwashes, they may treat all clubs as failures, and fail to reward any firm for its club participation. Such problems could lead to a "lemons market" (Akerloff 1970) for voluntary environmental clubs in which weak clubs drive effective ones out of the market. What is important for clubs—and perhaps even central—is that they build and communicate a brand identity that stakeholders understand and find credible.

10. See Rees (1997) work on communitarian regulations in this regard.

11. Monitoring can have four variants: first-party (internal auditing), second-party (conducted by firms in the same industry, as in Responsible Care prior to 2002), third-party (conducted by accredited auditors but paid for by the audited party), and fourth-party (conducted by accredited auditors that have no financial relationship with the audited party). First- and second-party auditing are not considered credible. To keep our framework simple, we do not discuss them. Fourth-party auditing is very rare and therefore less

interesting to examine from a policy perspective. By and large, third-party auditing is the gold standard in voluntary clubs.

12. Kotchen and Van d'Veld (2009) are notable exceptions.

13. However, there are situations where industry clubs are established not by firms but by nongovernmental organizations that wish to regulate firms' environmental policies. In the forestry industry, non-governmental organizations established the Forest Stewardship Council and began lobbying forestry firms to join it. Forestry firms were not comfortable with this club, simply because they did not want an adversarial actor to decide the stringency of club standards (Sasser et al. 2006). Thus, key forestry firms sought to and succeeded in establishing an industry-sponsored club, the Sustainable Forestry Initiative.

14. http://www.sfiprogram.org/erp.cfm; accessed 8/21/07.

15. http://www.iso.org/iso/en/stdsdevelopment/whowhenhow/how. html; accessed 08/21/07.

16. http://www.isealalliance.org/; accessed 8/21/07.

17. In addition to industry reputation, firms have reputations and so do their products. Toyota Camry's aggregate reputation is a function of Camry's reputation, Toyota's reputation, and the Japanese automobile industry's reputation. Which reputation type will dominate in specific contexts and why, is a question worthy of further research.

REFERENCES

Akerlof, G. A. 1970. The market for "lemons": Quality uncertainty and the market mechanism. *Quarterly Journal of Economics* 84, no. 3: 488–500.

Barnett, M. L., and A. A. King. 2006. Good fences make good neighbors: An institutional explanation of industry self-regulation. Paper presented at the Academy of Management Best Paper Proceedings, Atlanta, GA.

Bartley, T. 2009. Standards for sweatshops: The power and limits of club theory for explaining voluntary labor standards programs. In *Voluntary programs: A club theory perspective*, ed. Matthew Potoski and Aseem Prakash. Cambridge: MIT Press.

Bessen S. M., and G. Saloner. 1988. *Compatibility standards and the market for telecommunication services*. Santa Monica: Rand.

Buchanan, J. M. 1965. An economic theory of clubs. *Economica* 32: 1–14.

Carpenter, D. P. 2001. *The forging of bureaucratic autonomy.* Princeton: Princeton University Press.

Cashore, B., G. Auld, and D. Newsom. 2004. *Governing through markets.* New Haven: Yale University Press.

Coase, R. H. 1960. The problem of social cost. *Journal of Law and Economics* 3: 1–44.

———. 1991. Nobel Prize lecture. http://www.nobel.se/economics/laureates/1991/coase-lecture.html; Retrieved on 08/15/2007.

Coglianese, C., and J. Nash, eds. 2001. *Regulating from the inside.* Washington, DC: Resources for the Future.

Cornes, R., and T. Sandler. [1986]1996. *The theory of externalities, public goods, and club goods.* 2nd edition. Cambridge: Cambridge University Press.

Cutler, Claire A., Virginia Haufler, and Tony Porter. eds. 1999. *Private authority and international affairs.* Albany: State University of New York Press.

Darnall, N. and J. Carmin. 2005. Greener and cleaner? *Policy Sciences* 38, no. 2–3: 71–90.

Delmas, M., and A. Keller. 2005. Strategic free riding in voluntary programs: The case of the US EPA Wastewise Program. *Policy Sciences* 38: 91–106.

Dolsak, N., and E. Ostrom, eds. 2003. *The commons in the new millennium.* Cambridge: The MIT Press.

Economist 2007. Economist Intelligence Unit Democracy Index 2006. http://www.economist.com/media/pdf/DEMOCRACY_TABLE_20 07_v3.pdf; accessed 08/08/2007.

Farrell, J., and G. Shapiro. 1985. Standardization, compatibility, and innovation. *Rand Journal of Economics* 16: 70–83.

Fiorinio, D. J. 1999. Rethinking environmental regulation. *Harvard Environmental Law Review* 23: 441–69.

Gunningham, N. A., R. A. Kagan, and D. Thornton. 2003. *Shades of green.* Stanford: Stanford University Press.

Harbaugh, R., J. Maxwell, and B. Roussillon. 2006. The Groucho Effect of uncertain standards. Working paper. Indiana University, Kelly School of Business Department of Business Economics and Public Policy.

Hardin, G. 1968. The tragedy of the commons, *Science* 162: 1243–48.

Haufler, V. 2009. The Kimberly Process, club goods, and public enforcement of private programs. In *Voluntary programs: A club theory perspective,* ed. Matthew Potoski and Aseem Prakash, Cambridge: MIT Press.

Hobbes, T. 1651. *Leviathan*. http://oregonstate.edu/instruct/phl302/texts/hobbes/leviathan-c.html; accessed 03/02/2007.

Hoffman, A. J. 1997. *From heresy to dogma*. San Francisco: New Lexington Press.

King, A., and M. Lenox. 2000. Industry self-regulation without sanctions: The chemical industry's Responsible Care Program. *Academy of Management Journal* 43 (August): 698–716.

Kotchen, M., and Klaas van 't Veld. 2009. An economics perspective on treating voluntary programs as clubs. In *Voluntary programs: A club theory perspective*, ed. Matthew Potoski and Aseem Prakash. Cambridge: MIT Press.

Lenox, M., and J. Nash. 2003. Industry self-regulation and adverse selection: A comparison across four trade association programs. *Business Strategy and the Environment* 12, no. 6: 343–56.

March, J., and J. Olsen. 1989. *Rediscovering institutions*. New York: The Free Press.

McGuire, M. 1972. Private good clubs and public good clubs. *Swedish Journal of Economics* 74: 84–99.

North, D. C. 1990. *Institutions, institutional change, and economic performance*. New York: Cambridge University Press.

North, D. C., and Weingast, B. 1989. Constitutions and commitment: Evolution of institutions governing public choice in 17th-century England. *Journal of Economic History* 49: 803–32.

Olson, M., Jr. 1965. *The logic of collective action*. Cambridge: Harvard University Press.

Ostrom, E. 1990. *Governing the commons*. Cambridge: Cambridge University Press.

———, Walker, J., and R. Gardner. 1994. *Rules, games, and common-pool resources*. Ann Arbor: University of Michigan Press.

Pigou, A. C. 1960[1920]. *The economics of welfare*. 4th ed. London: McMillan.

Potoski, M., and A. Prakash. 2004. Green clubs and voluntary governance: ISO 14001 and firms' regulatory compliance. *American Journal of Political Science* 49, no. 2: 235–48.

———. 2005. Covenants with weak swords: ISO 14001 and firms' environmental performance. *Journal of Policy Analysis and Management* 24, no. 4: 745–69.

———, eds. 2008. *Voluntary programs: A club theory perspective*. Cambridge: MIT Press.

Prakash, A. 2000. *Greening the firm*. Cambridge: Cambridge University Press.

Prakash, A., and M. Potoski. 2006. Racing to the bottom? Globalization, environmental governance, and ISO 14001. *American Journal of Political Science* 50, no. 2: 347–61.

———. 2007a. Collective action through voluntary environmental programs: A club theory perspective. *Policy Studies Journal* 35, no. 4: 773–92.

———. 2007b. Investing up: FDI and the cross-national diffusion of ISO 14001. *International Studies Quarterly* 51, no. 3: 723–44.

———, and M. Potoski. 2006a. *The voluntary environmentalists*. Cambridge: Cambridge University Press.

Porter, M., and C. van der Linde. 1995. Toward a new conception of the environment-competitiveness relationship. *Journal of Economic Perspectives* 9: 97–118.

Rees, J. 1997. The development of communitarian regulation in the chemical industry. *Law and Policy* 19, no. 4: 477–528.

Rivera, J., P. de Leon, and C. Koerber. 2006. Is greener whiter yet? The Sustainable Slopes Program after five years. *Policy Studies Journal* 34, no. 2: 195–224.

Rivera, J., and P. deLeon. 2004. Is greener whiter? The Sustainable Slopes Program and the voluntary environmental performance of western ski areas. *Policy Studies Journal* 32, no. 3: 417–37.

Sasser, E., A. Prakash, B. Cashore, and G. Auld. 2006. Direct targeting as NGO political strategy: Examining private authority regimes in the forestry sector. *Business and Politics* 8, no. 3: 1–32.

Schultz, M., J. Mouritsen, and G. Gabrielsen. 2001. Sticky reputation. *Corporate Reputation Review* 4, no. 1: 24–41.

Stigler, G. 1971. The theory of economic regulation. *Bell Journal of Economics* 2: 3–21.

Tiebout, C. M. 1956. A pure theory of public expenditure. *Journal of Political Economy* 64: 416–24.

Weigelt, K., and Camerer, C. 1988. Reputation and corporate strategy: A review of recent theory and applications. *Strategic Management Journal* 9, no. 5: 443–54.

Welch, E. W., A. Mazur, and S. Bretschneider. 2000. Voluntary behavior by electric utilities. *Journal of Policy Analysis and Management* 19 (Summer): 407–25.

Winter, S. C., and P. J. May. 2001. Motivation for compliance with environmental regulations. *Journal of Policy Analysis and Management* 20, no. 4: 675–98.

Wiseman, J. 1957. The theory of public utility—An empty box. *Oxford Economic Papers* 9: 56–74.

3

THE DEMOCRATIC LEGITIMACY OF
PRIVATE AUTHORITY IN THE FOOD CHAIN

DORIS FUCHS AND AGNI KALFAGIANNI

INTRODUCTION

The objective of this chapter is to explore the implications of private
authority in global food governance for democratic legitimacy. It starts
from the recognition that global food and agricultural governance is
increasingly being created not only by (inter)governmental actors but
also by private actors. Food retail corporations, in particular, have
become key players in the governance of the global food system
through the creation of governance institutions such as private standards, corporate social responsibility initiatives, and public-private or
private-private partnerships (PPPs). In the interest of time and space,
however, we will concentrate on private standards in the context of this
chapter. Private retail standards, while targeting key problems of the
global food system, such as food safety and environmental sustainability, also reflect and to some extent strengthen the exercise of power by
retailers in global food governance, raising questions about their democratic legitimacy.

Such questions become particularly relevant when standards fail to
improve, if they don't actually worsen, the sustainability of the global
food system. As we have shown elsewhere, the implications of private
standards for sustainability are indeed ambivalent (Fuchs, Kalfagianni,
Arentsen 2009). While some positive effects on food safety and some

quality can be recognized in Western countries, domestic food quality in developing countries has not benefited accordingly as these positive effects are often restricted to food products for export markets. Furthermore, the introduction of environmental standards may have led to some environmental benefits, yet these environmental improvements are not as big as retailers want consumers to believe. Moreover, they may not be the most pressing concerns at the moment. Especially in developing countries, a trend toward the marginalization of small farmers and retailers, and subsequently an increase in economic inequality due to the stringent retail standards, can be observed. This chapter then, analyzes the implications of private retail standards for democratic legitimacy, taking into account their ambivalent sustainability effects.

In its endeavor, the chapter is based on an analytic governance approach combined with a critical power-theoretic perspective in order to present the link between retail power, especially its structural and discursive facets, and private governance institutions. In discussing the democratic legitimacy of these institutions, the chapter uses the criteria of participation, transparency, and accountability proposed by Porter and Ronit (this volume). Since there is currently no agreement as to which concept of democracy is more appropriate for governance beyond the state, the chapter evaluates, with the help of the proposed criteria, three frequently discussed concepts of democratic legitimacy: input legitimacy, output legitimacy, and deliberative democracy. In developing and applying these concepts to global food governance, the chapter finds that private standards are deficient and need to be more strongly linked to public forms of authority if democratic legitimacy in this issue area is to be ensured.

The following section presents a conceptual discussion of power and democracy before turning to the case. The third section then will show that private standards can be linked to the growth in the structural and discursive power of retail corporations. The fourth section will assess the democratic legitimacy of food retail standards, while the fifth section concludes our chapter by summarizing our findings and delineating their implications for research and policy.

CONCEPTUAL ISSUES: POWER AND DEMOCRACY

Power

The rise in private food governance and its implications cannot be understood without reference to the increasing economic and political power of retail corporations. Before starting our empirical analysis, then, we briefly lay out our conceptualization of business power. We assume that state and non-state actors play an important role in global politics. In other words, this analysis treats governance as "multi-actor, multi-level political decision-making" (Rosenau and Czempiel 1992; Messner and Nuscheler 1996, 2003). Moreover, we assume that actors draw power from material and structural as well as ideational and normative sources. In other words, we apply a critical power-theoretic approach, which is positioned close to Lukes's (1974; 2004) work on the three faces of power and Levy and Egan's (2000) analysis of business power in climate change politics (see also Fuchs 2005; 2007).

The different facets of power are conceptualized as follows. Instrumental power is characterized by its direct influence on other actors' decisions, thereby affecting the output side of the political process. Although contributing significantly to the analysis of (business) actors' power, for instance via lobbying and campaign/party financing, this first facet neglects those sources of power that predetermine actors' behavioral options. Therefore, structural power as the "second face" of power focuses on the input side of the political process, emphasizing the influence on actors' behavioral options through existing material structures. Structural power is either indirect (agenda-setting) or direct (rule-setting power). In this chapter, we are interested in rule-setting power, which endows business actors that have access to and control over pivotal networks and necessary resources with the capacity to adopt, implement, and enforce quasi-binding rules, thereby affecting other actors as well.

Finally, an analysis of both instrumental and structural power still neglects the systemic sources of power that preexist decisions and non-decisions by actors. Discursive power, therefore, adds a third, sociological perspective to the analysis of power. This facet emphasizes the importance of norms and ideas and treats policy decisions as a function of discursive contests over the framing of policies, actors, as well as underlying societal norms. In addition, it recognizes the importance of symbols, story lines, and compelling arguments in the public debate. Discursive power is closely tied to the question of legitimacy, as it relies on the willingness of recipients to listen and also to trust these actors. Furthermore, the success of self-regulatory practices largely depends on the perception of business as a legitimate political actor.

In an analysis of the democratic implications of business power, all three forms of power would be equally important. Such an analysis, for instance, would stress the pluralistic character of the policy process in a democracy and investigate the influence of private actors in decision making, through lobbying, agenda setting, and rule setting, and the influence of issue-specific as well as broader societal norms and ideas. In the interest of space and time, however, we restrict our analysis to the democratic implications of private governance institutions in this chapter. In other words, we are interested in the democratic functions, structures, and outcomes of institutions created and controlled by private actors within the context of a global "public" space. Since, as we will show below, the rise of such institutions, specifically food retail standards, is based primarily on the structural and discursive facets of business power, we neglect the instrumental facet in the context of this chapter.

Democracy

In this section, we present three frequently discussed conceptualizations of democratic legitimacy beyond the state: input legitimacy, output legitimacy and deliberative democracy. We will subsequently explore the democratic legitimacy of private food governance from each of these three perspectives based on the criteria of participation, transparency, and accountability (see chapter 1).

According to input-oriented-arguments, legitimacy derives from democratic procedures and formal arrangements. These procedures and arrangements (i.e., individual rights, participation in law formation, elections, etc.) are in place to ensure the autonomy of the individual and the collectivity, which are fundamental for the self-governance of a democratic society. Autonomy means that individuals feel free under law even though constrained by it because it is they who have created the law in the first place. As such, autonomy presupposes equality, as it is difficult to imagine freedom under law if it is not equally possible for all to participate in the positing of the law (Castoriadis 1997). According to output-oriented arguments, on the other hand, legitimacy derives from the effectiveness of the specific governance institution in designing policies that promote the public good. In that latter type of legitimacy, two notions are entailed; one that the public good rather than private interest (from private or public actors) is served and the other that the public good is served effectively (Scharpf 2003).

Finally, deliberative democracy bases its understanding of democratic legitimacy on the discursive quality of the procedures leading to the design and implementation of the governance institution. As the term itself suggests, in a deliberative democracy, these procedures are discursive. Influenced by Habermasian ideas, the rationale is that individuals (and indeed any actor) increasingly accept the force of arguments. Hence, the main concern of deliberative democracy is how to optimize the discourse about which goals are to be achieved by utilizing and fostering the deliberative competence of those involved in it (Wolf 2002). Democratic legitimacy, in turn, derives from the quality of the discursive process.

THE CASE OF PRIVATE FOOD STANDARDS

The democratic legitimacy of global food governance is fundamental for the well-being of societies worldwide. Democracy is the major political achievement of mankind. Today's global food governance, however, is characterized by an increasing role of private governance institutions. Significantly, public rules and norms also exist in food governance, and have since World War II. These include for example, the Food and Agriculture Organization (FAO), the Codex Alimentarius Commission, or the Biosafety Convention and Cartagena Protocol. The Codex Alimentarius Commission, in particular, has developed a multitude of food standards covering aspects of safety, quality, and transparency since its creation (Sklair 2002). Moreover, regulations regarding standards of food production have existed for a long time at the European Union level.

Against this background, the increasing spread of private governance institutions is of pivotal importance. We argue that this spread can be linked to developments in retail power, in particular its structural and discursive facets. Hence, before we turn to the analysis of the democratic legitimacy of private institutions in food governance, we first present some examples of expanding private institutions and then discuss the links between private governance and power.

Examples of Private Retail Standards

Standards are defined as a rule of measurement established by regulation or authority (Jones and Hill 1994). Private standards tend to be voluntary in nature and rely on certification mechanisms to identify actors complying with the principles defined in the standard. Often, these retail standards are developed collectively (either at the national or international level) in order to strengthen their structural power and induce supplier participation. As we discuss below, by adopting the same standards retailers, for instance, can constrain market choices and thereby basically force suppliers to accept them (Busch 2000). The British Retail Consortium (BRC), the Global Food Safety Initiative

(GFSI), GLOBALGAP,[1] and FOODTRACE are examples of such standards in global food governance.

Let us present these standards in more detail. The British Retail Consortium Technical Standard was created by the BRC in 1998 in order to evaluate manufacturers of retailers' own brand products. It consists of more than 250 requirements including comprehensive norms for food safety and quality schemes, products and process management, as well as personal hygiene of personnel. For most UK and Scandinavian retailers, BRC certification is required in order to consider business with these suppliers (www.brc.org.uk). Following the Packaging Standard in the previous year, the Consumer Products Standard was introduced in August 2003 by the BRC. Each of these standards is revised and updated at least every three years.

The Global Food Safety initiative was initiated in 2000 by a group of international retailers and global manufacturers such as Unilever. With fifty-two members and 65 percent of worldwide food retail revenue, it aims for consumer protection and the strengthening of consumer confidence. Furthermore, the initiative sets requirements for food safety and intends to improve efficiency costs throughout the food chain.

GLOBALGAP was developed in 1997 by a group of retailers belonging to the Euro-retailers Produce Working Group (EUREP). While initially only applying to fruits and vegetables, it now covers meat products and fish from aquaculture as well. Completion and verification of a checklist consisting of 254 questions is required in order to acquire GLOBALGAP certification. This checklist is divided into 41 "major musts," 122 "minor musts," as well as 91 recommendations, or "shoulds." Traceability and food safety are covered by major must practices while minor musts and shoulds include environmental and animal welfare issues. Currently, GLOBALGAP covers more than eighty thousand producers in eighty countries and, like the rest of the business-to-business standards presented here is not visible to consumers (see also Levi-Faur, this volume).

FOODTRACE, finally, was initiated by the European retail association for the promotion of a European concerted action in the development of a traceability scheme for the whole chain. Their goal is to create a practical framework for all actors involved in the chain, including the international level, thereby allowing for traceability throughout all stages of the chain. In order to ensure its application in developing countries, the proposed scheme is supposed to be technology independent but technologically supported.

ASSESSING THE POWER OF THE FOOD RETAILERS
AND THEIR STANDARDS

The rise in private food governance and its implications cannot be understood without reference to the increasing economic and political power of retail corporations. We currently recognize a global development toward retail concentration. According to economists, six large supermarket chains will dominate global markets in the future. Their representatives will buy on site and use global networks to distribute the products to their stores around the world (MacMillan 2005). This trend toward concentration is particularly staggering in Europe and the United States. In the United States, the five largest supermarket chains have more than doubled their market share between 1992 and 2000 (Konefal et al. 2005). In Europe, likewise, increasing retail concentration can be seen even in countries in which it was still low in the beginning of the 1990s, for example, Portugal and Spain (OECD 2006).

What are the implications of this increasing market power of retailers? First and foremost, these trends suggest the ability of retail chains to put pressure on suppliers in terms of prices (monopsony power) reaching all the way to farmers in both industrialized and developing countries. For instance, studies have shown a dramatic drop in farmers' selling power in Norway, where four grocery chains (Norgesgruppen, Ica Norge, Coop Norgeand, Reitan Narvesen) control nearly 100 percent of the groceries sold (OECD 2006). Furthermore, by selling and distributing the premium national and international brands, the large grocery chains significantly limit the possibility for small or local farmers to get their products in the grocery chains (op. cit.). In other words, due to their position retail chains are able to exercise significant structural power in both national and international markets.

Most importantly for the current analysis, however, retail power is not only reflected in the ability to determine market prices. The increasing presence and relevance of private standards also reflect a facet of the political power of retail corporations. After all, these standards allow retail corporations to affect the input side of the political process, that is, to determine the focus and content of rules governing the international food system. This power is a form of structural power insofar as the position of corporations in the global economic networks provides them with a strong influence on which private standards and labels are widely adopted. In other words, corporations can punish and reward NGO-created standards and labels, for instance, for their choice of criteria, just as the traditional notion of structural power identified the ability of TNCs to punish and reward governments for their policy choices.

Finally, the increasing discursive power of food retail corporations is noteworthy. Retailers' successful representation of themselves as guardians of consumer interest, both in terms of prices and quality, is one of the best examples of this discursive power. By arguing that public actors are not fast enough and lack the necessary expertise to develop the most efficient standards, and simultaneously emphasizing their own efficiency in production, distribution, and, most importantly, in the design and monitoring of such standards, retailers have secured legitimacy as political actors in global food governance for themselves.

Private standards constitute an important part of PR strategies and advertising through which discursive power can be exercised. With standard guidelines not included in product labeling, retail brands are used to create a loyal and stable customer base (Burch and Lawrence 2005; Codron, Siriex, and Reardon 2006).[2] In this context, retail brands are used to communicate the existence of private standards in order to frame and point out quality assurances. According to studies, one of every five products bought in supermarkets in the United States is of retail store brand, thereby indicating the success of the incorporated "quality claim." Moreover, further growth with regard to these brands can be expected and similar developments can be observed in several European countries (Nemeth-Ek 2000). For instance, with 44.7 percent share (by volume) of the retail market, the United Kingdom leads in sales of retail brands, followed by Belgium (34.8 percent), Germany (33.4 percent), the Netherlands (21.1 percent), and France (22.2 percent). Within the next few years, experts predict a dominance of retail brands in the global food industry, with the biggest retailers being the primary actors (AgraEurope 2002).

Rule-setting power and discursive power in food retail are closely linked to the question of consumer power. Both business and government actors frequently refer to the consumer as the main decision maker, emphasizing the notion of "consumer sovereignty." Yet, while it is true that consumers do have some power, this power is limited by information asymmetries concerning products, production processes, and other actors in the supply chain, as well as high transaction costs for "political" consumers. After all, in order to be able to exercise significant market power thousands of consumers have to be mobilized. Furthermore, consumer power is constrained by business actors' active manipulations of demand (see media presence) and choice editing. And while it is true that consumers are not free of liability concerning the economic, social, and ethical implications of their decisions, within the political framework of the food governance regime they obviously find themselves in a much weaker position vis-à-vis the retail industry.

In sum, the power of retailers (as well as the importance of food as a source of nourishment and income) makes it crucial to assess the democratic legitimacy of private food standards. After all, these private governance institutions are more than business practices companies use to organize their activities. They reflect rules and standards that have fundamental implications for the allocation of values and resources in society, the core business of politics, according to Easton (1971). They embody the triumph of one rule or norm over other potential ones and may prevent or undermine public rules and norms. Accordingly, the fundamental question of how to create a level playing field, institute checks and balances on power, and ensure the accountability of those setting rules and standards in global food governance can no longer be neglected.

ASSESSING THE DEMOCRATIC LEGITIMACY OF THE PRIVATE GOVERNANCE OF FOOD

Input Legitimacy

Privatizing food governance is highly problematic from the perspective of input legitimacy. Regarding the procedural dimension, critical observers draw attention to a lack of transparency and access that characterizes many private or public-private schemes. A lack of access provides a serious obstacle to the provision of equal opportunities to different societal actors to influence the norms and rules that govern the food system. The lack of participation in the development of the institutions, with which individuals and groups have to abide, is a fundamental detriment to autonomy and equality. For the private standards discussed in this chapter, such discrimination in access primarily affects civil society and actors from developing countries, but also smaller business actors and those that are farther away from the consumer, for example, farmers. In the development of GLOBALGAP, for instance, while committees for standard requirements have 50 percent retailer and 50 percent producer participation, participants from industrialized countries, Europe in particular, dominate.[3] Such dominance can be explained by the criteria of expertise instead of nationality on the basis of which membership and participation in committees is granted (Levi-Faur, this volume) as well as resource constraints. Thus, even in multi-stakeholder initiatives, participation from developing countries is considered problematic and North-South inequities remain (Schaller 2007).

An interesting question in this context is, then, to what extent private actors still would be interested in creating private governance institutions if they were forced to allow wide participation and ensure accountability.[4] The Forest Stewardship Council (FSC) is a private governance institution that suggests ambivalent insights in this context. On the one side, the FSC is frequently lauded as a success due to its participatory structure and associated relatively stringent criteria. On the other side, it still covers a small share of world timber markets only, as important timber industries have decided to create competing and weaker labels rather than joining the FSC.

A lack of transparency also weakens the democratic legitimacy of private governance mechanisms from the perspective of input legitimacy. If private actors develop their own rules, then at least these rules should be open to public scrutiny. The lack of transparency can render access, even in cases where it exists, meaningless by obscuring the real options actors can "vote" for. This is related to the exclusion of civil society in the monitoring and implementation of standards in most cases.

Next to questions of participation and transparency, finally, accountability is a crucial issue when it comes to democratic input legitimacy. While public actors are not always superior as creators of governance institutions, it is on the issue of accountability that we find them in a clear advantage. Public actors (in functioning democracies) have to be accountable to more interests and criteria than private actors. With private governance institutions, accountability and mechanisms to ensure it are not predefined. Multinational business actors are at best accountable to only a fraction of the people affected by their activities. Moreover, accountability is difficult if not impossible to enforce for vague standards and CSR initiatives. The same applies to many public-private partnerships, by the way. In the area of biotechnology and development aid, for instance, the collaboration between public and private actors is quite obscure. In the large network of actors around USAID and the GMO corporations, who is to be held accountable if genetically modified seeds accidentally mix with local corn in African countries, and how?

Accountability to the people in a democracy differs from accountability to the people ruled by a nondemocratic, potentially corrupt government, of course. Thus, one may be inclined to argue that in the case of a lack of democratically elected and accountable public actors, private governance institutions will be able to provide a more legitimate form of governance. As long as these private governance institutions are not held to some standard of accountability, however, such an assumption does not stand on firm ground.

The institution of measures providing input legitimacy for private governance institutions clearly is not an easy task. Ensuring a level playing field in participation would require first a definition of who should have the right to participate. Who are those "governed" by a private governance institution? Should only those "directly" affected by such an institution have the right to participate, or everybody even remotely affected? Secondly, such measures would require support for those facing resource or collective action constraints in participation. In terms of accountability, similar questions arise: Accountability to whom? And how can those governed be provided with sufficient support to allow them to actually enforce this accountability in the context of huge information asymmetries and collective action problems?[5]

Output Legitimacy

The above discussion points out that private institutions do not fulfill the criteria of input legitimacy most of the time. According to a more functionalist account, however, concerns about input legitimacy would be less relevant if output legitimacy was provided. Output legitimacy refers to the effectiveness of private governance institutions in promoting the public good. Yet, we will show that claims to democratic legitimacy based on output-related criteria stand on equally shaky ground.

To be able to judge the performance of private governance institutions in terms of output, after all, one first needs to define "effectiveness" and "the public good" in the context of global food governance. Immediately, we face similar problems as those identified with respect to input legitimacy. More specifically, concerns about participation, transparency, and accountability play an important role here too. In terms of participation, different stakeholders will define different aspects of the global food system as "the public good." In consequence, there is also no objective measure of the "effectiveness" of a private governance institution in providing the public good. Rather, we can only define the public good and measure the effectiveness of its provision with respect to the definition and interests of certain publics. Retailers, for instance, will define the effectiveness of their standards in terms of traceability and the provision of food safety in the narrow sense. If we include consumers in the North in the relevant public, the effectiveness of the provision of public good will also have to be measured with respect to the promotion of some environmental norms. If, on the other hand, the public includes all those affected, then the public good is promoted effectively when safety, environmental, and

social norms are fostered simultaneously, that is, when farmer livelihoods in the South are included as well.

Accordingly, the definition of the relevant "public" is a crucial issue,
which is strongly linked to the question of participation, in turn. It is difficult to imagine that the norms and objectives relevant to a broader
public truly will be fostered without the participation of this public. How
are these norms and objectives going to be voiced otherwise? Who is
going to ensure their effective inclusion? Elements of private governance
institutions allegedly addressing questions of environmental or social
responsibility frequently turn out to be window dressing rather than serious efforts at performance improvements, for example (Gibson 1999;
Haufler 2001; King and Lenox 2000; von Mirbach 1999). Hence, output
legitimacy presupposes satisfying criteria of participation, after all.

Furthermore, one precondition for the pursuit of the public good in
global food governance is transparency. In a narrow sense, transparency in the global food system relates to the ability to trace the history of a product backward and forward through the entire production
chain from harvest through transport, processing, distribution, and sale.
This process is important in order to ensure the accurate and rapid
identification of product and process information up and down the
chain and therefore to be able to eliminate or confine a potential food
safety danger. In a broader sense, however, transparency also covers
the normative concerns of various societal actors regarding the environmental and social sustainability impacts of food production, for
instance. Normative transparency is important in order to help the various stakeholders make informed choices based on sound sustainability
criteria. Regarding the narrow conceptualization of transparency, the
standards presented in the third section illustrate significant efforts
toward an improvement of traceability and food safety. In contrast,
attention to sustainability in a broader sense has been either minimal or
incidental (see also Kalfagianni 2006). Thus, we can attribute output
legitimacy of private food governance institutions in terms of transparency only when transparency is narrowly defined.

Finally, advocates of the concept of output legitimacy will have to
acknowledge that accountability is important in terms of output legitimacy too. If the output provided by a governance institution does not
serve the public good, or not in a sufficiently effective way, the "governing" actors should be held accountable. In a narrow sense again,
accountability in private food governance can be interpreted in terms of
compliance with the rules provided by the private governance institutions, as well as the consequences of noncompliance. Regular checks
and controls by an independent, trusted authority, for instance, could

foster compliance and enhance the effectiveness of private governance institutions. Almost all private schemes mentioned earlier in the chapter include as a consequence of noncompliance that parties lose their license to produce. Hence, in this narrow sense, private governance actors can be held accountable for their conduct. That criterion would not necessarily satisfy those, however, who regard the broader public as the relevant stakeholders of private food governance. After all, the public cannot hold the "governors" of a private food governance institution accountable, if it feels that that institution does not serve the public good (sufficiently effectively).[6] In consequence, the concept of output legitimacy proves to be characterized by conceptual weaknesses.

In addition, we can identify significant challenges to the democratic legitimacy of private standards in global food governance from a substantive perspective. A key contemporary aspect of output legitimacy in global food governance necessarily has to be sustainability. Sustainability here includes aspects of food safety and security, environmental implications, and social implications, such as the creation of livelihoods. In a socioeconomic sense, more than half of the world's population is engaged in agricultural production. It thus provides a livelihood for a significant proportion of people on the planet. And food is a commodity that touches us all—we all eat, and thus are consumers of food as well. Food production and trade have important implications for socioeconomic outcomes and, depending on their organization and distribution, can work to either enhance or detract from economic opportunities and environmental and social living conditions. As we have shown elsewhere (Fuchs, Kalfagianni, and Arentsen 2009) and mentioned above, however, private food standards have conflicting impacts on these different aspects of sustainability. While some positive effects on food safety and quality for consumers in Northern markets can be recognized, the food quality in developing countries has not benefited accordingly, as these positive effects are often restricted to food products for export markets. Furthermore, the introduction of environmental standards may have led to some environmental benefits, but these benefits are limited and environmental issues may not be the most pressing concerns at the moment. Especially in developing countries, a trend toward the marginalization of farmers and retailers as well as an increase in economic inequality due to the retail standards can be observed. If we add these substantive concerns to the conceptual weakness of the concept of output legitimacy, we can clearly recognize that output legitimacy fails to provide the potential alternative source of democratic legitimacy for private food governance with which its advocates associate it.[7]

Deliberative Democracy

Deliberative democracy, as well as other conceptualizations of democracy beyond the state (e.g., cosmopolitan democracy), have been developed to respond to the challenges globalization poses to traditional,
territorial concepts of democracy. Deliberative democracy is relevant for
our present discussion because it makes a direct link between input
and output legitimacy. More specifically, it recognizes that the quality of
procedures on the input side influences the quality of the outputs.
Since the procedures in a deliberative democracy are discursive, the
context of deliberation takes profound significance. Two fundamental
conditions need to be fulfilled for the fostering of legitimacy according
to deliberative democracy theories: inclusiveness and unconstrained
dialogue (Dryzek 1990; Smith 2003; Young 2000). In terms of inclusiveness, the principle of stakeholding is central to the deliberative argument: all those affected by, or with a stake in, the decision have a right
to the voice in the governance of those matters (McGrew 2003). That
confines the relevant *demos* to those affected by the decisions. Regarding unconstrained dialogue, this requires the promotion of deliberate as
opposed to strategic arguments (Smith 2003). This, in turn, requires
interactions that are egalitarian, uncoerced, competent, and free from
delusion, deception, power, and strategy (Dryzek 1990).

While inclusiveness and unconstrained dialogue may seem to have
a great appeal for arguments regarding the democratic legitimacy of private institutions of food governance, there are a number of concerns
associated with the deliberative democracy thesis as well, however.
Regarding the selection of participants in the deliberations, the participation criterion for democratic legitimacy, proponents of deliberative
democracy appear to have a very clear proposal: those affected the
most by the decisions should participate in the deliberations. That automatically excludes those not or less affected by the decisions and, by
implication, restricts accountability and transparency of the decision-
making process to a narrowly defined public as well. However, who is
most affected by a specific governance institution may well be controversial. In terms of private food governance institutions, for instance,
who would those included in or excluded from the decisions be? Who
are those the most affected and who is going to decide about that?
After all, all the actors in the food chain, from the farmer to the consumer, are affected by private food standards.

Moreover, even if one happens to arrive at agreement on the point
of who is most affected by a given governance institution, the question
then becomes how to organize an inclusive, transparent, and egalitarian

deliberation. After all, that presupposes a level of equality in resources, organizing capacities, and reach that can hardly be said to exist between a transnational corporation and a small NGO, a transnational corporation and a small farmer or independent store, a small and a large NGO, and so on. In the same way, the structural power of these different actors is vastly different, as is their discursive power and associated capacity to influence other actors' ideas and perceptions.

In that respect, the relationship between consumer and retail discursive power is a complex one. Consumer demand for transparency, quality, and healthy food products, for example, overlaps with retail demand for higher standards. It may seem difficult to determine here whose discursive power is bigger, even though consumers do not have access to the media and advertising, which are the main discursive instruments for reaching mass audiences. It is the structural supremacy of retailers, however, that clearly creates difficulties in an open and egalitarian deliberative dialogue with consumers.

Perhaps, then, deliberative democracy ideas are more applicable when we talk about individuals as stakeholders rather than organized interests. Of course, there are several criticisms associated with that thesis too, such as the neglect of individuals' different cultures and understandings (Young 1996), the infinite time needed for deliberation in the face of pressing political decisions, the utopian character of deliberative democracy because of the large number of people that need to be involved for it to be meaningful (Farrelly 2004), and the assumptions about perfect information and perfect knowledge of the democratic procedures of the people involved (Castoriadis 1997). Yet, deliberative democracy sounds more plausible when it refers to individuals than when it refers to the foundation of democratic legitimacy in the context of private governance institutions in today's global political economy.

It may make more sense, then, to approach the question of the democratic legitimacy of private food governance institutions in terms of the democratic control of these institutions. How can such a democratic control be exercised, however? Here, public actors necessarily come back into the game. Indeed, private governance institutions need to be placed under the auspices of public regulatory frameworks. Such frameworks need to provide criteria for participation, transparency, and accountability in the creation of private governance institutions, if not for the inclusion of specific objectives and criteria.

The unwillingness of public actors to create the necessary and sufficiently effective governance institutions to solve the sustainability problems of today's global food system, for instance, has led to the opportunity and need for private governance institutions in the global food system, in the first place, however. Thus, it is certainly not immediately obvious, why these very public actors should be willing to provide the necessary framework for private governance now. In consequence, the recognition of the need for a public framework is not meant to suggest that one can be easily obtained.

Democratic control could, in principle, also be exercised by citizens directly. In that case, however, the questions regarding access, transparency, and accountability need to be addressed again, not to mention issues of resources and organizing capacities. Thus, even here additional regulatory and capacity building measures would be needed.

CONCLUSION

In this chapter, we have delineated facets of the increasing political and economic power of private authority in food governance and investigated their implications for democratic legitimacy. Concentrating on retail standards in global food governance, we have shown that retailers have acquired rule-setting power as a result of their material position within the global economy. Due to their control of networks and resources, retailers have gained the capacity to adopt, implement, and enforce privately set rules (standards), which then take on obligatory quality for suppliers and affect the choice set of consumers. In this context, they have benefited from their acquisition of political legitimacy and therefore discursive power, due to their alleged expertise and efficiency in relation to public actors, as well as used their rule-setting activities to enhance and maintain this power.

Assessing the implications of private retail schemes in terms of their democratic legitimacy, we found that neither input and output legitimacy nor the concept of deliberative democracy offer convincing solutions to the democratic deficit of private food governance institutions. Questions about participation, accountability, and transparency keep surfacing in all three concepts of democratic legitimacy considered in this chapter. In terms of input legitimacy, concerns have been raised about the unequal participation and lack of transparency in the development of private standards, as well as problems in attributing accountability to private governance institutions due to difficulties in identifying the relevant public. In terms of output legitimacy, we found that effectiveness in promoting the public good can only be evaluated subjectively, as participation determines definitions of the public good. Moreover, transparency and accountability can be attributed in private governance schemes in terms of output legitimacy only when the former are narrowly defined. Finally, we briefly explored the suitability of the concept of deliberative democracy as a basis for attributing legitimacy to food governance beyond the state. We raised concerns, however, regarding the stakeholding principle of deliberative democracy due to restrictions in the definition of the relevant public and therefore accountability and transparency of the relevant processes and decisions to society at large. Most importantly, we found it problematic to attribute democratic legitimacy deriving from a deliberative process to organized interests, primarily due to inequalities in the structural and discursive power of the relevant actors. This, in turn, makes egalitarian participation in the deliberative process, a fundamental requirement for deliberative democracy, extremely difficult.

The result of our discussion of the issue of democratic legitimacy then, is not an optimistic one. Rather than being able to explain on what sources of legitimacy private food governance can draw, we have to caution against too easily attributing democratic legitimacy here. Private food governance is certainly desirable in a number of ways, such as the improvements in food safety and quality, and even to some extent environmental conditions achieved. Yet, its potential negative consequences are sufficiently severe to remind us of the importance of participation, transparency, and accountability in its creation as well as the need for checks and balances for the power exercised by the different actors involved, especially the large retail corporations.

The difficulty of this endeavor does not escape us. The development of effective mechanisms to improve participation, transparency, and accountability will have to take into account the asymmetrical power relationships among the actors involved in global food governance. Our analysis does not aim to suggest that any attempt to improve these dimensions of democratic legitimacy is futile and will fail in its objectives. It serves as a reminder, however, that democratization of private food governance cannot be achieved without establishing mechanisms of control of corporate power.

Such mechanisms include, for instance, investment in collective action and networking and other forms of strategic alliances that help balance the power exercised by retail corporations (Cook and Iliopoulos 2000; Fulton 2001; Johnson and Berdegue 2004; Levins 2002). Moreover, international organizations should establish stricter measures to prevent further expansion of retail structural power. The European Commission, in this context, has stopped mergers between companies in cases where there were justified fears of monopsony power (OECD 2006).

Likewise, any attempt to attribute democratic legitimacy to private food governance will have to take a position on the definition of a "global public." In that context, critical scholars question whether democracy *for all* should include corporations (as citizens) (see contributions of May and Smith, this volume). Such scholars urge us to revisit the basics of the definition of corporations as legal persons with identities and rights comparable to physical persons. It is important, in that sense, to keep in mind the artificial character of concepts and practices in food and other areas of governance, as well as the constant redefinition of objectives, roles, and responsibilities actors assume therein. Democracy and democratic legitimacy as societally created concepts and practices require continuous vigilance about whose voice is being heard articulating what objectives and whose interests are being served in the global governance of food, in the end.

NOTES

1. Until September 2007 GLOBALGAP was known as EUREPGAP. In this chapter GLOBALGAP is used throughout to refer to both.
2. Experts report that there is a growing significance of "own brand" products promoted by the supermarkets, which gradually are replacing manufacturers' brands (Burch and Lawrence 2005).
3. Standards and requirements of certification are approved by working committees in each sector.
4. This does not apply to mere "coordination games," of course.
5. In this context, a great difficulty in ensuring the accountability of private governance institutions is that many countries lack the institutions that foster "individual and collective agency" (Marquez 2005). In China, where many of the Western retailers are opening new stores, for example, collective action by workers is forbidden. In general, collective action through unionization has declined considerably across the world. Research reports that it has dropped especially sharply in Latin America, with decreased levels of unionization by almost 50 percent in Argentina, Colombia, Peru, and Venezuela since 1980 (Sabatini and Farnsworth 2006).
6. One could argue that the public, as consumers, could punish such private governance institutions. However, that would presuppose that a level of consumer information and choice rarely existent in the current complex global food system and concentrated retail sector.
7. Potentially, this lack of output legitimacy could lead to challenges to business power, in particular its discursive facet, in the long

term. If retailers are unable to provide the public good because the "public" is difficult to define in global food governance, then their legitimacy as food governors could be threatened. Subsequently, the vulnerability of private governance institutions cannot be ruled out. This would also require, however, a transformation of how political and consumer elites think about food governance toward an endorsement of real global criteria in the design and implementation of food policies.

REFERENCES

ActionAid International. 2005. *Power hungry. Six reasons to regulate global food corporations.*

Agra Europe. 2002. The shape of things to come—Food industry report, Global brands to dominate food industry over next year.

Alvarado, I., and K. Charmel. 2000. Crecimiento de los canales de distribucion de productos agricolas y sus efectos en el sector rural de America Central. Paper presented at the International Workshop Concentration in the Processing and Retails Segments of the Agrifood System in Latin America: Effects on the Rural Poor. Santiago, Chile.

Aristotle. 1992 edition. *The politics.* London: Penguin Books.

Baines, R. 2005. Private sector environment standards: Impact on ecological performance and international competitiveness of UK agriculture. Research Paper, Royal Agricultural College, UK.

Balsevich, F., J. A.Berdegue, L. Flores, D. Mainville, and Th. Reardon. 2003. Supermarkets and produce quality and safety standards in Latin America. *American Journal of Agricultural Economics* 85, no. 5: 1147–54.

Barry, J. 1996. Sustainability, political judgment and citizenship. Connecting green politics and democracy. In *Democracy and green political thought. Sustainability, rights, and citizenship*, ed. B. Doherty and M. de Geus, 115–31. London: Routledge.

Burch, D., and G. Lawrence. 2005. Supermarket own brands, supply chains, and the transformation of the agri-food system. *International Journal of Sociology of Agriculture and Food* 13, no. 1: 1–18.

Busch, L. 2000. The moral economy of grades and standards. *Journal of Rural Studies* 16: 273–83.

Castoriadis, C. 1997. Democracy as procedure and democracy as regime. *Constellations* 4, no. 1: 1–18.

Codron, J. M., L. Siriex, and Th. Reardon. 2006. Social and environmental attributes of food products in an emerging mass market: Challenges of signalling and consumer perception with European illustrations. *Agriculture and Human Values* 23: 283–97.

Cook, M. L., and C. Iliopoulos. 2000. Ill-defined property rights in collective action: The case of US agricultural cooperatives. In *Institutions, contracts, and organisations: Perspectives from new institutional economics*, ed. Claude Menard, 335–48. Northampton: Edward Elgar.

Dries L., Th. Reardon, and J. F. M. Swinnen. 2004. The rapid rise of supermarkets in Central and Eastern Europe: Implications for the agrifood sector and rural development. *Development Policy Review* 22, no. 5: 1–32.

Dryzek, J. S. 1990. Green reason: Communicative ethics and the biosphere. *Environmental Ethics* 12: 195–210.

Easton, D. 1971. *The political system. An inquiry into the state of political science*. New York: Knopf.

Farrelly, C. 2004. *An introduction to contemporary political theory*. London: Sage.

Fuchs, D. 2005. Commanding heights? The strength and fragility of business power in global politics. *Millennium* 33, no. 3: 771–803.

———. 2006. Transnational corporations and global governance: The effectiveness of private governance. In *Globalization. State of the art of research and perspectives*, ed. Stefan Schirm, 122–41. London: Routledge.

———. 2007. *Business power in global governance*. Boulder: Lynne Rienner Publishers.

———, A. Kalfagianni, and M. Arentsen. 2009. Retail power, private standards, and sustainability in the global food system. In *Agrofood corporations, global governance, and sustainability*, ed. Jennifer Clapp and Doris Fuchs. Cambridge: MIT Press.

Fulton, M. 2001. Traditional versus new generation cooperatives. In *A cooperative approach to local economic development*, ed. Christopher D. Merrett and Norman Walzer, 11–24. Westport: Quorum Books.

Gibson, R., ed. 1999. *Voluntary initiatives*. Peterborough: Broadview Press.

Grain. 2005. *USAID: Making the world hungry for GM crops*. Grain Briefing, (April 2000).

Haufler, V. 2001. *A public role for the private sector*. Washington, DC: Carnegie Endowment for International Peace.

Johnson, N., and J. A. Berdegué. 2004. Collective action and property rights for sustainable development, 2020 vision for food, agriculture, and the environment. In *Collective action and property rights for sustainable development*. ed. Ruth S. Meinzen-Dick and Monica Di Gregorio. Brief 13 of 16. February. Washington, DC: International Food Policy Research Institute (IFPRI). Available at http://www.ifpri.org/2020/focus/focus11/focus11.pdf.

Jones, E., and L. D. Hill. 1994. Re-engineering marketing policies in food and agriculture; Issues and alternatives for grain grading policies. In *Re-engineering marketing policies for food and agriculture*, ed. D. I. Padberg, 19–129. Texas A&M: Food and Agricultural Marketing Consortium, FAMC 94-1.

Kalfagianni, A. 2006. *Transparency in the food chain: Policies and politics*, Enschede: Twente University Press.

King, A., and M. Lenox. 2000. Industry self-regulation without sanctions. *Academy of Management Journal* 43, no. 4: 698–716.

Levins, R. 2002. Collective bargaining by farmers: Fresh look? *Choices* (Winter 2001-2002): 15–18.

Levy, D., and D. Egan. 2000. Corporate political Action in the global polity. In *Non-state actors and authority in the global system,* ed. R. Higgott, G. Underhill, and A. Bieler, 138–54. LLondon: Routledge.

Lukes, S. 1974. *Power, a radical view.*London: Macmillan.

———. 2004. *Power, a radical view.* London: Palgrave Macmillan.

Marquez, I. 2005. Development ethics and the ethics of development. *World Futures* 61: 307–16.

McGrew, A. 2003. Models of transnational democracy. In, *The global transformations reader,* ed. D. Held and A. McGrew, 500–13. Cambridge: Polity Press.

Messner, D., and F. Nuscheler. 1996. Global governance. Challenges to German politics on the threshold of the twenty-first century. *SEF Policy Paper 2,* Development and Peace Foundation, Bonn.

———. 2003. *Das Konzept Global Governance. Stand und Perspektiven.* INEF-Report 67. Duisburg: Institut für Entwickluing und Frieden.

Meuwissen, M. P. M., A. G. J. Velthuis, H. Hogeveen and R. B. M. Huirne. 2003. Traceability and certification in meat supply chains. *Journal of Agribusiness* 21, no. 2: 167–81.

Miller, D. 1992. Deliberative democracy and social choice. *Political Studies*. Special Issue: Prospects for Democracy, 40: 54–67.

Mirbach, M. von. 1999. Demanding good wood. In *Voluntary initiatives,* ed. Robert Gibson. 211–23. Peterborough: Broadview Press.

Nemeth-Ek, M. 2000. Private label brands captivate Europe's consumers. AgExporter.

OECD. 2006. *Competition and regulation in agriculture: Monopsony buying and joint selling* (May). Paris: OECD.

Phillips, A. 1995. *The politics of presence*. Berkeley: University of California Press.

Reardon Th., C. P. Timmer, and J. A. Berdegue. 2004. The rapid rise of supermarkets in developing countries: Induced organisational, institutional, and technological change in agrifood systems, Paper presented at the Meetings of the International Society for New Institutional Economics, Tucson, AZ (September).

Reardon, Th., and E. Farina. 2002. The rise of private food quality and safety standards: Illustrations from Brazil. *International Food and Agribusiness Management Review* 4, no. 4: 413–21.

Reardon Th., J.-M. Codron, B. Lawrence, B. James, and C. Harris. 2001. Global change in agrifood grades and standards: agribusiness strategic responses in developing countries. *International Food and Agribusiness Management Review* 2, no. 3: 421–35.

Rosenau, J., and E.-O. Czempiel. 1992. *Governance without government: Order and change in world politics*. Cambridge: Cambridge University Press.

Sabatini, Ch., and E. Fransworth. 2006. The urgent need for labor law reform. *Journal of Democracy* 17, no. 4: 50–63.

Schaller, Susanne. 2007. The democratic legitimacy of private governance: An analysis of the Ethical Trading Initiative. INEF Report 91/2007. Institute for Development and Peace. University of Duisburg-Essen.

Scharpf, F. W. 1997. *Games real actors play: Actor-centered institutionalism in policy research*. Boulder: Westview.

———. 2003. Problem solving effectiveness and democratic accountability in the EU. MP1fG Working Paper 03/1 (February).

Smith, G. 2003. *Deliberative democracy and the environment*. London: Routledge.

Van der Grip, N. M., T. Marsden, and J. S. B. Cavalcanti. 2005. European retailers as agents of change towards sustainability: The case of fruit production in Brazil. *Environmental Sciences* 2, no. 4: 445–60.

Wolf, K. D. 2002. Governance: Concepts. In *Participatory governance. Political and societal implications,* ed J. R. Grote and B. Gbiki, 35–50. Opladen: Leske and Budrich.

Young, I. M. 2000. *Inclusion and democracy,* Oxford: Oxford University Press.

———. 1996. Communication and the other: Beyond deliberative democracy. In *Democracy and difference,* ed. S. Benhabib, 120–35. Princeton: Princeton University Press.

4

POWER, INTERESTS, AND THE
UNITED NATIONS GLOBAL COMPACT

JACKIE SMITH

INTRODUCTION

The relationship between global business and democracy has been hotly contested in ways that reflect deep differences in visions of how the world should be organized (Ayres 2004; Khagram 2004). Economic globalizers believe the best way to improving the human condition is through economic growth, the creation of globalized markets and the empowerment of business. They see democratic demands such as human rights and environmental protection as best addressed through "trickle down" effects of a growing economy. Opposing this view are what I have referred to elsewhere (Smith 2008) as "democratic globalizers," or collections of individuals and organizations articulating preferences for a global order governed by social norms of human rights, equity, sustainability, and democracy. Democratic globalizers point to evidence contesting the links between market liberalization and growth, and they object to the undemocratic nature of globalized markets (Cavanagh and Mander 2004; Couch 2004; Gray 1998; UNDP 2005). Rather than treating society as a support system for business, they argue for a system of global governance that subordinates the expansion of business to the democratically articulated needs of society (Chase-Dunn 2006; Elson 2004; Munck 2002; Polanyi, 1944).

This chapter examines the Global Compact, an arrangement that is an especially important test case of a third approach that has become prominent in the early twenty-first century. This third approach advocates cooperative "partnerships" between governments and private sector actors to address global problems and "see[s] no fundamental contradictions between the hope of human rights and the exigencies of competitive capital accumulation" (Elson 2004, 46). The Global Compact (GC) integrates businesses into the United Nations Framework as "partners" in the hopes that this will encourage corporate behaviors more consistent with the principles enshrined in the UN Charter.

The editors of this volume have urged us to explore the possibilities to "bind business to global policy processes in such a way that the interests of business and citizens more generally are aligned to the maximum extent possible" (chapter 1, 2). Proponents of the Global Compact suggest that it can do this. This chapter challenges this view, arguing that the Global Compact merely serves to enhance corporate dominance and to legitimate corporate practices that are incompatible with democracy. Analysts and practitioners need to recognize the tremendous asymmetries of power that prevent business "partners" from participating in negotiations that they see as impeding their ability to maximize profits. If our aim is to advance democratic models of global governance, we need to think more creatively about how to engage corporate actors in ways that don't privilege the profit motive over other social goals and that don't enable the private sector to overwhelm the voices of civil society and advocates of a public sphere.

THE GLOBAL COMPACT

The Global Compact (GC) was developed as a mechanism through which the international community might govern the behavior of corporations. Reflecting the relative weakness of global governance institutions, it adopted a nontraditional approach to governance, based on learning, normative pressure, and networks, rather than more conventional regulation, monitoring, and legal sanctioning. Using persuasion rather than coercive approaches, the architects of the GC hoped to engage businesses in the work of carrying out UN principles in their day-to-day operations. They argued that through demonstrations of "best practices," and through reporting on corporate practices as they relate to the GC's core social and environmental principles, corporations would learn to be better global citizens. They also defend the initiative as contributing to the effort to strengthen the UN's regulatory mechanisms, thereby strengthening global governance of business.

The Global Compact should, however, be seen as one part of a much longer-term effort by proponents of neoliberal globalization to transform global power relations in ways that advance their vision of economic globalization. Since the 1970s, supporters of what is now known as neoliberalism have led a sustained effort to use their behavioral power to discredit the United Nations and reduce its role in global economic policy making. In conjunction with Northern governments—especially the United States—business actors worked to mute the political impact of third world governments and their calls for a "New International Economic Order" by eliminating the UN's Center on Transnational Corporations, shifting responsibility for trade negotiations outside the United Nations, and by strengthening the influence of the World Bank and IMF on the policies of third world governments (see, e.g., Smith 2008; Bello 2003; McMichael 2003; Sklair 2001; Paine 2000; Bennis 1997; Karliner 1997). Also, through cultural lobbies such as the Heritage Foundation and the American Enterprise Institute, they worked systematically to discredit the United Nations in popular and elite discourse in the United States.

Starting from this weak position, Kofi Annan worked to transform the UN's relationship with the business community throughout his tenure.[1] Engaging the business community was part of his larger strategy of convincing the U.S. government to adopt a more constructive role in the UN. U.S. participation—including its financial cooperation—was seen as vital to achieving the organization's mission. Thus, in addition to attending private meetings with corporate leaders and the International Chamber of Commerce, Annan regularly attended the World Economic Forum, an annual gathering of corporate and political elite. He launched a plan to promote business "partnerships" with the UN body, and encouraged all UN agencies to cultivate innovative relationships with business as a means of securing new resources and legitimacy for the organization. The Global Compact became a central part of this strategy to bring businesses into the UN orbit, and Annan used his office to amplify attention to the initiative.

The Global Compact seeks to promote global governance of corporate practices through normative pressure. It works to sensitize corporate leaders to the values and norms of the UN system and to encourage them to implement its ten "core principles" in their corporate practices, including support and respect for human rights, respect for basic labor rights, and the adoption of anticorruption and pro-environmental principles.[2] To participate in the GC, a company must (1) send a letter to the UN Secretary General expressing an intention to integrate GC principles into the corporation's operations; (2) publicly advocate for the GC and its principles in its publications; (3) publish in its annual report a summary of how the company is working to advance the GC principles; and (4) participate in GC policy dialogues and operational activities.[3]

The GC essentially seeks to create "learning networks" made up of corporate, civil society, and governmental actors that work to sensitize corporate leaders to the values and norms of the UN. Corporate "partners" are asked to submit case studies of how they've attempted to implement Global Compact principles, and "the hope and expectation is that good practices will help to drive out bad ones through the power of dialogue, transparency, advocacy and competition" (Ruggie 2002). The UN uses its convening power to help bring civil society and governmental actors together to discuss ways to improve links between business practices and human rights. Examples of "best practices" are highlighted on the GC Web site as models for other corporations to follow. GC-sponsored "Global Policy Dialogues" aim to help partners internalize human rights and other global norms. In addition to these activities, the GC supports network building between corporations and local and national associations working to promote socially responsible corporate practices.

What is quite clear from the language of GC proponents and from the literature on the GC Web site is that the GC does not aim to challenge the market ideology that is inherent in predominant models of economic globalization. To the contrary, it draws heavily on the market logic and seeks to make the UN a more direct proponent of global markets as solutions to contemporary crises. As he promoted the initiative, Kofi Annan justified the GC by saying that, in the political arena, the UN can "help make the case for and maintain an environment which favours trade and open markets" (quoted in Martens,2007). In advance of its 2007 "Global Leaders Summit," the GC posted a link to a Goldman Sachs report touting the competitive advantages seen by companies implementing social and environmental practices into their operations.[4] UN press releases for the Summit claimed that the event was about "building the markets of tomorrow." And key GC architects George Kell and John G. Ruggie routinely use pro-market language to promote their cause, including this interesting justification: "One can readily appreciate why corporations would be attracted to the Global Compact. It offers one stop-shopping in the three critical areas of greatest external pressure: human rights, environment and labor standards, thereby reducing their transaction costs" (2000, 20).

Without rejecting out of hand the market model of economic development, we can and should ask whether it is the role of the UN to advocate so directly for this model, especially at a time when it has come under considerable scrutiny for its failures to promote human well-being and environmental sustainability. Why is it that the GC was only introduced *after* serious challenges to economic globalization emerged? Should any government adopt a single model of economic development without establishing mechanisms to critically evaluate its costs and benefits and to adjudicate among the arguments for and against alternatives? A further problem with the blatantly pro-market agenda of the GC is the fact that studies it has commissioned of its partners demonstrate that it is these very market principles that are limiting the ability of partners to integrate GC goals into their business operations. For instance, a McKinsey survey of GC partners done in advance of the 2007 Global Leaders Summit showed that CEOs of corporate partners listed the following most common reasons for not systematically implementing GC principles (respondents could list multiple answers):

- "Competing strategic priorities" (43 percent)
- "Complexity of implementing strategy across various business functions" (39 percent)
- "Lack of recognition from the financial markets" (25 percent)
- "Failure to recognize a link to value drivers" (18 percent)

All of these items signal that it is global market competition itself that undermines the ability of the GC to affect corporate behavior. The profit-imperative of corporations competes with the GC principles of protecting labor and other human rights. And the need to decentralize business operations as well as the failure of markets to respond positively to pro-labor and pro–human rights practices were seen as major obstacles to implementing GC principles. Somewhat surprisingly, another frequent answer from CEOs to this same question was a desire for a set of common standards of social and environmental responsibility. This suggests that even business leaders recognize the need for more global regulation to counter market pressures on social and environmental goods. The pro-market bias of the GC, however, prevents it from addressing the structural or systemic causes of the harmful practices it purportedly seeks to limit.

While its corporate partners are the centerpiece of the GC, the program also invites participation from civil society organizations (including labor) and academic institutions at the international, and increasingly the national and local, levels. It seeks to promote greater cooperation between businesses and civil society groups as a means of enhancing corporate social responsibility, and has encouraged the formation of local networks to support the GC principles. However, the success of the GC at engaging active civil society participation has been limited, mostly by the refusal of business partners to accept more transparency and openness in their reporting on their implementation of GC principles. Civil society partners and critics of the GC alike have urged the UN to establish mechanisms for independent monitoring of corporate practice rather than to rely solely on the claims of corporate partners about how their practices support human rights and environmental sustainability. But the business community has steadfastly rejected any monitoring scheme, insisting that the GC remain a purely voluntary program. As a result, the GC has not seriously challenged "partners" whose practices clearly violate the GC and other UN principles.[5]

Although some improvements have been made to the GC in response to critics, the Global Compact remains problematic for many observers both inside and outside the United Nations. This is because it allows corporations to claim an allegiance with the UN without requiring verifiable measures to ensure that the behavior of corporate "partners" is consistent with UN norms. Business leaders have refused to allow monitoring of their practices, and the GC has not made an effort to push for such measures. Thus, while businesses can gain favorable publicity by joining the Global Compact, they assume no costs, since compliance is voluntary. "Even [George] Soros noted that [the Global Compact] was nothing more than corporate image whitewash" (quoted in Robinson 2004, 171). Activists dubbed the program "blue wash," since it allows corporations to hide unscrupulous behaviors behind the UN's blue flag (TRAC 2000). Many member governments also remain highly critical of the GC. This is in part because the process by which the initiative was adopted involved no consultation with member governments from the Global South, and it amounted to an end run around the UN General Assembly. Critics see the GC as a decoy that corporations and their allies are using to obstruct efforts in the UN to more effectively govern their practices (Elson 2004).

THE GLOBAL COMPACT AND GLOBAL DEMOCRACY

The editors of this volume have rightly argued that we need to improve how we think about democracy and business at the global level (chapter 1, 2). They propose a definition of democracy that emphasizes participation, transparency, and accountability. These provide useful yardsticks against which we can measure the democratic content of the GC. Our editors have also addressed the question of power, and certainly any discussion of the impacts of the GC on democracy would be incomplete without serious attention to how it affects the distribution of material and symbolic resources that allow different groups to shape policy outcomes.

GC Impacts on Global Power Relations

The introductory chapter introduced several dimensions of power that are relevant to our consideration here. Behavioral power is the ability of an actor to intervene in political processes to obtain policy outcomes favorable to its interests. The discussion above of the historical context of the GC illustrates the power neoliberal globalizers have had within global political institutions, and how they used this power to create the GC and ensure that it operates in ways consistent with their interests. This power grows mainly from their vastly disproportionate control of financial resources, which allow business leaders to devote time and resources to monitoring political developments, crafting draft resolutions and proposals for policy initiatives that advance their interests, and influencing the agendas as well as the perspectives of policymakers. The ability to hire full-time lobbyists and legal assistants to determine how proposed international agreements will impact class interests gives neoliberal globalizers a substantial edge (to say the least) in advocating for their interest on the global stage (Millen et al. 2000). In contrast, even governments have difficulties supporting technical staff to protect their interests in global negotiations (Ostry 2007).

The GC itself may help amplify the behavioral power of transnational corporations by enhancing their formal roles and legitimacy as "partners" in global governance. This is because the United Nations has invited corporate involvement in its operations from a position of weakness rather than strength. It has sought to entice corporate players into the UN by offering them use of the "UN brand" to help them market their products and services (Kell and Levin 2002; Ruggie 2002). It has acquiesced to corporate pressure and refused to establish monitoring procedures in order to ensure corporate compliance with GC principles. And it has allowed corporate players to effectively thwart discussions about other initiatives to more effectively govern corporate practices by claiming that such discussions duplicate efforts already being taken in the GC (Bendell 2004; Hobbs, Khan, Posner, and Roth 2003; Martens 2003).

Within the GC, then, corporations have become players that should
be consulted about policy rather than regulated by it. The GC explicitly
disavows any responsibility for monitoring or ensuring corporate compliance with global norms, thereby allowing the persistence of a governance gap with respect to the application of international law. Since
international law as it is currently written applies only to states, currently only states can be held accountable to it. However, as corporations have eclipsed the power and capacity of many states,[6] they have
become both capable of serious violations of international law and
immune from prosecution for such violations.

While it strengthens the power of corporations, the GC simultaneously diminishes the power of civil society. By privileging corporations
as central players within the United Nations, the GC helps marginalize
civil society voices while promoting the idea that "the business of government is business" and that the "business of business is government"
(Hertz 2001, 166). In other words, to justify their failure to take on a
role of governing corporations, the GC has helped make corporations
appear as legitimate representatives of broad public interests who
deserve a special role in global decision making. Civil society actors, in
contrast, have been marginalized and overshadowed in the United
Nations because of their inability to compete with the agenda-setting
and ideological capacities of a more readily coordinated community of
business actors.[7] To further marginalize civil society actors from engagement in global economic policy discussions, the GC co-sponsored with
corporate partners a purportedly scientific study of NGO accountability
that was harshly (and unfairly) critical of NGOs that challenged economic globalization. The report offered a decidedly pro-business perspective on the role of civil society.[8]

In addition to behavioral power, the GC also fails to challenge and
possibly even strengthens the structural power of business actors. Structural power was defined in chapter 1 as flowing from the dependence
of governments on economic growth; the ability of businesses to pit
governments against each other in competition for investment dollars
and jobs; and from prevailing business-friendly cultural and institutional
tendencies such as individualism, consumerism, uncritical support for
economic growth, and hostility toward the public sector. Again, by providing corporations with a privileged position within the UN system
without requiring verifiable compliance with UN norms, the GC provides tacit support for the model of economic organization that reinforces corporate power over public institutions and that subordinates
public policy to markets. Elson refers to this as the "privatization of
relations between the UN and big corporations," which she defines as

"a process wherein UN agencies no longer see it as their role to strengthen member-states in their dealings with corporations, but rather facilitate the self-regulation of corporations and promote bilateral deals between UN agencies and corporations that bypass member-states" (2004, 52–53; See also Daly 2002; Mander and Goldsmith 1996).

While some might argue that the "learning networks" established within the GC can contribute to changes in the values and practices of corporations, nothing in the current procedures of the GC is likely to lead to any serious challenges to the cultural and competitive logics that define how corporations behave. While corporate players might clean up their images and possibly even some of their practices, in the end they still operate in a global economic system that values profit over other social values. Because the UN has engaged the business community as a supplicant rather than as a king (or president!), the GC is unlikely to advance global democracy or serve as a model for global economic governance. To do so, it would have to intervene to alter the balance of power among global actors—in particular to strengthen the hands of governments and civil society relative to corporations and to subject markets to democratic control.

GC Impacts on Democratic Practices

Clearly, power is closely related to the following discussion of the procedural impacts of the GC as they relate to global democracy. Disempowered actors are less able to participate, to demand transparency in the practices of more powerful actors, and to hold more powerful actors accountable to international norms. Thus, to the extent that the GC fails to remedy the significant inequalities of power between corporations and civil society and between corporations and governments, it is not likely to significantly advance these three measures of global democracy. Nevertheless, it is worth devoting some attention to the question of how the GC might impact each area.

Does the GC enhance participation in global policymaking? The first question we must ask is whether the GC provides opportunities for more people to be involved in policy discussions related to how global and national economies are organized. A related but often neglected question in this regard is how particular institutional arrangements affect the possibilities for *economic* participation, or the opportunities for people to exercise real choice in decisions about how they participate in the economy (see, e.g., Miller 2006; Mander and Goldsmith 1996; Daly 2002).

The first question about the participation in policy debates is some-what difficult to address for two reasons. First is the lack of detailed information about the extensiveness and representativeness of partici-pation in GC policy dialogues and in the local GC networks. A second problem is that we are unable to evaluate whether the GC model is better at expanding participation than some alternative model for gov-erning corporate practices. Nevertheless, I will try to present some evi-dence about the participation in economic policy dialogues that can be attributed to the GC.

The GC currently claims—after nearly eight years of operation—to have 5,600 participants, including around 3,700 active businesses. GC proponents argue that these business partners would otherwise be dis-engaged from the UN system and their practices regarding human rights and other global norms would remain outside of the UN arena. But when we consider that there are more than seventy thousand transna-tional corporations worldwide with hundreds of thousands of affiliates and millions of suppliers (Manalsuren 2007; Utting 2007, 699–700), this figure represents a mere drop in the bucket of the potential corporate participants in the GC. Moreover, critics of the GC note that the pro-gram's focus on the larger, transnational companies and their national affiliates overlooks the corporate trend toward subcontracting produc-tion to small, localized enterprises that engage in more precarious forms of employment and the casualization of labor (Utting 2007, 700). In short, corporate participation in the GC represents a very small tip of a very large iceberg, and it may in fact be obscuring systemic trends away from human rights. While some might argue that it is better to engage these few than none, we might also ask whether alternative institutional arrangements—i.e., those not dependent upon corporate acquiescence but upon government authority to regulate corporate practices and empower citizens—could achieve greater corporate participation.

We should also consider what participation in the GC actually means in qualitative terms. Do large corporations really take their obli-gations as partners in the GC seriously? There is some evidence that speaks to this question, and not very favorably. For instance, in 2007 the GC released its first study of participants, which was based in part on an analysis of an anonymous, online survey. The response rate achieved by the survey was just 15 percent (four hundred companies), far lower than most respected social science studies and also much lower than one would expect given the symbolic and material resources that were behind the study. Also, since 2006, the GC has withdrawn the memberships of 778 partners for their failure to file the requisite performance reports.[9] Given that there are now just 3,700 corporate partners, this is a rather high attrition rate. The recent study of the GC reported that of participants who were in the program for more than two years, 45 percent of Northern and 65–70 percent of Southern partners are "inactive" or "non-communicating."[10]

Civil society participation in the GC is similarly miniscule. As of July 2007, around nine hundred participants in the GC were from civil society, labor, and academic organizations. Just thirty-six "global" NGOs were listed as civil society partners to the GC. These included some groups more closely aligned with the corporate and government sectors than with civil society, such as the World Economic Forum and the New York Office of the High Commissioner for Human Rights, among others. A much larger list of several hundred "national" NGOs were listed, but it is not clear what their "participation" means.[11] This figure is a similarly tiny proportion of the many thousands of civil society groups that have participated in global conferences and the hundreds of thousands of participants in the World Social Forum process (Smith and Karides et al. 2008; Willetts 1996).[12] We should note, too, that this number is especially low, given that one important inducement for civil society participation in the GC is the promise of funding from corporate partners, which are encouraged to engage in joint initiatives with civil society groups to help implement the GC principles.[13]

The next important question that is often neglected in discussions of democracy is the extent to which particular institutional arrangements promote or limit more expansive popular participation in economic life. Most market proponents assume that free, open markets provide equal access to all participants, but considerable evidence challenges this assumption (see, e.g., New Economics Foundation 2006; UNDP, 2005). If economic globalization is the process of integrating local and national economies into a single, globalized market, then it effectively involves the transfer of economic control from local to global-level actors. When countries organize their economies to respond to global markets, they shift land and other resources toward production that is responsive to global rather than local demand. Thus, we find growing numbers of countries with tremendous food production capabilities suffering from national food insecurity (McMichael 2004; 2003). The choices of jobs available to residents are also lost, as globetrotting companies can cross borders in search of the cheapest workers, following the economic notion of "comparative advantage." Daly describes the (il)logical conclusion to policies that emphasize specialization for global market competitiveness:

In Uruguay, for example, everyone would have to be either a shepherd or a cowboy in conformity with the dictates of competitive advantage in the global market. Everything else should be imported in exchange for beef, mutton, wool, and leather. Any Uruguayan who wants to play in a symphony orchestra or be an airline pilot should emigrate. (2002, 3)

The rise of precarious labor and the casualization of labor, which has been enabled by the weakening of unions under economic globalization, reflects a considerable loss in the capacity of civil society to participate in the economic and social lives of their communities (Klein 1999; Moody 1997; Munck 2002). To the extent that the GC fails to challenge the power of the corporate sector and even lends legitimacy to the market-oriented model of economic globalization, it helps to reduce rather than enhance the effective participation of civil society.

Does the GC enhance transparency in global decision making? The GC should in theory contribute to greater transparency in global affairs by requiring corporate partners to provide information about how they are trying to implement global principles. As is stated above, partners are required to submit annual "communications on progress" (COPs) to the GC Web site. We can also assume that they have an incentive to do so, since it can contribute to favorable public relations and corporate visibility with little cost. Table 4.1 shows the numbers of COPs filed by corporate partners to the GC between 2002 and 2007.

The number of COPs received by the GC office reached a high of nearly 1,700 in 2006. This figure, however, does not reflect the total numbers of GC partners reporting, since it can include multiple filings by the same company.[14] In 2007, despite a presumed growth in the numbers of GC corporate partners, the number of COPs filed dropped by more than 20 percent, and the numbers for 2008 don't seem to be on track to reverse the decline.[15] Similarly, the percentage of reports that were deemed notable as models of how to report on progress and/or how to implement GC principles[16] declined sharply since 2003, the first year for which complete records were available. However, one sign that the "learning network" principle is having an impact is that an increasing number of COPs contain specific information about actions the company has taken to help further GC principles.[17]

This mixed record raises questions about the ability of the GC to generate greater transparency in global economic governance. Given that partners are not required to demonstrate, in a verifiable way, that their actual practices match the claims made in these reports,[18] the failure of such large numbers to submit reports in a timely way is rather surprising.

Table 4.1. Global Compact Table
Communications of Progress (COP) Filings 2002–2007*

	2002	2003	2004	2005	2006	2007
Number of COPs filed	36	205	701	1245	1692	1310
# COPs describing practical actions taken	27	137	438	781	1446	1195
Percent notable COPs	0	0	11%	7%	4%	2%

Figures obtained 7 July 2008.
Source: www.unglobalcompact.org/
*GC Partners are required to submit a COP every two years. There is no standard template for COPs, and some companies submit COPs for two-year time periods or for irregular time-frames. Thus, an estimated 30–40 percent of the annual totals include dual-counts.

Complicating the question of transparency, moreover, is the absence of any meaningful attempt by the UN to monitor the extent to which corporate words match their deeds. As Utting notes, most independent analyses have found a "[s]erious gap between stated intentions and actual implementation of [corporate social responsibility]" (Utting 2007, 700). Most civil society partners have remained highly critical of the absence of monitoring and enforcement of principles, and Ramesh Singh, chief executive of ActionAid, a major development NGO, called the project a "happy-go-lucky club" for its reliance on purely voluntary compliance. And the UN's Special Rapporteur on the right to food, Jean Ziegler, called for active resistance to the GC because it was being used as a public relations operation by major TNCs (Capedevila 2007). In short, it is clear that if the GC does not establish measures that enhance the credibility of corporate claims, the value of COPs for enhancing transparency is minimal to none.

Beyond these details of reporting and monitoring compliance with global norms, we must also ask about the extent to which the GC framework enhances global transparency in terms of the discussion of the relative merits of market-based development models for the global community. Utting notes the irony of the fact that companies might be deemed model citizens in terms of their performance measures as outlined by corporate social responsibility schemes, while at the same time they are "lobbying forcefully for macroeconomic, labour market and other social policies associated with forms of labour market flexibilisation, deregulation . . . that can result in the weakening of institutions and systems of social protection" (Utting 2007, 701). In other words, schemes such as the GC might generate improvements in some corporate practices "without questioning various contradictory policies and practices that can have perverse consequences in terms of equality and equity" (Utting 2007, 701). The GC thus obfuscates the social impacts of global market competition and corporate practices.

Does the GC enhance accountability of powerful actors? Political accountability can be defined as "being obliged to explain one's actions to others and being held responsible to a broad-based public" (Wapner 2002, 59).[19] While the failures of transparency described above suggest that little is being done through the GC to facilitate accountability of powerful actors, there are other elements of the GC that we can examine in an attempt to assess its prospects for strengthening accountability in the global system.

A look at the history of the GC provides insights into its limitations as a mechanism for increasing global accountability. As was mentioned earlier, the GC was formed at the initiative of the Secretary General, and largely due to pressure from a single—albeit very powerful—UN member state, the United States. While the move was certainly within the realm of the Secretary General's authority, it bypassed the usual procedures for establishing new offices to address important global problems. The General Assembly is the body authorized to launch major initiatives, and certainly any substantial UN project would require the support of most of its member states. More importantly, it ensured that the GC would not be shaped by the preferences of a majority of member governments that had already signaled their interest in strengthening the UN's ability to regulate TNCs and strengthen member governments' negotiating power relative to them. And although the GC operates in their name, as an initiative of the Secretariat, the GC is not accountable to most member states.

This failure of accountability to the full membership of the UN in questions about how the UN should relate to global corporations has prevented the GC from being linked with other UN negotiations and conventions. For instance, references to the GC were deleted from final declaration at the Copenhagen +5 Social Summit (Elson 2004, 51). And a search of the UN Web site revealed that the only references to the Global Compact were by the GC office.[20] Given that the GC is being promoted as the key process for addressing the crucial question of how to apply international law to the practices of transnational corporations, we would certainly expect more widespread incorporation of the GC program into the wider UN system. The fact that, eight years after its launch, it remains such an isolated entity shows that it has little legitimacy even within the UN itself.

Another important failure of accountability in the GC is that there is no procedure for verifying the claims made by participants, nor is there evidence of an attempt to develop one. The GC Web site indicates that the office makes no attempt to verify the accuracy of claims made in partners' Communications of Progress, but it does not provide space for even its own civil society participants to comment on corporate partners' claims.[21] Under pressure to remedy this serious shortfall, the GC adopted a series of "integrity measures" in 2005, which included a provision allowing third parties to report serious violations of the GC principles to the GC office (Global Compact 2005). However, the new measures provide only for internal negotiations among GC and corporate entities involved, preventing complainants from making public statements regarding the matter "until it is resolved." So while there is some effort to hold GC members accountable, the audience of accountability—and its potential impact on corporate practices—is extremely limited.

The GC's limited attempt to hold partners accountable means it will not have a substantial impact on the practices of its corporate partners. And the evidence we have to date suggests that this expectation is being borne out, as "relatively few of the over 2500 participating companies provide comprehensive evidence of compliance with the 10 principles" (Utting 2007, 704). And a study of GC participants conducted in 2004 found that only 6 percent of participating companies were taking actions that they would not have taken if they remained outside the initiative (Blair, Bugg-Levine, and Rippin 2004).[22]

A further serious problem with the GC is that it undermines other efforts to advance a more rigorous model for effective corporate governance within the United Nations. For instance, the GC completely bypasses existing institutional arrangements in the International Labor Organization regarding the treatment and rights of workers. By establishing a separate framework of reference, the GC shifts the attention of policymakers away from efforts to strengthen existing foundations for human rights and international law, attempting to focus them on the development of entirely new institutional arrangements. In this case, it is serving to marginalize important elements of the UN—including member states—from discussions of global corporate governance.

Although GC proponents argue that the initiative is designed to complement and promote stronger regulatory mechanisms within the UN,[23] they haven't done much either to support specific initiatives or to encourage their "partners" to accept these. Most evidence points to the contrary. For instance, the proposed "Norms on the responsibilities of transnational corporations and other business enterprises with regard to human rights" (UN Draft Norms for Business) are being advanced by a coalition of civil society groups including Rights and Accountability in Development (RAID), Amnesty International, and the Economic Social and Cultural Rights Action Network, together with other corporate accountability groups and coalitions (International Network for Economic Social and Cultural Rights 2005; Amnesty International 2004). The initiative has support within the United Nations and from some member governments, [24] and it has already been adopted by the UN Sub-Commission on the Promotion and Protection of Human Rights, a first step in achieving a binding international treaty.[25] But the GC is used to justify arguments by corporate actors that self-regulation works and that mechanisms like the draft Norms are unnecessary. Because the GC involves no oversight mechanism, it can provide no credible evidence that voluntary compliance actually works, but it has, nevertheless, effectively slowed down other efforts to promote changes in corporate practices.

CONCLUSION

The above analysis shows serious limitations of the Global Compact as a model for global governance of business. It shows that its proponents' claims that the GC will draw business into normative commitments more effectively than strong public sector rules are wrong. The failures of the GC as a form of global corporate governance stem largely from the fact that the project itself emerged from the disproportionate power of corporations relative to other actors in the global system—including governments, international officials, and civil society. A more democratic and effective system of corporate governance is impossible without efforts to address the inequities of power between corporations, civil society, and states.

The GC is not likely to provide a solid foundation for change in this direction because it is shaped by these very power inequities that allow violations of social and ecological norms to continue. It reflects the disproportionate behavioral power of business, since corporate lobbyists were able to influence the design of the project in ways that preempted other UN initiatives to regulate the practices of transnational corporations. In its work to advance the GC, the behavioral power of business overrode the interests and preferences of a majority of UN member governments and civil society. Any attempt to remedy the accountability gap in the GC would require steps to transform this imbalance between corporate actors and governments and civil society. The GC is also problematic in that it serves to replicate rather than counterbalance the structural power of business actors. The mandate of the GC reinforces the assumption that governments' main task is to promote economic growth over other social values. This undermines governments' roles in promoting global public goods such as human rights and environmental sustainability. More importantly, by allowing corporate partners to develop privileged relationships with international officials and governments, the GC serves to reinforce the structural power of business and marginalize the voices of less powerful actors (Korten 1997a; 1997b; Beausang 2003).

In sum, the process of governing global business practices should begin with an authoritative mandate that grows from a transparent and democratic process and that works to decrease the behavioral and structural power of business relative to other global actors. Thus, the GC framework should be abandoned in favor of an arrangement that strengthens governments and civil society relative to business actors, enabling these actors to effectively defend a culture of peace and human rights against the predominant, pro-business model of globalized markets. This follows the analyses of Karl Polanyi and of many contemporary analysts who argue for a "re-embedding" of the global economy in a system of norms and values that emerge from a democratic global society (Elson 2004, 60; Munck 2002). Substantial material and authoritative resources must be shifted toward states and civil society if this is to happen. Also, any effort to develop a coherent and democratic structure for governing global business should revive entities such as the UN Center on Transnational Corporations and UNCTAD. If the CG continues to exist, it should be subordinated to these two entities, which fall within the jurisdiction of the General Assembly (not the Secretariat alone).

The Global Compact is ultimately an arrangement that privatizes relations between the UN and transnational corporations, thereby insulating corporations from public scrutiny while tying the hands of the UN, thereby limiting its capacities to ensure the implementation of international law and norms. It reflects an elite model of governance, which assumes that business leaders and policy experts are best equipped to determine how society should be governed, and that democratic processes and public scrutiny are inefficient and counterproductive to the task of governance. While such a model may be appealing in many ways, it cannot survive over the long term, as it will ultimately be challenged for its lack of legitimacy. While its goal of educating and providing corporations with models for better corporate practices may indeed help realize the principles it promotes, without a structure that subordinates corporations to governments and to public scrutiny and democratic accountability, it will not bring the interests of business and citizens into greater alignment.

NOTES

1. Annan was a graduate of MIT's Sloan School of Business, and thus he was very familiar with, if not sympathetic to, the principles guiding neoliberal globalization. His appointment as UN Secretary General was favored by the United States, and his effort to launch the GC was in part an effort to help re-engage the United States in the activities of the UN.
2. See http://www.unglobalcompact.org/AboutTheGC/TheTenPrinciples/index.html.
3. Nongovernmental organizations or NGOs, in contrast, must go through an elaborate accreditation process that is subject to review by a committee of member state representatives. They must demonstrate for this committee that their work contributes to the work of the United Nations, among other requirements.
4. The GC Web site announcement proclaimed that "an increasing number of business leaders see corporate responsibility as a way to compete successfully and to build trust with stakeholders"—and that sustainability front-runners in a range of industries can generate higher stock prices.
5. In 2005, the GC responded to these criticisms by establishing "integrity measures" that specified that GC partners that failed to file the required reports to the GC would have their memberships suspended (Global Compact 2005). It also established procedures through which complaints could be filed against partners for alleged violations of GC principles. I address this further later in the chapter.
6. Of the world's top fifty economies (based on revenues) in the early 2000s, just fifteen were national governments and thirty-five were corporations (Sklair 2002).
7. The fact that business actors share a common interest in securing global rules that enable and enhance their ability to accumulate profits makes it far easier to coordinate their global strategy—even

without formal efforts to do so—than it is for civil society groups that are poorly funded and focused on a wide array of issues (Smith 2008).

8. The study, "The 21st Century NGO: In the Market for Change" was co-sponsored by a business lobby, Sustainability, the UN Global Compact, and UN Environment Programme, along with business "partners" such as Dow Chemical.

9. This figure was reported on the GC Web site in July 2007. The site has since been reorganized, and there is no clear report on the number of companies that have had their GC membership withdrawn for failing to comply with basic requirements. A whole section on enhancing accountability of GC partners has been removed from the Web site, or if it is there, it is not as transparent as it was in 2007.

10. An active partner is one that has produced a COP within two years of joining the Global Compact or within one year of its previous COP.

11. A review of the list of civil society participants as well as of some of these participants' Web sites suggests that their identification with the GC may have come from their participation in policy dialogues and other GC-sponsored events. In other words, it is more the convening power of the UN than the compelling nature of the GC program that appears to be inducing civil society participation in the program. Many groups have signed public statements criticizing the GC for its failure to monitor corporate practices.

12. The numbers of participants in the most recent (second) Global Compact Leaders Summit in 2007 showed similar patterns of participation. A total of 1,027 people registered for the Summit—638 from companies, 95 from government entities, 76 from international organizations, 65 from international business organizations, 62 from international NGOs, 45 from academia, 28 from the Global Compact network, 13 from foundations, and 5 from international labor organizations.

13. For instance, civil society groups can receive corporate grants for running training programs for business leaders in environmental sustainability or human rights protection.

14. For instance, in 2006 Air France submitted nine separate COPs, each containing a distinct claim to have helped advance GC principles.

15. By mid-2008, just 268 COPs were filed for 2008, and most of those were reports that had been filed in earlier years (and already

counted in those totals). These patterns mirror analyses by other scholars (see, e.g. Bendell 2004; Martens 2003).

16. Notable COPs are chosen because they represent "emerging best practices in communicating progress." In particular, these COPs include notable examples of one or all of the following: (1) a statement of continued support for the Global Compact from the chief executive officer, chairperson, or other senior executive; (2) references, links or descriptions of policies, commitments, and systems the company has created in order to implement the Global Compact principles in its operations; (3) a description of actions taken in implementing the Principles and/or in furthering broader UN goals; (4) indicators that are used to determine success and/or failure in meeting the company's corporate citizenship goals; (5) information about progress made and/or future plans with respect to all ten Global Compact principles; (6) a description of how the COP is being disseminated among the company's stakeholders.

17. Further scrutiny is in order, however, to determine whether GC partners are actually learning new corporate behaviors or simply learning to file effective reports. For instance, one might ask about the practical significance of Air France's claim in one of its 2006 COPs to have helped advance GC principles by providing for "transportation of disabled passengers or those with limited mobility." This is certainly not a new policy, or one that the company would not have taken if it wasn't a GC partner. But, to be fair, we might hope that Air France's participation in the GC program would make it think hard about cutting services to disabled passengers as it cuts overall operating costs. The point is that we don't know the actual effects of the GC on corporate practices from these self-reports.

18. The GC Web site includes a disclaimer noting that the accuracy of partners' claims is not verified by the GC. While there is an indicator in the GC search engine of whether or not a COP was "third party assured," it is not clear how this designation is made. In any case, very few reports have this designation.

19. Wapner discusses accountability as it relates to governmental and civil society actors, but his conceptualization and analysis is applicable here as well.

20. The search was conducted on July 19, 2007. Examples of the handful of items that this search of the UN Web site produced include an office of procurement document urging all vendors to join GC, and a press release promoting a new, "GC-branded" Sri Lankan tea.

21. In contrast, the ILO has online business and social initiatives database that includes corporate claims as well as third-party evaluations (Elson 2004). If the aim of the GC is to make corporate practice conform to global norms, it is crucial that some effort be made for greater accountability, and the ILO practice can serve as a model.

22. The McKinsey survey included 311 respondents, drawn from around 1,800 GC partners (a 17 percent response rate). No further details are known about the survey methodology, and therefore it is impossible to determine the possible effect of selection bias in survey results. I suspect that respondents would be relatively more engaged in the GC process and more likely to report its impact on practices, and therefore this very low figure suggests that the GC is not having much overall impact on corporate practices. Responses relating to how GC participation affected partners' practices were as follows: No changes in practices since joining: 33 percent; Change would have occurred anyway: 27 percent; Change would have happened, but participation significantly facilitated change: 34 percent; Change would have been difficult to implement without participation: 4 percent; Change would not have happened without participation: 2 percent.

23. For instance, its recent first annual report stated that the program aims to continue to revise and strengthen its communication practices in order to "Position[ing] the Global Compact as a frame of reference for other initiatives and explore stronger linkages with implementation, accountability and certification schemes" (54). It is uncertain how serious this statement is, given the limited corporate participation in even the existing minimalist, voluntary codes and the vociferous corporate opposition to any more binding arrangements.

24. Many civil society partners in the GC support the Global Norms for Business, arguing that the GC should be seen as simply a first step toward a more comprehensive system of corporate governance. They argue that serious steps are needed to monitor the practices of companies to ensure compliance with international law.

25. The Draft "Norms on the responsibilities of transnational corporations and other business enterprises with regard to human rights" (E/CN.4/Sub.2/2003/12/Rev.2 26 August 2003) was prepared in the UN Sub-Commission on the Promotion and Protection of Human Rights. The broader UN Commission on Human Rights has challenged the legal standing of this document since it did not explicitly commission the draft.

REFERENCES

Ayres, J. M. 2004. Framing collective action against neoliberalism: The case of the "anti-globalization" movement. *Journal of World Systems Research* 10: 11–34.

Beausang, F. 2003. Is there a development case for United Nations–business partnerships? Development Studies Institute, London School of Economics, London, Working Paper No. 03-44.

Bello, W. 2003. *Deglobalization: New ideas for running the world economy.* London: Zed Books.

Bendell, J. 2004. Flags of inconvenience? The Global Compact and the future of the United Nations. Nottingham University Business School, Nottingham, UK.

Bennis, P. 1997. *Calling the shots: How Washington dominates today's UN.* New York: Olive Branch Press.

Blair, M. E., A. J. Bugg-Levine, and T. M. Rippin. 2004. The UN Global Compact has become a major force promoting corporate social responsibility, but not enough US companies are participating. *McKinsey Quarterly.* At: http://www.mckinseyquarterly.com/article_page.aspx?ar=1499&L2=33&L3=117&srid=18&gp=1.

Capedevila, G. 2007. Global compact with business "Lacks Teeth"—NGOs. *IPS News,* July 6. At: http://ipsnews.net/news.asp?idnews=38453.

Cavanagh, J., and J. Mander, eds. 2004. *Alternatives to economic globalization: A better world is possible.* 2nd ed. San Francisco: Berrett-Koehler Publishers.

Chase-Dunn, C. 2006. Social evolution and the future of world society. *Journal of World Systems Research* 11: 171–92.

Couch, C. 2004. *Post-democracies.* London: Polity.

Daly, H. 2002. Globalization versus internationalization, and four economic arguments for why internationalization is a better model for world community. In *Globalizations: Cultural, economic, democratic,* vol. 2004. College Park, MD. At: www.bsos.umd.edu/socy/conference/newpapers/daly.rtf.

Elson, D. 2004. Human rights and corporate profits: The UN Global Compact—Part of the solution or part of the problem? In *Global tensions: Challenges and opportunities in the world economy,* ed L. Benería and S. Bisnath, 45–64 New York: Routledge.

Global Compact. 2005. Global Compact Integrity Measures. At: http://www.unglobalcompact.org/AboutTheGC/integrity.html.

Gray, J. 1998. *False dawn: Delusions of global capitalism.* New York: The New Press.

Hertz, N. 2001. *The silent takeover: Global capitalism and the death of democracy.* New York: The Free Press.

Hobbs, J., I. Khan, M. Posner, and K. Roth. 2003. Letter to Louise Fréchette raising concerns on UN Global Compact. At: http://web.amnesty.org/pages/ec_briefings_global_7April03.

Karliner, J. 1997. *The corporate planet: Ecology and politics in the age of globalization.* San Francisco: Sierra Club.

Kell, G., and D. Levin. 2002. The evolution of the Global Compact Network: An historic experiment in learning and action. Conference paper. Academy of Management Annual Conference, Denver, vol. 2005. At: http://157.150.195.47/Pubs/chronicle/2002/issue3/denver.pdf.

Kell, G., and J. G. Ruggie. 2000. Reconciling economic imperatives with social priorities: The Global Compact. Paper Presented at Carnegie Council on Ethics and International Affairs, New York.

Khagram, S. 2004. *Dams and development: Transnational struggles for water and power.* Ithaca: Cornell University Press.

Klein, N. 1999. *No logo: Taking aim at the brand name bullies.* New York: Picador.

Korten, D. C. 1997a. Memo to United Nations General Assembly President, Mr. Razali Ismail. People Centered Development Forum.

———. 1997b. The United Nations and the corporate agenda. At: http://www.pcdf.org/1997/PKortenUNcorporate.htm.   People Centered Development Forum, August 5.

Manalsuren, N. 2007. Global compact expands, impact still hazy. *IPS News*, July 3. At: http://ipsnews.net/news.asp?idnews=38411.

Mander, J., and E. Goldsmith. 1996. *The case against the global economy and for a turn towards the local.* San Francisco: Sierra Club Books.

Martens, J. 2003. Precarious partnerships: Six problems of the Global Compact between business and the UN. *Global Policy Forum.* At: http://www.globalpolicy.org/reform/business/2004/0623partnerships.htm.

———. 2007. Multistakeholder partnerships: Future models of multilateralism? Friedrich-Ebert-Stiftung (FES), Berlin. At: http://www.globalpolicy.org/reform/business/2007/0107multistake.pdf.

McMichael, P. 2003. *Development and social change: A global perspective.* 3rd ed. Thousand Oaks, CA.: Pine Forge.

———. 2004. Biotechnology and food insecurity: Profiting on insecurity? In *Global tensions: Challenges and opportunities in the world economy*, ed. L. Benería and S. Bisnath, 137–54. New York: Routledge.

Millen, J. V., E. Lyon, and A. Irwin. 2000. The political influence of national and transnational corporations. In *Dying for growth: Global inequity and the health of the poor*, ed. Jim Yong Kim, Joyce V. Millen, Alec Irwin, and John Gershman, 225–45. Monroe, ME: Common Courage Press.

Miller, E. 2006. Other economies are possible: Organizing toward an economy of cooperation and solidarity. *Dollars and Sense* (September 9).

Moody, K. 1997. *Workers in a lean world: Unions in the international economy* . New York: Verso.

Munck, R. 2002. *Globalization and labour: The new great transformation* . London: Zed Books.

New Economics Foundation. 2006. Growth isn't working: The unbalanced distribution of benefits and costs from economic growth. New Economics Foundation, London. At: http://www.neweconomics.org/gen/uploads/hrfu5w555mzd3f55m2vqwty502022006112929.pdf.

Ostry, S. 2009. The World Trade Organization: System under stress. In *Unsettled legitimacy: Political community, power, and authority in a global era*, ed. Steven Bernstein and William Coleman. Forthcoming. Vancouver: University of British Columbia Press.

Paine, E. 2000. The road to the Global Compact: Corporate power and the battle over global public policy at the United Nations. New York: Global Policy Forum. At: http://www.globalpolicy.org/reform/papers/2000/road.htm.

Polanyi, K. 1944. *The great transformation* . Boston: Beacon Press.

Robinson, W. 2004. *A theory of global capitalism*. Baltimore: Johns Hopkins University Press.

Ruggie, J. G. 2002. The theory and practice of learning networks: Corporate social responsibility and the Global Compact. *Journal of Corporate Citizenship 5* (Spring): 27–36.

Sklair, L. 2001. *The transnational capitalist class*. Cambridge: Blackwell.

———. 2002. *Globalization and its alternatives*. New York: Oxford University Press.

Smith, J. 2008. *Social movements for global democracy*. Baltimore: Johns Hopkins University Press.

———, M. Karides, M. Becker, et al. 2008. *Global democracy and the world social forums*. Boulder: Paradigm Publishers.

TRAC. 2000. Tangled up in blue: Corporate partnerships at the United Nations. Transnational Resource and Action Center, San Francisco.

UNDP. 2005. *Human development report 2005: International cooperation at a crossroads.* New York: Oxford University Press.

Utting, P. 2007. CSR and equality. *Third World Quarterly* 28: 697–712.

Wapner, P. 2002. Introductory essay: Paradise lost? NGOs and global accountability. *Chicago Journal of International Law* 3: 155–60.

Willetts, P., ed. 1996. *The conscience of the world: The influence of NGOs in the United Nations system.* London: C. Hurst.

SECTION 2

THE INDUSTRY LEVEL

The Organizing Capacities of Industries and Their Regulation

5

BUSINESS AUTHORITY AND GLOBAL FINANCIAL GOVERNANCE

Challenges to Accountability and Legitimacy

GEOFFREY R. D. UNDERHILL AND XIAOKE ZHANG

INTRODUCTION

Financial governance reforms emphasizing market efficiency, privatization, and financial openness have not only placed private firms at the center of a more market-oriented system, but also increased their role in global financial governance. Transnational policy networks have emerged involving close public-private interaction and fully self-regulatory regimes at the international level, yielding a system of market-based governance built on the wide recognition and prevalence of private authority in the public domain.[1] While domestic financial governance has always involved the consultation of private interests, the emerging global pattern of business participation is an important departure from the traditional pattern of international financial architecture during the early postwar period. A range of empirical studies demonstrate how and why private market agents have influenced global policies and institutions (Mattli and Büthe 2005; Porter 2005; Sinclair 2002; Tsingou 2003). As global economic integration has eroded national policy capacities and arguably increased the need for global governance, official and scholarly proponents of enhanced business involvement in global financial governance (IMF 2001; Cline 2000; Slaughter 2000) have seen private sector involvement as an essential mechanism to enhance the efficiency of collective goods provision such as market regulation or crisis management.

The focus of this volume on the relationship between globalization, business authority, and democracy provokes skepticism about the emerging pattern of global monetary and financial governance. Firstly, there is the problem of fulfilling traditional nationally based democratic standards in an increasingly multilevel system of governance (Held 1997; Zürn 2004) in which the problems for democracy increase commensurately. Secondly, increased market orientation and business influence in public policy processes invokes the central issues of the book: the breadth of constituency participation as well as the transparency and accountability of private authority to the public domain, and therefore also concerning the nature/choice of the collective goods to be provided and for whom. This chapter addresses these two issues by examining the relationship between the new forms of business participation in the global financial order, and the prerequisites for an efficient and democratically legitimate governance of international finance, employing two seminal case studies of public-private interaction: (1) the supervision of international financial institutions centered on the Basle I & II agreements of the Basle Committee on Banking Supervision, and (2) international securities market regulation and the International Organization of Securities Commissions (IOSCO).

The central claim is that the emergence of public-private transnational regimes has reduced the participation (we opt here for the stronger notion of representation)[2] of other constituencies in the decision-making process, leaving public authorities vulnerable to dependence on the information and expertise provided by private agents in a fast-moving market environment, in turn compromising the transparency and accountability functions of democratic governance. Secondly, while these developments (often encouraged by states themselves: Helleiner 1994; Underhill 1997) have brought a range of important (if unequally distributed) benefits, they also involved instability and crisis for many societies to a degree that has led to challenges to the process of integration and global governance itself. The result is policy that has been consistently aligned to private sector preferences to a degree which should raise fears of capture and does little to enhance democratic accountability or legitimacy. This problem of capture and the ongoing dependence of public authorities on private information flows and expertise lies in no small way behind the current and most important episode of financial crisis since the Great Depression.

The most powerful business interests in the financial sector, which in turn pose the greatest risks to the financial system as a whole, have succeeded in establishing a system of financial supervision that confers competitive advantages upon themselves while exposing the public to systemic collapse and the costs of rescue. This is not a healthy development in terms of democratic legitimacy. The implication is clear: the process of global financial governance needs to be more inclusive, and policy processes where private constituencies threaten or manifest capture must be rendered transparent and accountable to a broader public. As long as taxpaying citizens remain the ultimate guarantors of the financial system, then their preferences and broad interest in a safe and stable financial architecture must be better represented to policymakers.

In line with the arguments of this volume, the point here is not that business involvement is as such a negative factor for democracy. Self-regulation and private authority is historically a common form of financial sector governance because it *can* improve the transparency of the public and private sectors, foster better risk assessment, and reduce the incidence of financial crises (IMF 2001). Nor is the argument that the proper functioning of private markets, financial or otherwise, is contrary to the public interest. However, business participation is problematic if the notion of the public good is aligned excessively with the private interests of those actors most likely to benefit from it. There is so far little evidence that intergovernmental organizations provide a meaningful counterweight to the power of private business in the sector. On the contrary, business input into the policy processes of intergovernmental organizations such as the Basle Committee or IMF, operating both transnationally and via member governments, appears more effective than the influence of many sovereign members of these policy processes and certainly more effective than "civil society." In this way this chapter is perhaps more pessimistic about the potential for broader societal input than, for example, chapter 9 by Kellow and Murphy, and this implies that the structural power of business to determine outcomes may apply at least as much at the global as at the national level. This power of business at the national and transnational levels is not necessarily balanced by the interests of civil society constituencies, and much would need to be done to align business with broader public interests and achieve what Levi-Faur sees as possible in relation to "regulatory capitalism" in chapter 8. The analysis fits better that of chapter 10 by Lavelle on the sovereign debt restructuring issue, which also points to the considerable power of private business to affect outcomes in financial governance. There the defeat of the Sovereign Debt Restructuring Mechanism (SDRM) was ensured by a combination of business lobbying backed by U.S. power and, crucially, the fear of emerging market economies that their endorsement of the proposal would lead to serious and negative reactions of the private financial sector to their policy choice such as to engender capital flight.

The first section argues that rendering business involvement in multilevel governance compatible with democracy requires that those who make rules at the global level should be answerable to those broadly affected by these rules, especially where there are substantial risks of negative externalities such as financial crisis. Using the standard distinction between the input versus the output sides of legitimacy, the chapter argues that while an outcome perceived as broadly efficient and legitimate is the ultimate test, a more representative and transparent policy process on the input side is more likely to lead to such an outcome, including a reassessment of the underlying policy norms themselves. This implies a third "phase" of democratic legitimacy, which the literature on global and regional governance tends to ignore, the accountability phase. The case material indicates that the input, output, and accountability phases of legitimacy in global monetary and financial governance reveal themselves as problematic, and much of the problem relates to the way in which private business interests are integrated into the process. In all, better consideration of all three "phases" of legitimacy and their interrelationships is likely to enhance the political underpinnings and legitimacy across levels of governance.

The second section employs the two cases to analyze the challenges posed by enhanced business authority for democracy in global financial governance, demonstrating that two prominent transnational regulatory organizations are flawed in terms of their input, output, and accountability phases. The third and final section summarizes the arguments and advances a range of normative prerequisites for the better democratic governance of global finance in relation to growing private authority.

THE ARGUMENT

Democracy should enhance the legitimacy of complex collective decision-making processes, yet legitimacy remains an elusive concept in the best of circumstances. Legitimacy is defined as "a property of a rule or rulemaking institution which itself exerts a pull towards compliance on those addressed normatively because those addressed believe that the rule or institution has come into being and operates in accordance with generally accepted principles of right process" (Franck 1990, 24). Steven

Bernstein (2004) contends that the best way to view the relevance and importance of legitimacy in global governance is through a sociological perspective. In this view, legitimacy is concerned with the social construction of intersubjective beliefs in a defined community and will be rooted in accepted norms of social justice if forms of democratic accountability of decision makers to those affected prevail.

When political communities accept rules as legitimate, they are motivated to comply with these rules by an internal sense of obligation rather than by the fear of retribution or by a calculation of self-interests, which are more costly and whose effects tend to be ephemeral (Hurd 1999). The legitimacy of political choices thus derives more easily from shared norms linking decision makers to individuals and their social constituencies, yet achieving these conditions is considerably easier where a defined (e.g., national) community has developed shared norms over time, and lines of representation and accountability are well institutionalized and understood.

Over time, the legitimacy of authorities becomes less dependent on "specific" support or short-term performance-related legitimacy (Easton 1965, 265) and a reserve of "diffuse" support will build up wherein legitimacy survives poor performance in the shorter run (Easton 1965, 273). Nonetheless, as the cross-border integration of the monetary and financial system intensifies, the effectiveness of domestic governance and of forms of democratic accountability are increasingly undermined, presenting challenges to reliance upon solely national-level policies. The development of global governance presents a potential solution to the problem (Zürn 2004, 286), but legitimacy is fragile: there is a weak sense of defined political community, accountability is underdeveloped, and citizens/constituencies may be poorly represented and distant from decision-making processes, and this means that diffuse support is likely to be in short supply. The system will rely on successful short-term outcomes in line with broad constituency preferences, yet these constituencies are also likely to be sufficiently poorly represented as to render outcomes in line with a sufficient range of preferences unlikely.

An accountability gap therefore emerges as a crucial problem that can be better comprehended by using the distinction between the input and output sides of legitimacy (Scharpf 1999; Wolf 2004) and what here is referred to as the accountability phase. The most important consideration is the interrelationships among these three "phases" of legitimacy. The input side refers to the broader representation of interests and the transparency of the decision-making process. The output side concerns the capacity of rule makers to resolve problems and achieve collective goals in line with accepted and shared preferences or norms of the community. An uneasy relationship between the input and output phases underpins legitimacy: if the output is perceived as legitimate, the process might not matter, yet consistently poor outcomes (e.g., financial crisis) may undermine a legitimate process. A highly legitimate process may consistently produce poor results that undermine diffuse legitimacy, whether decision makers can meaningfully influence the circumstances or not. That said, a democratic process with input from those who bear the costs of decisions is more likely to lead to acceptance of poor results over time; legitimate input and output combined are most likely to contribute to strengthening diffuse support. In particular, a more representative and transparent input side is more likely to lead to output reflecting norms that are perceived as legitimate. This is because input-side interaction is closely linked to how the sense of community and accountability is defined, and over time should help emergence of sense of community as outcomes correspond better to an accepted set of norms around particular issues.

This relationship implies a third accountability phase of legitimacy, which the literature on global and regional governance often ignores (notable exception Keohane 2006). This concerns the (democratic) accountability of global policy processes *and* outcomes to the broad range of constituencies, beyond the rather narrow often technical policy communities that currently participate in decision making, which are affected by the output phase. More effective accountability across the multilevel institutional layers of monetary and financial governance should facilitate both a more thorough assessment of outcomes and their distributional impact, and assessment of the balance between decision-making efficiency and representation, eventually bringing new constituencies and issues into the input phase. In this sense accountability enhances transparency as well.

There emerges a circular relationship among these three "phases" of legitimacy where problems or shifts in one phase may lead to ongoing pressures for change in the others. One must not, however, forget that focused business interests are likely to prove easier to organize in the first place, a standard Mancur Olson point (Olson 1965), that they have considerable organizational and resource advantages relative to other interests (see introduction to this volume), and that they consequently operate on the transnational level with greater facility than many organized constituencies with countervailing power at the domestic level. Extrapolating to the current state of global financial governance, the cases reveal the input, output, and accountability elements of legitimacy as problematic, starting with an input side that advances the interests of transnational private actors at variance with the broader political and economic imperatives of developing countries and developed country constituencies as well. Recent developments indicate that private agent preferences have dominated the representation of interests in decision making, with little representation of wider constituencies despite the fact that citizens have borne the cost of financial system failure and rescue. How has this happened?

To summarize a complex situation,[3] decision making that led to financial globalization was based on close and relatively exclusive relationships between private sectors and regulatory agencies, with frequent delegation to self-regulatory institutions. This is reinforced by common professional norms, the specialized and technical nature of expertise in the financial sector, and the shared need to maintain public confidence in the financial system itself. Cross-border market integration itself brought into question the effectiveness of national-level institutions, which decision makers sought to resolve through cross-border cooperation with their peers. Crucial information and expertise for the process remains the proprietary domain of firms which supervisors admit they cannot match. As cooperative and eventually transnational decision making became more removed from national-level systems of accountability and broader constituency representation, a shift in the balance of power between public authority and private market interests across the G7 leading economies (Baker 2005) provided private actors with greater influence and the potential to capture the input side. Finally, decisions made in relatively unaccountable policy processes were often aimed at increasing the levels of internationalization and marketization of economic policy making, benefiting those private market interests best able to respond to the new market opportunities. As they interacted more exclusively with private agents, authorities developed market-oriented approaches to regulation, supervision, and corporate risk management. This crucial aspect of public policy, the safety and stability of the financial system, became dominated by the preferences of those private market makers who stood to benefit from it most.[4] State jurisdictions were both responding to problems facing domestic policy capacity and the legitimacy problems that might result, and producing outcomes challenging traditional democratic accountability, giving way to a poorly defined sense of community and public interest at the international level. This situation is worsened by frequent recourse to self-regulation, yielding a system of financial governance reliant on private institutions centered on the financial markets (Cerny 1996, 96–99; Porter 1999). An input side representing a limited range of constituencies and admitting of reduced transparency meant that the clear definition of the public interest distinct from the particularistic claims of private market actors in relation to the financial system became more difficult (Underhill 1997; 2000). The processes that regulate and govern the financial markets and monetary order have become separated off from traditional means of accountability as well as from the influence of broader social constituencies.

This unrepresentative policy process shaping international financial market governance would matter little were it not for the high output-side stakes in terms of potential negative externalities for states and their societies, as the current financial crisis illustrates. This suggests that the output side of the legitimacy of global financial governance is also flawed, and the lack of accountability mechanisms at the global level provides little opportunity for a review of either the input or the output sides of the equation. While financial markets may be more integrated and regulatory standards more harmonized, these have been achieved at the cost of financial system instability, macroeconomic adjustment difficulties and weakened credibility of democratically elected governments with the majority of the population (Cerny 1999; Pharr, Putman, and Dalton 2000). The dénouement of the Argentine crisis is the clearest illustration: there, IMF conditionality in loan negotiations and private sector demands concerning debt workout directly confronted the outcome of democratic elections bringing President Kirchner into office. The outcome was painful for investors and the economy alike, as Kirchner largely chose to follow his electoral constituencies.

To summarize the argument so far, the current institutions of financial governance in which private market agents play a dominant role fail on the both the input and output criteria of political legitimacy. The input from broader social constituencies or developing countries has been at best limited, and while there have been benefits, these interests have often paid a considerable price in terms of externalities. The system of financial supervision and regulation quite simply failed. Public and private actors alike have yet to be held properly responsible for the decisions and actions that have affected the lives of people outside their jurisdictions and policy spheres, and the process of policy reform has been dominated by the same set of interests that fostered cross-border integration and its mixed results in the first place. This points to a flawed accountability phase as well.

TWO EMPIRICAL CASES

To substantiate the preceding argument, this section explores the changing nature of private sector involvement in international banking supervision via the Basle Committee on Banking Supervision (BC), and global securities markets regulation structured around the International Organization of Securities Commissions (IOSCO). These two cases are selected, first, because of their central importance to the emerging global financial architecture, and secondly because the financial governance functions involved have migrated out of the national domain and developed multilevel, indeed global-level characteristics. Thirdly, both banking supervision and securities regulation have traditionally involved public-private sector interaction at the domestic level in the postwar period, and the transnationalization of each policy process allows one to correlate the emergence of multilevel governance to potential observable shifts in the balance of public versus private authority in the policy process. Furthermore, a range of existing studies have characterized public-private interaction in the BC and IOSCO as largely benign or positive, a proposition with which this chapter differs. On these grounds, an analysis of these two cases should shed light on the challenges to democracy that growing private authority has posed to global financial governance.

The BC and Bank Supervision

The BC was founded in 1974[5] and consists of the banking supervisor from the central bank[6] of each G-10 member country (there were in fact thirteen though crisis reforms in 2009 expanded the committee to include the G20 and other systemically important countries, for a total of twenty-seven).[7] The BC quickly gained a reputation for "Olympian" detachment and guardian of the public interest, with an institutional culture of strict secrecy and relative insulation from public and private institutions of government and market. Global financial integration was in its early stages and the strong "public domain" of the Bretton Woods postwar era in financial systems governance underpinned the committee's role and decision-making processes. The conclusion of the Basle Capital Adequacy Accord (B-I) in 1988[8] was the crowning achievement of the BC and occurred with little formal consultation with "outside" interests, private or otherwise.

Doubtless up until the Market Risk Amendment to B-I (BC 1996), the committee did operate in a considerably more detached manner than is the case today, but "Olympian detachment" obscured a more prosaic reality. The relatively closed and exclusionary national financial policy communities, with central banks and autonomous regulatory agencies at their core, were often characterized by "business corporatism" and the delegation of public authority to private agencies via self-regulation (Coleman 1996; Moran 1986). National central banks and financial supervisors develop policy in close cooperation with a small community of private interests that share more with their "principals" than with other sectors of the economy and society. This close relationship is in fact enhanced by the "Olympian" distance of central banks and other autonomous agencies with supervisory responsibilities from the rough and tumble of traditional policy making in democratic governments.

Cross-border integration meant regulatory bargains reached at the national level had to be adapted, and B-I achieved this in relation to capital adequacy. The outcome of the agreement meant some national banking sectors had to raise substantial amounts of new capital, sharply affecting the cost of their lending (Oatley and Nabors 1998). Calls thus emerged for the BC to consider more closely the relative impact of its decisions on the banking sector and that led to more BC consultation with the private sector, including with the Institute for International Finance (IIF) based in Washington.[9] This process expanded with the committee's 1993 proposals to amend B-I to include banks' securities market risks (BC 1993).

This at first informal and until then unprecedented consultation process with IIF began when the IIF issued a position paper sharply criticizing the 1993 BC document: the proposals "fail[ed] to create sufficient regulatory incentives for banks to operate more sophisticated risk measurement systems than those necessary to meet the regulatory minimum,"[10] meaning it failed to stimulate the use of internal control mechanisms. A well-circulated and authoritative paper by Dimson and Marsh (1994) of the London Business School, arguing that internal control mechanisms were more effective than the committee's proposed approach, added to the pressure to revamp the proposal. Two consecutive new consultative documents embraced the approach advocated by the IIF (BC 1995a and 1995b). The pressure had worked, but the committee's new and soon to become formal interlocutor was hardly representative of the range of interested parties that would be affected by the amended accord. There was no emerging market representation in the BC[11] and the process did not extend beyond the traditionally close relationships between banks and regulators. Situated at the transnational level, one may argue, the emerging policy community was even farther removed from traditional lines of democratic accountability in the policy-making process.

The private sector began playing an even stronger agenda-setting role. Following the successful translation of IIF preferences into committee policy, the committee began to consider a new capital adequacy accord (B-II) in the face of ongoing criticisms of unchanged B-I treatment of credit risk. The review of B-I began with a study group report on systemic risk by the Group of Thirty (G30 1997), a private think tank–like body of members drawn from official and private institutions in the financial sector alike, many of whom had held prestigious appointments in both.[12] In the foreword to the report, G30 chairman Paul Volcker eulogized the role of B-I in the development of international regulatory and supervisory frameworks and emphasized collaborative efforts between global banks and their supervisors as an effective and broadly acceptable contribution toward the process (G30 1997, ii).

The report argued that internal risk management should play a central role in the supervision of financial systems and that "core" financial institutions should take the initiative to develop a new system along with "international groupings of supervisors." In essence, financial globalization had rendered the supervisory process increasingly difficult and beyond the reach of national supervisors. The conclusions of the report implied that regulatory agencies should rely more on the private institutions that they supervised and that these institutions themselves would accept the responsibility to improve the structure of, and the discipline imposed by, their internal control functions and risk management mechanisms (G30 1997, 12).

Here lie the origins of the market-based supervisory approach contained in the three pillars of B-II.[13] In 1998 the IIF issued its own report specifically urging the BC to update B-I on the basis of banks' market-based internal rating approach (IIF 1998). Although the BC invited consultations on its three sets of proposals for B-II, the IIF remained the principal interlocutor, and comments came overwhelmingly from financial institutions in Europe and North America, and to a lesser extent from officials from agencies, a few academics, chambers of commerce, and industry producer associations.[14]

While a claim that the BC in the mid- and late-1990s was a victim of policy capture might be considered by some as an exaggeration, there is little doubt that it was far more likely the BC and its member institutions would take into the account the preferences of private sector interlocutors in developed countries than the interests of developing country supervisors and their corresponding financial sectors. The long-institutionalized relationship between regulators and the regulated in financial supervision, which approximates conditions of capture, had developed at the transnational level by the mid-1990s. And if B-II derived directly from an agenda set by proposals from the private sector, supervisory failure and the undercapitalization of major systemically important banks belonging to the IIF were among the most important contributors to the outbreak of the current crisis.

It is not surprising that the advantages of the accord accrue to those large banks best able to operate the advanced internal rating-based systems permitted under special circumstances by the accord.[15] According to the BC's own estimates, this "advanced" approach will tend to lower their regulatory capital and reduce the cost of their lending operations relative to their smaller brethren using the "standard" approach (BC 2006, 5–11 and Table 5), and banks (and clients) using the latter will find their capital reserves more likely to rise, hurting their competitive position. The "standard" approach relies on external credit rating agencies (e.g., Moody's, Standard and Poor's). Claims on highly rated clients require lower capital charges, which negatively affects the many low- or non-rated small banks and SME clients, even though they are not necessarily riskier,[16] and are certainly less significant in systemic terms. B-II thus implies a clear relative capital cost disadvantage for both rated and unrated banks specializing in lending to (low-/unrated) small and medium enterprises (SME).

Developing countries were largely excluded from the BC policy-making process, and the situation for unrated banks or their clients in developing countries is worse yet: for otherwise creditworthy entities within those countries, capital costs are set to increase relative to Basle I (BC 2006, 21–23). Developing country submissions to the BC identified this as a problem, arguing that some banks and corporations in developing countries were sounder than the sovereign and that the ratings of the bank and corporations should be considered separately from that of the sovereign and based on the real risks of lending to the bank or corporation itself.[17] Yet their pleas were ignored. B-II thus has negative implications for the cost of capital for developing countries, likely reducing the quantity of lending to these borrowers.[18] A final problem of specific implications for developing countries concerns high compliance costs generated by the complicated risk management procedures and mechanisms of B-II. Complexity raises the relative compliance costs more for smaller and less sophisticated banks, erecting barriers to entry and hindering competition. Again, this especially affects banks in developing countries, which tend to be smaller and less sophisticated, putting them at a competitive disadvantage relative to large banks from developed countries yet where risks are not necessarily higher.

If the accord most likely contributed to the problem of undercapitalization of systemically important banks, there are further reasons why the risk management practices associated with B-II are unlikely to improve the safety and soundness of the financial system it is supposed to protect. For one, this is because it may enhance the pro-cyclicality of lending, again a particular problem for developing countries. B-II's reliance on asset price and ratings market signals may produce objective assessments of individual banks, but whether the aggregation of good individual practices leads to systemic level stability is more doubtful. If a wide range of banks responds simultaneously and in the same way to perceived market trends¾as reflected in prices and ratings in the market—downturns and upturns may be reinforced as banks downgrade or upgrade clients on a large scale. This issue may be of particular concern for emerging markets whose asset prices and ratings are already more volatile than those of developed countries. It could make their external financing more volatile and domestically lead to more severe business cycles.

Extensive quantitative analyses (Claessens et al. 2008; see also Bailey 2005; Griffith-Jones 2002; Powell 2004) provide evidence that B-II implies higher capital adequacy requirements for, in particular, small banks located in developing and emerging-market countries. Their clients are most likely to see their capital costs rise and access to external financing decline. These analyses also demonstrate that B-II has an adverse impact on the cost and volume of capital flows to some lower-rated developing countries, although the effects on average are small. Importantly, they establish that the pro-cyclicality of capital flows to developing countries may increase with the use of internal ratings by internationally active banks. The increase in fluctuations in the availability of external financing would be a very unfortunate outcome, given that developing countries already suffer from volatile capital flows.

While a reformed Basle II may yet contribute to the general efficiency of the global financial markets, its effects are skewed, and what may be efficient for international banks involves costs for developing countries as well as some (SME) social constituencies in developed ones. In the end, efficiency for *whom* is a valid issue to address, and in this sense the contribution of B-II to global financial market efficiency and to the quality of supervision may be called into question. The clear implication of our analysis is that if BC standards have such an obviously global impact as the BC itself claims and to which the evidence here attests, affecting the terms of competition among financial institutions, the cost of capital, and the stability of capital flows, a committee more representative of the broader interests of the global community is required, and one with an accountability mechanism that connects the input and output phases with ongoing attempts at reforming global financial governance. The interests of those who bear the cost of crisis must also be better represented in terms of both the input and output sides of the ledger.

IOSCO and Regulatory Harmonization

The International Organization of Securities Commissions (IOSCO) was founded in 1984 in a market environment in which national regulators alone could no longer cope. Members are official national securities regulators, usually autonomous government agencies mandated by legislation,[19] supplemented by "associate" members (e.g., important official securities regulators at sub-national/provincial level, or other market authorities that work closely with the "national" regulator) and "affiliate" members, which are self-regulatory organizations (SROs), securities exchanges, or trade associations with self-regulatory responsibilities. The latter do not vote but are considered crucial to the policymaking process of IOSCO. IOSCO also maintains contacts with international organizations involved in financial architecture issues, such as the OECD, the IMF, and the multilateral development banks, including a long record of interaction with the Basle Committee on capital adequacy issues (Underhill 1997, 33–38).

The close relationship between official regulators and SROs is particularly important to the argument: most official regulators retain full legal powers of supervision and regulation, yet operate by delegating to SROs composed of private member firms.[20] Equally significant, IOSCO works in close consultation with private international regulatory bodies as such the World Federation of Exchanges (WFE)[21] or the International Capital Markets Association, a self-regulating association of dealers on primary and secondary international capital markets.[22] As a result of these linkages, IOSCO considers itself a nongovernmental international organization (Underhill 1995, 261). IOSCO officials consistently stress the importance of incorporating industry inputs to the standard-setting process in order to focus on policy matters of relevance to practitioners and industry bodies (IOSCO 2004, 14–15; 2005a, 11–12; 2006, 5). Proposals are thus developed in close consultation with IOSCO's SRO Consultative Committee (SROCC, founded in 1989), while market innovations have made regulators heavily dependent on the expertise of industry analysts for the skills involved in developing regulation. This closely knit transnational policy community constitutes a typical case of Michael Moran's "esoteric politics" (1986), wherein an elite group works out the management of its own vital interests without wider public involvement.

Many IOSCO regulatory functions are outrightly delegated to private-sector associations and think tanks. For example, IOSCO has relied almost entirely upon the International Accounting Standards Board (IASB) for developing and harmonizing accounting standards, which is crucial to facilitating the globalization of securities trading and the leveling of the playing field for major market players (IOSCO 2005b; Vaughan and Felderhof 2002). In the late 1980s IOSCO vested the Group of Thirty with the authority to deal with clearance and settlement issues in international securities markets; in 1993 the G30 issued the first major report on derivatives regulation and has since played a leading role in shaping an international framework for regulating derivatives markets (Tsingou 2003; 2006). In short, IOSCO forms the hub of a constellation of private industry associations and self-regulatory organizations with a private sector membership. This increases its acceptance by the industry, but it also means that the IOSCO "input phase" is relatively closed.

IOSCO's primary goal has been to provide globally the regulatory benefits of the domestic level, chiefly by harmonizing cross-border securities market regulation (Guy 1992; IOSCO 2006, 18). The Technical Committee (TC) of the fifteen "most developed" market members (Guy 1992, 293)[23] in consultation with the SROCC is the chief forum for achieving these aims by focusing on multinational disclosure and accounting, regulations of secondary markets and intermediaries, the enforcement and exchange of information, investment management, and, more recently, corporate governance (IOSCO 2006, 6–9). These efforts have stimulated the global integration of securities markets, with broader political economy and welfare effects on a range of constituencies. These output-side effects are beneficial where they strengthen (weak) domestic financial governance. Given the tendency of (especially short-term) capital to flow "uphill" from developing to developed country markets (Prasad, Rajan, and Subramanian 2007), they also involve costs by extending capital market openness to crisis-prone emerging markets; such integration can also have negative consequences for financial development and therefore growth in lower income countries (Law and Demetriades 2006).

IOSCO realized in the late 1980s that cross-country regulatory harmonization (e.g., disclosure, clearing, and settlement arrangements, fraud and bankruptcy standards, market transparency) would reduce the cost of international equity offers and securities dealing and encourage market integration. If the most developed segment of the market were properly internationalized, more thoroughgoing cross-national harmonization and integration would follow (IOSCO 1989; 1991; 1992), arguably leading to more efficient capital markets and thus economic growth. Behind this rationale lay the advancement of private and particularistic interests seeking relief from saturated U.S. markets. Regulatory convergence within the IOSCO policy community to establish international (largely American) standards would permit U.S. investment bank expansion into European and fast-growing East Asian markets where they might also have a competitive edge, and would also enhance the role of private interests in the emerging transnational policy processes (Simmons 2001; Zaring 1998).

The powerful TC and its five standing committees pushed for a single common prospectus for the leading securities exchanges, similar disclosure requirements and harmonized clearing arrangements (Underhill 1995, 265–66), while recognizing that any changes would have to be consistent with the legal mandates of the member organizations. In doing so, IOSCO actively incorporated G30 and WFE proposals (IOSCO 1989; 1991). In the mid-1990s, the TC began work on a comprehensive set of international securities market regulations as a code of conduct for global market integration, all in close cooperation with the SROCC, global private-sector associations such as the WFE, IASB, and the G30, and market participants (IOSCO 1999). The result was the promulgation of the thirty "Objectives and Principles of Securities Regulation" in 1998, a revised version of which was published in 2003 along with a comprehensive implementation "methodology." The three main objectives of the thirty principles were investor protection, market efficiency and transparency, and the reduction of systemic risks (IOSCO 2003), thereby reducing the risks and costs of cross-border transactions and issuance and further accelerating capital market openness. This of course heightened the need for national governments to develop the institutions of multilevel governance further in order to cope with the outcome, and brought a series of differentiated costs and benefits to the various players of the global financial system.

More recently, following the financial fraud and major corporate failures of the late 1990s and early 2000s, IOSCO formed the Securities Fraud Task Force to strengthen corporate governance. IOSCO first endorsed the OECD Principles of Corporate Governance and prioritized minority shareholder protection and board member independence (IOSCO 2005a, 12–13; 2006, 6), and then launched a program of reform and institutional change along those lines (IOSCO 2006). Senior IOSCO officials argued that good corporate governance was integral to internationally acceptable principles of sound capital market regulation (Cooper 2006; IOSCO 2005a; 2006), and few would argue the contrary. Nonetheless, their emphasis was consistent with the interests of private actors within and beyond the IOSCO policy community who promoted convergence on the basis of the "shareholder value" model and who would initially benefit in competitive terms from the adjustments this would impose on others (Nölke 2004; Useem 1998).

The TC essentially designed the standards, and while the Emerging Markets Committee (EMC) played a consultative role, much of the discussion concerned the implementation and not the content of the standards (IOSCO 2005a; 2006). The further integration of emerging market and developing economies into the global financial system was one of the objectives in this regard, and adjustment to the new standards would be difficult for some. Whether or not there was evidence that such a development would assist development prospects, failure to adopt the standards might send negative signals to potential investors and creditors in developed countries.

IOSCO regards its crowning achievement to be its multilateral system of Memoranda of Understanding (MOUs) developed in 2002. Replacing a system of bilateral deals, the multilateral MOU aims to speed up the commitment of national securities regulators to the thirty IOSCO Principles, in particular the exchange of information and cross-border enforcement of market regulations (IOSCO 2004, 8–10; 2006, 10–11), both essential ingredients of functional transnational markets. The process went farther in 2005 with all-member endorsement of both the principles and the MOU as the core international regulatory standards to ensure against systemic risk (the crisis certainly invites skepticism as to the attainment of this objective in particular), investor protection, and market efficiency, with firm targets in terms of implementation and to expand the network of signatories by 2010.[24]

While the IOSCO policy process enjoyed a substantial degree of autonomy from typical norms of accountability in (democratic) governance, it had relatively little independence from the private interests it supervised and worked with. Members and firms alike shared a commitment to market-based integration and governance. Private sector control of crucial specialized knowledge in a dynamic market context increased the dependence of regulators on particularistic interests. The system of membership was far from open despite the broad impact of IOSCO's policies, and this implies flawed input. There were also problems on the output side. Regulatory convergence accelerated the transnationalization of segmented national financial systems, opening developing countries to often volatile short-term capital flows and imposing important adjustment burdens on weak legal and regulatory systems. Rapid changes in the mode of financial and corporate governance in the direction of market principles may destabilize the often-delicate institutional and

political underpinnings of developing societies. Increased capital mobility makes macroeconomic policy management difficult and constrains
the ability of developing states to implement the fiscal and welfare policies often crucial to political legitimacy (Underhill and Zhang 2003), thus
playing a part in the regular outbreak of crises. As with the Basle case,
the output was most beneficial to those who designed the policies in the
first place, with important potential costs for more vulnerable constituencies, particularly in developing countries. This rather exclusionary
process also included a low level of accountability to broader, external
constituencies affected by decision making, especially if the financial
crisis may be considered one of the outputs. Arm's-length IOSCO members were more accountable to SROs and private market participants
than to traditional government oversight, yielding a poorly defined sense
of broader public interest and community in international regulatory
convergence. There is no institutionalized process to shift IOSCO's convergence and harmonization financial governance reform debate to a
broader forum.

It should be noted that there is change in the air, which may lead
to the considerable enhancement of developing country regulator input
into the process, though with little effect on broader constituencies outside the sector. IOSCO has recognized that successful realization of the
MOU process will require better input and participation of developing
country members. Governance structures in IOSCO have begun to
reflect this change: developing countries are being brought into the
inner sanctum of the TC (currently only Mexico is there); regional
standing committees have begun to play a greater role; the membership
of the executive committee (the effective decision-making body, which
decides upon the measures proposed by the TC, for example) has
broadened considerably; and the vice-chair of the executive committee
has for the past three years been the member from China (confidential
interview, July 2008; see also IOSCO Web site, consulted September 23,
2009). The full effect of these changes cannot yet be fully determined,
but over time IOSCO sensitivity to the concerns of developing country
securities commissions must surely increase, and the denouement of
the current financial crisis may lead to yet further change.

CONCLUSION:
POLICY IMPLICATIONS AND NORMATIVE PREREQUISITES

The two cases demonstrate that private business interests dominate the
input side of global financial and monetary governance, yielding out-

comes with some "public interest content" but largely in line with a narrow range of interests and imposing externalities on other constituencies. Private financiers from the leading financial markets and their public counterparts made decisions without being held accountable to constituencies negatively affected by these decisions, while the same private interests that promoted the outcome benefited the most. These important examples of business authority in multilevel governance are hardly compatible with the enhancement of democracy. The world is now struggling in the aftermath of a costly financial crisis, the origins of which have much to do with the nature and quality of financial governance as output. Meanwhile, important segments of the financial services industry are carrying on with business as usual, including the award of substantial bonuses to those whose risk taking in the past contributed to the calamity so recently experienced. Better representation and transparency on the input side and improved external and internal accountability mechanisms might produce more broadly acceptable outcomes, thus enhancing democracy and the political underpinnings of the system. Much must change if the more optimistic scenarios of some of the chapters in this volume are to prevail.

This assessment suggests that global financial governance requires appropriate institutional changes. The crucial input phase could be substantially enhanced through better and broader constituency representation based on a range of principles, thus increasing the likelihood of better outcomes and that a more acceptable spectrum of norms come to be shared in global financial governance. This issue is especially relevant for developing countries, whose access to decision making in financial governance is less than that of private business interests at the moment: in the BC there was no representation until the April 2009 G20 crisis summit, and in IOSCO emerging markets have only a consultative role in the EMC. Progress firstly involves looking closely at the policymaking autonomy of regulatory agencies from national to global levels. Where autonomous public agencies such as financial supervisors maintain close interactive relationships with private actors and associations prone to policy rent-seeking, governments and their international offshoots should establish effective and representative decision-making and accountability mechanisms involving a much wider range of constituencies in their electorates (Campos and Root 1997, 153–71). The power of private actors and potential for capture in situations of delegated authority could be counteracted by including a broader range of social groups in policy processes and by fashioning more inclusive state-society relations (Biddle and Milor 1997). To ensure the responsiveness of private interests to the countries and peoples most affected by their decisions, key international financial institutions should also engage actively with transnational social forces and stakeholders (Held 1995; Woods 2001). This is of course easier said than done, and would certainly run into the fierce opposition of the transnational corporate interests that most enjoy the benefits of global markets. But the absence of more democratic forms of governance also has a cost. States find it increasingly difficult to augment their policy capacity by pooling sovereignty while finding themselves simultaneously constrained by the sociopolitical tensions and legitimacy problems associated with cross-border integration and international regulatory processes on the domestic front.

NOTES

This chapter is an abridged and revised version of the article "Setting the Rules: Private Power, Political Underpinnings, and Legitimacy in Global Monetary and Financial Governance," first published in *International Affairs* 84, no. 3 (May 2008); 535–54. Generous financial support from the World Economy and Finance Programme of the UK Economic and Social Research Council, grant RES-156-25-0009, is gratefully acknowledged, as is support from the EU Framework 6 program Network of Excellence "GARNET" and Framework 7 consortium "PEGGED."

1. The literature on private business participation in the broader context of global economic governance is too voluminous to view here. For two recent examples see Schirm (2004) and Streeck (2005).
2. We argue that "representation" implies more systematic and institutionalized forms of involvement in decision-making processes wherein it is more difficult to circumvent constituencies that are properly represented than those that merely "participate." Sound representation of a range of stakeholders, we argue, also increases the constraints on the structurally most powerful constituencies and their potential alliances with government by enhancing the availability of alternative arguments and information (see Held and König-Archibugi 2004), and thereby enhancing the accountability of decision making to the broad range of interests in democratic societies.
3. See Cohen (1999); Helleiner (1994); Underhill (1997).
4. Some analysts cast serious doubts on whether market-based supervisory methods will lead to stability at all; e.g., see Persaud (2000).

5. For more on the history of the BC, see Wood (2005).

6. If this is not the banking supervisor, then there is an additional representative of the national supervisory agency, though this does not add an extra "vote" and the committee anyway operates on a consensus basis.

7. The thirteen members before expansion were Belgium, Canada, France, Germany, Italy, Japan, Luxemburg, Netherlands, Spain, Sweden, Switzerland, the UK, and the United States. After expansion the members were Argentina, Australia, Belgium, Brazil, Canada, China, France, Germany, Hong Kong SAR, India, Indonesia, Italy, Japan, Korea, Luxemburg, Mexico, the Netherlands, Russia, Saudi Arabia, Singapore, South Africa, Spain, Sweden, Switzerland, Turkey, the United Kingdom, and the United States. The present chairman of the committee is Mr. Nout Wellink, president of the Netherlands Bank.

8. Capital adequacy refers to the amount of liquid or near liquid capital reserves a bank must put aside to ensure its ongoing soundness in the event of rapid withdrawal of deposits. Capital reserves are measured as a percentage of total bank assets, hence capital adequacy ratios.

9. The IIF was originally formed as a consultative group of major U.S. and European banks during the debt crisis of the 1980s, and became a more broadly based organization representing some 350 member banks worldwide.

10. The IIF, Report of the Working Group on Capital Adequacy (Washington, DC: IIF, 1993), cited in *Financial Regulation Report*, December 1993, 3.

11. The IIF membership did eventually include some emerging market financial institutions, and the BC eventually began an "outreach" process involving emerging market economies. As mentioned in Note 7 above, since the crisis reforms of 2009, the BC does now include major developing country members but this was clearly a long time coming.

12. The report includes the names of study group participants (ix–x), and members of the G30 itself (47–48).

13. The three pillars consist of minimum capital requirements, supervisory review of capital adequacy, and public disclosure and market discipline. Under the three pillar system, bank supervisors are no longer exclusively responsible for the supervisory process and specifying levels of capital adequacy; rather bank owners and risk managers, supervisors, and market forces combine to oversee banks. For a more technical discussion, see the BC (2003).

14. See Committee web site section on comments on proposals at http://www.bis.org/bcbs/cacomments.htm (comments on second consultative document) and http://www.bis.org/bcbs/cp3comments.htm (comments on third consultative document).
15. See Claessens et al. (2008), on which this account draws, for a detailed discussion of the welfare effects of B-II.
16. See, e.g., submissions on http://www.bis.org/bcbs/cp3comments. htm by Austrian Banking Industry, the German *Bankenfachverband*, the European Co-operative Banks, the World Council of Credit Unions, or the *Kredittilsynet-Norges* Bank (Norwegian central bank) submission.
17. See, e.g., submission of the central bank of Belize (http:// www.bis.org/bcbs/cp3/belcenban.pdf) and of Burundi (http:// www.bis.org/bcbs/cp3/burcenban.pdf).
18. For additional literature reinforcing these points, see, e.g., Persaud (2002); Griffith-Jones et al. (2002a; 2002b).
19. This could involve a division of a national finance ministry, a self-regulatory institution (for instance a stock market), or even a central bank. See IOSCO Web site section on membership and other rules at http://www.iosco.org/lists/index.cfm?section=general.
20. For example, the SEC delegates to what was the National Association of Securities Dealers, plus the relevant stock exchanges, which are now all merged in the self-regulatory Financial Industry Regulatory Authority.
21. Formerly the International Federation of Stock Exchanges.
22. A merger of the Int. Sec. Markets Assoc. and the Int. Primary Mkts. Association; *Trading Places* (Mondo Visione), 02/05/05, http:// www.exchange-handbook.co.uk/index.cfm?section=news& action=detail&id=51279.
23. Mexico recently became the first emerging market member.
24. See IOSCO Web site, http://www.iosco.org/about/index.cfm?section=history. For a broader discussion of how nongovernment regulatory bodies influenced capital flows through their coercive power, see Soederberg (2003).

REFERENCES

Bailey, R. 2005. Basle II and developing countries. Working paper 05-71. Development Studies Institute, London School of Economics.

Baker, A. 2005. *The Group of Seven finance ministries, central banks, and global financial governance*. London: Routledge.

Basle Committee. 1993. *The supervisory treatment of market risks*, consultative paper. Basle: Bank for International Settlements.

———. 1995a. *Proposal to issue a supplement to the Basle Capital Accord to cover market risks*. Basle: Bank for International Settlements.

———. 1995b. *An internal model-based approach to market risk capital requirements*. Basle: Bank for International Settlements.

———. 1996. *Amendment to the capital accord to incorporate market risks*. Basle: Bank for International Settlements.

———. 2003. *Overview of the new Basle Capital Accord*. Basle: Bank for International Settlements.

———. 2006. *Results of the fifth quantitative impact study*.

Bernstein, S. 2004. The elusive basis of legitimacy in global governance. Working Paper GHC 04/2. Hamilton: McMaster University Institute on Globalization and the Human Condition.

Biddle, J., and V. Milnor. 1997. Economic governance in Turkey. In *Business and state in developing countries*, ed S. Maxfield and B. R. Schneider, 277–309. Ithaca: Cornell University Press.

Bohman, J. 1999. International regimes and democratic governance. *International Affairs* 75, no. 3: 499–513.

Buira, A. 2005. The IMF at sixty, in *The IMF and the World Bank at sixty*, ed. Ariel Buira. New York: Anthem Press.

Campos, E., and H. Root. 1996. *The key to the Asian Miracle*. Washington, DC: Brookings Institution.

Cerny, P. 1995. Globalization and the changing logic of collective action. *International Organization*, 49, no. 4 (Autumn): 595–625.

———. 1996. International finance and the erosion of state policy capacity. In *Globalisation and public policy*, ed. Philip Gummet, 83–104. Cheltenham: Edward Elgar.

———. 1999. Globalisation and the erosion of democracy. *European Journal of Political Research* 36, no. 2: 1–26.

Claessens, S., G. Underhill, and X. Zhang. 2008. The political economy of Basle II: The costs for poor countries. *The World Economy* 31, no. 3: 313–44.

Cline, W. R. 2000. The role of the private sector in resolving financial crises in emerging markets. Paper prepared for the National Bureau of Economic Research Conference on Economic and Financial Crises in Emerging Market Economies, Woodstock, VT, October 19–21.

Cohen, B. J. 1999. *The geography of money.* Ithaca: Cornell University Press.

Coleman, W., and G. Underhill. 1998. Introduction, in *Regionalism and Global Economic Integration,* ed. Coleman and Underhill. London: Routledge.

Cooper, J. 2006. Corporate governance. Paper presented to the OECD-ADBI 8th Round Table Capital Market Reform in Asia, Tokyo, October 11–12.

Dimson, E., and P. Marsh. 1994. *The debate on international capital requirements.* London: London Business School.

Easton, D. 1965. *A systems analysis of political life.* New York: John Wiley and Sons.

Franck, T. 1990. *The power of legitimacy among nations.* New York: Oxford University Press.

Group of Thirty (G30). 1997. *Global institutions, national supervision, and systemic risk.* Washington, DC: Group of Thirty/Study Group Report.

Guy, P. 1992. Regulatory harmonization to achieve effective international competition. In *Regulating international financial markets: Issues and policies,* ed. R. Edwards and H. T. Patrick, 291–96. Dordrecht: Kluwer.

Held, D. 1995. *Democracy and the global order,* Stanford: Stanford University Press.

———. 1997. Democracy and globalization. *Global Governance* 3, no. 3: 251–67.

———, and M. König-Archibugi. 2004. Introduction. Special issue on global governance and accountability. *Government and Opposition* 39, no. 2: 127.

Helleiner, E. 1994. *States and the re-emergence of global finance: From Bretton Woods to the 1990s.* Ithaca: Cornell University Press.

Hurd, I. 1999. Legitimacy and authority in international politics. *International Organization* 53, no. 2: 379–408.

Institute for International Finance (IIF). 1998. *Recommendations for revising the regulatory capital rules for credit risk.* Report of the Working Group on Capital Adequacy. Washington, DC: IIF.

International Monetary Fund (IMF). 2001. *Reforming the international financial architecture—Progress through 2000.* Washington, DC: IMF.

IOSCO. 1989. *International equity offers.*

———. 1991. *Annual report.*

———. 1992. *Annual report.*

————. 1999. *Annual report.*

————. 2003. *Objectives and principles of securities regulation.*

————. 2004. *Annual report.*

————. 2005a. *Annual report.*

————. 2005b. *The development and use of international financial reporting standards.*

————. 2006. *Annual report.*

Keohane, R. 2006. Accountability in world politics. *Scandinavian political studies* 29, no. 2 (June): 75–87.

Law, S. H., and P. Demetriades. 2006. Openness, institutions, and financial development. Working Paper WEF0012. World Economy and Finance Research Programme, Economic and Social Res. Council of the UK.

Mattli, W., and T. Büthe. 2005. Global private governance: Lessons from a national model of setting standards in accounting. *Law and Contemporary Problems* 68, no. 3/4: 225–62.

Moran, M. 1986. Theories of regulation and changes in regulation. *Political Studies* 34, no. 2: 185–201.

Nölke, A. 2004. Transnational private authority and corporate governance. In *New rules for global markets*, ed. Stefan A. Schirm, 212–42. London: Palgrave Macmillan.

Oatley, T., and R. Nabors. 1998. Redistributive co-operation: Market failure, wealth transfers, and the Basle Accord. *International Organization* 52, no. 1: 35–54.

Olson, M. 1965. *The logic of collective action: Public goods and the theory of goods.* Cambridge: Harvard University Press.

Persaud, A. 2000. Sending the herd off the cliff edge. First Prize, Jacques de la Rosiere essay competition, Institute for International Finance, Washington, DC. Published in E-Risk Erisk.com, December.

Pharr, S. J., R. D. Putnam, and R. J. Dalton. 2000. A quarter-century of declining confidence. *Journal of Democracy* 11, no. 2: 5–25.

Porter, T. 1999. The transnational agenda for financial regulation in developing countries. In *Financial globalisation and democracy in emerging markets*, ed. Leslie Elliott Armijo, 91–114. London: Macmillan.

————. 2005. Private authority, technical authority, and the globalization of accounting standards, *Business and Politics* 7: 1–30.

Powell, A. 2004. Basle II and developing countries. Working Paper 3387. Washington, DC: World Bank.

Prasad, E., R. Rajan, and A. Subranmanian. 2007. The paradox of capital. *Finance and Development* (March): 16–19.

Scharpf, F. W. 1999. *Governing Europe: Effective and democratic?* Oxford: Oxford University Press.

Schirm, S. A., ed.. 2004. *New rules for global markets,* London: Palgrave Macmillan.

Simmons, B. 2001. The international politics of harmonization. *International Organisation* 55, no. 3: 589–620.

Sinclair, T. 2002. Private makers of public policy: Bond rating agencies and the new global finance. In *Common goods: Reinventing European and international governance,* ed. Adrienne Heritier, 279–92. New York: Rowman and Littlefield.

Slaughter, A.-M. 2000. Governing the global economy through government networks. In *The role of law in international politics,* ed. Michael Byers, 177–205. Oxford: Oxford University Press.

Soederberg, S. 2003. The promotion of Anglo-American corporate governance in the South. *Third World Quarterly* 24, no. 1: 7–27.

Streeck, W., ed. 2005. *Governing interests: Business associations in the national, European, and global political economy.* London: Routledge.

Tsingou, E. 2003. Transnational policy communities and financial governance. CSGR Working Paper No. 111/03. Centre for the Study of Globalisation and Regionalisation, University of Warwick.

———. 2006. The governance of OTC derivatives markets. In *The political economy of financial market regulation,* ed. P. Mooslechner, H. Schuberth, and B. Weber, 168–90. Aldershot: Edward Elgar.

Underhill, G. R.D. 1995. Keeping governments out of politics. *Review of International Studies* 21, no. 3: 251–78.

———. 1997. Private markets and public responsibility. In *The new world order in international finance,* ed. Geoffrey R. D. Underhill, 17–49. London: Macmillan.

———. 2000. The public good versus private interests in the global financial and monetary system. *International Comparative and Corporate Law Journal* 2, no. 3: 335–59.

———, and Xiaoke Zhang, eds. 2003. *International financial governance under stress.* Cambridge: Cambridge University Press.

Useem, M. 1998. Corporate leadership in a globalising equity market. *Academy of Management Executive* 12, no. 4: 43–59.

Vaughan, S., and S. Felderhof. 2002. International mineral resources and mineral reserve. Paper presented to the 48th Annual Rocky Mountain Mineral Law Institute, Lake Tahoe, 24–26 July.

Wolf, K. D. 2004. Private actors and the legitimacy of governance beyond the state. In *Governance and democracy,* ed. Arthur Benz and Yannis Papadopoulos, 200–27. London: Routledge.

Woods, N. 2001. Making the IMF and the World Bank more account-able. *International Affairs* 77, no. 1: 83–100.

Zaring, D. 1998. International law by other means. *Texas International Law Journal* 33: 281–330.

Zürn, M. 2004. Global governance and legitimacy problems. *Government and Opposition* 39, no. 2: 260–87.

6

BUSINESS AND DEMOCRACY?

Pharmaceutical Firms, Intellectual Property, and Developing Countries

SUSAN K. SELL

INTRODUCTION

The brand name pharmaceutical industry has been quite assertive in U.S. trade policymaking in recent years. Beginning in the 1970s when it pushed for stronger intellectual property protection, through the 1980s and 1990s when it achieved many of its goals in the multilateral Agreement on Trade-Related Intellectual Property Protection (TRIPs) in the World Trade Organization (WTO), and continuing into the 2000s with its influence over intellectual property provisions in regional and bilateral Free Trade Agreements (FTAs), the industry has maintained pressure on foreign governments to better protect its patents. Foreign governments, nongovernmental organizations (NGOs), and affected patients have not been passive in responding to this pressure.

Overall, however, the scorecard is tipped in industry's favor. Not in terms of reputation by any means, but by results. As this chapter demonstrates, the brand name pharmaceutical industry has deployed its significant power, resources, and energy to press its preferred outcomes at every conceivable level. Its actions are often nontransparent, exclusionary, and elude accountability. To the extent that this is the case this suggests decay. With very few exceptions, industry's role in this instance has outpaced the development of democracy in deliberations over intellectual property protection of brand name pharmaceutical products.

Readers will note a decidedly bleaker assessment here than that offered by Kellow and Murphy in this volume. Kellow and Murphy highlight an increasingly productive relationship between government, business, and civil society in multiple venues. While this may generally be the case in the multilateral arena, this chapter adopts a wide angle lens to explore multiple arenas. Indeed, vertical forum shifting (from multilateral to regional, bilateral, and even individual targets of opportunity) may well be a consequence of the phenomenon that Kellow and Murphy describe. Perhaps the multilateral forums have become too democratic to suit the global brand name pharmaceutical firms.

Examining the impact that this activity may have on democracy requires the exploration of these activities at multiple levels. Following Tony Porter and Karsten Ronit's framework, this chapter begins at the most macro level, that of structural power within a global capitalist system, and continues its analysis through the sectoral or industry-wide level, down to the level of the firm. Brand name pharmaceutical firms have ample structural power, but perhaps more noteworthy has been their close relationship with the U.S. government and the government's willingness to support their goals and strategies. Given the importance of the U.S. economy globally, this close relationship has significant repercussions abroad. What one might find surprising in examining the role of business is the extent of its influence and the depth of its efforts to effect change abroad. Business is engaged at the multilateral level, the regional level, the bilateral level, the domestic level, and in some instances has targeted specific individuals abroad to challenge them in their regulatory role. The implications for democracy as defined by Porter and Ronit can be troubling.

This chapter demonstrates that political conflicts extend far beyond traditional democratic mechanisms such as voting and lobbying, although such mechanisms continue to remain relevant. The exercise of business power, and conflicts related to this, can move from the most global and structural levels to very personal conflicts involving individuals. Similarly, they range across public sector and private sector institutions, with developments and outcomes in one area affecting those in another, often in unexpected ways. This reflects the complexity of the relationship between global business and democracy and suggests that this relationship is not predetermined, but rather is in an ongoing process of construction. This means that the elements of democracy that this volume focuses on—transparency, participation, and accountability—require new and complex initiatives, practices, and institutional arrangements as well.

The chapter begins by describing a central controversy over pharmaceutical drugs in developing countries. The next section analyzes the structural power of global corporations. Then it examines the pharmaceutical sector, its relationship to policymakers, and its deployment of its power in a variety of negotiating contexts. The chapter traces a number of significant episodes of controversy at multilateral, regional, bilateral, and even individual levels, as well as concerted efforts to curb this industry's power and push back. It concludes by assessing the impact of these episodes on the democratic features of participation, transparency, and accountability, and more broadly, on the prospects for further decay or renewal going forward.

THE CONTROVERSY

The battle over access to essential medicines revolves around the right to issue compulsory licenses and to manufacture and export generic versions of brand name drugs to *expand* access. Global brand name pharmaceutical corporations seek to restrict the ability of generic manufacturers to produce and distribute essential medicines; they seek to *ration* access. African countries in the grip of the HIV/AIDS pandemic, Brazil, India, Thailand, and their nongovernmental organization (NGO) advocates have sought to clarify interpretations of TRIPS that permit compulsory licensing, parallel importing, generic manufacture, and export. The debate over TRIPS and access to medicines has galvanized a broad range of stakeholders. Brand name pharmaceutical companies, developed and developing country governments, the United States Trade Representative (USTR), NGOs representing public health and consumer interests, and generic drug manufacturers are all participating in this vigorous debate. Among the competing values embedded in TRIPS are the generation of knowledge, the facilitation of "undistorted" trade, and the protection of public health (Shaffer 2004, 460).

On one side of the TRIPS and access to medicines debate are those who support strong intellectual property protection for pharmaceuticals and argue that, if anything, TRIPS is too weak. These advocates highlight the high costs of developing new drugs, the importance of strong property rights as incentives for innovation, and the need for substantial compensation for providing life saving drugs (Grabowski 2002, 850–53). The brand name global pharmaceutical industry, the United States, and the USTR promote this perspective. It has also been influential in the World Trade Organization (WTO) and the World Intellectual Property Organization (WIPO). The industry fears that any expansion of cut-rate drugs will undermine its markets, particularly if they find their way into high-income industrialized country markets. It also is eager to develop markets in middle-income countries in Asia and Latin America. The global brand name pharmaceutical industry highlights the potential health dangers of widespread generic production, "piracy," and the use of drugs without the supervision, dosing instructions, and regulatory controls covering global pharma's products (Symposium 2002, 729).

Substantively, advocates of the position taken by the Pharmaceutical Research and Manufacturers of America (PhRMA) object to any weakening of intellectual property protection through public health exceptions. They reject compulsory licensing as a policy tool to bring the costs of essential medicines down. They reject parallel importing (Symposium 2002, 727), whereby states can take advantage of differential pricing policies and import the cheapest version of the brand name patented pharmaceutical product. Harvey Bale of International Federation of Pharmaceutical Manufacturers (IFPMA) criticized a World Health Organization (WHO) report for its repeated references to compulsory licensing "as a panacea for fundamental poverty and structural problems in developing countries' health care systems" (IFPMA 2006). In fact, no one has ever touted compulsory licensing as a panacea for poverty but rather as an instrument for promoting competition thus lowering prices. Instead, PhRMA advocates promote increased foreign aid and drug donations from firms.

On the other side of the debate is an alliance of developing country governments and NGOs campaigning for access to essential medicines. They argue that patent protection *is* a barrier to access and that public health exceptions to patent rules are necessary to prevent needless deaths. They advocate compulsory licensing, generic competition, parallel importation, and fixed rates of compensation for pharmaceutical companies.

Among the most outspoken advocates of this position are James Love of Knowledge Ecology International and Ellen 't Hoen of Médecins Sans Frontières (MSF). They consistently have attacked PhRMA's positions on these issues. Ellen 't Hoen points to strong intellectual property protection as one important barrier to access; she argues that patent protection leads to high prices and limited access (2002, 29). MSF and other NGOs have expressed a number of concerns about TRIPS, including high drug prices, reduced availability of quality generic alternatives, inadequate research and development into tropical diseases, and bilateral pressures on developing countries to adopt patent protection that exceeds TRIPS' requirements ('t Hoen 2002, 29–30) Furthermore, Love has challenged PhRMA's claims that its companies spend $500–800 million developing each new drug, and has argued that the majority of important HIV/AIDS drugs were actually developed by the public National Institutes of Health (NIH), and funded by taxpayers' dollars (CPTech 2000).

Brazil, India, and the African group of countries have been leaders in the intergovernmental efforts to address their public health emergencies. Health care activists have praised Brazil's policies of providing universal access to HIV/AIDS drugs (Rosenberg, T. 2001, 26). Brazil has used the threat of compulsory licensing to negotiate steep drug discounts with global pharma. It also has committed resources to producing generic drugs. Its policies have helped to create a market for high quality generic drugs (Symposium 2002, 702). Creating a market has encouraged competition that has brought HIV/AIDS drugs prices down from $10,000 to $150 a year per patient.[1] As a WHO report concludes, "Competition is perhaps the most powerful policy instrument to bring down drug prices for off-patent drugs" (quoted in Abbott 2005, 472). Above all, the access to medicines campaign endorses the right of developing countries to compulsory license drugs, to produce, export, and import generic drugs, and to take advantage of parallel importing to seek out the lowest cost patented medicines.

STRUCTURAL POWER: GLOBAL CORPORATIONS

At the most abstract level, one can argue that the structural power of global corporations in an era of capital mobility has increased the political power of such corporations. Many have argued that capital mobility has increased the power of private enterprise vis-à-vis the state (Strange 1996). Insofar as governments and societies depend upon business to generate economic growth they may defer to the interests of the most profitable of these corporations. Among the most profitable are global brand name pharmaceutical companies. Therefore, one should not be too surprised to find U.S. policymakers sympathetic to the concerns of these firms as they expand their activities abroad. This is especially true to the extent that the issues are framed in terms of U.S. economic competitiveness in global markets. Thinking of intellectual property, it is not surprising that the tropes of "piracy" and "theft" have particular resonance in the private property-revering consumer culture of American capitalism. Highlighting intellectual property as a particular form of private "real" property triggers an appeal to deeply held and unquestioned norms of private property rights in the American context. Furthermore, these global corporations are eager to point out shortcomings in foreigners' laws and regulatory environments that reduce their attractiveness as potential investment sites. "If you do not protect our property rights we will either pull investment out of your country or refuse to invest there in the first place." Therefore, at least three core forms of structural power are in evidence in this issue area: public policy supportive of business success; resonance with business-friendly cultural and institutional tendencies; and business opportunities to withhold or withdraw investment conditional on policy change (Porter and Ronit, this volume, 13).

Thus far, global corporations, conceived of at this level, have neither exerted substantial agency nor deployed significant resources in securing their desired outcomes. To do so business must mobilize and make policy preferences explicit. In the 1980s a handful of global business firms with substantial intellectual property holdings banded together to form the ad hoc Intellectual Property Committee (IPC). The IPC's purpose was to mobilize its European and Japanese counterparts to press for a high standard multilateral intellectual property agreement. The IPC included global corporations that represented pharmaceutical, agricultural chemical, software, and entertainment sectors. The different concerns of these varied sectors and regions meant that some compromises were inevitable in fashioning an acceptable agreement. The pharmaceutical companies, in particular, had to soften some of their demands in order to keep the copyright interests and the Europeans and Japanese on board. Nonetheless, in TRIPs the IPC achieved "95%" of what it wanted (Sell 2003, 115). Many analysts and activists have criticized the process as being insufficiently transparent and the outcome as being illegitimate (Drahos and Braithwaite 2002).

To understand the post-TRIPS process and the events discussed in this chapter, it is necessary to focus more sharply on the pharmaceutical sector. Since the late 1990s, some of the TRIPs advocates have found themselves to be in sharp disagreement about the extent of optimal patent protection; in particular software and consumer electronics corporations have stood opposed to biotechnology and pharmaceutical corporations (Thomas 2006). Insofar as the consumer electronics business model is to create multifunctional hand-held devices such as Blackberries and iPhones, without some relaxation of patent standards they are bound to infringe. On the other hand, the biotechnology industry is pushing for ever higher standards of patent protection at home and abroad.

The Brand Name Pharmaceutical Sector

Brand name pharmaceutical firms have become increasingly profitable and politically powerful, especially in the United States trade policy-making context. The pharmaceutical sector is characterized by marked economic concentration that has only increased over the past several decades. The combination of expanded intellectual property rights and relaxed antitrust enforcement has led to economic concentration in the life sciences industries. In pharmaceuticals just since 1999, Zeneca acquired Astra, Hoescht acquired Marion Merrel Dow, Sandoz and Ciba-Geigy merged, Glaxo Wellcome and SmithKline Beecham merged, Pharmacia and Upjohn merged with Monsanto, Sanofi-Syntelabo SA was the object of a hostile takeover by Aventis, and Pfizer's acquisitions made it the world's largest pharmaceutical company with revenues of $53 billion in 2004 (roughly 40 percent more than number two, Glaxo-SmithKline) (Rosenberg 2006, 65). The global market shares of the largest nongeneric pharmaceutical companies in 2003 were as follows: Pfizer, 11 percent; GlaxoSmithKline, 6.9 percent; Merck and Co., 5 percent; AstraZeneca, 4.8 percent, and Johnson and Johnson, 4.7 percent (Rosenberg 2006, 68). This situation has translated "economic power into greater influence over policymaking that has hitherto been seen as the realm of the public sphere" (Buse 2002, 261).

The increasing commercialization of medicine means that the diseases of the poor will be ignored by firms for sound economic reasons (Dutfield 2003, 495). As a number of commentators point out, across a broad range of products, the current system skews research toward rich and middle-income countries' markets and sectors (Barton 2003; Lettington 2003; Rai and Eisenberg 2003). In the public health sector this means the neglect of tropical diseases in favor of cancer and so-called lifestyle drugs (i.e., for obesity, balding, and erectile dysfunction). For example, only thirteen of 1,233 new drugs marketed between 1975 and 1997 were approved for tropical diseases. "As a result, the rhetoric of strong intellectual property rights leading to innovation that meets social needs rings particularly hollow in this setting" (Hammer 2002, 888).

According to Peter Drahos the United States and its IP activist industries have been engaged in a "one-way ratchet" for intellectual property, systematically obtaining higher levels of protection (2004, 55–61). Industry lobbyists are eager to point out that nothing in TRIPS prevents states from adopting *stronger* forms of protection, and the United States and its industries increasingly are coordinating enforcement through a number of venues. The structural power of global firms is reflected in the membership of key policymaking committees in U.S. trade institutions. These committees assist U.S. trade negotiators in designing policies for multilateral, regional, and bilateral trade. The USTR's Industry Functional Advisory Committee (IFAC) on Intellectual Property Rights includes representatives for Pfizer, Eli Lilly and Co., PhRMA, Merck and Co., Inc., Biotechnology Industry Organization, and Intellectual Property Owners Association. None of these firms or organizations is pressing for more balance between private rights and the public domain. The reach of these advisory committees can be quite broad and U.S.-based firms work with their subsidiaries abroad to develop support for their positions. Significantly, in the November 2002 U.S. congressional elections a group of global PhRMA firms, headed by then-Pfizer CEO Hank McKinnell, raised $30 million for Republican congressional campaigns (Ireland 2006). Not coincidentally, the Bush administration responded to and supported global pharma's objectives and strategies.

Industry representation in the USTR advisory committees, overlapping memberships in industry associations such as the PhRMA, Business Software Alliance (BSA), and the International Intellectual Property Alliance (IIPA) increase the information exchange among private actors and the USTR to monitor compliance, negotiate and enforce TRIPS-Plus[2] deals and lobby at national and multilateral levels. For example, Microsoft is a member of the IIPA, BSA, and IFAC-3 (Drahos 2004, 69). In addition to these more formal vehicles for representation and influence, firms also participate in ad hoc mobilization groups such as the American BioIndustry Alliance (ABIA).[3] Jacques Gorlin founded the ABIA in 2005. Gorlin was a key player in the original TRIPS negotiations as consultant to the Intellectual Property Committee (IPC). The IPC, made up of twelve CEOs of U.S.-based global firms with large intellectual property portfolios, mobilized transnational private sector and governmental support for TRIPS and drafted major portions of TRIPS (Sell 2003). Gorlin formed the ABIA to continue industry advocacy in multilateral, bilateral, and U.S. government forums. Member companies include: Bristol Myers-Squibb, Eli Lilly, Hana Biosciences, General Electric, Merck, Pfizer, Procter and Gamble, and Tethys Research (ABIA). At least half of these firms participated in the original IPC. Gorlin serves as president, and Susan Finston, formerly of PhRMA, serves as executive director. ABIA is leading the lobbying fight to preserve and promote patents on life forms and is targeting activities at WIPO, WTO, and Convention on Biological Diversity (CBD). The ABIA plans to lobby its allies, the United States, Australia, Canada, Korea, Japan, and New Zealand, as well as work with India's biotechnology industry to try to soften India's negotiating stance (IP-Watch, Mar. 2, 2006). This thick and overlapping network has resulted in a centralized system of private governance that enlists the USTR for legitimation and enforcement and heightens opportunities for rent seeking (Drahos 2004, 77).

Patents: The Power to Withhold

Patents confer withholding power, the ability to restrict use, by *constructing* scarcity (May and Sell 2006, 36). Patent owners can refuse to license patented products or processes. Patent owners can refuse to make their products or processes available. The following pharmaceutical cases illustrate how this power to withhold can imperil public health.

Brand name pharmaceutical companies responded to developing country and NGO access campaigns by announcing generous price reductions and expanded availability of their products for HIV/AIDS patients in developing countries. However, having earned their public relations kudos and positive reactions from their shareholders, they have not always followed through on their pledges. For instance, in 2002 the sole producer of tenofovir disoproxil fumarate (Viread®), an important antiretroviral drug with fewer side effects for AIDS patients, Gilead announced that it would make Viread available at reduced prices to ninety-seven developing countries through its Viread Access Program (MSF 2006, Feb. 7). More than three years later, Viread was registered for use in only six countries.[4] Gilead had not even *requested* marketing clearance in most developing countries.

Abbott Laboratories received approval of Kaletra in the United States in October 2005. Kaletra is a second-line fixed dose combination of protease inhibitor lopinavir and booster ritonavir (LPV/r) that has particular advantages for developing countries' HIV/AIDS patients. Patients need only take four pills a day (versus six) and the pills require no dietary restrictions. Crucially, the formula is heat stable, requiring no refrigeration (Doctors without Borders 2006a, March 14). WHO has recognized LPV/r as an essential medicine as part of a second-line HIV/AIDS therapy once first-line failure has occurred. Since May 2002 Abbott has been selling an earlier, non–heat stable formulation in Africa and Least Developed countries for $500 per patient per year. MSF has asked Abbott to register the new drug in developing countries and to set an affordable differential price for it in developing countries. Abbott has claimed that it first needs to acquire a Certificate of Pharmaceutical Product (CPP) from Europe (the drug is manufactured in Germany) before it can register the new drug in developing countries. However, according to WHO guidelines and U.S. regulations CPP's may be issued by the *exporting* country (the U.S. FDA in this instance) (DWB 2006b, March 14). MSF placed a Kaletra order for four hundred MSF patients in nine countries in March 2006. While Abbott announced that it would make the new drug available for $500 per patient per year in African and least developed countries, the drug is unavailable for purchase because Abbott has not registered it anywhere but South Africa. As MSF states, "[I]f access to needed drugs depends on the marketing policies of pharmaceutical companies, then the lives of millions of people with HIV/AIDS remain at risk" (DWB 2006, April 27).

German Velasquez argues that in recent years developing countries have won an important victory in the WTO for access to medicines (2004, 63). The Doha Declaration of November 2001 affirmed WTO Member States' rights to implement TRIPS in such a way as to protect public health and to promote access to medicines for all (WTO 2001, November 14). After extensive and protracted negotiations, Member States also resolved the question of countries' ability to export generic drugs produced under compulsory license to countries lacking pharmaceutical manufacturing capacity (the so-called Paragraph 6 agreement). The deal authorized any member state lacking sufficient pharmaceutical manufacturing capacity to import necessary medicines from any other member state. This waiver of TRIPS Article 31(f) (restricting compulsory licensing only to supply one's domestic market) included procedural safeguards to prevent diversion of cheap medicines to rich countries' markets (WTO 2003; Matthews 2003, 73). Now, generic copies of drugs made under compulsory license can be exported to countries lacking production capacity (IP-Watch 2005, Dec 6a).

The decision also included a Chairman's Statement, emphasizing the "Members' 'shared understanding' that the Decision will be interpreted and implemented on a 'good faith' basis in order to deal with public health problems and not for industrial or commercial policy objectives" and their agreement to take steps to prevent drug diversion to third markets (Matthews 2004, 11). According to Love, the Chairman's Statement was approved by Pfizer CEO Hank McKinnell and the office of President Bush's Deputy Chief of Staff in charge of policy (who at that time was Karl Rove) (2005). This highlights the close relationship between this industry and the top levels of government. In December 2005, Member States adopted the waiver as an amendment to TRIPS that includes Article 31bis, the waiver, one annex on terms and conditions, and an appendix on the assessment of pharmaceutical manufacturing capabilities (IP-Watch 2005, Dec. 6a). A number of African delegations were pleased with the outcome and one delegate expressed relief that the uncertainty generated by the waiver was resolved as it is now a permanent part of TRIPS (IP-Watch 2005, Dec. 6b). Nonetheless, Velasquez warns that TRIPS-Plus provisions of FTAs may "dash the hopes raised by Doha" (2004, 65).

On one hand, individual firms have used the power to withhold their drugs in order to maximize revenue, despite public relations campaigns that suggest otherwise. On the other, developing countries and their NGO allies have succeeded in amending TRIPS to facilitate access. However since then, the action has moved to regional and bilateral arenas that tend to reduce developing countries' bargaining power.

FTA TRIPS-PLUS PROVISIONS: BARRIERS TO ACCESS

In recent years intellectual property protection has been dramatically expanded in bilateral and regional free trade agreements (FTAs). The baseline for property rights has moved quite far in the direction of private reward over public access. To insist that all countries adopt high protectionist standards of protection denies them the opportunity to pursue the public policy strategies that every "developed" country enjoyed. Lax intellectual property protection, compulsory licensing, working requirements, keeping certain sectors off-limits in terms of property rights, parallel importing, and discriminating against foreign rights holders were all key features of the developed countries' public policy strategies (May and Sell 2006, 107–131).

The United States and the EU have been able to exploit resource disparities and shift forums whenever it suits their interests. This holds true of the horizontal shift from WIPO to WTO and back again (Sell 1998; Drahos and Braithwaite 2000), as well as the vertical shifting between multilateral, bilateral and regional negotiations. Bilateral and regional agreements threaten to undermine any gains that developing countries may bargain for or achieve in multilateral settings. At the end of the Uruguay Round negotiators from the United States and the European Union saw TRIPS as a floor—a minimum baseline for intellectual property protection. By contrast, developing country negotiators saw it more as a ceiling—a maximum standard of protection beyond which they were unwilling and/or unable to go.

The United States and the EU aggressively have been pursuing efforts to ratchet up TRIPS standards, to eliminate TRIPS flexibilities and close TRIPS loopholes. Playing a multilevel, multiforum governance game, countries such as the United States have been able to extract a high price from economically more vulnerable parties eager to gain access to large, affluent markets (Abbott, 350–54; Correa 2004, 331; Vivas-Eugui 2003). Bilateral Investment Treaties, Bilateral Intellectual Property Agreements, and regional FTAs concluded between the United States and developing countries, and between the European Union and developing countries, invariably have been TRIPS-Plus (Drahos 2001, 6; Dutfield 2003). According to Dylan Williams, "[A] recent US Congressional Research Service report states that the United States' main purpose for pursuing bilateral FTAs is to advance US intellectual property protection rather than promoting more free trade" (2006).

The United States has offered countries WTO-Plus market access in exchange for TRIPs-Plus policies (Shadlen 2005, 11). Particular provisions in these bilateral and regional trade agreements include: (1) data exclusivity provisions; (2) prohibitions of parallel importation; (3) linkage between drug registration and patent protection; (4) highly restrictive conditions for issuing compulsory licenses; (5) expanded subject matter requirements; and (6) patent term extensions. All of these provisions have been crafted by the brand name pharmaceutical industry and serve to reduce the availability of affordable drugs. I will discuss each of these in turn.

Brand name pharmaceutical firms favor data exclusivity provisions because they offer new rights and opportunities to maximize returns on their products by delaying competition. Under Article 39.3 of TRIPs WTO members must protect undisclosed test data on pharmaceutical products against unfair competition. Brand name pharmaceutical companies are required to submit efficacy and safety test data as part of the drug approval process. However, the FTA provisions require signatories to grant at least five years of data exclusivity counted from the date on which the product was approved, (ten years for agrochemicals), whether or not it was patented and whether or not the data was disclosed. It also covers chemical entities that are not new (Correa 2006, 401). As Musungu and Oh point out, "[T]he first registrant of a new pharmaceutical product may obtain data protection even in the case of old and well known products" (2005, 59–60). These provisions are designed to require generic pharmaceutical producers to generate their own clinical trial test data, rather than rely on safety and efficacy findings of the brand name drugs in the generic drug approval process. This could lead to a five- to ten-year delay in a state's ability to authorize marketing approval of certain drugs (Reichman 2004, 1). Brand name pharmaceutical companies, in effect, have acquired a new form of intellectual property right in their test data and information generated by that data (Shadlen 2005, 19).

Parallel importation is the importation of patented goods from another country. Under TRIPs, countries are free to determine the type of exhaustion regime they want to have. The principle of patent exhaustion refers to the patentee's ability to control the first sale of a product where the product is patented. The United States has a *national exhaustion* regime, which has been incorporated into a number of FTAs. Under the United States' national exhaustion regime the patent holder is the *only* person who has the authority to make the first sale of the product in the United States. This prevents the importation of the patented product from another country without the permission of the U.S. patent holder, drastically curbing the opportunities for parallel importation. This policy drove many American senior citizens in the past several years to take buses to Canada to purchase cheaper versions of brand name drugs. By contrast, proponents of access to medicines recommend an *international exhaustion* regime. Under this TRIPS-compliant alternative regime, the first sale of a patented product *anywhere* exhausts the patent holder's right to block parallel importation. For example, using parallel importation, countries can take advantage of differential pharmaceutical pricing policies in order to obtain cheaper patented goods. If a brand name pharmaceutical company sells a patented product more cheaply in country x than in country y, country y could import the drug from country x. By mandating *national* exhaustion regimes, the FTAs are TRIPs-plus by eliminating a TRIPs-compliant opportunity to access more affordable patented drugs; this is especially crucial in the case of second-line HIV/AIDS drugs that are patented and for which no generics are available.

Patent protection and drug registration are linked in many TRIPs-Plus agreements. Under these provisions national health authorities are required to refuse to provide marketing approval to a generic drug if a patent on the drug is in force, unless the patent owner consents to such approval. Additionally, the health authorities must inform patent owners of any applications for generic product approval (Correa 2006, 401). This linkage and the data exclusivity provisions have a chilling effect on generic competition and compulsory licensing. Unless the patent holder acquiesces to marketing approval, which is highly unlikely, it will be nearly impossible to use compulsory licensing as permitted by TRIPS.

TRIPs permits compulsory licensing, albeit with some significant restrictions. While the December 2005 Paragraph 6 agreement incorporated some cumbersome procedural requirements, TRIPs retained far more flexibility to issue such licenses than have the bilateral and regional agreements. The FTAs restrict compulsory licensing to a very limited set of circumstances. For example, in both the US-FTAs with

Singapore and Jordan compulsory licenses may not be issued except in the event of "national emergency or other circumstances of extreme urgency" (US-Singapore FTA, Article 16.7[6][b]). Chapter 15 of the US-Morocco FTA limits use of TRIPs flexibilities to particular diseases (HIV/AIDS, malaria and tuberculosis, and other epidemics) and to circumstances of "extreme urgency" or "national emergency." The United States had pushed for these exact limits during the deliberations over Paragraph 6 of the Doha Declaration but was rebuffed. Now it seeks to incorporate its preferred language in the FTAs with the aim to sharply curtail the possibility of generic competition and compulsory licensing (Correa 2001, 10). Chapter 15.9(2) of the US-Morocco FTA also requires Morocco to give up its right under TRIPs 27.3(b) to exclude plants and animals from patentability, thereby effectively expanding the subject matter available for patent protection (Correa 2001, 10).

Finally, a number of the FTAs incorporate automatic patent term extensions beyond TRIPs' twenty-year term. Unlike U.S. law, which limits extensions to compensate for delays in marketing approval to five years; the FTA provisions are not limited in time. Therefore the bilateral and regional agreements are not only TRIPs-Plus but are in fact, *U.S.-Plus*. These agreements provide for automatic extensions for delays in patent examination and marketing approval. This is troubling in developing countries because their patent offices are understaffed and stretched to the limit. According to Correa:

> Nothing seems to prevent a patent from being extended for x years due to a delay in its granting process, and for y more years due to a delay in the marketing approval process. . . . These mechanisms will . . . generate increased flow of payments to pharmaceutical companies that can hardly be justified by any additional benefits to patients in developing countries. (2006, 401)

Significantly, these provisions inject considerable uncertainty into the calculations of would-be generic competitors and could delay the introduction of competing and affordable products (Correa 2006, 401).

Former USTR-turned-PhRMA lobbyist Mickey Kantor offered a vigorous defense of TRIPs-Plus provisions in the bilateral and regional trade agreements reflecting the brand name pharmaceutical industry position. He takes issue with critics who "allege" that TRIPS-plus provisions "extend beyond those expressly set forth in the TRIPS Agreement and thus violate TRIPS" (Kantor 2005, 3). He argues that the provisions are TRIPS-compliant. His rhetoric misses the point. Provisions that "expressly extend beyond those set forth in TRIPS" are *by definition*

TRIPS-Plus. He himself states that the "provisions often are more specific and provide greater intellectual property protection (Kantor 2005, 3)." No one has ever charged that TRIPS-Plus provisions were *illegal* or *violated* TRIPS. Indeed, TRIPS explicitly provides that states may adopt provisions that exceed requirements of TRIPS. Critics of TRIPS-Plus provisions question their merits on public health, moral, human rights, and economic development grounds.

These TRIPS-Plus agreements reflect business power, backed by the USTR. In them we see business gaining advantages that were rejected in the more democratic, multilateral process. Business has deftly exploited power asymmetries to maximize its advantages.

RESISTANCE TO TRIPS-PLUS TRENDS

In recent years developing countries have begun to challenge the discrepancy between the multilateral rules and the TRIPS-Plus standards proposed in regional and bilateral agreements (Chon 2006, 2821).[5] In late 2005, Ecuador and Colombia broke off talks with the United States over TRIPS-Plus provisions and had refused to agree to TRIPS-Plus standards. However, in late February 2006 the United States and Colombia concluded an agreement that includes TRIPS-Plus standards despite the best efforts of some Colombian negotiators to counteract them (IP-Watch 2006, March 3).

In May 2006 South American Ministers of Health from Argentina, Bolivia, Brazil, Chile, Colombia, Ecuador, Paraguay, Peru, Uruguay, and Venezuela issued an important declaration on intellectual property, access to medicines and public health.[6] Noting the link between patents and the high cost of medicines, the ministers endorsed their commitment to the Doha Declaration and expressed their intent to maintain TRIPS flexibilities such as compulsory licensing, parallel importing, and Bolar exceptions (which speed the registration of generic drugs). Furthermore, they explicitly rejected all TRIPS-plus provisions.

Resistance also has been emerging from WHO activities, and protests over the US-Thai FTA negotiations have become particularly sharp. This section first discusses activities at WHO, then the US-Thai FTA protests. It ends with a discussion of how these two threads intersected with U.S. industry lobbyists' efforts to interfere with the WHO and the Thai resistance in early 2006. The intersection between the US-Thai FTA and WHO processes provide a particularly vivid illustration of Drahos's discussion of the murky, deliberately opaque thicket that is industry-driven "nodal governance" (2004).

WORLD HEALTH ORGANIZATION

The WHO is a specialized agency of the UN system. Its mandate is to direct and coordinate authority for health work (Stein 2001, 497). Since TRIPS, the WHO increasingly has been drawn into trade issues, and NGOs have had considerable access to the institution (Stein 2001, 498). Even though global pharma has an important voice in the WHO through its powerful OECD member states, which contribute significant funding, at times the WHO has been criticized for its "failure to cooperate with the private sector" (Stein 2001, 498).

WHO has adopted access to essential medicines as an element in compliance with the human right to health (Seuba 2006, 405). Under a human rights rubric, intellectual property is recast as "a social product with a social function and not primarily as an economic relationship" (Chapman 2002, 867). According to critics of the access campaigns:

> By advocating these human rights of access, IP skeptics seek to create a conflict with intellectual property rights, which give their owners the right to control and exclude others. . . . Since advocates view "human rights obligations" as having "primacy" over economic policies and agreements, then it follows that intellectual property rights are secondary, to be treated as limited exceptions. (Schultz and Walker 2005, 84)

The human rights rubric seeks to elevate the rights of *patients* over patents, and to provide avenues for reporting violations of international human rights agreements.

The May 2003 World Health Assembly (WHA) meeting on improving access to essential medicines resulted in a resolution calling for the establishment of a time-limited independent commission, the Commission on Intellectual Property Rights, Innovation and Public Health (CIPIH). The resolution prominently featured the Doha Declaration and endorsed the NGO/developing country approaches to the medicines issue by emphasizing the Doha Declaration's recognition that pharmaceutical products require special treatment, and that patent protection has negative effects on drug pricing (WHO 2003, May 28) and by underscoring the importance of making full use of TRIPS flexibilities.

In April 2006 the CIPIH issued its report making numerous recommendations for improving health in developing countries (WHO 2006).[7] The report's definition of "innovation" represented a major discursive breakthrough. For the first time, innovation was defined as including not only the standard "discovery" and "development" components, but also *"delivery."* As Ellen't Hoen of MSF points out, "The report stresses that innovation is only meaningful when people can have access to the results of the innovation" (2006, 421). This is the first time that access has been linked to innovation. It is significant insofar as it changes the debate. Just as today one cannot talk about intellectual property without talking about public health, perhaps several years from now people will begin to assume a necessary relationship between innovation and *access.* Furthermore, the report explicitly characterizes intellectual property protection as a means and not an end ('t Hoen 2006, 421). The report recommends that governments avoid provisions in bilateral trade agreements that could restrict access to medicines (WHO, CIPIH 2006, 351).[8] Overall, it highlights how the current patent-based system of drug development is inadequate to serve the needs of the poor.

A former Bush aide and USAID lawyer sharply criticized the CIPIH report for its bias in favor of generic drugs and its criticisms of U.S. FTAs, which he defends as "the best tool to raise economic growth, and therefore health, in the developing world" (Gardner 2006). This focus on macroeconomic growth typically obscures these policies' distributional effects. The CIPIH Report explicitly acknowledges the limitations of this prevailing instrumental perspective and calls for new approaches to medical R&D to better serve the poor. While it did not go as far as some health activists would have liked (Correa 2006b, 198–99), it is still a significant step forward for WHO in addressing health gaps.

Addressing intellectual property in a public health context shifts the metric of successful policy from strict economic gain to delivery of health care benefits. Broadening the discourse can provide openings for changes that could benefit a larger range of stakeholders beyond business.

THAILAND, FTA NEGOTIATIONS, THE UNITED STATES AND WHO

Thailand is another noteworthy site of resistance to the one-way TRIPS-Plus ratchet. Thailand was one of the first to suffer in the HIV/AIDS pandemic and the United States has targeted Thailand as a culprit in numerous trade disputes over intellectual property and pharmaceuticals. PhRMA consistently has complained about Thailand and the USTR placed Thailand on its Section 301 Watch List every year between 1996 and 2000 (Sell 2003, 128). In 2001 Thai activists challenged Bristol-Myers Squibb over its antiretroviral drug didanosine (DDI) because the public U.S. National Institutes of Health developed the drug. That same year the United States threatened to impose trade sanctions against

Thailand if it pursued compulsory licensing to produce DDI. "In 2002, a Thai court cited international statutes when it ruled that Thai HIV/AIDS patients could be injured by patents and had legal standing to sue if drug makers holding patents restricted the availability of drugs through their pricing policies. This verdict was upheld in January 2004" and Bristol Myer Squibb settled out of court, surrendering its version of the drug to the Thai Department of Intellectual Property (Williams 2006).

The United States has been trying to negotiate a US—Thai FTA, and these deliberations became embroiled in a national political crisis. In April 2006, "after one of the longest anti-government mobilizations in Thailand's history" (Williams 2006) caretaker prime minister Thaksin Shinawatra relinquished his post. While initially protesters focused on Thaksin, the People's Alliance for Democracy (PAD) expanded its attack to include the US-Thailand FTA negotiations. In a nontransparent process, acting prime minister Thaksin had been conducting these negotiations unilaterally without consulting Parliament (Williams 2006). Eager to develop and expand Asian markets for its firms' pharmaceutical products, the United States hoped that a US-Thai FTA would provide a template for similar deals with Malaysia and Indonesia (Williams 2006).

On January 9, 2006, the chief American WHO representative to Thailand, Dr. William Aldis, published an opinion piece in the *Bangkok Post* warning Thailand about the high stakes involved in the US-Thai FTA negotiations. His op-ed appeared in the midst of the sixth round of US-Thai FTA negotiations in Chiang Mai. He wrote:

> If the outcomes of other US bilateral trade negotiations are anything to go by, Thailand may well be in for a rough ride. . . . To the surprise of many observers, these countries[9] have bargained away reasonable flexibilities and safeguards in the implementation of intellectual property rights provided by the World Trade Organization. (Aldis 2006)

He went on to point out that of more than six hundred thousand Thais living with HIV/AIDS over eighty thousand have access to life-prolonging treatments "thanks to the supply of cheap locally produced generic drugs, and the target is 150,000 by 2008. As a result, Aids [sic] deaths in Thailand have fallen by an extraordinary 79%" (Aldis 2006). He concluded by stating that "giving up internationally agreed flexibilities in the implementation of intellectual property rights would put at risk the survival of hundreds of thousands of Thai citizens, and would likely bankrupt the 30 baht scheme in the process" (Aldis 2006).

In late March 2006, the late WHO director general Lee Jong-wook[10] transferred Dr. Aldis from Bangkok to a research position in New Delhi. An *Asia Times Online* investigative report into this transfer revealed U.S. industry lobbying behind what amounted to a demotion. At the time of his death in May 2006, according to the report, "Lee had closely aligned himself with the US government and by association US corporate interests, often to the detriment of the WHO's most vital commitments and positions, including its current drive to promote the production and marketing of affordable generic antiretroviral drugs" (Williams 2006). Lee recalled Dr. Aldis after serving just over fifteen months in what is traditionally a four-year posting (Williams 2006). While a regional WHO official in New Delhi attributed Aldis's removal to his "inefficiency," "Thai officials who worked alongside him through the 2004 tsunami and on-going avian-influenza scare have privately contested this characterization" (Williams 2006).

In fact, it appears that Dr. Aldis was being punished for his January op-ed opposing the TRIPS-Plus provisions of the US-Thai FTA proposals. The British medical journal *The Lancet* implied as much in its June article in which it characterized Dr. Aldis's transfer as a direct result of the editorial and "was a clear signal of US influence on WHO" (Benkimoun 2006, 1806). Aldis was critical of the United States' mixing of commercial and public health agendas and "chafed at WHO regional headquarters' instructions to receive representatives from US corporations and introduce them to senior Thai government officials to whom the private company representatives hoped to sell big-ticket projects and products" (Williams 2006). During the spring of 2006, Pfizer and IBM requested WHO personnel in Thailand to facilitate access to senior Thai officials; "[S]ome senior WHO staff members have expressed their concerns about a possible conflict of interests, as the requested appointments were notably not related to any ongoing WHO technical-assistance program with the Thai government" (Williams 2006).

On March 23, 2006, a U.S. ambassador to the UN in Geneva met with Lee privately and expressed concerns about Aldis's editorial. "A follow-up letter from the US government addressed to Lee impressed Washington's view of the importance of the WHO to remain 'neutral and objective' and requested that Lee personally remind senior WHO officials of those commitments" (Williams 2006). The next day Lee contacted the regional WHO New Delhi office and told it of his decision to recall Aldis (Williams 2006). A Bangkok-based U.S. official leaked the news of Aldis's transfer. A senior WHO official believes that Lee's decision and the U.S. government's news leak were "specifically designed to engender more self-censorship among other WHO country representatives when they comment publicly on the intersection of US trade and WHO public-health policies" (Williams 2006). Williams concludes that the Bush administration's tactics of trying to bring UN agencies into line with U.S. commercial and political interests come at the expense of the WHO's "stated mission, commitments and global credibility as an impartial and apolitical actor" (2006). In the meantime, Suwit Wibulpolprasert, senior adviser to the Thai Public Health Ministry, has requested that WHO provide an explanation for Dr. Aldis's abrupt removal (*Bangkok Post* 2006, June 20). This issue has sparked considerable consternation about lack of transparency and suppression of freedom of speech for WHO employees, but remains unresolved.

This case demonstrates the power of citizen activism in protesting TRIPS-Plus provisions. Yet it also reveals a disturbing antidemocratic pattern of business interests using nontransparent back channels to subvert more democratic processes and to impede openness and public debate.

FIRMS CHALLENGING DIVERSE ACTORS AT THE SUBSTATE LEVEL

Thus far, this chapter has examined structural power, agency to mobilize and achieve a global agreement, some foot dragging in making particular drugs available as promised, and pressure from firms on particular foreign governments and international organizations. This section explores firm behavior at a more micro level as the firm interacts with patients as a group, AIDS NGOs, and targets particular individuals as strategies to achieve its goals.

Several brand name pharmaceutical firms have shocked some observers by bullying patients, AIDS NGOs, and particular individuals. This section looks at three cases: Novartis's targeting of leukemia patients in South Korea, Abbott Laboratories' threatening legal action against ACT-UP Paris, and Pfizer's aggressive lawsuits against two individuals in the Philippines.

Gleevec[11] is a leukemia drug that was developed with assistance from the U.S. Orphan Drug Act, under which the U.S. government paid for 50 percent of the private sector costs of clinical trials (Ip-Health 2001). Swiss drug maker Novartis owns the patent. The drug costs roughly $27,000 per year per patient in the United States, keeping it out of reach of most. In late 2001 Novartis suspended supply of Gleevec to South Korea because Novartis failed to get the price it sought from the South Korean government. The United States, Switzerland, and Japan had accepted the price of US$19.50 per pill[12] during the Novartis–South Korean negotiations. Novartis directly approached Korean leukemia patients offering them a co-payment exemption if they would convince the South Korean government to accept that price. The patients refused. Rather than negotiating a lower price, the South Korean government sought to contain costs by excluding chronic phase chronic myelogenic leukemia (CML) patients from insurance coverage. Hae-joo Chung, Director of Equipharm project, issued a plea on behalf of the People's Health Coalition for Equitable Society for global consumer and health groups to endorse its quest to get the South Korean government to restart negotiations with Novartis and resume supply—even if it meant resorting to compulsory licensing in line with the Doha Declaration on TRIPS and Public Health (IP-Health 2001). These health groups appealed to the Korean Intellectual Property Office and requested adjudication for the grant of a nonexclusive license to import generic Gleevec from India for the public interest, because Korean CML patients were imperiled by unstable supplies and high prices (IP-Health 2003).

While Novartis is a Swiss company, the USTR supported Novartis in this case. Facing declining profitability in the European market, makers of potentially high profit drugs such as Gleevec are turning to emerging middle-income markets in Asia and Latin America to make up the difference (Benvenisti and Downs 2004, 21–52). In order to ensure the success of this strategy they must fend off generic challengers in these markets. As Benevisti and Downs suggest, the USTR intervened on behalf of Novartis in order to "prevent a precedent that might eventually damage the profitability of products manufactured by its own firms" (2004). Indeed, the Korean decision to reject the generic importation option under compulsory license incorporated the very language that USTR Robert Zoellick had been promoting in his efforts to limit the scope of the Doha Declaration on TRIPS and Public Health. The Korean government denied the petition on the grounds that CML was neither "infectious" nor likely to cause "an extremely dangerous situation in our nation" (IP-Health 2003; Abbott 2005, 328–36). This example highlights the intrusive reach of what Drahos calls the "nodal enforcement pyramid" that global IP-based firms and their governments deploy (2004). Given the expansion of intellectual property rights and unequal distribution of economic and political power across the globe, developing countries face substantial challenges in navigating the system to their benefit.

In early 2007, Abbott Laboratories threatened to withdraw all of its pending drug applications in Thailand after Thailand announced plans to issue compulsory licenses for several drugs, including the heat stable

HIV/AIDS drug Kaletra. Thai AIDS patient groups appealed to ACT-UP Paris to protest Abbott's actions by attacking Abbott's Web site. ACT-UP Paris posted a link on its Web site that protestors could click on to overwhelm Abbott's server on the eve of its annual shareholder meeting (*WSJ* 2007). On May 23, 2007, Abbott filed suit in France, charging ACT-UP Paris with launching a cyber attack on Abbott's Web site. This abruptly broke a long-standing taboo against harassing AIDS patient groups. As Justine Frain, of GlaxoSmithKline PLC pointed out, "Early on we realized it was important to work with the activist groups" (*WSJ* 2007). Other pharmaceutical executives indicated that Abbott's actions regarding Thailand were a public relations disaster for the industry as a whole. ACT-UP Paris defended its actions as the lawful exercise of free speech. While Abbott eventually withdrew the lawsuit, its public reputation was in tatters. Furthermore, Abbott refused to reverse its "deadly blockade of its lifesaving HIV medication Aluvia" (ACT UP Paris 2007), underscoring the withholding power of patent owners. And in April 2007, the USTR named Thailand to its Section 301 Watchlist on the basis of its compulsory licensing activity.

While the 1998 South African case in which brand name pharmaceutical firms sued Nelson Mandela is well known (Bond 1999, 765), an ongoing case in the Philippines demonstrates that these bullying tactics persist. Pfizer is suing the Philippine government for parallel importing the Pfizer drug Norvasc for high blood pressure. In the Philippines, this product is only available from Pfizer. There, Norvasc costs twice as much as it does in Indonesia and Thailand. India sells the drug for 650 percent less than the Philippine price. The Philippines imported and registered, but did not market, two hundred tablets of the patented drug from India (IP-Watch 2006, April 30). The Bureau of Food and Drug (BFAD) provided Pfizer with written assurances that it would not market the drug until Pfizer's patent expired. Pfizer charged the government with infringement, and is not only suing the BFAD and Philippine International Trading Corporation (PITC) but is also suing BFAD director Leticia Barbara Gutierrez and Emilio Polig (a BFAD officer) *in their personal capacity* for damages. Pfizer claims that it is acting to protect its patent and denies that it is a parallel importation case because Pfizer does not believe that the Indian supplier was a Pfizer-authorized source. PITC has filed a countersuit against Pfizer. Stanford alumni and graduate students launched a signatory campaign to oust Pfizer CEO Henry McKinnell from the Stanford Advisory Board over Pfizer's "bullying" of Philippine government drug regulators (IP-Watch 2006, April 30; WHO 2006).

In attacking portions of the 2006 WHO CIPIH report (IP-Watch 2006, April 30), Eric Noehrenberg of IFPMA argued that the report repeated the "myth that patents give the power to set prices" (2006, 419). He goes on to state that "such a misrepresentation ignores the effect of competition between drugs." (Noehrenberg 2006, 419). However, in the Philippines case it is precisely the *lack* of competition that has caused the problem, and Pfizer actively is seeking to prevent or at least delay competition.

This behavior clearly poses dangers to public health. Expanded intellectual property rights, economic concentration, and strong-arm tactics against vulnerable populations highlight the vulnerabilities associated with relying only on the decisions of private companies. It also demonstrates the surprising reach of these firms into domestic affairs abroad—bypassing governments to reach patients directly, suing specific individuals because of their regulatory roles, and filing lawsuits against NGOs.

PUSHING BACK: CHALLENGING FIRMS

This section reviews recent successful challenges to some of the brand name firms' tactics. The cases are: Novartis's challenge to Section 3(d) of Indian patent law; and setbacks for PhRMA in the United States.

When India drafted its Patents Act in January 2005, it incorporated Section 3(d) to try to ensure that only truly innovative products would receive patent protection. Section 3(d) is designed to prevent the widespread practice of "evergreening" in which a firm gets a patent on minor improvements to old drugs. Evergreening lengthens the time in which the owner can reap monopoly rents. Each WTO member is free to devise its own patent regimes within the broad guidelines of TRIPS, and India has forbidden "the patenting of derivative forms of known substances (e.g., salts, polymorphs, metabolites, and isomers) unless they are substantially more effective than the known substance" (Mueller 2007, 542). On the basis of 3(d) the Indian Patent Office denied Novartis a patent on Gleevec. In response, Novartis filed suit in the Chennai High Court claiming that Section 3(d) violated TRIPS, which requires that patentable inventions be new and involve an "inventive step" (Mueller 2007, 542).

Supporters of the decision to deny Novartis a patent on Gleevec point out that TRIPS does not define "inventive step" and gives states some freedom to craft their own criteria for this, along the lines of the concept of "non-obviousness" in U.S. law. While some protestors insisted that India reject Novartis's case outright, Mueller points out that since "India has an independent judiciary and an established rule-of-law tradition" it is important to let the Novartis litigation go forward to subject India's new law to judicial analysis and set an important precedent in sharpening and clarifying the law (2007, 543). In August 2007, the Madras High Court rejected Novartis's challenge, finding that the new drug was insufficiently different from the previous version. This means that Indian generics producers will be free to continue making versions of the drug. Subsequently Novartis asked the Swiss government to support a challenge to Section 3(d) in the WTO, and the Swiss government declined. This represents a big change from when even the USTR was willing to support the Swiss company Novartis in its campaign against developing countries.

In the spring of 2007, the U.S. Supreme Court unanimously decided a major case that underscored the importance of obviousness as a criterion for denying a patent. In *KSR International v. Teleflex*, Justice Kennedy wrote: "Granting patent protection to advances that would occur in the ordinary course without real innovation retards progress" (*Washington Post*, May 1, 2007, D1). This landmark case opens the way for generic drug companies to sue the brand name firms. As John Thomas, an intellectual property professor at Georgetown University, noted, "The bottom line is that interested parties have a greater ability to challenge patents and a greater possibility of prevailing" (*Washington Post*, May 1, 2007, D3). The parallel logic between this outcome and the Indian 3(d) case is noteworthy. In another interesting twist, Pfizer's patent on Novarsc (the drug at issue in the Philippines case) was rejected in U.S. courts for obviousness (Zuhn 2007)!

Tensions between the interests of pharmaceutical and biotechnology companies on the one hand, and high-technology electronics and computing firms on the other have boiled over in heated debates over patent reform in the United States. This is significant insofar as the conflict could be a harbinger of fundamental change. These two sectors were in lockstep promoting stronger intellectual property protection worldwide at the time of TRIPS negotiations. Now, Emory Simon, of the Business Software Alliance and former supporter of TRIPS, is arguing that patent law discourages innovators and should be relaxed. By contrast Billy Tauzin, president of PhRMA is ardently defending the current system. The House of Representatives voted in favor of patent reform and it also is on the Senate's agenda. On September 7 the House passed a comprehensive patent reform bill that endorses the technology and financial services sectors at the expense of PhRMA's preferred position (*Washington Post*, September 8, 2007, D1). This split between two important sectors over intellectual property offers an opportunity for fundamental change that could have important effects on the way the United States and its firms conduct themselves abroad. If U.S. law were to weaken, it would be hard to maintain aggressive tactics vis-à-vis smaller and weaker trading partners without inviting widespread condemnation.

CONCLUSION: RENEWAL, STALEMATE, OR DECAY?

Contemporary trends are both disturbing and hopeful. The disturbing side of the ledger points to decay. For example, the close ties between PhRMA, USTR, and campaign contributions mean that U.S. policy will likely remain aggressive in the immediate future. This raises questions of accountability when current and former public servants may be more accountable to donors and potential future employers than they are to a broad range of citizens. Furthermore, the revolving door that allows former high-level policymakers such as Mickey Kantor to turn around and profit as lobbyists also erodes any image of policymakers as disinterested stewards of the "public interest." Further, there has been very little accountability for strong-arm tactics against vulnerable populations, as in the Korean Gleevec case.

The lack of transparency characterizing many of the episodes recounted here also points to decay. Inappropriate interference with organizations, such as WHO, in pursuit of corporate agendas compromises the very integrity of the organizations. These murky and opaque ways of conducting business provide ample opportunity for policies that put profits ahead of people. The recall of Dr. Aldis was a particularly ham-fisted example of U.S. interference behind the scenes. In terms of democracy it also had a chilling effect on freedom of speech for WHO employees who came to fear that free speech would be punished.

In terms of participation, excluding the Thai Parliament from the US-Thai FTA negotiations is antidemocratic. However, Thai leaders were made to pay for that breach of democratic process, as protestors called for the prime minister's ouster. Patients and consumer groups have certainly not had the kind of access to policymakers that industry has had. Clearly these are all instances of what the editors call "decay."

On the other hand, there are hopeful glimmers of renewal as well. For instance, one may hope that revelations of inappropriate interference will provoke enough outrage to lead to new measures to ensure transparency and wider participation in policymaking. The South American health ministers' unity behind TRIPS flexibilities and against TRIPS-Plus provisions is another hopeful development. They have pledged to be involved in trade policymaking; to the extent that they are able to do so they can work to keep access to medicines a priority in trade negotiations. They seek to participate in order to hold negotiators accountable to a public health metric. In any event, it seems clear that they will not stand on the sidelines and let their governments bargain away TRIPS flexibilities without a fight. India's efforts to use its political and judicial processes to ensure that only truly innovative products receive patent protection are another example of renewal. Asserting its right to determine its own standards may give other countries the confidence to do so in ways that reflect their levels of economic and technological development. Finally, recent changes in OECD countries hold some promise. The Swiss government ultimately declined to support Novartis in challenging India's law at the WTO. Recent decisions of the U.S. Supreme Court and legislative activity promoting fundamental patent reform provide some evidence of renewal and suggest that democratic processes may, in the end, serve to constrain the less admirable behavior of brand name pharmaceutical firms.

The case of pharmaceuticals illustrates the remarkable complexity of conflicts between business and democracy. Democracy in this issue area has a protean quality, appearing in multiple forms in a great variety of settings. The structural power of business, reframing of issues by those who wish to challenge this structural power, lobbying, legislation, the use of state power in court cases, conflicts between industries and firms—all play their part in this story. At the same time, the role of the state, and the U.S. state in particular, continues to be crucial. The stakes are high, and the outcomes are not predetermined. Identifying and analyzing the conflicts that this chapter addresses are necessary if global business is to be reconciled and aligned with democracy rather than subvert it. This chapter suggests that while not impossible, that is likely to be a tall order.

NOTES

1. But see MSF on the continued high costs of second-line therapies, www.msf.org.
2. TRIPs-Plus refers to provisions that either exceed the requirements of TRIPS or eliminate TRIPS flexibilities.

3. At http://www.abialliance.com.
4. Ibid. The six countries are: the Bahamas, Gambia, Kenya, Rwanda, Uganda, and Zambia.
5. This resistance is neither limited to medicines nor to the trade arena. See Chon (2006, 2821, 1).
6. *Declaratoria de Ministras y Ministros de America del sur Sobre Propiedad Intelectual, Acceso a los Medicamentos y Salud Publica* Geneva, 23 May 2006. I thank Maria Auxiliadora Oliveira for alerting me to the significance of this declaration, and to Nicoletta Dentico for sending me both the full text and an unofficial English translation (on file with author).
7. CIPIH Report, *at* http://www.who.int/intellectualproperty (2006).
8. World Health Organization, *CIPIH Report: Main Recommendations*, 84 BULLETIN OF THE WORLD HEALTH ORGANIZATION 351 (2006). (emphasis is mine).
9. Australia, Chile, Morocco, Singapore, Bahrain, and Central American countries.
10. He died of a sudden brain hemorrhage on the eve of the WHA meeting in late May 2006.
11. Known as Glivec outside of the United States.
12. Daily dosages range from four to eight pills a day.

REFERENCES

Abbott, F. 2004. The Doha Declaration on the TRIPS agreement and public health and the contradictory trend in bilateral and regional free trade agreements. Quaker United Nations Office, Occasional Paper, April 14. At: http://www.quno.org.

——. 2005. The WTO medicines decision: World pharmaceutical trade and the protection of public health. *American Journal of International Law* 99, no. 2 (April): 317–58.

ACT-UP Paris. 2007. Abbott drops lawsuit, maintains deadly blockade. July 22. At: http://www.actupparis.org/article3111.html.

Aldis, W. 2006. It could be a matter of life and death: Thailand should think carefully about surrendering its sovereign right under WTO and access to cheap medicine in exchange for an FTA with the United States. *Bangkok Post,* January 9. At: http://www.bangkok-post.com/News/09Jan_new19.php.

Bangkok Post. 2006. String pulling: Aldis warned against Thai-US free trade pact. June 20. At: http://www.bangkokpost.com/News/20Jun2006_news03.php.

Barnes, R., and A. Sipress. 2007. Rulings weaken patents' power. The *Washington Post*, May 1: D1.

Barton, J. 2003. *Nutrition and technology transfer policies* at: http://www.iprsonline.

Benvenisti, E., and G. Downs. 2004. Distributive politics and international institutions: The case of drugs. *Case Western Reserve Journal of International Law* 36, no. 1 (Winter): 21–51.

Benkimoun, P. 2006. How Lee Jong-wook changed WHO. *The Lancet* 367(9525) (June 3): 1806–08.

Bermudez, J., and M. A. Oliveira, eds. 2004. *Intellectual property in the context of the WTO TRIPS agreement: Challenges for public health*. Rio de Janeiro: WHO/PAHO Collaborating Center for Pharmaceutical Policies, National School of Public Health. Sergio Arouca, Oswaldo Cruz Foundation.

Bond, P. 1999. Globalization, pharmaceutical pricing, and South African health policy: Managing confrontation with U.S. firms and politicians. *International Journal of Health Services* 29, no. 4: 765–92.

Braithwaite, J., and P. Drahos. 2000. *Global business regulation*. Cambridge: Cambridge University Press.

Buse, K., N. Drager, S. Fustukian, and K. Lee, 2002. Globalisation and health policy: Trends and opportunities. In *Health Policy in a Globalising World,* ed. Kelley Lee, Kent Buse, and Suzanne Fustukian, 251–80. Cambridge: Cambridge University Press.

Carreyrou, J. and A. Johnson. 2007. Abbott breaks with industry, sues AIDS group. *Wall Street Journal* (Eastern edition), June 18: B1.

Chapman, A. R. 2002. The human rights implications of intellectual property protection. *Journal of International Economic Law* 5 (December): 861–82.

Chon, M. 2006. Intellectual property and the development divide. *Cardozo Law Review* 27, no. 6 (April): 2821–914.

Chomthongdi, J. 2006. Thaksin's retreat: Chance for a change or consolidation of power? April 5. At: http://www.ftawatch.org.

Consumer Project on Technology. 2000. Background information on fourteen FDA approved HIV/AIDS drugs. Jun. 8. At: http://www.cptech.org/ip/health/aids/druginfo.html.

Correa, C. 2004. Investment protection in bilateral and free trade agreements: Implications for the granting of compulsory licenses. *Michigan Journal of International Law* 26, no. 1: Article 11.

———. 2006. Implications of bilateral free trade agreements on access to medicines. *Bulletin of the World Health Organization* 84, no. 5 (May): 337–424.

————. 2006. The Commission on IPRs, Innovation, and Public Health –A critique. *South Bulletin* 122. April 15. At: http://www.south-centre.org.

Doctors without Borders. 2006. Abbott's new and improved Kaletra: Only in the U.S.—But what about the rest of the world? March 14. At: http://www.doctorswithoutborders.org/news/hiv-aids/kaletra_briefingdoc.cfm.

————. 2006. Unnecessary delays by Abbott: the "CPP" myth debunked. March 14. At: http://www.doctorswithoutborders.org/news/hiv-aids/kaletra_cppdoc.htm.

————. 2006. More empty promises: Abbott fails to supply critical new AIDS drug formulation to developing countries. April 27. At: http://www.doctorswithoutborders.org/pr/2006/04-27-2006_1.cfm.

Drahos, P. 2004. Securing the future of intellectual property: Intellectual property owners and their nodally coordinated enforcement pyramid. *Case Western Reserve Journal of International Law* 36, no 1 (Winter): 53–77.

————. 2001. BITS and BIPS: Bilateralism in intellectual property. *Journal of World Intellectual Property* 4, no. 6: 791–808.

————, and J. Braithwaite. 2002. *Information feudalism.* London: Zed Books.

Dutfield, G. 2003. Should we terminate terminator technology? *European Intellectual Property Review* 25, no. 11: 491–95.

————. 2003. Sharing the benefits of biodiversity: Is there a role for the patent system? *Journal of World Intellectual Property* 5, no. 6: 899–931.

Gardner, J. 2006. Healthcare in the developing world: Obstacles and opportunities. *Tech Central Station.* May 9. At: http://www.tcsdaily.com/article.aspx?id=051906B.

Grabowski, H. 2002. Patents, innovation, and access to new pharmaceuticals. *Journal of International Economic Law* 5 (December): 849–60.

Hammer, P. 2002. Differential pricing of essential AIDS drugs: Markets, politics, and public health. *Journal of International Economic Law* 5 (December): 883–912.

Ignjatovic, T. 2007. Abbott: AIDS group lawsuit attracts negative publicity. June 20. At: http://www.pharmaceutical-business-review.com/article_feature_print.asp?guid=E468F441-.

International Federation of Pharmaceutical Manufacturers. 2006. WHO commission report on biomedical innovation, patents, and public health contains many sound proposals but underestimates the vital role of patents. April 3. At: http://www.ifpma.org/News/ NewsReleaseDetail.aspx?nID=3D4628.

IP-health. 2003. Text of Korean decision in Glivec case. March 10. At: http://lists.essential.org/pipermail/ip-health/2003/March.

———. 2001. Re: Call for endorsements on Glivec (sic) from South Korea. November 30. At: http://listsessential.org/pipermail/ip-health/2001.

IP-Watch. 2006. Biotech industry fights disclosure in patents on three IP policy fronts. March 2. At: http://www.ip-watch.org.

———. 2006. Groups decry impact of IP and health terms in US trade agreements. March 3. At: http://www.ip-watch.org.

———. 2006. Pfizer fights IP flexibilities in the Philippines. April 30. At: http://www.ip-watch.org.

———. 2005. African countries ready to accept TRIPS and public health deal. December 6. At: http://www.ip-watch.org.

Ireland, D. 2006. Under the counter. *POZ Magazine.* At: http://www.poz.com/articles/1056_7008.shtml.

Kantor, M. 2005. U.S. free trade agreements and the public health. Submission to WHO CIPIH, at: http://www.who.int.

Lettington, R. 2003. Small-scale agriculture and the nutritional safeguard under Article 8(1) of the Uruguay Round agreement on trade-related aspects of intellectual property rights: Case studies from Kenya and Peru. At: http://www.iprs.online.

Love, J. 2005. No gift to the poor: Strategies used by the US and EC to protect big pharma in WTO TRIPS negotiations. *Working Agenda* at: http://workingagenda.blogspot.com/2005/12/no-gift-to-poor-strategies-used-by-us.html.

Matthews, D. 2004. WTO decision on implementation of paragraph 6 of the Doha Declaration on the TRIPS agreement and public health: A solution to the access to medicines problem? *Journal of International Economic Law* 7 (March): 73–107.

———. 2004. Is history repeating itself? Outcome of the negotiations on access to medicines. *Electronic Law Journal LGD* at: http://www2.warwick.ac.uk/fac/soc/law/elj/lgd/2004_1/matthews2004.

May, C. and S. K. Sell. 2006. *Intellectual property: A critical history.* Boulder: Lynne Rienner.

Medecins sans Frontieres. 2006.Gilead's Tenofovir "access program" for developing countries: A case of false promises? February 7. At: http://www.doctorswithoutborders.org/pr/2006/02-07-2006.htm.

Mueller, J. 2007. Taking TRIPS to India—Novartis, patent law, and access to medicines. *The New England Journal of Medicine* 356, no. 6: 541–43.

Musungu, S., and C. Oh. 2005. The use of flexibilities in TRIPS by developing countries: Can they promote access to medicines? CIPIH Study 4C, August. At: http://who.int.org.

Noehrenberg, E. 2006. Report of the commission on intellectual property rights, innovation, and public health: An industry perspective. *Bulletin of the World Health Organization* 84, no. 5: 419–20.

Rai, A. and R. Eisenberg. 2003. The public domain: Bayh-Dole reform and the progress of biomedicine. *Law and Contemporary Problems* 66 (Winter/Spring): 289–314.

Rampell, C. 2007. House approves comprehensive patent overhaul. *Washington Post,* September 8, D1.

Reichman, J. 2004. Undisclosed clinical trial data under the TRIPS agreements and its progeny: A broader perspective. At: http://www.iprsonline.

Rosenberg, B. 2006. Market concentration of the transnational pharmaceutical industry and generic industries: Trends in mergers, acquisitions, and other transactions. In *Negotiating health: Intellectual property and access to medicines,* ed. Pedro Roffe, Geoff Tansey, and David Vivas-Eugui, 65–81. Geneva: International Centre for Trade and Sustainable Development.

Rosenberg, T. 2001. Look at Brazil. *The New York Times* January 28, Section 6 (magazine).

Schultz, M. and D. Walker. 2005. How intellectual property became controversial: NGOs and the new IP agenda. 6 *Engage* at: http://www.ngowatch.org.

Sell, S. K. 2003. *Private power, public law: The globalization of intellectual property rights.* Cambridge: Cambridge University Press.

———. 1998. *Power and ideas: The North-South politics of intellectual property and antitrust.* Albany: State University of New York Press.

Seuba, X. 2006. A human rights approach to the WHO model list of essential medicines. *Bulletin of the World Health Organization* 84, no. 5 (May): 405–407.

Shadlen, K. 2005. Policy space for development in the WTO and beyond: The case of intellectual property rights. Working Paper No. 05-06. At: http://ase.tufts.edu.gdae.

Shaffer, G. 2004. Recognizing public goods in WTO dispute settlement: Who participates? Who decides? *Journal of International Economic Law* 7 (June): 459–82.

Sipress, A. 2007. Patently at odds: Drug and tech sectors battle with reform high on agenda. *Washington Post,* April 18, D1.

Spicy IP. 2006. First mailbox opposition (Gleevec) decided in India. March 11. At: http://spicyipindia.blogspot.com/2006/03/first-mailbox-opposition-gleevec.html.

Stein, E. 2001. International integration and democracy: No love at first sight. *American Journal of International Law* 95, no. 3 (July): 489–534.

Strange, S. 1996. *The retreat of the state.* Cambridge: Cambridge University Press.

Symposium. 2002. Global intellectual property rights: Boundaries of access and enforcement. *Fordham Intellectual Property Media and Entertainment Journal* 12: 805–57.

't Hoen, E. 2002. TRIPS, pharmaceutical patents, and access to essential medicines: A long way from Seattle to Doha. *Chicago Journal of International Law,* 3, no. 1: 27–46.

———. 2006. Report of the commission on intellectual property rights, innovation, and public health: A call to governments. *Bulletin of the World Health Organization* 84, no. 5 (May): 421–23.

Thomas, R. 2006. Vanquishing copyright pirates and patent trolls: The divergent evolution of copyright and patent laws. *American Business Law Journal* 43, no. 4 (Winter): 689–739.

Velasquez, G. 2004. Bilateral trade agreements and access to essential drugs. In *Intellectual property in the context of the WTO TRIPS agreements: Challenges for public health,* ed. Jorge Bermudez and Maria Auxiliadora Oliveira, 63–70. Rio De Janeiro: WHO/PAHO Collaborating Center for Pharmaceutical Policies, National School of Public Health Sergio Arouca, Oswaldo Cruz Foundation.

Vivas-Eugui, D. 2003. *Regional and bilateral agreements and a TRIPS-Plus world: The free trade area of the Americas.* Quaker United Nations Office at: http://www.quno.org.

Williams, D. 2006. World health: A lethal dose of US politics. *Asia Times Online,* Jun. 16t. At: http://www.atimes.com.

World Health Assembly. 2003. Resolution of the World Health Assembly: Intellectual property rights, innovation, and public health. WHA56.27 at: http://www.who.int.

World Health Organization. 2003. Intellectual property rights, innovation, and public health. May 28. At: http://www.who.int.

———. 2006. CIPIH report: Main recommendations. 84 *Bulletin of the World Health Organization* at: http://www.who.int.

———. 2006. Commission on intellectual property rights, innovation, and public health: Report. At: http://www.who.intellectualproperty.

———. 2006. Public health, innovation, essential health research on intellectual property rights: Towards a global Strategy and plan

of action. A59/A/Conf.Paper No. 8. May 27. At: http://www.
who.int.

World Trade Organization. 2001. *Declaration on the TRIPS agreements
and public health.* Ministerial Conference, Fourth Session, Doha.
WT/MIN(01)DEC/W/2. Nov. 14.

World Trade Organization Council on TRIPS, WTO decision on implementation of paragraph 6 of the Doha declaration on the TRIPS
agreement and public health. IP/C/405 at: http://wto.org.

Zuhn, D. 2007. Pfizer, Inc. v. Apotex, Inc. (Fed. Cir. 2007). May 22. At:
http://patentdocs.typepad.com/patent_docs/2007/05/pfizer_inc_
v_ap.html.

7

THE CORRUPTION OF THE PUBLIC INTEREST

Intellectual Property and the Corporation as a Rights-Holding "Citizen"

CHRISTOPHER MAY

INTRODUCTION

The corporate legal form is a key consideration in analyzing the relationship of global business to democracy. Although corporations are organizations made up of groups of people, various social and internal institutions and capital (and other) assets mobilized toward a set of economic (and sometime extra-economic) ends, corporations also are usually treated as having a single personality for legal purposes. This pays clear organizational dividends, within contract law for instance: the corporation can be dealt with as a single signatory to agreements and undertakings. However, the legal personality of the corporation also has a distinct political role that must be considered in assessing the relationship of business to democracy. Moreover, this legal form, which arguably was subject to some democratic deliberation in the UK and the United States as it was developed during the nineteenth and twentieth centuries, has been adopted (to various degrees) across the global system, with little chance for local political groups to have any

significant impact on its articulation. The ability of other governments
and populations to develop methods for holding businesses to account
that reflect important local traditions and mores has consequently been
undermined. Therefore, focusing especially on the case of intellectual
property, and relating this to the history of the corporation in Britain
and latterly the United States, below I seek to explore the political role
of the corporate form.

Although there are other modes of corporate organization, the
Anglo-Saxon legal form is influential and widespread. For many corporations the need to compete to raise capital in London or New York,
and thus seek stock market listings in the UK or United States, has a
significant impact on the adoption of specific legal arrangements to
deliver specified accounting and financial reporting requirements
(Hansmann and Kraakman 2000). Thus, through compliance with such
regulations, the Anglo-Saxon legal form is exported to countries with
differing legal traditions and practices. The convergence of corporate
form, however has not been beneficial for the accountability of business; the increasing adoption of Anglo-Saxon modes of limited liability
within the governance of subsidiaries has shielded companies and their
shareholders from accountability across their international networks
(Sahni 2005). Likewise the globalization of the protection of intellectual
property is often a case of the adoption (albeit not always happily) of
Anglo-Saxon modes of regulation with little local accountability for the
formulation of policy. This suggests the discussion set out below will
have resonance far beyond the scope of the cases cited.[1]

The legal personality of the corporation is an aspect of the structural power of business that largely operates outside the types of political contestations associated with elections and other traditional
democratic practices. Nevertheless, it can excessively empower business
and constrain policy options in a way that is detrimental to democracy.
Most traditional democratic discussions take the corporate form as so
self-evidently a standard functional feature of society that it is not
worthy of comment—or even noticed. Legislative changes to the corporate form are often presented as relatively minor adjustments and
almost exclusively involve corporate lawyers, courts, and specialized
legislative committees, with no involvement of the general public, even
though, as this chapter will show, there are important public interest
issues at stake. The establishment of the common sense of corporate
personhood in effect limits participation, accountability, and transparency, the defining properties of democracy highlighted in the first
chapter of this book.

While the taken-for-granted status of the corporate form is an important aspect of structural power, this status is also based on two powerful myths that justify the power of business. These myths are especially important when that form is challenged. The first of these myths is that the corporation is like an individual person in a way that makes it deserving of rights, including the intellectual property rights that are examined below. The second myth is that the corporate form is economically efficient. This chapter challenges these myths to open up the issue of the corporation's legal personality to the participation, accountability, and transparency that it deserves.

In addition to offering a critique of corporate structural power, I also highlight an alternative way to think about the corporate form. To reconcile the corporate form with democracy, we need to return to the original logic of the corporate form; a grant of authority by the state to carry out certain public purposes. In the seventeenth century, when this first became widely used, these public purposes were defined by the state with relatively little public participation, but nevertheless were framed as public interests and opposed to rights to private enrichment. Since then democracy has grown in importance as a crucial element in legitimizing the authority of the state and in identifying and implementing the public interest.

As we enter a world in which the possibility of globalized democracy has become increasingly proclaimed, the (multinational) corporation stands before us, its supporters again arguing that its forms and practices are not political but merely technical. However, the public interest, the treatment of the corporation as legally constituted individual, and the assumption that it necessarily contributes to economic well-being all need to be subjected to scrutiny and democratic deliberation if business and democracy are to be truly reconciled within a nascent global (democratic) society.

THE CORPORATION FINDS ITS PERSONALITY

Most corporations do not have the institutional longevity of established states, nevertheless their enjoyment of legal personality (and the attendant rights of that personality) allow them to deploy greater social power than the natural persons on whose rights, corporate rights are often modeled. Three distinct legal personalities are generally recognized in law: naturally existing people (that is, individuals in a particular jurisdiction); the state (in its role as collective location of sovereign and legal authority); and the legally constituted corporation, a collective organization recognized for the purposes of regulation as having a single legal personality. This division is hardly natural, and while the division between (sovereign) political authority and individual subject (or later citizen) might be said to have emerged almost organically from the historical and legal requirements of nation-state politics, the assumption of legal personhood by the corporation was more of a politically engineered legal innovation.

As Steve Russell and Michael Gilbert have pointed out, "Corporations have many advantages over natural persons: effective immortality, superior resources, and with globalisation, mobility on a scale available to few human beings" (Russell and Gilbert 2002, 45). Indeed, the divergence between the legal protection available to all (legally constituted) people, and the effective position of the various types of individuals claiming the protection of the law have been central to much critical discussion of modern corporations. While certainly corporations remain outside the scope of international law, like other persons they are subjects only of national law, corporations' recourse to legalized personality is a relatively internationalized legal structure even if it remains a national jurisdictional matter. While corporations may be influenced by international "soft law," little regulation at the international level has been solidified into (hard) positive law (Muchlinkski 2007, 111). This has the advantage of offering opportunities for transnational organizational convergence with its associated efficiency benefits, but with few of the accountability costs of formal legislative development.

Although the origins of the corporate idea (that a group organized for a specific task or goal can be treated as a single person for legal purposes) are far from clear, and may stretch back more than two millennia (Moore and Lewis 1999), here I will limit my historical treatment to a shorter period.[2] The practice of incorporation was relatively normal (with various entities enjoying something analogous to personality) in the late sixteenth century when the common-law assumption of legal personality began to be extended to business enterprises that reached beyond the relatively local horizons of the guilds. The East India Company, the Royal African Company, and the Hudson's Bay Company were among the first to be incorporated by charter, and were the first corporate entities to reach out beyond the borders of their home country strategically rather than merely as opportunistic response to specific circumstances (Jones 2000). They were in many ways, previous commercial activities notwithstanding, the first international corporations.

Although the law of corporations was only finally codified by William Blackstone in his *Commentaries on the Law of England*, as John

P Davis pointed out, he "did little more than to bring together the principles scattered through [Sir Edward] Coke's Institutes and Reports, and to present them in a more compact and serviceable form" (Davis 1905, vol II, 210). Most importantly for the argument here, Coke finally established that the law differentiated between a corporation and its members (and hence the debts of the corporation were not the debts of its members). Thus, whatever the organizational history of corporations, the modern law on which their incorporation is based finds its beginnings in the common-law upheavals in the early seventeenth century (Coke's Institutes and Reports was published in 1628) and in a number of cases incorporation became caught up in the disputes between the Crown and Parliament regarding monopoly grants (Jones 1926, 930–33).[3] By the end of the century, however, the legal structures had become standardized and incorporation was being utilized much more widely than the previous guild arrangements.

In 1702, the increasingly important role that corporations were playing in the organization of the British economy prompted the anonymous publication of the first book devoted to the subject of "The Law of Corporations" (Williston 1909, 201). Both in this book and in the charters of the new corporations, one of the key corporate undertakings was the public goal of the better management and ordering of the trade in which it engaged, alongside any private goals of profit for its members. Hence, the legal personality of the early corporation was conditional on a clear public regarding role in promoting economic development. In return for providing such public benefits, investors were able to limit their liability, which further consolidated the idea of the corporation as a separate legally constituted individual. Thus, during the nineteenth century, it became established in law that a corporation was separate from its shareholders and other groups: the corporate person was finally made concrete; although for some time it had had a de facto existence in law, now it was firmly de jure.[4]

The ability to effectively shield wealth from claims against corporate liability had already allowed shares-based investment to flourish, but the final formal/legal establishment of corporate personality consolidated the corporation as the key method of organizing economic activity. Indeed, the limitation of liability was an important mechanism underpinning the growth in size and resources of corporations, allowing them access to disparate and unconsolidated capital to a much greater extent than partnerships. From this point on, in the United States (Chandler 1977; Resnick and Wolf 2003) and elsewhere (Micklethwait and Wooldridge 2003, 83–101), this corporate form became the dominant organizational design for commercial enterprise.

In the last one hundred years the professional manager has become the key corporate player, exercising the rights of the corporate personality on behalf of its owners (Chandler 1977; Galbraith 1985). Thorstein Veblen referred to this development as the rise of "Absentee Ownership," where those who interacted with the corporation had no chance of meeting an "owner" (and final beneficiary of corporate profits) and thus were alienated from the power of ownership. Drawing a direct parallel with absentee landlords, Veblen wanted to stress the impersonal governance of the (American) corporation and its carelessness of the interests of the small holder, supplier, or customer (Veblen 1923 [1997]). While certainly formally accountable to the board of directors and through them to the shareholders, a new highly rewarded professional business class has emerged, that while not necessarily completely separate from owners, nevertheless has great latitude for independent management of the corporation (a further distancing device in Veblen's eyes). However, this independence has also produced a style of management that has had only a very narrow conception (based on profitability) of the social responsibilities linked to incorporation.

Incorporation, and the assumption of corporate personality, was originally linked with the notion that such organizations enjoyed this privilege because they undertook to serve the public interest. Thus, David Korten has suggested that this legal protection should be foregone when the practices of specific corporations no longer do so (Korten 1995, 54). Likewise, Joel Bakan has argued that one key mechanism for policing corporate actions that is currently underrecognised is the revocation of corporate charters by regulators (Bakan 2004, 156). As yet this final sanction has never been deployed against a major corporation, although it is frequently used against smaller companies for all sorts of procedural infractions, although not for what we might regard as social activities that are detrimental to the public realm/domain.

Before examining the manner in which this assumption of corporate personality has played out in the realm of intellectual property, we should be clear about the general dimensions and characteristics of this particular aspect of corporations' political economy.[5] These characteristics, as Phillip Blumberg has pointed out, involve "the recognition of particular rights and responsibilities—one by one—that shapes the juridical contours of the legal unit for which they have been created" (Blumberg 1993, 207). Hence the character of the legally constituted corporate person is not natural but rather has been established and molded by the law, through statutory regulation, through judicial precedent (in common-law systems) and via emerging international "soft law" regulatory models. The core of the rights that are generally recognized in most developed country jurisdictions, and elsewhere, are:

- the right to a name (and thus to have an identity);
- the right to sue and be sued;
- the right to acquire, hold and dispose of property;
- the right to contract; and
- rights under various constitutional and legislative provisions (and specifically as regards corporations) to:
  - continued existence, notwithstanding a change in membership or share ownership;
  - limited liability of members for organizational legal responsibility; and
  - central direction of management. (Blumberg 1993, 209, 210)

While there are also some possible responsibilities these are generally somewhat circumscribed by the impact of limited liability, and the frequent difficulty of establishing the location of decisions that might have led to sanctionable offenses under law (Sahni 2005). In the UK the difficulty of establishing a single "directing mind" has undermined past attempts to prosecute corporate manslaughter, despite its statutory introduction as a crime.

Having set out the historical contours of corporate personality, we can now turn to the issue at the heart of this chapter: its impact on the political economy of intellectual property. Clearly, intellectual property rights are not the only rights enjoyed by corporations; other rights of ownership and deployment of resources (gathered together under property law more generally, and articulated through contract law) often conflict with rights of employees and other groups. As in any political system different rights will likely conflict, and one of the key defining motives of democracy is to provide a forum where decisions over social conflicts such as these can be deliberated and (often only partly) resolved. As the case of IPRs demonstrates however, corporations have managed to establish a privileged position in this political process.

CORPORATIONS AND INTELLECTUAL PROPERTY

As Susan Sell and I have laid out elsewhere at some length, the history of intellectual property has been a history of political contest, dispute, and bargaining (May and Sell 2005). At the forefront of these political debates for the last half-millennium have been commercial interests; originally these were represented by guilds (the British Stationers for instance) and other collective organizations such as trade associations, but as corporations established their socioeconomic position, and as they grew larger, specific commercial interests began to represent themselves. Trade associations and other corporate-based organizations continue to seek to influence governments, but large corporations themselves (especially where they enjoy a dominant market position) also have sought to directly influence government. Perhaps the key mechanism for individual corporate influence, in the realm of intellectual property, has been the numerous attempts (some very successful) to encourage the adoption of specific corporate technologies/protocols as industry standards, supported by governmental bodies. Therefore, corporate influence has usually taken place in two dimensions, in some areas of political-legal debate the corporation has represented its own interest (in specific intellectual property courts cases), while at other times they have used their considerable political economic resources to lobby (and support) politicians/legislators to move the law of intellectual property in specific directions. Moreover, the notion that corporations should be encouraged through the award of intellectual property rights has also often been presented as a central part of the "logic" of modern capitalism.

The narratives of justification that have underpinned intellectual property for much of its existence have always included (drawing on the work of John Locke) a claim that the grant of (intellectual) property rights both rewards previous effort but, perhaps more importantly, also stimulates further innovation and economic activity (May and Sell 2005, chapter 2). Thus, Adam Smith in his *Lectures on Jurisprudence* (published in 1766) saw patents as a "rare example of a harmless exclusive privilege" that had clear benefits as regards the support of invention (MacLeod 1988, 197). And in his famous *Inquiry into the Nature and Causes of the Wealth of Nations* (first published in 1776) Smith justified patents and copyrights as monopolies on the grounds that they were "the easiest and most natural way in which the state can recompense [companies] for hazarding a dangerous and expensive experiment, of which the publick is afterwards to reap the benefit" (Smith 1776 [1993], 418). These views were echoed and consolidated in the subsequent two centuries leading to their central role in underpinning the Trade Related Aspects of Intellectual Property Rights (TRIPs) agreement under the auspices of the World Trade Organization.

Paradoxically, now that intellectual property has finally been incorporated into the mechanisms of global governance, the corporate interest seems to tell two very different stories about the history of development. As far as IPRs are concerned, the long-contested (nationally based, and differentiated) history of the development of intellectual property should be ignored; developing countries should immediately adopt the standards that have only relatively recently been adopted in the richest, most developed economies (Kellow and Murphy, this volume). Thus, while it has taken the best part of five hundred years for the now developed countries to establish the contemporary forms of intellectual property, rather than also work through this developmental trajectory, developing countries (for their own good) should immediately adopt a robust and wide-ranging commodification of knowledge and information. Conversely, in the realm of wages, corporations and their representatives argue that remuneration must reflect the local levels of development (to accord for differences in productivity and skills), while the prices paid for local inputs reflect local market conditions. Differential treatment is fine when it reflects the corporate interest, but is not acceptable when it might threaten important sources of corporate profitability.

Rather than merely assert that the corporate control of intellectual property presents a problem in the global political economy, I shall demonstrate why the unalloyed adoption of commercialized intellectual property rights may not indeed serve the political purpose it was historically intended to serve. This is not to say that all IPRs are illegitimate or problematic: intellectual property as a policy device was developed by various governments (from Venice in the fifteenth century to the United States in the eighteenth and nineteenth) to serve specific social or public ends, and as such may certainly have a role to play in contemporary global society. However, this has become distorted and misdirected through the assumption that corporations should enjoy (intellectual property) rights that were originally developed to reward and encourage real people (or as they are termed in international trade law, "natural persons"). Intellectual property has always been a mechanism to encourage and reward innovation in technology and other socially useful creative endeavors, on the grounds that this would serve national governments' ends in encouraging and expanding social economic activity and development. However, the manner in which IPRs have often been deployed by corporations has not always achieved these ends in any meaningful manner.

THE SKEWERING OF DEVELOPMENTAL IMPERATIVES

As with all awards of monopoly rights, IPRs allow a single operator to gain control of a market in a specific good/product for a certain period, and this is intended to promote rewards from the market that would not be otherwise be able to be captured. These rewards are intended to support behavior that would not be profitable or economic within a market that was not so limited. Thus, for instance, in the past many public utilities (such as water or gas) that require extensive investment in infrastructure, that would be possibly be inefficiently provided (or even duplicated) can be provided through monopoly in a more open market situation.[6] However, there is also always the danger that the enjoyment of monopoly in a new market may skewer the development of the market, and prompt its movement in a direction that while in the direct interests of the monopolists may be less clearly in the wider social interest.

As Michael Perelman points out in the early history of petrol (or gasoline) while there were significant scientific advantages to the use of alcohol-based additives, these could not be controlled through patent rights (not least of all as it utilized already well-known practices). However, an alternative lead-based process utilizing Tetraethyl-lead was as yet undeveloped and could therefore be subject to a claim for patent protection. Thus, General Motors set out to develop leaded petrol and were granted a patent on the rights to the process by which it could deliver usable fuel for motor cars. Once the patent had been secured GM used its significant resources to support scientific research that seemed to establish that this was a safe technology and it was more than half a century before the persistent doubts about the safety of lead-based fuel additives finally prompted a move toward safer alternatives (Perelman 2002, 160–61). This delay in introducing cleaner fuel produced severe costs to public health.

With a swiftly expanding technology such as automobiles in the early years of the last century, a monopoly over a key element of the technology led the development of automobiles to be locked in to one possible fuel system. The control of fuel additive technology at the very same time that the first major wave of infrastructural development was taking place (the building of a network of petrol stations) made the switch to a different technology much more difficult in subsequent years. Certainly, the patent grant did not in itself preclude the development of fuel alternatives, but the support by the industry for this one patented process by a major player ensured that building an alternative system subsequently would be expensive and difficult (indeed, as was the final, and drawn-out process of moving to unleaded petrol across the world).

To take a more recent example, the role of copyright protection for software has had a major role to play in the domination of the Windows operating system in personal computing. Here, the key developments took place before there was significant recourse to copyright claims in software. In the early years of the history of computer development, source code was shared and work was collaborative and essentially unowned. However, after the U.S. Department of Justice prosecuted IBM for antitrust violations, the use of software and hardware was separated, allowing a separate software industry to develop which sought to "own" the software's code, so as to profit from it. This separation prompted IBM to set up a standard processor architecture based on the xx86 series of computer chips which would allow the expansion of a market for personal computers, and subcontracted the development of software for this new smaller form of computer to the fledgling Microsoft.

By controlling the copyright on the initial and subsequent versions of the operating system that would become Windows, Microsoft has managed to dominate and control the software market for home computing. In other areas, such as bespoke software, enterprise software, and device-dedicated software, Microsoft has proved much less able to compete successfully. However, in the realm of its monopoly it now dominates the market. While this domination is now being challenged by the continued rise of the Free and Open Source Software movement, as yet the MS-Dos/Windows lock-in continues to allow Microsoft an essentially monopolist position. It is commonly held across the software community that even if at one time Microsoft may have been a technological innovator, those days have long since passed: network effects (the fact that most people use Microsoft products and thus it makes sense for others to do so too) may still support Microsoft's quasi monopoly, but this can hardly be said to support the further innovation and improvement of software.

As these two brief examples indicate, in theory the award of a monopoly can prompt and reward the development of new technologies. However, especially where this is granted at the beginning of a period of accelerated social deployment of the broad technological mode (of which the patent grant covers an important or vital element), IPRs can actually underpin "lock-in." This, quite apart from any positive corporate actions mentioned below, actually limits and shapes the technological trajectory of a particular society. The question is whether this presents an in insurmountable problem, whether some sort of reform of the system is possible, or whether it is a "price worth paying" for the other benefits the system might currently deliver.

This is a question for policymakers, and in the past has been dealt with by the compulsory licensing of specific technologies when social need has been perceived to outweigh the requirements of corporate profitability (for instance, during wartime). Certainly, reform and tightening of patent examination as suggested by Adam Jaffe and Josh Lerner in their recent discussion of the problems of the current U.S. system (Jaffe and Lerner 2004) may solve some of the perceived problems with the system. In the realm of copyright, the problems are rather different, revolving around questions of allowable fair-use/fair-dealing (i.e., noncommercial use without the owner's permission), and the scope of information and knowledge that is regarded as subject to copyright and associated rights. Here, until recent technological developments, there was a grey area between ownership and (commercial) counterfeiting that hid the social problem to a large extent.[7]

The key issue here, however, remains that while the award of intellectual property is meant to reward and encourage effort and innovation, in the hands of corporations such grants are actually entirely tied up with commercialization and market control. Indeed, As John Kay (2002) has pointed out, in many cases, rather than related to a direct reward for innovation, rights are enjoyed arbitrarily because they can be purchased by any buyer once awarded or recognized. Here the interests of the corporate personality and the individual are subtly different; although we can imagine that some innovators and inventors have no limit to their desire for wealth, we can also be relatively sure that after a certain level of wealth and welfare has been attained, there is little extra motivation or reward to be gained by the individual. However, the corporation has an insatiable demand for reward (profits) and indeed this logic underpins the entire capitalist system. Thus, lock-in and market control or advantage are exactly what a corporation seeks (and it make little difference whether this is obtained through innovation or not). The developmental imperative encapsulated in the logic and justification of intellectual property is skewered by awarding IPRs to corporations.

LITIGATION COSTS AND THREATS

It is not only through the imposition of specific market trajectories that corporations distort the notion of intellectual property's broader social role. Corporations have used their control of IPRs to litigate and to mobilize the threat of litigation seeking to halt the development of competing technologies. Again, the example of software is apposite, with the emergence of threats of IPR-related litigation as regards elements of LINUX, one of the key open source programs. A number of corporations are claiming they may have patent rights over elements that are deployed within the LINUX source code. Although as yet no cases have made their way through the legal process, corporations may use litigation to halt competition, and have already deployed this possibility to scare open source providers' prospective customers with the possibility of expensive court cases.[8] However, this problem is hardly recent.

James Watt, perhaps Britain's most famous inventor of the Industrial Revolution, did not patent a specific steam engine, but rather sought to patent the "method of diminishing the consumption of fuel" in steam engines. He already understood that to patent a specific engine would lead his competitors to specify some small changes and claim their steam engine was a new invention. Thus, he sought a wider-ranging patent to cover the technological method (May and Sell, chapter 4). Even so, Watt and his business partners believed that the term of his main steam patent was not long enough to recoup their investment, not least of all as Watt could not immediately manufacture a steam engine that worked. In 1775, six years into the term of the patent, Watt sought an extension from Parliament. The extended period that was secured allowed Watt to enjoy a thirty-one-year patent on his invention.

This caused two problems in the supply of steam technology. Firstly, unless prospective users were prepared to wait, or could afford the license fees, they had to settle for inferior engines or build illegal machines. Secondly, the patent also stifled and constrained further innovations of this important technology for at least two decades through fear of litigation (Watt himself was no stranger to the courts, being a voracious litigant). Most strikingly, it halted the development of steam driven rotary movement for some years, until Watt's business partners could convince him of its utility. Likewise, high pressure steam had to await the end of the patent to be developed into a usable improvement. Indeed, the patent so alienated the Cornish mining industry that at the beginning of the nineteenth century various mine owners and others instigated a more collective approach to innovation, publishing improvements to their steam engines in *Lean's Engine Reporter* which published each month a report of improvements and incremental inventions made.

The full exploitation of a patent grant (by Watt, acting with his partners as a corporate entity) instilled a reaction by innovators who did not regard patenting as the best way to spur inventive activity, and looked to a more collective innovation model instead. To some extent the relatively small community of Cornish mine owners enhanced the possibility of developing technologies outside the patent system.[9] However, for our purposes here, as this suggests, one of the key elements that arose from Watt's strategy was the threat of the costs of litigation.

Likewise, in the decade after World War II, although revolving around a slightly different set of questions (not least the control by Fergusson of the innovations of its chief engineer, who defected to Ford), the dispute between Ford and Fergusson over agricultural tractor technology required both corporations, who were already active in the sector, to spend large amounts of money to settle a case regarding the ownership of specific elements tractor-related technology (Fraser 1972: chapters 23 and 24). While both corporations could clearly afford the expenditure, the final result of the case, was little more than a settlement to differ, and can hardly be said to have served the social good of agricultural development.

Much more recently, and in another development of some advantage to corporations, under the TRIPs agreement in the area of process patents, the burden of proof has been switched from the plaintiff (the owner of the patent) to the defendant. If a product has been produced that might have used the patented process, it is up to the defendant to prove that the patented process has *not* been used. Thus, if the manufacturer is to prove that no infringement has occurred in circumstances where the patent's "owner has been unable to determine the process actually used" the details of manufacture will be forced into the public domain (article 34). And while there is provision for the "legitimate interests of the defendant in protecting his manufacturing and business secrets [to] be taken into account," once again the balance of rights has shifted quite significantly to the owner of the original process patent (May and Sell 2005, chapter 7). Thus, where reverse engineering has failed there is now a recourse to law to force competitors to reveal how they are competing. Although such a case does not yet appear to have been litigated, if it is, the historical legal notion that defendants might be innocent until proven guilty has been eradicated where the interests of corporate intellectual property holders deem it obstructive to the benefits they enjoy from their property. Thus, rather than support innovation and the development of new technologies, in the hands of corporations eager to consolidate control of specific market sectors, the patent system supports legal strategies that can at the very least tie up competitors in court and force them to spend money on fighting these cases rather than on research and development.

THE QUESTION OF PROFIT

Because of their predominantly commercial character when used and deployed by corporations, IPRs have tended to encourage the development of technologies and innovations that will serve to underpin potentially profitable activity. Hence, when there are clear markets for technologies and the good or services that they support, then whatever other arguments may be made about the plausibility of their justifications, there is some clear logic to this part of their story: IPRs underpin profits in new technologies; provided a potential market exists. However, for those potential inventions and technological solutions that might be regarded as politically or socially useful but do not immediately seem to establish a possibility for profitable commercialization, intellectual property offers little motivation for development.

Certainly, the point of intellectual property in the first instance is to establish a market, through the commodification of information or knowledge, and thus allow commercialization where none was previously possible. Thus, IPRs' construction of scarcity of use in the market relations that surround the use of knowledge and information are meant to constitute the *possibility* of a market.[10] However, once this initial moment of commodification has been achieved, it still requires the possibility of profitable exploitation of a market for potential commodification to work as an incentive to innovation and development. This is perhaps most obviously (but by no means exclusively) a problem in the realm of pharmaceuticals.

While certainly highly proficient at the commercialization of specific pharmaceuticals (the development of mass production of compounds), the pharmaceutical sector as a whole continues to rely for its basic scientific work, which is then commercialized, on the public sector. Indeed, much of the expenditure that is supported by the grant of patent has little to do with innovation or research, but rather underwrites the sector's massive advertising and marketing spend. These issues have become the subject of disputes between the representatives of "big pharma" on one side and the (often self-appointed) representatives of (global) civil society on the other.[11] The role of profits has ensured that the commercialization of innovation has been frequently and significantly patterned by wealth effects, or "effective demand."

Whereas in the past this effect might have mitigated through compulsory licensing (or the threat of such action), since the TRIPs agreement has largely halted such practices by WTO members, the profit motive has now become a key element in the manner in which IPRs encourage specific innovations.[12] Where there is little hope of profitable enterprise based on market exchange, the current (global) system of IPRs does little to encourage innovation. As might be expected, only those innovations and developments that a corporation can expect to turn a profit are actually stimulated, and thus it is predominantly the rich countries whose "needs" are served by innovation.

WHO GETS THE REWARDS?

Finally, one more general problem stems directly from what Kay see as IPRs' essentially arbitrary character. Intellectual property is generally owned and controlled by corporations despite the rhetoric of rewards and encouragement being set out in narratives of the heroic inventor or genius creator. However, to exploit these rights it is often (although not always) difficult for the individual "natural person" to take advantage of the monopoly that she or he has been awarded. Hence, there is a significant level of transfer of rights from natural persons to corporate persons. Given that most often IPRs are effectively rights to commercialization, it is seldom the case that real innovators capture as much income as those corporations that commercialize a specific advance. (This should not be taken as an argument that commercialization deserves *no* reward, but rather a question of the effective distribution of reward relative to the claimed justification for granting or awarding IPRs in the first instance.)

With the increasing industrialization of innovation, the picture of the individual inventor in a lonely laboratory waiting for a "eureka moment" is largely a fantasy, although there continue to be many independent inventors working around the world. Nowadays, most innovation and invention is undertaken by large teams of employed researchers either in the public or private sector. In the private sector this work is conducted under "work-for-hire" provisions; inventions and innovations are the property of the employer, not the innovator. Likewise, while creators may sometimes work with profit in mind, many work for other reasons as well. Likewise, when artists have produced a creative artifact, they often need to sell the rights to a company that will be able to mass-produce and distribute their work to an audience, but they frequently are unable to successfully negotiate a large share of any future earnings (with the exception of certain superstars in any specific field). Thus, while different in form from patents, copyright also produces inequities due to the need to commercialize to profit from creative production; again, this privileges rewards to mass production, rather than the original creative act(s).

Because the patent system is oriented toward the needs and interests of large companies, the costs of patenting innovations is prohibitively expensive for individuals and often ensures that it is impossible for innovators to remain independent rights holders. Indeed, the costs of patenting have sometimes allowed large companies to use independent innovators' inventions without their permission because they have been unable to fund the protection of their rights through the patent system.

Generally speaking, for a patent to stay live, for it to continue to be a legal deterrent to infringement, renewal fees have to be paid to the Patent Office. In Britain, James Dyson (the inventor of the cyclone vacuum cleaner) has twice challenged these fees in the European Court of Human Rights and lost. Dyson's case was prompted by his losing elements of his vacuum cleaner technology when he was unable to afford to renew all his patents early in his career. A major manufacturer was able to use the ideas covered by the nonrenewed patents, and he had no rights to payment. These renewal fees can run into the tens of thousands for a complex technology (Halstead 1997). For instance, Kane Kramer invented a paint he calls *Metalcoat,* which he now distributes himself under patent protection. However, maintaining the patent cost him in the first three years around £30,000, three times the one-off fee ICI were willing to buy the idea for (Martin 2002). Renewal fees may be small change for large companies, but for individual inventors they are often enormous sums. While renewal fees are (rightly) intended to ensure that ideas are only protected if they are being used commercially, for Dyson, Kramer, and others it suggests the system serves the commercial needs of large companies rather than the rights of inventors.

Furthermore, companies often try to avoid paying any fees to inventors if possible. In one case Electrolux was sued by John North over another aspect of vacuum cleaner design. North met with executives from Electrolux in the 1990s and nothing came of the meetings. However, subsequently the company launched a new cleaner that incorporated aspects of North's designs. In May 2004, Electrolux settled a court case before it concluded for $300 million, although they admitted no liability. North had not patented his idea, but had signed nondisclosure contracts that he claimed the company had subsequently violated (Matthiason 2004; Reuters 2004). Having secured the backing of a law firm on a no-win-no-fee basis, North unlike many small inventors was able to assert his rights. Although not strictly a case of infringement of IPRs this case illustrates the lengths some inventors need to go to gain a reward *despite* the well-developed intellectual property system in Europe.

Moreover, the multinational corporate control of intellectual property facilitates some level of tax avoidance by large corporations. To take one example from medicine: Ezetrol, an anticholesterol absorption inhibitor manufactured by Merck Sharp & Dohme Ltd. and Schering-Plough in Europe, has a trademark registered by a joint venture between these companies in Singapore. This enables the Singaporean arm of the corporation to charge a license fee (set by the corporation itself) for use of the trademark, which facilitates transfers of profits from European tax jurisdictions to a lower tax regime in Singapore. Clearly, this is about tax planning and not any public-regarding information function of trademarks, nor the public interest more generally, as it robs the European jurisdictions of tax income that might be spent on various public programs.[13]

Therefore, although the rhetoric of the intellectual property system is set out as a set of arguments about the natural rights of inventors, creators, and other "natural persons," what the system actually rewards is commercialization and often facilitates tax planning; this is undertaken not by innovators but by corporations who have been able to secure the rights initially generated by innovative and creative activity. Again, I stress that this is not an argument that commercialization deserves no reward, but rather a question of how specific rights are legitimated and justified to those who (in one way or another) are being asked to pay the price of protecting these rights. If there is a disjuncture between rhetorical narrative and the effects of the law, then this is a political problem, as continued support for the system of IPRs is being maintained on the basis of misleading or even false accounts of how the system benefits society, which through its representative institutions extends these rights to corporate individuals.

CONCLUSION: TWO PROBLEMATIC MYTHS

The ownership and deployment of intellectual property by corporations is the product of two myths that have been effectively and progressively globalized since the second half of the twentieth century. One myth tells us that IPRs are basic political rights that can, and indeed, should be awarded to the innovators and creators of our (now global) society to encourage them in their efforts, and by doing so increase the social stocks of innovation and creative artifacts for us all. Then, another complimentary myth tells us that we should recognize corporations as legally constituted persons so that they can function more efficiently. This second myth has also encompassed the claim that political rights should be extended to these "persons" to allow them to enjoy the same protections from interference in their affairs as "real" persons.

This latter myth has been fostered and expanded by corporate practice and influence, and through the globalization of Anglo-Saxon regulatory models. This has distorted the democratic ideals of individual rights by extending them to non-natural persons. The history of democracy has been concerned with the protection of the rights of individuals against the power of organized (political) groups; extending rights to corporations (which are themselves organized groups) corrupts and undermines this aspect of democracy. Too often these myths have been taken as largely unproblematic and as such, until recently at least, have often not been widely commented on; indeed they have often been regarded as self-evident truths, not myths at all.

However, as I have attempted to demonstrate, what this mythical structure reveals is a clear sociopolitical purpose: the attempt by corporations to establish their privileges as rights across the world; to obscure the preference they receive through the practice of particular legal mechanisms. In both cases, the rights extended were developed with the express purpose of serving well-specified social ends, however in their modern and globalized use they have become corrupted, their original social/policy purpose obscured and any elements of accountability diluted through the (as yet only partial) detachment from national regulatory authority. Indeed, especially for IPRs, the deployment of a political (or natural) rights discourse has been intended exactly to obscure and mystify the original social purpose of legislation.

Rather than argue that therefore the legal underpinnings of both myths should be dismantled, a more plausible (and more legitimate) political project is to return these legal instruments to their original public-regarding emphasis, recognizing their contingent existence, dependent on the ends required being served. Thus, while it may well be the case that both legal regimes (IPRs and incorporation) can serve worthwhile social ends, it is a mistake to imagine that these are political rights in the sense of natural (and thus universal) rights that cannot be rescinded. International policy discussion needs to return to an understanding of these mechanisms as being contingent on the behavior and action of their recipients rather than merely being used to discipline and punish so-called pirates and social forces aiming to constrain corporations activities in one way or another.

Regarding, and acknowledging the history of these two sets of rights allows us to recognize that their current manifestation in developed countries' legal systems is not a foregone conclusion, nor the necessary end point of legal refinement and development, but rather a contested, and contestable, settlement that needs to be subject to political scrutiny, not acquiescence and accommodation. Therefore, the convergence on Anglo-Saxon corporate legal forms, alongside the TRIPs agreement's globalization of a specific mode of regulating knowledge and information, must prompt a recovery of examples of earlier political settlements around these issues, which were potentially more accommodating to modes of democratic accountability. However, in national jurisdictions, at best, this was uneven in its practical operation, and therefore the real challenge is to link an emerging global polity to reengineered mechanisms that will facilitate the holding to account of globally active corporations.

This might lead us to (paradoxically) conclude that the regulation of corporations was more democratic prior to the age of mass democracy: this would be a mistake. However, what *is* notable is that corporations have been able to represent their interests as equal to those of other groups within the demos. Whereas in its early history the corporation was regulated with specific public interests in mind (albeit those decided on by an elitist authority), corporations have managed to reduce (or even eliminate) the separation between themselves and other "citizens." While democracy may certainly be more developed than in the past, we might also suggest that in this aspect (only?) societies were perhaps more "democratic" when political authorities recognized that corporations are different from natural persons. The question is: whether (global) democracy *should* include corporations; currently corporations enjoy many citizenship rights, but it is not clear that this is completely beneficial to (global) society as a whole as the example of intellectual property clearly demonstrates.

NOTES

1. Comments by the editors of this volume on an earlier draft helped me refine and clarify my argument for which I extend thanks; the remaining shortcomings are of course my own.
2. For legal personality linked to the rise of Benedictine orders, see Brown (2003); for developments during the eleventh century, in Britain and on the European continent, including the incorporation of universities, ecclesiastical orders, and boroughs, see Davis (1905, 35–88); for the incorporation of guilds, see Williston (1909) and Jones (1926).
3. Ironically, this is the same period in which intellectual property (although as yet not so named) was being consolidated in English law as part of the regulation of monopolies (May and Sell, 2005, chapter 4).

4. Space precludes a full exploration of the historical aspects of the legal recognition of corporate personality, but the contributions to Grantham and Rickett (1998) map out the range of issues well.

5. Here I am going to leave aside the distinction between entity based law (focusing on the corporation as an individual actor) and the notion of enterprise law (focusing on the relations between the multinational and its subsidiaries), as this has little impact on the issues around intellectual property that are the focus of the main part of the paper. However, more generally this is an important issue and an extensive treatment can be found in Blumberg (1993) and Sahni (2005).

6. Obviously, there are a number of caveats to this brief description of the economics of monopoly that in an extended treatment one might want to offer, not least that technological change itself may change the character of the market sufficiently to make monopoly provision no longer socially advantageous.

7. See the extended discussion in May (2007).

8. For a study of the legal threats (based on disputes over ownership and licensing of elements of LINUX's source code) mounted by proprietary corporations, see Omar (2005).

9. The non-patent development of Cornish mining technology is discussed at length in Nuvolari (2001).

10. I shall leave this question to one side having written at length about this issue in my previous work, most recently in May (2006).

11. For a full discussion of the question of intellectual property and the pharmaceutical sector, see Sell (this volume).

12. I leave aside here any discussion of the Doha Declaration of the TRIPs Agreement and Public Health, due to the lack of any real (rather than rhetorical) impact on the global flow of medicines.

13. Space precludes a full discussion of the political economy of transfer pricing, but see Webb (2006) for an excellent overview of the issues.

REFERENCES

Bakan, J. 2004. *The corporation. The pathological pursuit of profit and power*. New York: Free Press.

Blumberg, P. I. 1993. *The multinational challenge to corporation law. The search for a new corporate personality* New York: Oxford University Press.

Brown, B. 2003. *The history of the corporation*. Vol. 1. Sumas, WA: BF Communications.

Chandler, A. D. 1977. *The visible hand. The managerial revolution in American business.* Cambridge: Belknap Press/Harvard University Press.

Davis, J. P. 1905. *Corporations. A study of the origin and development of great business combinations and their relation to the authority of the state.* New York: G. P. Putnam's Sons.

Fraser, C. 1972. *Harry Fergusson: Inventor and pioneer* London: John Murray.

Galbraith, J. K. 1985. *The new industrial state,* 4th ed., with a new introduction. Boston: Houghton Mifflin.

Grantham, R., and C. Rickett. 1998. *Corporate personality in the 20th century* Oxford: Hart Publishing.

Halstead, R. 1997. Inventor takes DTI to European Court. *Independent on Sunday* (Business section), 12 January, 1.

Hansmann, H., and R. Kraakman. 2000. *The end of history for corporate law.* Yale Law School: Law and Economics Working Paper no. 235. New Haven: Yale Law School.

Jaffe, A. B., and J. Lerner. 2004. *Innovation and its discontents* Princeton: Princeton University Press.

Jones, F. D. 1926. Historical development of the law of business competition. *Yale Law Journal* 25, no. 8 (July): 905–38.

Jones, G. 2000. *Merchants to multinationals: British trading companies in the nineteenth and twentieth centuries.* Oxford: Oxford University Press.

Kay, J. 2002. Arbitrary rights. *CentrePiece* (Summer): 28–32.

Korten, D.C. 1995. *When corporations rule the world.* London: Earthscan.

Martin, P. 2002. Inventors and invention: Eureka UK. *Sunday Times Magazine,* 14 July, 22–24.

Matthiason, N. 2004. Inventor sues Electrolux over "Theft" of his design. *The Observer* (Business section), 9 May, 2.

May, C. 2004. Capacity building and the (re)production of intellectual property rights. *Third World Quarterly* 25, no. 5: 821–37.

———. 2006. The denial of history: Reification, intellectual property rights and the lessons of the past. *Capital and Class* 88 (Spring): 33–56.

———. 2007. *Digital rights management: The problem of expanding ownership rights.* Oxford: Chandos.

———, and S. Sell. 2005. *Intellectual property rights: A critical history.* Boulder: Lynne Rienner.

Micklethwait, J. and A. Wooldridge. 2003. *The company. A short history of a revolutionary idea.* London: Weidenfeld and Nicolson.

Moore, K. and D. Lewis. 1999. *Birth of the multinational: 2000 years of ancient business history—from Ashur to Augustus.* Copenhagen: Copenhagen Business School Press.

Muchlinski, P. T. (2007) *Multilateral enterprises and the law.* 2nd ed. Oxford: Oxford University Press.

Nuvolari, A. 2001 Collective invention during the British Industrial Revolution: The case of the Cornish pumping engine. Eindhoven Centre for Innovation Studies: working paper 01.04. Eindhoven: ECIS/Technische Universitiet Eindohoven.

Omar, I. 2005. The penguin in peril: SCO's legal threats to Linux. *First Monday* 10, 1. September 19, 2007. At: http://firstmonday.org/issues/issue10_1/omar/index.html.

Perelman, M. 2002. *Steal this idea: Intellectual property rights and the corporate confiscation of creativity.* New York: Palgrave.

Resnick, S. and R. Wolff. 2003. Exploitation, consumption, and the uniqueness of US capitalism. *Historical Materialism* 11, no. 4: 209–26.

Reuters. 2004. Electrolux settles legal dispute for $30mln. May 19, at: http://uk.biz.yahoo.com/040519/80/eu19s.html (now removed).

Russell, S. and M. J. Gilbert. 2002. Social control of transnational corporations in the age of marketocracy. *International Journal of the Sociology of the Law* 30, no. 1 (March): 33–50.

Sahni, B. 2005. The interpretation of the corporate personality of transnational corporations. *Widener Law Journal* 15, no. 1: 1–45.

Veblen, T. 1923 [1997]. *Absentee ownership. Business enterprise in recent times: The case of America.* New York: B. W. Heubsch [reprinted with a new introduction by Marion J Levy. New Brunswick: Transaction Publishers].

Webb, M. C. 2006. Shaping international corporate taxation. In: *Global corporate power* (IPE Yearbook 15), ed. C. May, 105–26. Boulder: Lynne Rienner.

Williston, S. 1909. The history of the law of business corporations before 1800. *Select essays in Anglo-American legal history. Vol. III.* Cambridge: Cambridge University Press.

SECTION 3

THE GENERAL LEVEL

Trans-Industry Business Action and Policy Processes

8

REGULATORY ARCHITECTURES FOR A GLOBAL DEMOCRACY

On Democratic Varieties of Regulatory Capitalism

DAVID LEVI-FAUR

INTRODUCTION

Should we worry about the future of democracy given the acceleration of economic, social, and political globalization? Does globalization, and the liberalization processes that are associated with it, constrain or invigorate democratic policymaking? These are not easy questions to answer, and there are many fruitful strategies to confront them. This chapter places these questions in the context of the emergence of a global order of "regulatory capitalism" (Levi-Faur 2005; Braithwaite 2008). The answers the chapter provides for the above questions, the challenges it identifies, and the solutions it suggests—all demand an attentive view of the global expansion of rule-based governance. All are contingent on the characteristics of hundreds, or even thousands, of micro-regimes at the global level that govern many aspects of our daily lives. These regimes are never entirely private or entirely public but are hybrids. They have some aspects of public governance and some aspects of the private governance at the same time. The different elements that make the hybrids are likely to coexist, mutually adjusting, cooperating, complementing, and competing with each other.

The production and delivery of the products we consume, of the services we buy, and our environment are all shaped by hundreds and thousands of regulations that were decided outside our respective national parliaments and executives and beyond the jurisdictions of our national courts (Braithwaite and Drahos 2000). These regulations shape the medicines and food we consume, the quality of the air we breathe and the water we drink, and the safety of our kids' toys. Many of these regimes have been established, and flourish, beyond the nation-state, yet they exert influence within its borders. These global regimes are often created and maintained by business corporations and trade associations but also by nonprofit advocacy groups. Whatever the motives of these organizations and groups—be they moral or material—the scope of their operation and the institutions they create go well beyond the nation-state. Consequently, scholars have identified the emergence and proliferation of "private authority regimes" and "private governments," and discuss the effects they have on effective governance, democratic legitimacy and quality, and the changing balance of power between corporations and states (Strange 1996; Weiss 1999; Haufler 2002; Hall and Biersteker 2002).

Private regulatory regimes, however, do not exist in vacuum. They are part of complex hybrids that include private and public. It is the effect of these hybrids that determines the characteristics and qualities of these regimes. On the basis of this assumption, we pose the question: Does the emergence of the global, in the form of these multitudes of international micro regulatory regimes, suggest a renewal of democratic policymaking, or does it attest to its stagnation or decay? Two very different responses are often given to these questions. The pessimistic response stems from the expectation of decay in the role and authority of public institutions. Accordingly, the democratic challenges identified suggest that the global is the domain of business; liberalization implies deregulation; civil and voluntary regulation[1] replace coercive state regulation; and the retreat of the nation-state signifies a decline in popular sovereignty. In such a world, the scope for public control, the demand for and supply of accountability, and the options for participation are either limited or in decline. The optimistic response, meanwhile, flows from the expectation of an institutional renewal of democratic practices at the global level. Accordingly, the democratic challenges that the optimists identify are grounded in the assertion that the global is *not* primarily the privileged domain of busi-

**Table 8.1. Democratic Challenges in the Age of Globalization:
The Antipodes**

Pessimists	Optimists
Decay in the role and authority of public institutions	Expectation of institutional renewal at the global level. Global democracy is emerging
The global is the privileged domain of business	The global is *not* primarily the domain of business but the place where new forms of civil action emerge
Liberalization implies deregulation	Liberalization is not only or mainly about deregulation but mostly about reregulation
Civil regulation replaces coercive state regulation	Civil regulation co-expands rather than replaces state regulation
The retreat of the nation state signifies a decline in popular sovereignty	Global governance represents an opportunity to reinvigorate popular sovereignty.

ness but *the* place where new forms of civil action emerge; liberalization is not only or mainly about *de*regulation but mostly about *re*regulation; civil regulation co-expands rather than replaces state regulation; and global governance represents an opportunity to reinvigorate popular sovereignty. In this fairly bright world, the scope for public control, the demand for and supply of accountability, and the options for participation are considerable and even expanding.

This chapter presents a point of view that is neither pessimistic nor optimistic. A measure of optimism might be gained from the recognition that the intellectual hegemony of neoliberalism blurs in all that concerns the regulatory dynamics of present-day capitalism. We are supposed to live in an era of *de*regulation, and yet the empirical evidence of the expansion of regulation does not support this gloomy assumption. There are wide gaps between the dominant narrative on neoliberal deregulation and the emerging realities of a regulatory explosion (Levi-Faur 2005). Braithwaite (2008) bluntly calls this narrative the "neoliberal fairy tale," suggesting that regulation is too important a feature of the current order simply to be left out of political economy and public policy accounts of change. Similarly, to note a couple of recent examples, both Moran (2003) and Levy (2006) reported findings that the state "after statism" remains an activist state. Its missions are evolving rather than eroding, and "reinventing government" is mainly or significantly a process of the transformation of the service-provision state into the regulatory state (Moran 2002, 391; Loughlin and Scott 1997; McGowan and Wallace 1996; Hood et al. 1999). Our pessimism, or a better recognition of the scope of the challenges, is not motivated so much by the privileged position of business (or its structural power). The gravest challenges are derived from the fragmentation of policy and politics into a multitude of decentralized arenas of regulation, which give rise to technocratic politics and also to a culture of distrust. This in turn results in punitive forms of accountability and panopticonic forms of transparency.

This chapter makes two major assertions. First, the rise of the regulatory state at the national level and the emergence of a multitude of issue-specific regimes at the global level consolidate a regulatory order that may best be described as "regulatory capitalism." The architecture of regulation is increasingly also the architecture of global governance, and it is in this context that democratic stalemate, decay, or renewal should be evaluated. To put it more bluntly, the chapter asserts that theories of democratic control and democratic participation cannot deal properly with the challenges of global democracy without taking into account the emergence, consolidation, and expansion of the new order of regulatory capitalism. In this new global order, rule making, rule monitoring, and rule enforcement are becoming major instruments of governance. The interaction between different types of regulators exercising powers of varying scope gives rise to four varieties of regulatory capitalism: laissez-faire, pluralist, corporatist, and étatist.

Second, the chapter asserts that one of these four varieties, namely, "regulatory corporatism," may best align public and business interests within international regulatory regimes. A major conceptual effort is directed, therefore, at clarifying the meaning and the implications of the notion of regulatory corporatism. In this sense, the chapter contributes to the renewal of corporatist theory, but it significantly departs from the association of corporatism with the tripartite arrangements of labor, business, and the state (on this postwar neocorporatism, see Schmitter 1974; Katzenstein 1984). The "neo-neo" global regulatory corporatism is more consensual, voluntary, and deliberative than its predecessors. It is rule-based in the sense that its direct and immediate effects are mainly procedural rather than distributive, and it reflects the co-expansion and co-functioning of state and civil rules at different and multiple levels of analysis. At the same time, it serves as an alternative theoretical framework to realist and liberal conceptions of the global order.

The first section of the chapter presents the notions of regulatory capitalism and regulatory state. The second focuses on the civil aspects of regulatory capitalism and discusses certain forms of civil regulation that are very rarely brought together in the literature. The third section proceeds to develop some distinctions between different varieties of regulatory capitalism—in particular, between laissez-faire, corporatist, pluralist, and étatist types of regulatory capitalism. The arguments and discussion in these three sections are mostly analytical and theoretical. Empirical examples are provided with regard to the governance of food safety, and especially with regard to the democratic challenge of a particular private governance regime—GLOBALGAP (known as EurepGap before September 2007).[2] GLOBALGAP is a private sector body that is said to set "voluntary standards" for the certification of agricultural products (see also Fuchs and Kalfagianni, this volume). It brings together agricultural producers and retailers who want to establish certification standards and procedures for Good Agricultural Practices (GAP). Certification covers the production process of the certified product from before the seed is planted until it leaves the farm. As a so-called business-to-business label, it is not directly visible to consumers, nor does it attract the direct scrutiny of governments. GLOBALGAP's advocates suggest that it leads to an upgrade of food safety standards and reduces both red tape and compliance costs. Its opponents point out that GLOBALGAP is taking over state functions, and is a form of private government that is neither accountable to the public nor transparent to important stakeholders (Campbell 2005; 2006; Freidberg 2007; Guthman 2007). The fourth section of the chapter examines and evaluates the basic democratic qualities of regulatory corporatism, especially with regard to participation, transparency, and accountability. The fifth section concludes.

REGULATORY CAPITALISM AND THE REGULATORY STATE

The way capitalism is organized and governed is changing (Rosenau and Czempiel 1992; Braithwaite and Drahos 2000; Slaughter 2004). A regulatory explosion—the proliferation of different mechanisms of control at both the national and the global level—is balancing the effects of neoliberal reforms and is creating a new global order that is characterized in important ways by regulation (Levi-Faur 2005). Our democratic worries and hopes, constraints and opportunities, strategies and ad hoc reactions are all defined to a significant extent by this new, emerging order of regulatory capitalism.

How should we best define the new global order of regulatory capitalism? One definition was offered in a lecture by the then-chairman of the U.S. Federal Communication Commission (FCC), William E. Kennard. For Chairman Kennard, regulation is too often used as a shield to protect the status quo from new competition, as well as a sword to cut a pathway for new players to compete by creating new networks and services. It is always easier for business to prowl the corridors of Congress, Chairman Kennard claims, than to compete in the rough and tumble of the marketplace. Accordingly, he suggests that regulatory capitalism is when companies work to change the regulations instead of working to change the market. Or, more succinctly: "Regulatory capitalism is when companies invest in lawyers, lobbyists and politicians, instead of plants, people and customer service. . . . Regulatory capitalists would rather litigate than innovate . . . it works best for companies that have the resources and know-how to play the regulatory game." Chairman Kennard thus presents a morbid view of regulatory capitalism, not much different from the portrayal of "interest group liberalism" offered by Theodore Lowi in the late 1960s, whereby single-issue groups pursue their narrow and short-term interests at the expense of the overall public interest. This, together with the sprawling, unaccountable, and octopus-like bureaucracy, represents *The End of Liberalism* (Lowi 1969). Leave aside the different era and context and the different ideological bent of the two: Lowi and Chairman Kennard are expressing the same sentiment, namely, that the interaction between government and big business is leading to the degradation of democracy.

Unlike both Lowi and Kennard, this chapter suggests a more open-ended and often contradictory view of regulatory capitalism, one that allows regulation to be both strong and weak, derived from public but also civil demand, with positive as well as negative results. This view contrasts relational-based to rule-based governance and does not reduce rules and rule making to a mere instrument of the powerful (Li 2003). Rule-based governance, to the extent that it is effective and legitimate, constrains both the powerful and the powerless, though not necessarily to the same extent. In order to elaborate such an open-ended concept of regulatory capitalism, this chapter defines regulatory capitalism as a political, economic, and social order where it is regulation, rather than the direct provision of public and private services, that is the expanding part of government, and where legal forms of domination are increasingly organized around functional roles and problem solving rather than national demarcation lines. The distribution of power and the corresponding form of interest intermediation in each issue arena and functional arena are shaped by the particular interaction of civil and state forms of regulation.

The notion of regulatory capitalism challenges and complements the notion of the regulatory state (Moran 2002, 391; Loughlin and Scott 1997; McGowan and Wallace 1996; Hood et al. 1999). One of the major manifestations of the rise of the regulatory state is the creation of autonomous agencies to regulate social and economic life. A recent survey of the establishment of regulatory agencies across sixteen different sectors in sixty-three countries from the 1920s through to 2007 reveals that it is possible to find an autonomous regulatory agency in about 73 percent of the possible sector-country units that were surveyed (Jordana, Levi-Faur, and Fernandez i Marin 2008). The number of regulatory agencies rose sharply in the 1990s. The rate of establishment increased extremely dramatically: from fewer than five new autonomous agencies per year from the 1960s to the 1980s, to more than twenty agencies per year from the 1990s to 2002 (rising to almost forty agencies per year between 1994 and 1996). Probably more than anything else, it is the establishment of these agencies that makes the regulatory state an attractive concept for social scientists (Majone 1994; 1997), Latin America (Manzetti 2002; Jordana and Levi-Faur 2006), East Asia (Jayasuriya 2001), Germany (Muller 2002), Britain (Moran 2003), and even China (Pearson 2005).

A useful definition of the term *regulatory state* suggests that "modern states are placing more emphasis on the use of authority, rules and standard-setting, partially displacing an earlier emphasis on public ownership, public subsidies, and directly provided services. The expanding part of modern government, the argument goes, is *regulation*" (Hood et al. 1999, 3). Alternatives to regulation, mostly distributive and redistributive policies, according to this view, are either stagnating or altogether in decline.[3] While the regulatory state signifies most often governance at the national level, in the European context the notion of the "regulatory state" often indicates a European Union–centered policy analysis where the steering functions are mainly located in Brussels rather than in the member states. This understanding of the European regulatory state is mostly associated with the work of Giandomenico Majone, who suggests that regulatory functions are migrating upward toward the European Union (Majone 1997). This migration challenges, of course, the notion of national and popular sovereignty, and therefore calls for discussion of its democratic qualities. To a large extent it mirrors the agenda of this book on the democratic challenges of economic, social, and political globalization.

Before I turn the reader's attention to the notion of civil regulation, let me exemplify the notions of regulatory capitalism, the regulatory state, and the European regulatory state as they apply to the issue of food safety and, more concretely, to the GLOBALGAP regime. Recall that GLOBALGAP is a private sector body that sets voluntary standards by bringing together agricultural producers and retailers who want to establish certification standards and procedures for Good Agricultural Practices. Certification covers the production process of the certified product from before the seed is planted until it leaves the farm. Note that it covers crops, livestock, and aquaculture, and covers more then eighty thousand certified producers in no fewer than eighty countries. Yet what we have had to say so far on regulatory capitalism doesn't directly apply to it. As a business-to-business standard, it does not directly represent what Chairman Kennard was warning against. It does not mainly or directly rely on lobbying government or using political capital in national or intergovernmental arenas. It also does not involve the creation of, or reliance on, regulatory agencies that serve as the major signifiers of the emergence of the regulatory state. GLOBALGAP, despite its European origins, is not part of the EU governance structure. It is therefore more a challenge to than a validation of Majone's notion of the European regulatory state. To better understand GLOBALGAP, we need to turn our attention from state and intergovernmental politics to the "regulatory society" and, more concretely, to a new type of social movement, namely, the business movement.

CIVIL REGULATION: BEYOND THE REGULATORY STATE

Regulatory capitalism is not only a political or economic order. It reflects sociological developments that are best expressed via the term *Regulatory Society* (Clarke 2000; Braithwaite 2003). The regulatory society represents the arena where non-state actors demand and supply their own regulatory solutions. These non-state actors can act within national boundaries or beyond them. In either case, they represent the existence and the importance of civil forms of regulation. The regulatory society interacts with the regulatory state and this interaction makes the order that we label as "regulatory capitalism." Yet, before we deal with this interaction, it might be best to discuss it on its own and to portray the different mechanisms of civil regulation that are associated with it.

Civil regulation (often also described as private regulation) refers to the institutionalization of global and national forms of regulation through the creation of private (non-state) forms of regulation to govern markets and societies (cf. Vogel 2005; 2006). Civil regulations are the product of the advocacy of non-state groups: nongovernmental organizations (NGOs), international nongovernmental organizations (INGOs), corporations, formal and informal networks of professionals, lobby groups, industry associations, terrorists, criminals and the like. While the boundaries between civil and state organizations are often blurred, we expect civil organizations to have significant degree of autonomy and formal constitution as societal organization (Hall and Biersteker 2002, 3). The literature on international private-interest regimes (Cutler, Haufler, and Porter 1999; Cutler 2003, Hall and Biersteker 2002; Sell 2003), private legal orders (Williams 2006), and global civil society (Kaldor 2003) probably reflects the growth of civil forms of organization and regulation (Cutler, Haufler, and Porter 1999, 3; Büthe 2004, 282).

Civil regulations attempt to embed markets and social groups in a normative and regulatory order that prescribes responsible business conduct and citizenship. "What distinguishes the legitimacy, governance and implementation of civil regulation," David Vogel tells us, "is that it is not rooted in public [i.e., state] authority. Operating beside or around the state rather than through it, civil regulations are based on 'soft law' rather than legally binding standards: violators are subject to market and civil penalties rather than legal ones" (Vogel 2006, 2–3). Market and other civil penalties should be understood here not only as direct and immediate economic outcomes, but also as penalties that are related to the standing and reputation of business corporations, civil organizations, and their managers and employees. Because penalties can be high, even if they are not based on legal norms and state enforcement, it might be useful to distinguish between voluntary and coercive forms of civil regulation. Coercive regulation derives from various forms of power that market and other social actors possess vis-à-vis other actors, sometime even vis-à-vis state actors. Coercive power is not only a property of the state, and thus can be used by civil regulators to enhance their interests and worldviews. This is exactly the type of power that increasingly acquired by big retailers in Europe and North America vis-à-vis domestic and international growers (see, Fuchs and Kalfagianni, this volume).

Voluntary regulation is not new; it precedes modernity and is recognized in wide areas of business and social activity (Potoski and Prakash, this volume). Scholarly and public interest in voluntary regulation derives from four shortcomings of "regulatory formalism," including (1) expensive and cost-ineffective regulatory strategies (Breyer 1993); (2) inflexible regulatory strategies that encourage adversarial enforcement (Bardach and Kagan, 1982); (3) legal constraints on the subject matter, procedure, and scope of regulatory discretion; (4) and *regula-tees'* resentment, which leads to noncompliance or "creative compliance" (McBarnet and Whelan 1997). While the turn to voluntary regulation is partly a response to the failures of formal regulation, it has its own flaws and weaknesses The basic puzzle of why firms and other social and economic organizations would take upon themselves responsibilities that are not mandated by law is still in need of more scholarly attention, and the scope and implications of voluntary regulation need to be more clearly delineated (Arora and Cason 1996; Prakash 2001; Porter and Ronit 2006).

Considering GLOBALGAP, it is tempting to accept its self-presentation as a voluntary organization. But this can be done only while turning a blind eye to apolitical, non-state forms of power. GLOBALGAP was established by retailers in an increasingly concentrated retail market, which allows retailers to exert significant control over producers. These retailers are generally located in the North and are organized as giant corporations, while the producers often come from the South and are organized in family farms. Better food safety in the North may come at a high price to the South. Civil regulation does not necessarily mean voluntarism. In the food sector, the power of retailers over other parts of the food industry is very significant and coercive aspects are at least part of the convergence of producers on stricter standards.

GLOBALGAP is also a form of self-regulation. According to Porter and Ronit, self-regulation "has recently come of age. In governments and in intergovernmental organizations, as well as among many private organizations in business and civil society, self-regulation is seen as an alternative to market and state" (Porter and Karsten 2006, 41). Self-regulation is a basic and common form of civil regulation and is often, but not always, voluntary. Figure 8.1 therefore distinguishes between self-regulation (when the regulator is voluntarily also the regulatee) and enforced self-regulation (when the regulatory is also the regulatee under some form of coercion).

Enforced self-regulation occurs where "the government would compel each company to write a set of rules tailored to the unique set of contingencies facing that firm. A regulatory agency would either approve these rules, or send them back for revision if they were insufficiently stringent" (Ayres and Braithwaite 1992, 106). Rather than the government enforcing the rules, most enforcement duties and costs would be internalized by the *regulatee*, which would be required to establish an internal independent compliance administration. The primary function of government inspectors would be to ensure the integrity and transparency of the work of the compliance group of the

Figure 8.1. Types of Civil Regulation

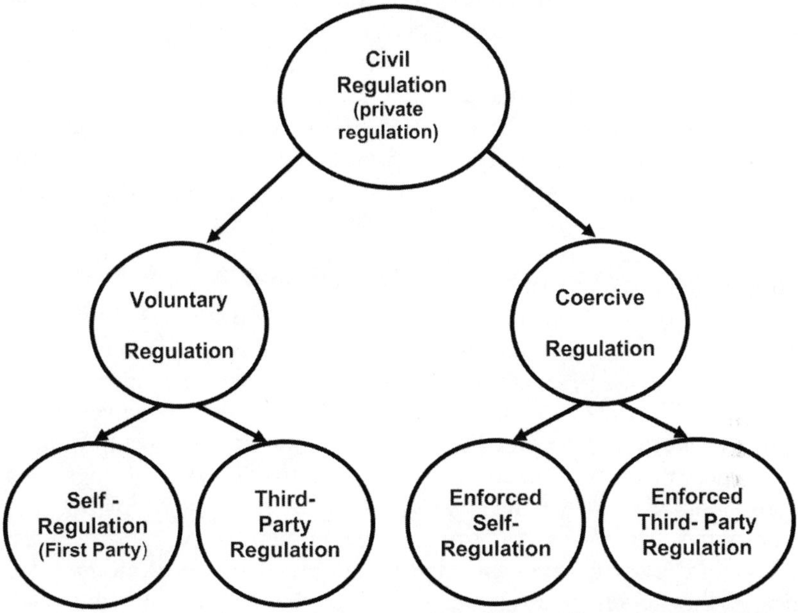

regulatees. State involvement would not stop at monitoring, however. Violations of the privately written and publicly ratified rules would be punishable by law (Ayres and Braithwaite 1992).

The self-regulatory regimes, enforced or voluntary, are based on a certain level of agreement and willingness to cooperate among various stakeholders, including professional and business competitors. Self-regulation may include a wide variety of techniques and instruments covering various facets of collective action. It may be defined in terms of one or all of the following aspects: entry regulation (e.g., having a license to operate a service); exit regulation (e.g., the withdrawal of a license to operate a service); cost regulation (e.g., the price of professional services); service regulation (e.g., the level of service expected from the provider); content regulation (e.g., degree of violence); and standard regulation (e.g., degree of acceptable noise). It should be obvious by this stage that GLOBALGAP is a self-regulatory mechanism of control. Legally, it is owned by FoodPlus, a not-for-profit limited company based in Cologne, Germany. As a system of food quality certification, it includes a set of normative documents. The standards and requirements of certification are approved by working committees in each sector. These committees have 50 percent retailer and 50 percent producer representation. Membership and participation are on the basis of expertise rather than nationality.

Third-party regulation is yet another common form of civil regulation. Again, it can come in a voluntary form but also as a coercive form, as Enforced Third-Party Regulation. Here, processes of accreditation by third parties are a central enforcement strategy and "a voluntary contractual relationship between regulated entities and the party auditing the facility in place of relying solely on the regulatory agency as enforcer" (Kunreuther, McNulty, and Kang 2002, 309). Third-party regulation is a prevalent feature of modern life. One of its more popular forms is "auditing." Indeed, the notion of auditing is now used in a variety of contexts to refer to growing pressures for verification requirements (Power 1997). Third-party regulators are sometimes called "gatekeepers" (Kraakman 1986). These include senior executives, independent directors, large auditing firms, external lawyers, securities analysts, the financial media, underwriters, and debt-rating agencies (Ribstein 2005, 5–6). Volunteerism is a measure and characteristic, however, of the *regulatee*, and not necessarily the third party. The incentives to the third party to enter into these relations might be economic, and indeed they often are, but they can also be enforced by the legal regime (either by the state or by the civil organization that shapes the regulatory regime). Note that, in the context of the GLOBALGAP regime, the accreditation of the eighty thousand or so producers is delegated to independent certifiers. In this process these certifiers are the third party that provides the accreditation for the producers. Yet, at the same time they are undergoing an accreditation process themselves by GLOBALGAP.

The particular dynamics of these various forms of civil regulation—in particular, whether they are on the rise or in decline—and the question of their origins, effects, and democratic legitimacy are still mostly open and subjects for further empirical research. Yet it is certain that at least in theory they can constitute an alternative arena and method of democratic governance. While the theory and practice of democracy always had close historical ties with the state, we are living in an age of globalization, and at least some theorists are suggesting that the major challenges we face are in the global or transnational arenas (Dryzek 1996; 2000). Transnational democracy suggests increasing use and application of civil regulation where state regulation is on the margins rather than at the center of regulatory regimes. However, in order to fully appreciate the challenges and promises that it represents, the interaction between civil and state regulation is discussed.

VARIETIES OF REGULATORY CAPITALISM

The consolidation of the regulatory state and regulatory society, and the more general expansion in the number of rules, orders, bylaws, administrative guidelines, statutory instruments, and the like, are the preconditions for the emergence of regulatory capitalism. This order is defined, sustained, and legitimized by the expansion in the number and scope of rules, rule making, rule monitoring, and rule enforcement. The dynamics and content of such rule activity is shaped by the interaction of varying degrees of civil and state regulation. A typology of the modes of regulation, as they emerge from this interaction, is presented in Table 8.2. For the sake of convenience, a simple distinction is drawn between "strong" and "weak" forms of regulation. This scheme not only offers some order in the various forms of regulation that govern business and society but also allows us to suggest that GlobalGap, the civil regulator that stood at the center of our empirical examples, can not be analyzed on its own. Its interaction with state regulation is what makes the current order more complex, more hybrid, and yes, also, potentially more effective and open than the proponents and opponents of neoliberalism often suggest.

This distinction gives rise to four types of regulatory capitalism. Under *étatist* regulatory capitalism, civil regulation is weak and state regulation is strong. It represents the adaptation of the Westphalian order to the regulatory arena, and in particular the expectation of its adaptation to the realities of multilevel governance. The ideal types of supranational and intergovernmental forms of European public policy *both* fall within this category of regulatory order. In the literature on regulation, étatist forms of regulation are often described as systems of command and control with prescriptive types of rules. Prescriptive rules tell regulated entities and individuals what to do and how to do it, and tend to be highly particularistic in specifying required actions and the standards for adhering to them (May 2007, 9). This variant of regulatory capitalism usually enjoys a high degree of capacity to impose sanctions,

Table 8.2. Varieties of Regulatory Capitalism

		Civil Regulation	
		Strong	*Weak*
State Regulation	*Strong*	Regulatory Corporatism	Étatist Regulatory Capitalism
	Weak	Pluralist Regulatory Capitalism	Laissez-faire Regulatory Capitalism

as well as clear-cut lines of responsibility and thus accountability. Yet these advantages come at a price: strict authoritarianism, unreasonable rule, and capricious enforcement practices impose needless costs and generate adversarial relations between regulators and regulatees.

Laissez-faire regulatory capitalism emerges from the interaction of weak forms of civil and state regulation. Both civil and state regulations are rudimentary elements of the regulatory order, which rests on rather limited, soft forms of rules. This variety of regulatory capitalism represents the ideal of the neoliberal enthusiast, who sees both state and civil forms of regulation as constraining economic and political liberties, and therefore advocates deregulation. Laissez-faire forms of regulatory capitalism represent the contraction of the political (and not only the state) and the expansion of market mechanisms of control. The dynamics of governance in this type of regulatory capitalism either face backward to the transformation of rules into principles (that is, unspecified or vague rules, often also known as standards), or forward, toward the consolidation of regimes that are based on principles from their very outset (Braithwaite 2003).

Pluralist regulatory capitalism emerges from the interaction of weak forms of state regulation and strong forms of civil regulation. This variety of regulatory capitalism represents the Americanization of the global order in the sense that group competition and contestation create public arenas of regulation that do not rest on public sanctions and public authority. The growth in scope and diversity of voluntary forms of regulation suggests that this variety of regulatory capitalism is gaining ground at the expense of other forms of regulatory capitalism. When compared with other forms, this particular type of regulatory capitalism is characterized by adversarialism, frequent changes within the regulatory regime, and high rates of regime demise. The types of rule that may best represent this kind of regulatory capitalism are process-based regulation (sometimes also called management-based regulation) or performance-based regulation. Process-based regulation advances systems for monitoring risks by the regulatees (May 2007, 10; Coglianese and Lazer 2003); performance-based regulation emphasizes regulatory outcomes and focuses on results, while leaving it to the regulated entities to determine how best to achieve the desired results (Coglianese et al. 2002). In doing so, these two types of rule avoid conflicts that may arise from prescriptive behavior and reduce enforcement and monitoring costs. These types of rule are most likely to proliferate in systems where state coercion and other sanctions are limited.

Finally, *corporatist regulatory capitalism* results from the interaction of strong forms of both civil regulation and state regulation. In arenas of redistribution these conditions may lead to the consolidation of a corporatist order. In arenas of distribution, and especially in the context of issues of economic development, they may lead to the creation of coordinated forms of capitalism. The type of rule that is most likely to result from the interaction between strong civil regulation and state regulation varies with the particular hybrid form of regulation. In what follows, I explore the democratic qualities of this last variant of regulatory capitalism. It might well be, and this should be a subject for further research, that it is not only that civil forms of regulation such as Global-Gap are on the rise but also state and intergovernmental forms of regulation are expanding. If this is the case, we may expect the emergence of corporatist forms of regulatory capitalism for the governance of the food safety industry.

ON THE DEMOCRATIC QUALITIES OF REGULATORY CORPORATISM

To what extent is regulatory corporatism a participatory order? I suggest that participation is best expressed and sustained in the coexistence of various forms of state and civil regulators side by side and in a way that does not threaten the autonomy or the scope of the responsibilities of the civil regulators. Four participatory variants are of particular importance. The first is co-regulation, where responsibility for regulatory design or regulatory enforcement is shared by the state and civil actors. The particular scope of cooperation may vary as long as the regulatory arrangements are grounded in cooperative techniques, and the legitimacy of the regime rests at least partly on public-private cooperation.

A second form of participatory regulatory corporatism is manifested in enforced self-regulation, which was discussed earlier. A third form of regulatory corporatism is meta-regulation. The notion of meta-regulation is closely related to the notion of enforced self-regulation as formulated above; however, unlike enforced self-regulation, it allows the *regulatee* to determine its own rules. The regulatory role of the state is confined to the institutionalization and monitoring of the integrity of the work of the compliance group of the regulatees. In this sense, it is about meta-monitoring (Grabosky 1995). In Christine Parker's formulation, the notion of meta-regulation has been used as a descriptive or explanatory term within the literature on "new governance" to refer to the way in which the state's role in governance and regulation is changing (Parker 2002). Meta-regulation "entails any form of regulation (whether by tools of state law or other mechanisms) that regulates any other form of regulation" (Parker, forthcoming). Thus, it might include the legal regulation of self-regulation (e.g., putting an oversight board above a self-regulatory professional association), nonlegal methods of "regulating" internal corporate self-regulation or management (e.g., voluntary accreditation to codes of good conduct), or the regulation of national lawmaking by transnational bodies (such as the EU) (Parker forthcoming). In the words of Bronwen Morgan, it captures a desire or tendency "to think reflexively about regulation, such that rather than regulating social and individual action directly, the process of regulation itself becomes regulated" (Morgan 2003, 2).

Finally, a fourth form of regulatory corporatism is often known as "multilevel regulation." Here, regulatory authority is allocated to different levels of territorial tiers—supranational (global and regional), national, regional (domestic), and local (Marks and Hooghe 2001). There are various forms of multilevel regulation depending on the number of tiers that are involved and the particular form of allocation. Regulatory authority can be allocated on a functional basis (whereby regulatory authority is allocated to different tiers according to their capacity to deal with the problem), or on a hierarchical basis (where supreme authority is defined in one of the regulatory tiers); alternatively, it may simply be a product of incremental, path-trajectory processes (where the regime is the result of the amalgamation of patches, each designed to solve a particular aspect as it occurred on the regulatory agenda). While much of the discussion on multilevel governance (which is a broader term than multilevel regulation) focuses on the transfer of authority between one tier and another, one should also note that the overall impact of multilevel regulation can be that of accretion. Indeed, the possibility that multilevel regulation may involve the co-development of regulatory capacities in different tiers is only rarely recognized. To summarize, these four forms of hybrid regulation allow participation of civil regulators without confining civil politics to lobbying, pressuring, or plain submission.

CONCLUSIONS: TOWARD REGULATORY CORPORATISM?

A major assertion of this volume is that it is important to bind business to global policy processes in such a way that its interests and the interests of citizens are aligned to the maximum possible extent. This chapter provides some support and elaboration of this assertion from the angle of regulatory governance. It asserts that, in order to assess business power in the context of democratic policymaking, and in order to design institutions that best align business and public interests, it is necessary to understand the regulatory features of national and global governance. Most intriguing among these regulatory features are the varieties of institutions and governance structures that emerge from the interaction of civil regulation and state regulation. Participation, regulation, and capitalism are increasingly intertwined, and new forms of capitalism are associated with new forms of regulation as well as with new forms and arenas for business and civil participation. Regulation—rather than privatization and deregulation—best captures the political aspects of the environment where business and civil actors are interacting with governmental actors.

In this spirit, and with some caution, it is suggested here that we should allow for the possibility that civil regulation and state regulation are not only competing forms of governance but also complementary. That their growth and co-expansion may reflect common general social trends—be they a declining tolerance of risk (Beck 1992; Furedi 1997), a continued quest for fairness and efficiency in the operation of markets, or harmonization of international rules (Vogel 1995; Vogel 1996). The notion of regulatory corporatism allows for further conceptualization and empirical assessment of this possibility of positive-sum relations between various sources of regulation. It is also intended to challenge the zero-sum assumptions that have characterized much of the debate on global regulatory change so far. These assumptions impair our understanding of the relations and interactions between the private and the public, the global and the local, the statist and the civil. First, what we conceive as private or public is constantly changing. The relations between the two can be, and indeed may often be, those of mutual reinforcement and mutual growth, and thus positive-sum. Second, the global is not a distinct arena that takes over the local. Regulatory controls at the local level can reflect and strengthen controls at the global level and vice versa. Third, the relations between civil regulation and state regulation can also be positive-sum, supporting and mutually enforcing each other rather than the opposite.

While it is still too early to conclude that civil regulation and state regulation are both expanding, we need to adopt a broader analytical view than is usual in social scientific research. The notion of regulatory corporatism allows us to assess regulatory developments in a more coherent and open way but also to experiment with institutional hybrids that may better align business and public interests. These hybrids are less likely to upgrade state-level command and control systems of governance to the global level than to create new forms of governance. The notion of regulatory corporatism requires us to revisit the theory of democracy itself. Civil organizations, business included, are the suppliers of government functions such as rules and regulations, but this does not necessarily mean less democracy; sometimes it means more. Iterative interactions and exchanges that are based on both competition and cooperation may produce better results than the alternative options of étatist, laissez-faire, or pluralist forms of regulatory capitalism. Global democracy in the age of regulation should be less about the creation of one centralized authority at the global level than about the development of general principles of accountability, transparency, and participation as well as about some general mechanisms and instruments for monitoring and regulating the application of those principles.

NOTES

Research on this paper was supported by a grant by the Lady Davis Institute for International Relations at the Hebrew University.

1. The notion of civil regulation is not identical or a derivative of the notion of civil law. Instead, it draws on the notion of civil society as a nongovernmental source of regulation.
2. EurepGap is the acronym for Euro-Retailer Produce Working Group for Good Agricultural Practice.
3. The regulatory state should first be differentiated from the welfare state and the developmental state. The politics, policies, and administration of the welfare state are primarily geared toward redistribution. Similarly, the developmental state focuses on distribution policy to a degree that marginalizes other instruments of policy-making, such as regulation and redistribution.

REFERENCES

Arora, S. and T. N. Cason. 1996. Why do firms volunteer to exceed environmental regulations? *Land Economics* 72, no. 4): 413–32.

Ayres, I. and J. Braithwaite. 1992. *Responsive regulation: Transcending the deregulation debate.* Oxford: Oxford University Press.

Baldwin, R., and M. Cave. 1999. *Understanding regulation: Theory, strategy, and practice.* Oxford: Oxford University Press.

Bardach, E. and R. A. Kagan. 1982. *Going by the book: The problem of regulatory unreasonableness.* Philadelphia: Temple University Press.

Beck, U. 1992. *Risk society: Towards a new modernity.* London: Sage Publications.

Braithwaite, J. 2003. Meta regulation for access to justice. Paper presented at the General Aspects of Law (GALA) Seminar Series, University of California, Berkeley, Novermber 13.

———. 2008. *Regulatory capitalism: How it works, ideas for making it work better.* Cheltenham: Edward Elgar.

———, and P. Drahos. 2000. *Global business regulation.* Cambridge: Cambridge University Press.

Breyer, S. 1993. *Breaking the vicious circle: Toward effective risk regulation.* Cambridge: Harvard University Press.

Buthe, T. 2004. Governance through private authority: Non-state actors in world politics. *Journal of International Affairs* 58: 281–90.

Campbell, H. 2005. The rise and rise of EurepGAP: The European (re) invention of colonial food relations? *International Journal of Sociology of Agriculture and Food* 13, no. 2: 6–19.

———. 2006. Consultation, commerce, and contemporary agri-food systems: Ethical engagement of new systems of governance under reflexive modernity. *Integrated Assessment* 6, no. 2: 117–36.

Clarke, M. 2000. *Regulation: The social control of business between law and politics.* Hampshire: Macmillan Press.

Coglianese, C., J. Nash, and T. Olmstead. 2003. Performance-based regulation: prospects and limitations in health, safety, and environmental regulation. *Administrative Law Review* 55: 705–28.

———, and D. Lazer. 2003. Management-based regulation: Prescribing private management to achieve public goals. *Law and Society Review* 37, no. 4: 691–730.

Cutler, A. C. 2003. *Private power and global authority: Transnational merchant law in the global political economy.* Cambridge: Cambridge University Press.

———, T. Porter, and V. Haufler, eds. 1999. *Private authority and international affairs.* Albany: State University of New York Press.

Dryzek, J. S. 1996. *Democracy in capitalist times: Ideals, limits, and struggles.* New York: Oxford University Press.

———. 2000. *Deliberative democracy and beyond: Liberals, critics, contestations.* Oxford: Oxford University Press.

Freidberg, S. 2007. Supermarkets and imperial knowledge. *Cultural Geographies* 14, no. 3): 321–42.

Fuchs, D., and A. Kalfagianni. (2009) Private authority in the food chain: Implications for democratic legitimacy. This volume.

Furedi, F. 1997. *Culture of fear: Risk-taking and the morality of low expectation.* London: Cassell.

Grabosky, P. 1995. Using non-governmental resources to foster regulatory compliance. *Governance* 8: 527–50.

Guthman, J. 2007. The Polanyian way? Voluntary food labels as neoliberal governance. *Antipode* 39, no. 3: 456–78.

Hall, R. B., and T. J. Biersteker, eds. 2002. *The emergence of private authority in the international system.* Cambridge: Cambridge University Press.

Haufler, V. 2002. *A public role for the private sector: Industry self-regulation in a global economy.* Washington, DC: Carnegie Endowment for International Peace.

Hood, C., C. Scott, O. James, G. Jones, and T. Travers. 1999. *Regulation inside government.* Oxford: Oxford University Press.

Jayasuriya, K. 2001. Globalization and the changing architecture of the state: The politics of the regulatory state and the politics of negative co-ordination. *Journal of European Public Policy* 8, no. 1:101–23.

Jordana, J., and D. Levi-Faur. 2006. Towards a Latin American regulatory state? The diffusion of autonomous regulatory agencies across countries and sectors. *International Journal of Public Administration* 29: 335–66.

———, and X. Fernandez i Marin. 2008. The global diffusion of regulatory agencies: Institutional emulation and the restructuring of modern bureaucracy. Unpublished ms.

Kaldor, M. 2003. The idea of global civil society. *International Affairs* 79, no. 3: 583–93.

Katzenstein, P. 1985. *Small states in world markets: Industrial policy in Europe.* Ithaca: Cornell University Press.

Kraakman, R. 1986. Gatekeepers: The anatomy of a third-party enforcement strategy. *Journal of Law, Economics and Organization* 2: 53–104.

Kunreuther, H. C., P. J. McNulty, and Y. Kang. 2002. Third-party inspection as an alternative to command and control regulation. *Risk Analysis* 22, no. 2: 309–18.

Levi-Faur, D. 2005. The global diffusion of regulatory capitalism. *The Annals of the American Academy of Political and Social Sciences* 598: 12–32.

———, and J. Jacint. 2005. The rise of regulatory capitalism: The global diffusion of a new order. *The Annals of the American Academy of Political and Social Science* 598.

Levy, J. 2006. *The state after statism: New state activities in the age of liberalization.* Cambridge: Harvard University Press.

Li, J. S. 2003. Relation-based versus rule-based governance: An explanation of the East Asian Miracle and Asian crisis. *Review of International Economics* 11: 651–73.

Loughlin, M., and C. Scott. 1997. The regulatory state. In *Developments in British politics*. ed. Patrick Dunleavy, Ian Holliday, Andrew Gamble, and Gillian Peele, 205–19. Basingstoke: Macmillan.

Lowi, T. J. 1969. *The end of liberalism: Ideology, policy, and the crisis of public authority.* New York : W. W. Norton.

McBarnet, D., and C. Whelan. 1997. Creative compliance and the defeat of legal control: The magic of the orphan subsidiary. In *The human face of law*, ed. K. Hawkins, 177–98. Oxford: Oxford University Press.

McGowan, F., and H. Wallace. 1996. Towards a European regulatory state. *Journal of European Public Policy* 3: 560–76.

Majone, G. 1994. The rise of the regulatory state in Europe. *West European Politics* 17: 77–101.

———. 1997. From the positive to the regulatory state. *Journal of Public Policy* 17, no. 2: 139–67.

Manzetti, L., ed. 2002 *Regulatory policy in Latin America: Post-privatization realities.* Miami: North-South Center Press.

Marks, G., and L. Hooghe. 2001. *Multi-level governance and European integration.* New York: Rowman and Littlefield.

May J. P. 2007. Regulatory regimes and accountability. *Regulation & Governance* 1, no. 1: 8–26.

Migdal, J. 2001. *State in society: Studying how states and societies transform and constitute one another.* Cambridge: Cambridge University Press.

Moran, M. 2002. Review article: Understanding the regulatory state. *British Journal of Political Science* 32: 391–413.

———. 2003. *The British regulatory state: High modernism and hyper innovation.* Oxford, Oxford University Press.

Morgan, B. 2003. *Social citizenship in the shadow of competition: The bureaucratic politics of regulatory justification.* Aldershot: Ashgate.

Muller, M. 2002. *The new regulatory state in Germany.* Birmingham: Birmingham University Press.

Prakash, A. 2001. Why do firms adopt "beyond-compliance" environmental policies? *Business Strategy and the Environment* 10, no. 5: 286–99.

Parker, C. 2002. *The open corporation: Effective self-regulation and democracy.* New York: Cambridge University Press.

———. 2007. Meta-regulation: Legal accountability for corporate social responsibility? In *The new corporate accountability: Corporate social responsibility and the law*, ed. Doreen McBarnet, Aurora Voiculescu, and Tom Campbell, 207–40: Cambridge: Cambridge University Press.

Pearson, M. M. 2005. The business of governing business in China: Institutions and norms of the emerging regulatory state. *World Politics* 57, no. 2: 296–322.

Potoski and Prakash, This volume.

Power, M. 1997. *The audit society: Rituals of verification*. Oxford: Oxford University Press.

Porter, T., and K. Ronit. 2006. Self regulation as policy process: The multiple and criss-crossing stages of private rule-making. *Policy Science* 39, no. 1: 41–72.

Ribstein, E. L. 2005. *Sarbanes-Oxley after three years*. Illinois Law and Economics Working Papers Series No. LE05-016.

Rosenau, N. J., and E.-O. Czempiel. 1992. *Governance without government: Order and change in world politics*. Cambridge: Cambridge University Press.

Schmitter, P. C. 1974. Still the century of corporatism? *The Review of Politics* 36, no. 1: 85–131.

Sell, S. K. 2003. *Private power, public law. The globalization of intellectual property rights*. Cambridge: Cambridge University Press.

Slaughter, A.-M. 2004. *A new world order*. Princeton: Princeton University Press.

Strange, S. 1996. *The retreat of the state*. Cambridge: Cambridge University Press.

Vogel, D. 2005. *The market for virtue: The potential and limits of corporate social responsibility*. Washington, DC: Brookings Institution.

———. 2006. *The role of civil regulation in global economic governance*. Paper prepared for the annual meeting of the American political Science Association, Philadelphia, September.

Vogel, S. K. 1996. *Freer markets, more rules: Regulatory reform in advanced industrial countries*. Ithaca and London: Cornell University Press.

Weiss, L. 1999. *The myths of the powerless state*. Ithaca: Cornell University Press.

Williams, J. W. 2006. Private legal orders: Professional markets and the commodification of financial governance. *Social & Legal Studies* 15, no. 2: 209–35.

9

DEMOCRATIC ACCOUNTABILITY
IN GLOBAL GOVERNANCE

Business and Civil Society in Multiple Arenas

AYNSLEY KELLOW AND HANNAH MURPHY

INTRODUCTION

Over the past few decades, global governance has become an increasingly complicated enterprise. Consisting of a large number of horizon-
tally differentiated issue-based arenas, global governance provides
numerous participation opportunities for business and civil society at
the international level, as well as via regional, national, and subnational
processes. The participation of business and civil society in global governance is a growing phenomenon that has some important implications for both business authority and democratic accountability at the
global level. In illustrating the variety of ways in which these nongovernmental actors are bound to global policy processes, we argue
that the institutional structures of international organizations have significant bearing upon the democratic potential and efficacy of global-level
policymaking. The design of these institutional structures holds the
potential to better align the interests of business and citizens, which is
the key to democratic renewal at the global level.

The multi-arena, issue-based nature of decision making in global governance has not resulted (and perhaps cannot result in) in the arrangement of participants into political parties as is typically the case at the national level. Instead, the fragmented nature of global governance has rendered the formation of more or less temporary, ad hoc groups of nation-states, business, and civil society actors. The variability and complexity of these groupings is demonstrated by the enormous range of different types of nongovernmental actors that have become prominent contributors to global-level decision making. For example, business actors have presented themselves as individual firms, or collectively within industry associations, for example the Japan Automobile Manufacturers Association, as business belonging to a particular nation as in the Business Council of Australia, or as general business associations such as the International Chamber of Commerce. In this chapter, we predominantly focus on business associations (rather than individual business firms) because business largely participates in global governance through these associations rather than via individual firms. We use the terms *civil society* and *civil society organization* (CSO) to refer to all other nonprofit organizations that claim to represent various public interests. CSOs are typically issue-based, for example, those that claim to represent the "South," the environment, human rights, sustainable development, or promote fair trade, and they are organized across all levels of governance from the local to the international level. The term *nongovernmental organization* is used to refer to all types of business and civil society actors collectively.

The chapter examines the participation of business and civil society at a range of intergovernmental organizations (IGOs) in the area of economic governance and discusses the implications for business and civil society authority at the international level. We argue that the particular institutional characteristics of IGOs have significant bearing upon the formation, participation, durability, and influence of groupings of actors within global governance, which comprise nation-states, business actors, and CSOs. The most significant IGO characteristics are related to the budget size, voting structure, organizational/management structures, strength of compliance mechanisms, the formal and informal engagement/participation mechanisms for nongovernmental actors, and the type of policy that an institution deals with. We adopt Theodore Lowi's categorization of policy type—regulatory, distributive, redistributive (1964)—as a tool for characterizing each policy arena. We seek to improve understandings of how these characteristics translate into incentives and constraints that affect the constitution and participation of groups in global governance and the consequences for democratic accountability at the international level.

Arild Underdal (1979) developed a Lowian "arenas of power" approach to foreign policymaking, suggesting there are "*several* foreign policy processes . . . and that patterns of participation, interaction, and influence tend to vary systematically with the kind of issues involved" (Underdal 1979, 1). However, Underdal was dealing with the level of the nation-state, whereas we apply the approach to international regimes that might tend to institutionalize particular policy types or deal with a number of different policy types in providing international governance. The fit is not always neat, and the dynamics of issues sometimes sit uncomfortably with institutionalized arena characteristics. To foreshadow one of our examples, the OECD provides institutionalized participation for peak business and labor organizations in a kind of transnational quasi-corporatist intermediation of redistributive conflict in pursuit of economic stability and growth, but many issues with which it deals are regulatory and divide business and labor on sectoral lines, which gives rise to problems. We follow here the version of arenas of power that includes both regulation between narrowly defined interests and of narrow interests in the public interest (Wilson 1973; Kellow 1988), especially because this type of policy captures many environmental and social regulatory policies that CSOs engage with at the international level. Underdal's analysis failed to anticipate the extent of this emergence of actors at the international level—individual firms and unions, sector groups and peak associations, and various CSOs.

In the first section of the chapter, we briefly examine the insights and limitations of the literature on the participation of CSOs and business actors in global governance. Second, we review the participation mechanisms for nongovernmental actors in place at the World Bank and International Monetary Fund (IMF), the World Trade Organization (WTO), and the Organization for Economic Cooperation and Development (OECD). All four IGOs are involved in global economic governance and are typically portrayed as providing privileged access for business actors. However, we show that this is not necessarily the case and that the different characteristics of each arena provide varying participation opportunities for both business and CSOs. For each IGO, we present a number of examples of how business and civil society have contributed to decision making in these arenas and specify the particular characteristics that created leverage for nongovernmental actors. The final section summarizes our findings about the significance of the institutional characteristics for the participation of business and civil society actors in global governance. We conclude with a discussion about the democratic accountability issues arising from the current participation patterns of nongovernmental actors at the IGOs.

APPROACHES TO UNDERSTANDING CIVIL SOCIETY AND BUSINESS AT INTERNATIONAL ORGANIZATIONS

Since the 1970s, direct exchanges between most major international institutions and nongovernmental actors have proliferated. Yet there is little consensus about how relations between nongovernmental actors and IGOs, especially those dealing with economic policy, should be conducted—each organization has engaged with nongovernmental actors in a different manner. Few scholars detail the different patterns of nongovernmental actor participation that have arisen in various fora and thus there is little analysis that elucidates the particular factors that have shaped such mechanisms. For example, many accounts of non-governmental activity in international politics focus exclusively on the role of CSOs as "norm entrepreneurs" that can "reconstitute" national sovereignty and affect international decision making (Haas 1992; Sikkink 1993; Wapner 1995; Klotz 1995; Price 1998; Keck and Sikkink 1998; Khagram, Riker, and Sikkink 2002). These contributions reveal little about the role of business in international politics because they have effectively sectioned off "principled issue" actors from other types of actors such as business (Ronit 2007, 23–24). The relative neglect of business actors in studies of global governance is at odds with the widespread inference about the risks of corporate power, which is said to have increased at an unprecedented rate in recent years (see Korten 1995). Ronit (2007, 11), reflecting upon the divide between civil society scholars and those that examine the role of business in global politics, also identifies the tendency to examine CSOs in terms of their issue-area focus, in particular human rights and the environment, stating that this emphasis has worked to sideline the study of those organizations that engage with economic issues such as international trade and finance (see also Nelson 2002).

Alternatively, a relatively small but growing number of contributions have employed governance-centered approaches, treating civil society and business as competing interest groups. For example, Ronit (2007) instead views both types of actors as private organizations and CSOs as a countervailing force to business in global public policymaking (see also Sell and Prakash 2004). Peter Willetts (2000) tests the suitability of a policy networks approach to the study of global economic relations, finding that policymaking occurs within both pluralist and corporatist policy networks at the major international economic institutions. O'Brien, Goetz, Scholte, and Williams (2000) also investigate relations between nongovernmental actors and the WTO, World Bank, and IMF, though they do not focus on business actors. They examine each institution's motivation for engaging with civil society and the extent to which each has modified its practices, illustrating how institutional characteristics mediate the influence of different types of civil society organizations. The most important factors in determining whether and how an international organization responds to civil society pressure are its raison d'être, organizational structure and culture, the role of the executive head, and the vulnerability of the institution to civil society pressure (O'Brien et al. 2000, 6). Despite the authors' acknowledgment that domestic political arenas have become "battlegrounds" for influencing international policy processes (O'Brien et al. 2000, 225–28), their focus on relations between the international institutions and issue-based CSOs largely neglects the utility of the national route of influence for some nongovernmental actors, which may be of paramount importance for business at the level of the firm and industry associations.

A related body of literature details the way in which the different characteristics of arenas are used strategically by actors to advance their agendas (see, for example: Meyer-Bisch 2001; Guiraudon 2000; Lachowski 1998; Sheingate 2000; Smythe 1998; Wendon 1998). Paul Nelson (2002, 388) recognizes that because international institutions are "fundamentally shaped by the political tasks for which they are formed," civil society (and business) must take note of the political environments in which it operates and adopt appropriate strategies to influence different economic issues and arenas. For example, depending upon their objectives in relation an institution, CSOs have often attempted to either weaken international authority while seeking to protect or restore national authority, or they have attempted to invoke international authority to constrain national behavior (Nelson 2002, 387; see also Keck and Sikkink 1998).

The idea of forum-shopping is an important concept in regard to the strategic use of arenas by nongovernmental actors. Braithwaite and Drahos (2000, 564–77) provide one of the few accounts of forum-shopping in the literature, showing the way in which different arenas shape opportunity structures for actors such as business firms and associations. In doing so, they provide valuable insights into how single firms and national associations can seek either harmonization or differentiation to their advantage, and how some IGOs suit single firm action (competitive issues) or provide a sufficiently shared set of stakes to favor association. Single firms have often played an important role at the international level, especially in telecommunications (seeking to write standards to favor technologies on which they hold patents), or at the Codex Alimentarius Commission where multinational corporations such as Nestlé, Coca-Cola, Unilever, and Monsanto seek to influence food standards to favor their products. This may be contrasted with the highly globalized maritime regulatory regime, where international business associations lobby directly at International Maritime Organization (IMO) meetings, with other (more common) regimes where the national arena is more important, and where national industry associations might seek to shape the law in a dominant state and then have that law become the model for less-powerful states and for global regimes (Braithwaite and Drahos 2000, 489). The IMO, they note, has not traditionally been a propitious arena for environment CSOs, with no participation in decision making between 1958 and 1972, and the recent attempt to strip Greenpeace of its consultative status, thwarted by Greenpeace only after it lobbied "friendly" member states.

Braithwaite and Drahos's (2000) analysis, however, is limited by the fact that they are dealing only with global business *regulation*. In an attempt to extend some of their ideas, we contend that there are differences in arena characteristics which depend upon the type of policy at stake (see also Kellow 2006). Thus, we follow Underdal (1979) in suggesting (after Lowi 1964) that different types of policy can affect the character of arenas at the international level by changing the incentives for different types of actors—in other words, by altering associability. Several of Braithwaite and Drahos's cases, such as the Codex Alimentarius, are distributive (to employ Lowi's terms) rather than regulatory, because they relate to the allocation of monopolistic property rights under patents, and individual firms mobilize at the international level on issues that are competitive with other members of the sector and the sector group is limited in its ability to act. A better understanding of the relationship between arena characteristics and actor participation can be gained by making this distinction according to policy type, a characteristic that has significant bearing upon whether and how nongovernmental actors may participate at an international institution. This characterization is also useful because the different types of policy arenas often affect the kind of decision-making procedures that are enacted at IGOs.

THE INTERNATIONAL FINANCIAL INSTITUTIONS:
THE WORLD BANK AND IMF

Together, the stated mission of the International Financial Institutions (IFIs), the World Bank and IMF, is to eradicate poverty and foster economic growth and employment (World Bank 2007a). Both IFIs underpin the international capitalist system, and are frequently targeted by the "peak labor" side in redistributive terms, but the IMF is essentially a regulatory policy arena because its most important work lies in setting terms ("regulations") under which assistance with monetary stabilization is granted. The World Bank should be considered predominantly a distributive arena, because it provides financial and technical assistance to developing countries for a range of development projects. Attempts to add conditionality to these loans are attempts to add regulatory dimensions.

The bank consists of five agencies, each with a specific, but interrelated role. The International Bank for Reconstruction and Development (IBRD) and the International Development Association (IDA) are the two major organizations, while the International Finance Corporation (IFC), the Multilateral Investment Guarantee Agency, and the International Centre for Settlement of Investment Disputes (ICSID) are affiliate agencies. In contrast, the IMF is a single organization that provides conditional financial assistance to developing countries and promotes international cooperation on monetary policy. The IMF has perhaps a more contentious role since the floating of currencies of developed countries in the 1970s and 1980s, when the conditions attached to loans between developed countries were effectively set in the OECD (by a working group of its Economic Policy Committee). Its activities are now directed much more toward developing countries and conditionality is seen as largely imposed on developing countries by the United States and other dominant members.

The IMF and World Bank share many organizational characteristics. They have a common membership of 185 states that have representation on each institution's board of governors, which is responsible for general oversight of decision-making processes. Descending the organizational structure, the executive board of each institution carries out the everyday work. It is staffed by just twenty-four executive directors and therefore does not represent all 185 member states equally (see Woods 2001, 84). The United States, Japan, the United Kingdom, Germany, and France each have their own executive director while all other members are represented in large groups by the remaining nineteen executive directors. Upon joining the institutions, a nation is allocated a quota intended to reflect its weight in the world economy, which determines its level of financial contributions and voting share in each of the IFIs (IMF 2006).[1] For example, the United States, the single largest contributor, holds more than 16 percent of the vote in both the IMF and the IBRD (World Bank 2007b; IMF 2007). Japan holds almost 8 percent in the IBRD and just over 6 percent in the IMF, while the United Kingdom, Germany, and France each hold between 4 and 6 percent of the vote at each institution (World Bank 2007b; IMF 2007). As a consequence, the "donor" nations, particularly the United States, hold a great deal of power at the IFIs. As the largest shareholder, the United States selects the World Bank president and may block major decisions because an 85 percent majority is required for all such decisions (Kahler 2001). At the IMF, the managing director is typically selected by Europe.[2] In contrast, and despite having large populations that are directly affected by the IFIs, developing member states or "borrowing" nations, hold little voting power, with most least-developed nations (LDCs) having less than one percent each.[3] As a consequence, the organizational structure of the institutions favors the industrialized nations that provide the institutions with the majority of their funds.

Although CSOs and business actors are not permitted a formal participatory role in decision making at either institution, the activities of the IFIs bring them into close contact with a range of nongovernmental actors (see Scholte and Schnabel 2002; this volume, chapter 5 in which Underhill and Zhang discuss business involvement in international banking supervision and the global securities markets regulation, and chapter 10 where Lavelle examines the debate at the IMF over the Sovereign Debt Restructuring Mechanism proposal). The World Bank lends between US$15 and $20 billion per year to developing countries to carry out various infrastructure projects, which effectively amounts to investment and business opportunities totaling approximately forty thousand contracts each year for both business firms and CSOs (World Bank 2007c; Nelson 2006, 702). As the World Bank's Web site states, the organization "works with other international institutions and donors, the private sector, civil society and professional and academic associations to improve the coordination of aid policies and practices in countries, at the regional level and at the global level" (World Bank 2007d). This is in marked contrast to the situation at the IMF where the major activities are promoting stability in the global economy and lending funds to nations in financial difficulty. As such, there is less scope for nongovernmental actors to undertake governance functions at the IMF. However, the nature of the IMF's work has drawn a great deal of criticism from CSOs, who disapprove of its conditionality policies that have required affected developing nations to adopt a range of neoliberal policy measures, the privatization of public utilities for example, in return for financial assistance. These same policies, however, have been perceived favorably by general business actors such as the ICC and the Coalition of Service Industries, which generally advocate market liberalization.

In recent years, both the IMF and World Bank have developed a number of formal and informal arrangements for engaging with nongovernmental actors (see Clarke 2002). In 1982, the NGO-World Bank Committee was established, which has become increasingly active as links with civil society have increased (Woods 2001, 95). In the 1990s, the World Bank instituted a civil society outreach program whereby it hosted a number of dialogues and consultations with CSOs, enhanced its Web-based communications and employed "civil society specialists." CSOs and business have also been granted access to World Bank complaints procedures such as the World Bank Inspection Panel and IFC Ombudsman. At the IMF, a similar process of granting increased recognition to nongovernmental actors got underway in the late 1980s. The IMF's Public Affairs Division, based within its External Relations Department, was created in 1989, the organization's publications program was also expanded, and a number of seminars for CSOs were held, especially for labor unions (Scholte 1998, 44). In 1996, the IMF began issuing biannual briefing letters in order to keep civil society abreast of its activities and more recently, the focus has been on strengthening ties with local CSOs through seminars and meetings (Dawson and Bhatt 2002).

Although there is substance to criticisms of the formal engagement mechanisms for nongovernmental actors at the IFIs (see O'Brien et al. 2000; Woods 2001; Scholte 1998, 44) these processes have helped to elevate the status of nongovernmental actors in global economic governance. Business associations and labor unions have benefited most from the IMF's attempts to improve relations with nongovernmental actors (O'Brien et al. 2000, 211–13), while at the World Bank, development and environment CSOs have had some success in having their concerns addressed (see Fox and Brown 1998; Nelson 2006). The IFIs have often treated CSOs and business as "consultants" to test the viability of certain infrastructure projects in developing countries (Scholte 1998: 44). For example, the World Bank Web site states that "[b]y tapping the knowledge of specialized CSOs and giving voice to the poor by consulting with CSOs whose membership comprises poor people, the Bank can have a richer and more complete basis on which to base its decisions" (World Bank 2007e). Similarly, the IMF's interest in engaging with CSOs has been directed at not only boosting the institution's legitimacy but at improving policymaking and implementation (Thirkell-White 2005, 251; O'Brien et al. 2000, 218). This suggests that business actors and CSOs can play important roles in global economic governance and that there is some potential for institutional structures to bring the goals of citizens groups and business actors into alignment. A more immediate challenge inhibiting this goal is that while there is demand for nongovernmental input, their organizational limitations, such as capacity constraints, often prevent them from contributing in an effective manner (Porter 2007, 90).

In addition to the formal engagement mechanisms offered by the IFIs, CSOs have lobbied particular member states as an alternative method for contributing to global economic governance. During the 1990s, CSOs intensified their campaigning against certain policies of both organizations. The highest-profile campaigns have revolved around issues of environmental sustainability, third world debt, and social justice in relation to the World Bank, while the IMF has also faced criticism from civil society in regard to debt relief, its lack of transparency, as well as its structural adjustment and conditionality policies that are tied to the provision of financial assistance (see Dawson and Bhatt 2002 and Clark 2002). Civil society campaigns that have attempted to incorporate environmental sustainability values into World Bank policy resulted in the cancellation of several high-profile infrastructure projects such as the Arun III dam project in Nepal during the 1990s. According to Fox and Brown (1998), success was dependent on CSOs from developed nations working with local groups to gain the support of the United States executive director. The CSOs also lobbied the executive directors of other donor countries, which led the German and Japanese governments to question the merits of the project and this increased the pressure on the World Bank to change course (Fox and Brown 1998, 486–87). Ultimately, in 1995, the concern of donor country representatives generated by the CSOs increased the controversy surrounding the project leading newly appointed bank president James Wolfensohn to abandon the project. During the 1990s, the debt relief campaigns, led by the CSOs European Network on Debt and Development (EURODAD), 50 Years is Enough, Jubilee 2000, and its successor Jubilee +, targeted both IFIs lobbying for the one-off cancellation of the debt of LDCs (see Evans 1999; Busby 2007; and Porter 2007, 100). These campaigns have encountered some success by influencing public opinion, the media and targeting the G-7/G-8 governments, which responded with initiatives that offered to cancel the multilateral debts owed by the developing countries most in debt to the World Bank, IMF, and African Development Bank (Busby 2007, 257–58).

These accounts of civil society advocacy directed at the IFIs illustrate how their institutional characteristics shaped the ways in which nongovernmental actors can and cannot affect decision making at the organizations. The environmental and debt relief campaigns reveal that some of the limitations of the formal mechanisms for civil society engagement encouraged CSOs to target individual member states as an alternative method of influence. The particular organizational characteristics that permitted civil society to exert influence on policy outcomes in this manner were the unequal power relations of the member states that are entrenched in the voting structures and the specification of nations as "borrowers" or "donors." This is a product of the nature of the policy arenas at both the IFIs in which the donor nations have considerable clout due to their lending capacity. As Woods (2001, 96) states, "Where NGOs have allied with or used political leverage in major shareholding countries, they have exercised considerable informal power and influence." The control that developed nations wield within the IFIs by way of voting power has meant that CSOs and other nongovernmental actors need only be successful in influencing the United States and other powerful member governments in order to exert some influence over decision making.

THE WTO

The WTO, like the IFIs, is among the small number of international organizations that do not allow nongovernmental actors to formally participate in decision making. In 1996, the majority of WTO members agreed that the nature of trade negotiations, characterized by bargaining and trade-offs among its 153 member states (as of September 2008), precludes the direct involvement of nongovernmental actors in its decision-making processes (WTO 1996). The WTO is essentially a governance mechanism for regulating international trade and should therefore be considered a regulatory area in Lowi's terms (1964). Thus, it contrasts with the IFIs in that it is not a funding pool for developing nations, though it does provide some technical assistance to boost the participation of developing nations in decision making at the organization. The chief governing body of the WTO is the Ministerial Council, comprising each member's trade minister or equivalent representative, while the day-to-day work is managed by the General Council, which consists of the diplomatic representatives of members. Due to the rules-based regulatory nature of this arena, the voting structure at the WTO is very different to that at the IFIs. Officially, WTO decision making is based on consensus and negotiations can only be finalized with the agreement of all members on every aspect of every agreement, on a "take it or leave it" basis (for more detail, see Steinberg 2002 and Sampson 2000). Members are formally considered equals and therefore there is no allocation of voting shares. The exception is the WTO's Dispute Settlement Mechanism (DSM) in which there must be unanimity for a decision to be rejected.[4]

Although nongovernmental actors cannot participate in decision making at the WTO, since 1996 the WTO secretariat has put in place a number of measures to enhance its relations with nongovernmental actors. The WTO has adopted a broad conception of civil society to include both public interest CSOs (as defined in this chapter) and business associations, so long as they are nonprofit. The WTO's engagement mechanisms comprise the attendance of CSOs and business organizations upon registration (as spectators, not participants) at the biannual Ministerial Conferences, issue-specific symposia and general briefing sessions organized by the WTO Secretariat, a range of Web-based communications and initiatives, the annual WTO Public Forum open to civil society, parliamentarians, business, the media, and academia, and general day-to-day contact between the WTO Secretariat and CSOs and business groups. Like the mechanisms at the IFIs, the WTO's arrangements have been criticized on a number of grounds including shallowness, lack of reciprocity, and the alleged privileged access for business over public interest CSOs (Scholte, O'Brien, and Williams 1999; Charnovitz 2002 and 2004; Nanz and Steffek 2004). In particular, the WTO's decision to view civil society as encompassing organizations that represent business (peak associations at the subnational, national, regional, and international levels, not individual firms) has been a source of contention among critics (see Scholte et al. 1999).

In addition to the formal relations between nongovernmental actors and the WTO itself, business and civil society are increasingly pursuing the national route to affect decision making at the WTO. Since the Singapore Ministerial Conference, representatives of business and CSOs have managed to gain a place on national delegations to WTO ministerial conferences, effectively giving them insider status as official delegates rather than as nongovernmental spectators. Several member states have established national consultation programs in regard to their nations' participation at the WTO, though as Capling and Nossal (2003) note, these differ in their effectiveness in informing national positions on international trade issues. The organizations most successful in obtaining a place on the official delegations to the WTO have been trade union and business sector representatives, however,

CSO representatives are increasingly being granted access via the national route especially within developing country delegations (Ddamilura and Noor Abdi 2003). Business at the level of the firm may also gain representation at the WTO. When aggrieved by another nation's rules or processes that affect their market share, individual firms and/or specific industries lobby their states to address the issues through the DSM on their behalf (on nongovernmental actors and the DSM see Charnovitz 2000 and 2004).

In attempting to affect WTO decision making, the formation of productive relations between business, civil society, and nation-states is becoming increasingly common. This is well illustrated by the history relating to the WTO's Trade-Related Intellectual Property (TRIPS) Agreement (see Sell and May 2005). During the Uruguay Round of trade negotiations that resulted in the establishment of the WTO, prominent business associations within the United States from the pharmaceutical, media, and entertainment industries successfully lobbied the U.S. government to pursue multilateral trade rules relating to intellectual property (Sell 2003; see also chapter 6 in this volume, in which Susan Sell illuminates important aspects of the relations between the nation-states and business from the macro to the firm level, and chapter 7 by Christopher May). Following the establishment of the WTO, research pharmaceutical lobbies in the United States and Europe pressured developing WTO members to install intellectual property rights higher than those required by the WTO's TRIPS Agreement, effectively seeking to limit production of generic medicines. However, the goals of these business lobbies and powerful nations were tempered by the emergence of another grouping in international trade politics. CSOs (including Oxfam International, Médecins Sans Frontières, and ActionAid), generic pharmaceutical companies and their associations (such as CIPLA and the European Generic Medicines Association), and developing countries (notably South Africa, India, and Brazil), together fought against U.S. and European Union (EU) attempts to pressure developing countries to increase their IP protection ('t Hoen 2002; Ford 2004; and He and Murphy 2007).

In regard to the issue of a foreign investment agreement at the WTO (one of the four "Singapore issues") the political actors were similarly polarized.[5] A prominent group of CSOs (including Friends of the Earth International, Third World Network, and the South and East African Trade Institute) encouraged developing country governments to oppose the launch of investment negotiations at the WTO, providing them with research and analysis about the potential negative impacts of such an agreement. This helped foster agreement among what became the Group of 90 (G-90) developing countries at the WTO's Cancún ministerial conference in 2003. On the other side, the EU and Japan strongly supported a WTO investment agreement and were backed by general business interests such as the ICC. Debate over investment at the WTO was one of the contributors to the collapse of the 2003 Cancún ministerial conference, at which a number of CSO representatives had gained a formal seat at the table via the official delegations of African nations (see Murphy 2007).

The particular institutional characteristics of the WTO as a regulatory arena with a decision-making process based on consensus, combined with variations in the distribution of costs and benefits of different WTO agreements to different members, has resulted in the formation of group contests at this IGO. CSOs and developing countries have formed relationships that have boosted the latter's negotiating power at the WTO, where, unlike at the IFIs, the most powerful nations do not always control the agenda at ministerial conferences. Business actors have pursued a different approach, attempting to influence the WTO by lobbying powerful member governments, especially the United States. While this strategy was successful during the Uruguay Round, the creation of the WTO in 1995, where (officially) members have equal rights and decision making is based on consensus, has tempered the potency of this strategy. For business groups, then, lobbying powerful nations in order to exert influence at the WTO has resulted in mixed success. For example, business actors in service industries have seen some of their objectives realized through the development of the General Agreement on Trade in Services (GATS), the research pharmaceutical industry did not achieve all their objectives in relations to TRIPS, nor were general business interests served by the failure to launch a WTO investment agreement negotiations despite the support of the EU and the United States. However, these outcomes may be contrasted with bilateral and regional free trade agreements involving the United States in which business has exerted a greater level of influence. The WTO's role as a regulatory arena rather than a distributive policy arena means that it has a relatively small operating budget and therefore threats by powerful states to withdraw funds also results in little leverage.

THE ORGANIZATION FOR ECONOMIC COOPERATION AND DEVELOPMENT

The substantive purposes of the OECD are set out in the preamble to the Paris Convention that established it (OECD 1960). The members' goals were to promote the highest sustainable growth of their economies while improving the economic and social well-being of their peoples and acknowledging a responsibility to developing countries. Article 1 of the OECD Convention says that the organization shall promote policies designed:

- to achieve the highest sustainable economic growth and employment and a rising standard of living in Member countries, while maintaining financial stability, and thus to contribute to the development of the world economy;
- to contribute to sound economic expansion in Member as well as nonmember countries in the process of economic development; and
- to contribute to the expansion of world trade on a multilateral, nondiscriminatory basis in accordance with international obligations.

The goals of the OECD, therefore, correspond to the traditional goals of economic policy: macroeconomic stabilization, efficient resource allocation, and the distribution of income. It is quintessentially a redistributive arena in which member governments agreed from the outset to make provision for participation by peak business and labor interests, intermediating potential redistributive conflict in a quasi-corporatist fashion, and as a result sometimes struggles to handle regulatory issues that divide along sectoral lines. Decision making also proceeds on a consensus basis, although funding is in accordance with a formula based upon the relative size of the economies of members, and the largest funding member (the United States) occasionally reminds others of its relative contribution in order to secure enhanced influence.

In the 1990s, the OECD was the subject of one of the first Internet-based activist campaigns when it sought to develop a convention to liberalize the conditions under which foreign investment was to be permitted by member states, the Multilateral Agreement on Investment, or MAI (Witherell 1995). While it proposed only that states should not discriminate between rules for foreign and domestic investors, NGOs feared that the MAI would undermine the ability of members to provide effective regulation on environmental, social, or consumer grounds (see, for example, Singer and Stumberg 1999). Negotiations that had commenced in 1995 were abandoned in 1998 after a fierce NGO campaign, and the OECD subsequently moved to improve its engagement with civil society. It is often assumed that the NGOs sank the MAI (Böhmer 1998) and that this prompted the OECD to open itself up to civil society, but this is a misunderstanding of the facts of the case: the negotiations were killed by the effective withdrawal of France (Henderson 1999); and the process of opening itself up had commenced before the MAI negotiation, with only more symbolic aspects of engagement being added in response to the MAI. Indeed, CSOs were consulted during the MAI negotiation, but chose to withdraw.

It is instructive to examine the reaction by the OECD to its experience with the MAI.[6] In setting out his strategic objectives for the next two years, Secretary-General Johnston had in late 1998 noted the need to strengthen relations with civil society and secure a more productive dialogue where there were mutual interests and benefits. In the communiqué from their 1999 ministerial meeting, the member states "looked to the Organization to assist governments in the important task of improving communication and consultation with civil society."

In considering how to better engage with civil society, the OECD placed great importance upon its work and working methods, which placed limits on the extent to which it might open up to civil society. In particular, much of the value of the OECD lay in providing an intergovernmental forum where more or less confidential discussions could occur between governments. One of its core functions also consisted of a process of peer review using individual country studies or sectoral studies in which the policies of all member countries were assessed. Both these functions would probably be changed substantially if they were opened to discussion by a wide range of interests, with their value reduced if openness inhibited the ability and willingness of governments and the secretariat to engage in vigorous discussion and robust criticism. For much of the OECD's analytical work, involvement of civil society was thought to be less problematic—and, indeed, many environment NGOs (for example) had begun to participate in relevant work programs by invitation.

But the OECD was also aware that many NGOs took either a sectoral approach, or were motivated by a broad concern with equity or quality of life, whereas much of the work of the organization was concerned with matters of economic efficiency and overall economic effects, underpinned by technical description and addressed directly to governments. This was not the kind of work likely to interest many NGOs, though they were quite likely to seek to be involved in matters that were of greater saliency.

The OECD in fact has a long history of consulting with various interests, primarily with business and labor through the Business and Industry Advisory Council (BIAC) and the Trade Union Advisory Council (TUAC). BIAC and TUAC date back to the predecessor institution to the OECD, the Organization for European Economic Cooperation, which had been established to administer the Marshall Plan. Shortly after the formation of the OECD in 1960, the OECD Council reached a Decision on Relations With International Non-Governmental Organizations setting out three criteria to be satisfied by NGOs if they were to be consulted by the Organization. These were that:

1. It has wide responsibilities in general economic matters or in a specific economic sector;
2. It has affiliated bodies belonging to all or most of the member countries in the organization; and
3. It substantially represents the nongovernmental interests in the field or sector in question (OECD, 1962).

In April 1962, the OECD Council recognized BIAC and TUAC and then extended recognition in July 1962 to the International Federation of Agricultural Producers (IFAP) and the European Federation of Agriculture (EFA). The International Association of Crafts and Small and Medium-Sized Enterprises (UIAPME) was also granted the benefit of the decision, but this relationship did not develop. The OECD Committee for Agriculture continues to maintain relations with international organizations of agriculture.

The 1962 Decision on Relations With International Non-Governmental Organizations invited the secretary-general to draw up for council approval lists of NGOs, but this power to list specific NGOs has not been employed since this early period. BIAC and TUAC may attend meetings, request meetings with the organization, attend meetings, and access documents as the secretary-general sees fit. BIAC and TUAC are not observers in any OECD body and do not, strictly speaking, enjoy a privileged position in relation to any other NGO in participation in OECD meetings, because Paragraph 9 of the 1962 Decision allows any NGO (listed or not) to be invited to participate in meetings or parts of meetings. In practice, BIAC and TUAC attend very few meetings of subsidiary bodies, and where appropriate their participation is confined to specific agenda items. They do, however, enjoy the opportunity of annual Liaison Committee meetings with the OECD Council and pre-ministerial consultations to offer their views, and thus receive some advantages as specially constituted consultative partners.

BIAC and TUAC maintain relatively small secretariats, and so face the problem of deciding the particular bodies on which to focus their scarce resources, although they can draw upon additional participants from their member organizations. BIAC frequently has difficulty in representing the full range of business interests, while TUAC is generally seen as having fewer difficulties in this regard. The rules on classification and declassification of documents were relaxed in 1997 to provide greater access and transparency, with initial classification to be more widely avoided, and from 1999, electronic access was granted to BIAC and TUAC secretariats to a wider (though limited) range of documents.

The various directorates also developed ad hoc arrangements for consultation with NGOs such as Consumers International and Greenpeace on specific issues and EPOC conducted a "multi-stakeholder" consultation with BIAC, TUAC, and NGOs in April 1998. The option of opening up the OECD to consumer and environmental NGOs was considered during the 1990s, but not pursued because it was decided that the NGOs concerned were unable to commit the necessary resources and because of the difficulties in establishing which NGOs were sufficiently representative. Most NGOs did not seek formal accreditation in the same manner as provided by the granting of consultative status in the United Nations, and therefore the relatively informal process was maintained. The directorates and committees of the OECD did, in fact, engage numerous business, union, environment, and consumer groups throughout the 1990s.

Some NGOs were granted observer status. For example, the Development Assistance Committee's Working Party on Development Cooperation and Environment granted observer status to the International Institute for Environment and Development, the World Conservation Union, and the World Resources Institute. The International Association of Insurance Supervisors was an observer on the Insurance Committee, and the Worldwide Fund for Nature was an observer on EPOC's Working Group on Pesticides. There were a few cases where NGOs were invited to participate as experts, as Greenpeace was on EPOC's Working Group on Waste Management and Consumers' International on the Consumer Policy Committee.

The experience with the MAI had a limited effect on the approach by the OECD to consultation with civil society. It was recognized that the negotiation of binding international instruments of such scope was a rare occurrence for the organization, and it was considered that (once member governments decided to open up the negotiating process) better communications and consultations on that issue had occurred. It was also recognized that very little of the organization's work attracted public attention on the scale that the MAI had. Rather, the response to the MAI was to enhance the preexisting mechanisms for consultation within directorates, establish an annual "Open Forum," publicize wherever possible such consultations, encourage committees to comment explicitly upon the concerns of civil society, and to use missions by senior members of the secretariat to establish contacts with NGOs in member countries. It also decided to enhance its Web site as a means of communication and consultation and to hold major high-level meetings with a range of representative NGOs. The 1999 Ministerial recognized the need for improved transparency and clarity in policymaking and sought to improve communication and consultation with civil society, resolving to establish an OECD Forum from 2000. The OECD Forum was initiated both as a means with engaging with civil society and with outreach to "economies outside its membership." By 2002, six hundred representatives from civil society organizations were participating in the OECD Forum.

PARTICIPATION OF BUSINESS AND CIVIL SOCIETY IN GLOBAL ECONOMIC GOVERNANCE: OUTCOMES FOR DEMOCRATIC ACCOUNTABILITY AND NONGOVERNMENTAL AUTHORITY

Our examples of business and civil society participation at the IFIs, the WTO, and OECD reveal that nongovernmental contributions to global economic governance are in large part structured by the dynamics and processes in place at the institutions themselves. Among these institutional characteristics, the formal participation mechanisms for nongovernmental actors, while important, represent only one factor in this regard. Other institutional characteristics, notably the type of policy arena, the decision-making procedures and interests of nation-states as formal members of the IGOs are also significant in providing incentives and constraints for nongovernmental actor participation. In particular, the decision-making procedures greatly affect power relations among nation-states and create leverage for nongovernmental actors to influence agendas and outcomes.

A crucial determinant of nongovernmental participation in global economic governance is the manner in which decision-making processes at the various institutions condition power relations among member states. For example, the United States is a significant actor in most intergovernmental arenas, but its influence can be seen to vary from one arena to the next, depending upon the decision-making procedures in place. At the IFIs, the United States is essentially a hegemon, because the voting structures allow it to use its funding preeminence to gain influence. This is substantially less the case in the OECD and WTO, where consensus is the rule and thus any member technically possesses a veto. However, budgetary contributions in the OECD are in

line with shares of GDP, so the United States is by far the largest contributor and not averse to reminding others of this. But there is also
ample scope through voluntary contributions for others to nudge agendas along paths they favor by making funds available for work programs. Thus, the enormity of the United States' financial support is the
source of its dominance in these institutions, thus making it an attractive target for civil society and business actors wishing to influence outcomes in these arenas. Environmental NGOs, for example, have been
able to persuade the World Bank to limit funding for hydroelectric
development simply because they have been able to persuade the
United States (and other powerful donor countries) to use its influence
within the bank (Fox and Brown 1998).

Civil society has achieved more success in the World Bank and
IMF because of U.S. hegemony than they have been able to achieve in
either accessing or influencing broader international economic policy
arenas such as the WTO. As the membership of the WTO has
expanded (with the incorporation of the GATT into the WTO in 1995)
the influence of the United States has declined. This is not to say that
the United States lacks influence, but it must often draw upon its
greater leverage in other arenas to amplify its influence in the WTO
(see Susan Sell's discussion of the U.S. government's attempts to institute TRIPS-Plus provisions in bilateral and regional free trade agreements in chapter 7, this volume). The civil society campaigns in regard
to TRIPS and investment show that the consensus-based decision
making at the WTO provided the NGOs with leverage to affect outcomes. In each case, the NGOs worked to boost the influence of
developing country members (and even work with affected business
associations representing the generic pharmaceutical industry, in the
TRIPS case) to achieve outcomes opposed by powerful members, the
United States and EU. At the OECD, the defeat of the MAI occurred
because of the effective veto by France (where there is bipartisan support for statism that runs counter to the aims of the MAI), assisted by
the civil society campaign, but not decided by it. The United States,
despite being the largest funder in the OECD, could not overcome the
French veto, illustrating the significant difference between the OECD
(and WTO) and the IFIs.

Delineated by policy type and arena characteristics, CSOs have
entrenched their place in global governance in two major respects.
First, they provide services of value to IGOs by lobbying national governments to support international policy measures and reporting on a
state's noncompliance—in both instances helping overcome the limitation (formal in the case of UN agencies) on IGOs becoming involved in

the domestic affairs of member states (Kellow 2000). Second, where a developing nation-state does not have the resources or technical capacity to adequately put its interests forward in international arenas, CSOs can act as "resource enhancers" (see Tuerk 2003; and Stairs and Taylor, 1992, 128). This is especially evident at the WTO where CSOs have provided developing nations with valuable research and analysis on trade policy matters. However, this outcome is dependent upon the CSOs and developing states sharing a common goal or interest. For example, at the World Bank, CSOs have frequently rallied against infrastructure projects that may have benefited developing nations. Likewise, investment rules, whether at the OECD or WTO may also have had the potential to benefit developing nations by providing stable and consistent rules and preventing a "race to the bottom" among developing nations seeking to attract foreign investors. In an extreme example, NGOs have filled the seats granted to developing nations in IGOs—for example, Greenpeace stacked meetings of the International Whaling Commission by recruiting new (and mostly non-whaling) nations, especially developing nations, and the Seychelles was even represented by Sidney Holt, a central figure in the Save-the-Whale movement who was once chairman of Greenpeace UK and was employed by the International Fund for Animal Welfare (Epstein 2005). Thus, the influence of civil society appears greatest where developing countries are constrained by resource limitations in effectively engaging in the multiple arenas that constitute the system of global governance or on issues and in arenas where their preferences either coincide or do not conflict with the interests of hegemonic actors. This suggests that caution is required on the part of those who extol the democratic potential of CSOs in global governance.

The globalization of business associability has not replicated that of civil society. As noted in this volume's introductory chapter, business associability is highly variable depending upon the sector and this is evident in that the ICC is one of the few general business associations that operate internationally. Instead, business actors have often been approached by states to give a business point of view at various international fora. For example, during the Uruguay Round, Europe and the United States sought the support of business involved in the services industries in regard to the development of the General Agreement on Trade in Services (GATS) at the WTO. In early 1998, the EU's trade commissioner, Sir Leon Brittan, requested key European business figures to form a European services lobby, in order to inform the GATS negotiations. This resulted in the establishment of the European Services Forum.

Attempts to solicit business participation, however, are sometimes ineffective because the ways in which arena characteristics shape the conditions for engagement are overlooked. For example, climate change is a regulatory issue that splits business at the sectoral level. Yet the Framework Convention on Climate Change (FCCC) secretariat routinely looked to the International Chamber of Commerce (ICC) for a business view on climate change, overlooking the point that the issue divides business on sectoral lines, not just energy producers versus energy consumers, but coal producers versus gas producers, nuclear energy companies, renewables industries, and so on. (At the same time, the FCCC secretariat was asking for *separate* inputs from Climate Action Network (CAN) Europe and CAN North America). As a result, the ICC could find little to say on behalf of *all* business, and this engagement merely encouraged different sector groups to retreat to the nation-state and use their "privileged position" to lobby hard to protect their interests in contests to determine national interest positions at that level. Small wonder then that nations such as Australia and the United States were not carried along by Kyoto, and many of those that were are a long way from meeting their obligations (Boehmer-Christiansen and Kellow 2003). Similarly, sectoral divisions do not always gel too readily with the peak association basis for engagement at the OECD via BIAC and TUAC, which is reflective of its overriding concern with redistributive policy issues. For example, Kellow (1999) recounts competitive struggles for representation on chemical risk reduction between the synthetic chemicals sector and the metals sector, with the former playing a dominant role in BIAC's representations on chemicals (and managing to ensure the focus was on metals) while the metals sector had to belatedly secure representation at a key meeting.

There is clearly a need for improvements to business representation on the international stage, because failure to foster engagement at that level is likely to result in business choosing to participate via the national route, where its "privileged position" will yield greater influence. This contributes to the "vertical disintegration of policy" (Hanf and Underdal 1998) in the form of international instruments that fail in their implementation, which must occur at the domestic level, where they are likely to be blocked by business. This illustrates that the structural power of business is not simply replicated at the international level. As our examples have shown, international organizations are largely indifferent to the location of business and do not derive their revenue streams directly from such sources. (They derive their revenue from nation-states and some, such as the United States, enjoy structural power because of the size of these contributions). However, the structural power of business gives them the capacity to "make or break" rat-ification and compliance at the level of the nation-state.

The demands of participation are not to be underestimated for either business or civil society. As the OECD example shows, business and trade unions find there are many more opportunities for participa-tion than they can take up, and this appears to have been the case for social, consumer, and environmental groups as well. Far from being excluded during the 1990s, they were invited to participate in the work programs of the OECD from at least the early 1990s, but the demands of taking up all available opportunities proved beyond them. This real-ity is in marked contrast to scholarship that promotes the formalization of CSO participation in multilateral decision making (see Charnovitz 2000 and 2004; and Nanz and Steffek 2004). Indeed, in the context of international trade policy, an Oxfam International representative stated that the organization did not seek full participation status at the WTO but aimed to provide high-quality analytical support on trade issues and foster constructive relations with WTO delegations.[7] Therefore, while participation in high-level meetings such as ministerials may seem appealing to some CSOs, the effective work in such organizations is conducted in meticulous detail away from the public gaze, and partici-pation in such processes may be better left to member nations, which can command greater resources—though even they must be selective about where they choose to participate.

CONCLUSION

Our observations of the interactions between nation-states, business and civil society in the area of global economic governance illustrate that the formal participation mechanisms for nongovernmental actors at IGOs only begin to tell the story about the nature of group contests in this area. Indeed, a range of institutional characteristics structure the participation and formation of groups in global governance. Our exam-ples drawn from the IFIs, the WTO, and OECD reveal that the type of policy issue/arena, decision-making procedures, and the extent to which power relations between the industrialized and developing nations are replicated within decision-making processes are significant factors in this regard, confirming a general institution-centered view that arena characteristics affect the kind of participation by groups (Pierson 1993). Overall, the examples show that CSOs are more likely to attempt to participate directly at the international level while busi-ness utilizes its domestic structural power to affect outcomes via the national route. However, there are numerous other opportunities for participation, and many subtle factors that affect participation and the effectiveness of participation.

There appear from this analysis to be some limitations for CSOs to serve as agents of democracy at the international level. We have not focused here on the problem of the representativeness or accountability of the CSOs themselves, but have identified some significant constraints related to arena characteristics. There are practical limits on how effectively they engage at the international level in the detail necessary for effective global governance. And, CSOs appear to be most effective when they can take advantage of either the hegemony of dominant actors such as the United States in the World Bank or the incapacities of developing nations—neither of which resonates loudly with democratic ideals. Ironically, when added to the problem of the vertical disintegration of policy that stems from the greater influence of business at the domestic level, which can bring undone hard-fought international successes, these factors suggest civil society might wish to rethink its desire for greater access to the deliberations of IGOs. Civil society might concentrate instead on more effective engagement with national governments, seeking to secure influence in global governance by affecting national negotiating positions and participating in delegations, but (perhaps most important of all) improving the quality of implementation, which must occur at the national level.

NOTES

1. Despite recent amendments to the method by which quotas are calculated at the IMF, which increased the quotas of some developing countries, the objective of reflecting a member's weight in the world economy has remained (see IMF 2006).
2. Based on a sixty-year-old unwritten convention, the major countries of Western Europe have always nominated the IMF managing director and the United States has always nominated the World Bank president. This convention was the result of a "gentleman's agreement" struck at the 1944 Bretton Woods Conference establishing the IFIs (Kahler 2001).
3. For example, at the IBRD and IMF respectively, China holds 3.67 and 2.78 of the voting share, Brazil holds 2.07 and 1.39, India holds 2.78 and 1.89, South Africa holds 0.85 and 0.86, and Indonesia holds 0.94 and 0.95. Among the LDCs for example, Vietnam holds

0.08 and 0.16, Uganda holds 0.07 and 0.09, while Haiti holds 0.08 and 0.05 at the IBRD and IMF respectively (World Bank 2007b and IMF 2007).
4. Since the winner from such a decision will never reject it, this rule in effect makes the decision that results from the DSM automatically binding. This aspect renders the WTO a strong and relatively effective international organization.
5. The other three "Singapore issues" are competition policy, government procurement, and trade facilitation. These issues first arose at the inaugural 1996 WTO ministerial meeting in Singapore.
6. This account is informed by interviews with former Secretary-General Donald Johnston, former Deputy Secretary-General Shigehara Kumiharu, and John West, OECD Public Affairs. This research was supported by the Australian Research Council.
7. Interview with Mr Romain Benicchio, Advocacy Officer, Oxfam International Geneva Office, September 27, 2006.

REFERENCES

Böhmer, A. 1998. The struggle for a multilateral agreement on investment—an assessment of the negotiation process in the OECD. *German Yearbook of International Law* 41: 267–98.

Boehmer-Christiansen, S., and A. Kellow. 2003. *International environmental policy: interests and the failure of the Kyoto process.* Cheltenham: Edward Elgar.

Busby, J. W. 2007. Bono made Jesse Helms cry: Jubilee 2000, debt relief, and moral action in international politics. *International Studies Quarterly* 51: 247–75.

Capling, A., and K. R. Nossal. 2003. The limits of like-mindedness: Australia, Canada, and multilateral trade. In *Parties long estranged: Canada and Australia in the 20th century*, ed. Margaret MacMillan and Francine McKenzie, 229–48. Vancouver: University of British Columbia Press.

Chandler, D. 2005. *Constructing global civil society: morality and power in international relations.* Basingstoke, Hampshire; New York: Palgrave Macmillan.

Charnovitz, S. 2000. Opening the WTO to non-governmental interests. *Fordham International Law Journal* 18, no. 2: 173–216.

———. 2004. The WTO and cosmopolitics. *Journal of International Economic Law* 7, no. 3: 675–82.

Clark, J. D. 2002. The World Bank and civil society. In *Civil society and global finance*, ed. Jan Arte Scholte and Albrecht Schnabel, 111–27. London: Routledge.

Dawson, T. C, and G. Bhatt. 2002. The IMF and civil society: striking a balance. In *Civil society and global finance*, ed. Jan Arte Scholte and Albrecht Schnabel, 144–61. London: Routledge.

Ddamilura, D., and N. A., Halima. 2003. *Civil society and the WTO: participation in national trade policy design in Uganda and Kenya.* London: CAFOD.

Epstein, C. 2005. Knowledge and power in global environmental activism. *International Journal of Peace Studies.* 10, no. 1: 47–67.

Evans, H. 1999. Debt relief for the poorest countries: why did it take so long? *Development Policy Review* 17, no. 3: 267–79.

Ford, N. 2004. Patents, access to medicines, and the role of non-governmental organizations. *Journal of Generic Medicines* 1, no. 2: 137–45.

Fox, J. A., and L. D. Brown. 1998. *The struggle for accountability: the World Bank, NGOs, and grassroots movements.* Cambridge: MIT Press.

Guiraudon, V. 2000. European integration and migration policy: Vertical policy-making as venue shopping. *Journal of Common Market Studies* 38, no. 2: 251–71.

Hanf, K., and A. Underdal.1998. Domesticating international commitments: Linking national and international decision making. In *The Politics of International Environmental Management*, ed. Arild Underdal, 101–27. Dordrecht: Kluwer.

Haas, P. M. 1992. Introduction: Epistemic communities and international policy coordination. *International Organization* 46, no. 1: 1–35.

He, B., and H. Murphy. 2007. Global social justice at the WTO? The role of NGOs in constructing global social contracts. *International Affairs* 83, no. 4: 707–27.

Henderson, D. 1999. The MAI affair: A story and its lessons. Pelham Paper No. 5 (Melbourne Business School) (also Royal Institute of International Affairs, Chatham House).

IMF (International Monetary Fund). 2006. IMF board of governors approves quota and related governance reforms. *IMF Press Release*, No. 06/205, September 18, 2006. http://www.imf.org/external/np/sec/pr/2006/pr06205.htm (accessed May 10, 2007).

———. 2007. About the IMF—IMF members' quotas and voting power, and IMF Board of Governors. http://www.imf.org/external/np/sec/memdir/members.htm (accessed May 10, 2007).

Kahler, M. 2001. *Leadership selection in the major multilaterals.* Peterson Institute.

Keck, M. E., and K. Sikkink. 1998. *Activists beyond borders: Advocacy networks in international politics*. Ithaca: Cornell University Press.

Kellow, A. 1988. Promoting elegance in policy theory: simplifying Lowi's arenas of power. *Policy Studies Journal* 16: 713–24.

———. 1999. *International toxic risk management: Ideals, interests and implementation*. Cambridge: Cambridge University Press.

———. 2000. Norms, interests and environmental NGOs: The limits of cosmopolitanism. *Environmental Politics* 9, no. 3: 1–22.

———. 2002. Comparing business and public interest associability at the international level. *International Political Science Review* 23, no. 2: 175–86.

———. 2006. Forum shopping, redundancy, duplication, omissions, and overlaps: Some reflections on multi-level and multi-arena governance. Paper presented at the Fulbright Symposium, *Maritime Governance and Security: Australians and American Perspectives*, Hobart, Australia, June 28–29, 2006.

Korten, D. C. 1995. *When corporations rule the world*. London: Earthscan.

Lachowski, Z. 1998. The ban on anti-personnel mines. *SIPRI Yearbook*, 545–58.

Levy, D. L., and D. Egan. 1998. Capital contests: National and transnational channels of corporate influence on the climate change negotiations. *Politics and Society* 26, no. 3: 335–59.

Lindblom, C. E. 1977. *Politics and markets: The world's political-economic systems*. New York: Basic.

Lowi, T. J. 1964. American business, public policy, case-studies, and political theory. *World Politics* 16, no. 4: 677–715.

Meyer-Bisch, P. 2001. Social actors and sovereignty in IGOs. *International Social Science Journal* 53, no. 4: 611–19.

Nanz, P., and J. Steffek. 2004. Global governance, participation, and the public sphere. *Government and Opposition* 39, no. 2: 314–35.

Murphy, H. 2007. NGOs, agenda-setting, and the WTO. Paper presented at the Australasian Political Studies Association Conference, Melbourne, Australia, September 24–26, 2007.

Nelson, P. 2002. New agendas and new patterns of international NGO political action. *Voluntas: International Journal of Voluntary and Nonprofit Organizations* 13, no. 4: 377–92.

———. 2006. The varied and conditional integration of NGOs in the aid system: NGOs and the World Bank. *Journal of International Development* 18: 701–13.

O'Brien, R., A. M. Goetz, J. A. Scholte, and M. Williams. 2000. *Contesting global governance: Multilateral economic institutions and global social movements*. Cambridge: Cambridge University Press.

OECD (The Organization for Economic Cooperation and Development). 1960. *The Organization for Economic Co-operation and Development*. Paris: OECD.

———. 1962. *Decision on relations with international non-governmental organizations.* (C(62)45).

Pierson, P. 1993. When effect becomes cause: Policy feedback and political change. *World Politics* 45: 595–628.

Porter, T. 2007. Governance and contestation in global finance. In *Global public policy: Business and the countervailing powers of civil society*, ed. Karsten Ronit, 89–109. London: Routledge.

Ronit, K., ed. 2007. *Global public policy: business and the countervailing powers of civil society*. London: Routledge.

Sampson, G. P. 2000. The World Trade Organisation after Seattle. *The World Economy* 23, no. 9: 1097–1117.

Sell, S. 2003. *Private power, public law: The globalization of intellectual property rights*. Cambridge: Cambridge University Press.

———, and C. May 2005. *Intellectual property rights: a critical history*. Boulder: Lynne Rienner.

———, and A. Prakash. 2004. Using ideas strategically: the contest between business and NGO networks in intellectual property rights. *International Studies Quarterly* 48: 143–75.

Scholte, J. A. 1998. The IMF meets civil society. *Finance and Development* 35, no. 3: 42–45.

———, R. O'Brien, and M. Williams. 1999. The WTO and civil society. *Journal of World Trade* 33: 107–23.

———, and A. Schnabel. 2002. *Civil society and global finance*. London: Routledge.

Sheingate, A. D. 2000. Agricultural retrenchment revisited: issue definition and venue change in the United States and European Union. *Governance* 13, no. 3: 335–63.

Singer, T. O., and R. Stumberg. 1999. A multilateral agreement on investment: Would it undermine subnational environment protection? *Journal of Environment and Development* 8, no. 1: 5–23.

Smythe, E. 1998. Your place or mine? States, international organizations, and the negotiation of investment rules. *Transnational Corporations* 7, no. 3: 85–120.

Stairs, K., and P. Taylor. 1992. Non-governmental organisations and the legal protections of the oceans: A case study. In *The international politics of the environment: Actors, interests, and institutions*, ed. Andrew Hurrell and Benedict Kingsbury, 110–41. Oxford: Oxford University Press.

Steinberg, R. H. 2002. In the shadow of law or power? Consensus-based bargaining and outcomes in the GATT/WTO. *International Organization* 56, no. 2: 339–74.

Thirkell-White, B. 2004. The International Monetary Fund and civil society. *New Political Economy* 9, no. 2: 251–70.

't Hoen, E. F. M. 2002. TRIPS, pharmaceutical patents, and access to essential medicines: A long way from Seattle to Doha. *Chicago Journal of International Law* 3, no. 1: 27–46.

Tuerk, E. 2003. The role of NGOs in international governance—NGOs and developing country WTO members: Is there potential for an alliance? In *International economic governance and non-economic concerns: New challenges for the international legal order*, ed. Stefan Griller, 162–211. Vienna and New York: Springer.

Underdal, A. 1979. Issues determine politics determine policies: The case for a "rationalistic" approach to the study of foreign policy decision-making. *Cooperation and Conflict* 14: 1–9.

Wendon, B. 1998. The Commission as image-venue entrepreneur in EU social policy. *Journal of European Public Policy* 5, no. 2: 339–53.

Willetts, P. 2000. Representation of private organizations in the global diplomacy of economic policy-making. In *Private organizations in global politics*, ed. Karsten Ronit and Volker Schneider, 34–58. London: Routledge.

Wilson, J. Q. 1973. *Political organizations.* New York: Basic Books.

Witherell, W. H. 1995. The OECD Multilateral Agreement on Investment. *Transnational Corporations* 4, no. 2: 1–14.

Woods, N. 2001. Making the IMF and the World Bank more accountable. *International Affairs* 77, no. 1: 83–100.

World Bank. 2007a. About us—Working for a world free of poverty. http://web.worldbank.org/WBSITE/EXTERNAL/EXTABOUTUS/0,,pagePK:50004410~piPK:36602~theSitePK:29708,00.html (accessed April 26, 2007).

———. 2007b. Boards of Directors—IBRD: votes and subscriptions. http://web.worldbank.org/WBSITE/EXTERNAL/EXTABOUTUS/ORGANIZATION/BODEXT/0,,contentMDK:20124831~menuPK:64020035~pagePK:64020054~piPK:64020408~theSitePK:278036,00.html (accessed April 26 2007).

———. 2007c. Business center. http://web.worldbank.org/WBSITE/EXTERNAL/OPPORTUNITIES/0,,contentMDK:20061685~menuPK:51199931~pagePK:95647~piPK:95671~theSitePK:95480,00.html (accessed April 2, 2007).

———. 2007d. Partners. http://web.worldbank.org/WBSITE/EXTER-

NAL/EXTABOUTUS/0,,contentMDK:20040606~menuPK:34639~pa gePK:51123644~piPK:329829~theSitePK:29708,00.html (accessed April 2, 2007).

———. 2007e. Outreach to civil society. http://web.worldbank.org/ WBSITE/EXTERNAL/TOPICS/CSO/0,,contentMDK:20094158~men uPK:220430~pagePK:220503~piPK:220476~theSitePK:228717,00.h tml (accessed April 2, 2007).

WTO (The World Trade Organization). 1996. Guidelines for arrangements on relations with non-governmental organizations, decision adopted by the General Council on 18 July 1996. WTO Document No. WT/L/162.

10

SOVEREIGN DEBT RESTRUCTURING

Alliances Crossing the Financial Services Industry, States, and Nongovernmental Organizations

KATHRYN C. LAVELLE

INTRODUCTION

As a range of actors have become involved in global decision-making processes, the new era of transnational capital mobility has marginalized some actors and expanded the potential for the democratic participation of others. Porter and Ronit point out in the introduction to this volume that democratic features cannot be neatly inventoried; nonetheless, participation, transparency, and accountability are assets that democratic processes comprise. Questions related to them are difficult to answer within traditional international relations theory, however, because the concepts are so closely linked to national systems and voting. Moreover, as globalization progresses, the venues associated with public and private business policy have changed.

The chapter compares two policy proposals for the creation of an international bankruptcy court to argue that participation, accountability, and transparency have not necessarily increased over time, but they have been reallocated according to changes in the composition of sovereign debt markets. Political groupings of actors have changed as well, but according to commonality of interests as would be expected by the nature of sovereign debt. The public, deliberative aspects of IOs and the activities of nongovernmental organizations (NGOs) cannot be overlooked as a component of the policy initiatives that carry the day. In the latter proposal for a sovereign debt restructuring mechanism (SDRM), the deliberations forced reconsiderations of collective action clauses that many had thought were unattainable. Therefore, this chapter examines the new, wider range of actors as Porter and Ronit propose by comparing the past with the present. It asks what, if any, commonality of interests exists among states that borrow money to finance economic development and for-profit and not-for-profit non-state actors? To answer this question, I borrow a hypothesis from literature in economic sociology that predicts political coalitions of state and non-state interests to form based on the unique circumstances inherent in sovereign borrowing, regardless of whether the lender is a state, international organization, bank, or bondholder.

Sovereign debt differs from other debt insofar as there is very little a sovereign can use as collateral, and there is no international court that can force a sovereign to comply with its wishes. The only penalty that exists for creditors to impose on debtors in default is to exclude them from future credit markets. Bruce Carruthers (1996) argues that this arrangement assigns interests to lenders and borrowers based on their material relationship. Debtors depend on creditors for money. Yet creditors are beholden to their debtors once a loan is made, because the creditor then has a stake in the ability of the debtor to repay the loan. Since political institutions that could enforce debt payment do not exist when the borrower is a sovereign state, sovereign lending has been particularly risky throughout history. The British state solved the domestic problem in the seventeenth century by creating liquid financial instruments that mobilized domestic capital. Liquid instruments spread risk and allowed for the Crown to create political allies out of a broader group of creditors who could transfer obligations among themselves according to different time frames (Carruthers 1996). Applying this logic to the international development finance sphere, similar rough alliances would be expected to form between current lenders and creditors, underpinned by their common material interest in repayment and future access to loans. In short, representatives of states would be expected to ally with providers of development finance because debtor states would seek access to credit markets in the future, whereas lender states would seek to ensure the ability of the debtor to repay outstanding loans.

To explore whether these rough alliances can be observed in the current era as actors and venues have changed, the chapter takes as an initial instance a proposal for an international debt workout mechanism from the late 1970s where governments negotiated among themselves within the United Nations Conference on Trade and Development (UNCTAD) framework. In the second instance approximately twenty years later, the material lending arrangements among banks, states, and bondholders had changed. Unlike the first, in the second example the IMF's statutory proposal for an SDRM was debated among states, the New York financial community, the IMF, and NGOs. Participation broadened, but was not necessarily more accountable or transparent.

The first section of the chapter examines the issue of sovereign debt as it developed within the Group of 77 (G77) developing states in UNCTAD. The second section considers the specific proposal for an SDRM the IMF framework, and its negotiation within the network of states, IOs, and civil society. The chapter concludes with some reflections on the changing nature of transnational financial interests in the global political economy.

BLOC REPRESENTATION:
UNCTAD PROPOSES AN INTERNATIONAL DEBT COMMISSION

Although some Southern states were members of the League of Nations in the 1920s, the sovereign representation of peoples in the developing world is a relatively recent historical phenomenon. Prior to the independence of India in 1947, much of the world's population was represented in IOs through some colonial vehicle. Regional groups existed in the United Nations since its founding, but these early groupings operated for administrative purposes, chiefly to decide on candidates for seats reserved for them in nonplenary organs of the UN system (Sauvant 1981). As decolonization progressed, new states called for an UNCTAD to address issues of trade and development in an integrated manner. During the preparations for the conference, the regional groups that had formed for administrative purposes came to acquire a political meaning as well. "Group A" represented Eastern Europe excluding Yugoslavia; "Group B" represented Western Europe, the United States, and Commonwealth countries not included in groups in C or D; "Group C" represented African and Asian countries and Yugoslavia; and "Group D" represented Latin American countries.

As these groups came to be institutionalized in the bloc voting system, "A" represented industrialized communist states, "B" represented industrialized market economies, and "C" and "D" represented developing countries. The groups did retain a certain degree of their

administrative origins. That is, for election purposes and for the definition of their own regional interests the regional groups always acted
separately; for intergroup negotiation purposes, they acted in unison.
While "Group C" represented African countries, Asian countries and
Yugoslavia, it never met as such; rather the African Group and Asian
Group met separately and the "Group C" delineation was used solely
for election to offices within the organization. Therefore, the groups
either operated as three (East, West, and South) in what came to be
known as the G77 coalition, or five (East, West, Latin America, Africa,
and Asia) "political parties."

When UNCTAD was eventually formed, statehood gave the developing countries an institutional advantage both at subsequent UNCTAD
conferences and within the UNCTAD secretariat because the governing
board of the UNCTAD secretariat between conferences, the Trade and
Development Board, consisted of fifty-five geographically distributed
representatives.[1] While voting in the Trade and Development Board was
according to a one-state, one-vote, system with a requisite two-thirds
majority of representatives present and voting on matters of substance,
developing countries could permanently outvote the West when they
voted as a bloc and the communists joined them. Thus, developing
countries were successful in structuring the way relations would be conducted within the central domain of the organization to their advantage.

At the regional (or "first round") of meetings, the groups sought to
define their positions before the G77 as a whole would meet. Thus, the
first round was among countries within a region and operated on a
quid pro quo basis. Countries would exchange support for each other's
special projects, resulting in a "package deal" of proposals. If concrete
diverging interests arose, countries "split the difference" to arrive at the
maximum common denominator (or the specific demands of various
parties would be added together for a maximum proposal). At the
second round of negotiations the G77 met in plenary. At that time,
members determined that the decision-making process would be
through consensus building since a majority vote would not resolve
controversial issues among sovereign states.

"Consensus building" meant that negotiations would continue until
a consensus was reached. Consensus did *not* mean that if a roll call had
been taken, all countries would have voted in the same manner. It
meant that no member delegation made any objections, that is, no state
took formal exception to the course of action proposed. Thus, votes
were not taken on any level. Moreover, no formal records were kept at
second round meetings to ensure that discussions would be open and
frank. The process proved to be extremely time-consuming and posi-

tions that resulted were not at all flexible. The G77's quid pro quo negotiating technique and lack of a permanent secretariat led to a certain degree of intragroup mutual suspicions. The third round of negotiations occurred at the UNCTAD conference itself among the G77, Groups B and D, and China. "Hard liners" were usually delegated to negotiate with the other groups to maintain G77 solidarity. This arrangement/strategy made it difficult to find the best solution to a given problem because any compromise at the late stage of negotiations was difficult considering what had transpired before. So when compromises were agreed upon, they were usually vague or only partial solutions. Many times the issue would be revisited in future negotiations (Sauvant 1981). Therefore, the group system in UNCTAD came to mean either "take the toughest line" or "use the least common denominator" of each group, handicapping intergroup negotiations throughout UNCTAD's early history (Cordovez 1968).

The democratic representation of peoples living in the developing world in the 1960s and 1970s thus took place through a state-based system of regional economic organizations, and ultimately the G77 bloc of developing states. Although the G77 itself never had a formal secretariat, the UNCTAD secretariat provided analyses of problems and proposals for remedial actions used by the G77. In many cases, UNCTAD secretariat proposals were directly embodied in the resolutions submitted by the G77 for negotiations with developing countries (South Centre 1994). Accountability in this system rested with states and their official representatives to IOs. Nonetheless, it was not transparent to individual citizens living in much of what was then called the third world.

The G77 and Sovereign Debt

The earliest discussion of problematic sovereign debt within international organizations took place at the fourth UNCTAD conference in Nairobi in 1976. It had been prompted by skyrocketing debt levels associated with the oil shocks of those years. Countries facing default on their official, bilateral, obligations had met in the informal Paris Club since 1956. In the 1970s, they began similar informal meetings in what became known as the London Club to restructure sovereign debt owed to commercial banks.[2] When first raised in international forums, the G77 proposed replacing the Paris Club with a more formal institution to favor their interests. Toward this end, UNCTAD convened a panel of experts. When the developing countries next met to prepare for the fifth conference in Manila, the G77 issued one of the earliest policy initiatives for better creditor coordination, and a formal restructuring process for international debt. This commission would be new, and permanent. It would replace both the Paris and London Clubs. It would consist of eminent public figures convened to address the debt situation within the broader context of development.[3] In sum, it would allow for debt reorganization, coordination of all parties, a neutral mediator, and continued new financing. It did not address the issue of private debt (other than the inclusion of the London Club in the commission), albeit little private sector lending to developing countries had occurred prior to the 1970s (Zettelmeyer 2002).

The outline for the international debt commission was generated in UNCTAD's Trade and Development Board when its meeting at the secretariat turned to the issue of generalized debt relief in March 1978 (Rieffel 1985). Only a small number of European-based advocacy NGOs participated in the Nairobi and Manila conferences. Although they lobbied the OECD governments in the areas of aid, financial resources, and trade on behalf of the G77, their efforts were constrained by their scant presence in the work of the Trade and Development Board, and its subsidiary intergovernmental bodies and the proposal failed to gain momentum (Hill 2002). By October 1980, the G77 had stopped pursuing it, and had returned to Paris Club procedures. A compromise of sorts had been reached wherein Paris Club negotiations were moved from one location in the city to another, and UNCTAD would participate in the debt restructurings as an observer (Rieffel 1985).

The Composition of Debt and the G77

The lack of success of the proposal was most likely due to the divisions that already existed within the Group of 77. Divisions existed between the Latin American bloc and the oil-producing (OPEC) states, as well as among primary commodity producers over the larger issue of the Integrated Programme for Commodities (Joshi 1980).[4] Alternate analyses concluded that the proposal died because moderate members of the G77 were convinced that creditors would not leave the Paris Club (Rieffel 1985). The G77 subsequently divided openly on the issue of debt (Lavelle 1996, 2001). When discussed in international forums in the 1980s, it was discussed in a regional context. Latin American states (with access to private capital markets) pursued it in the OAS, ECLAC, and the Cartegena Group; yet the Latins sought to reschedule agreements with commercial banks.

Despite the controversies associated with them, the reschedulings of the 1980s took place in a reasonably orderly fashion. A steering committee of approximately fifteen creditor members, responsible for holding approximately 85 percent of a given country's debt, could conduct a given rescheduling during those years. Most of the major creditors to Latin American states were commercial banks, and thus the negotiators had strong incentives to cooperate. They desired to maintain good relations with the debtor state to ensure future business. As similar financial institutions, they were subject to similar regulations. If a holdout creditor chose to pursue its claims through litigation, the creditor would have to share its proceeds with the others. This obligation rendered such action rare.

Other regions addressed debt according to its source. African states borrowed mostly from public sources and looked to debt forgiveness from these sources. Not confronting the same degree of crisis in those years, the Asians did not pursue the issue (Rieffel 1985). In reflecting on the North-South dialogue, the South Centre concluded that "meaningful North-South negotiations ended at that (UNCTAD 1981) conference in Manila (Commission 1990)." By 1987 at the seventh UNCTAD conference, meetings were held in informal committees. This change opened up the rigid bloc-system where consensus had been reached within regional groups and could not be altered after the group meeting ended.

Differences in the composition of debt became even more profound in subsequent years. Beginning with Mexico in the 1990s, the Brady Plan restructured a volume of syndicated bank debt to developing countries in "Brady Bonds." Loans were exchanged for bonds that would allow the debt to be traded in financial markets where it could be priced according to its market value. This value was enhanced by the use of U.S. Treasury securities to guarantee part of the interest and principal payments (Dodd 2002). As a result, Latin American debt was not only to private sources, it was disintermediated. In the current era, emerging market bond issues have grown four times as quickly as syndicated bank loans. The variety of debt instruments and derivatives used has also grown among the debt stock.

The rising use of disintermediated credit that had been propelled by the Brady Bonds changed the picture of commonality of creditors' interests. It even eroded the premise that all creditors seek repayment as their primary goal. Some bondholders continue to seek a rapid and orderly restructuring to preserve the value of their claims. Others prefer a disorderly process that results in debt that can be purchased cheaply on the secondary market. In general, bondholders have more legal leverage than banks, and are less subject to the influence of official regulators (Krueger). Although fears of disruptive litigation may prove to be overly pessimistic, an aggressive creditor holds the potential to upset the entire process of debt workout. In one notable case an aggressive hold-out creditor, Elliott Associates, bought US$20 million of Peru's debt on the secondary market for $11 million, which was approximately one-half its actual value. Elliott then persuaded courts in the United States and Europe to prevent Peru from servicing its Brady debt until Elliott was paid. Rather than go into default, Peru settled, and paid Elliott Associates $58 million (full payment of the debt plus capitalized interest). Individuals involved in this, and other such "vulture fund" cases have pursued similar activities with the debt of Panama, Ecuador, Poland, Cote d'Ivoire, Turkmenistan, and the Democratic Republic of Congo.

Therefore, the representation of peoples living in the developing world has thus evolved from one wherein officials from third world states perceive common economic interests and pledge solidarity, to one where they perceive their interests to be more parochial. The UNCTAD negotiations were state-based, and lending was state-based as well. As the composition of sovereign debt and the political organization of the world system at the close of the cold war era changed, so too did the representative mechanisms in IOs.

THE IMF PROPOSES A SOVEREIGN DEBT RESTRUCTURING MECHANISM

The Group of 77 never operated in the Bretton Woods financial institutions. Developing countries organized themselves through the Group of 24 (G24) and various other "issue groupings" led by the North.[5] G24 deputies discuss issues and approve a document that details the consensus views of member countries on them. Similar to the G77, decision making within the G24 is by consensus. However, unlike the G77, the G24 meets twice a year, preceding the spring and fall meetings of the International Monetary and Financial Committee, and the Joint Development Committee of the World Bank and IMF. The heads of the IMF and World Bank, and senior officials of the UN system address the G24 when it meets in plenary. As the composition of sovereign debt has changed, a group of "emerging markets" led by Mexico, Brazil, and South Africa has loosely organized within the G24 and negotiated on issues more relevant to private capital markets.

Coordinating the interests of developing states in the IMF and World Bank was problematic because the G77 never operated there. The G24 is an organization of finance ministers and thus has not always been in agreement with the policy proposals of the G77. Nonetheless, the G24 receives support from an UNCTAD project that prepares a collection of research papers to generate analytical capacity and negotiating strength among developing countries with respect to international monetary and financial issues (Ali Mohammed 2001).[6]

By the 1990s, public discourse concerning the North-South gap had moved beyond conceptualizing it as among states, and toward understanding the gap as one that exists in the global social order, that is, groups or classes of rich and poor people, which cut across state boundaries (Thomas 1997). These understandings of the South replaced the concept of "colonialism" as the cause of inequality, with the more amorphous concept of "globalization" as the cause of a new, and deepening, inequality. "Globalization" itself is a process whereby power is located in global social formations, and expressed through global networks, rather than through territorially based states. Globalization erodes the authority of states differently, according to this understanding (Mittelman 2000, 2002; Hardt 2000). Despite the amorphous nature of the term *globalization* various groups have organized themselves as supporting or opposing it. Copying other successful activist networks, these groups have expanded their participation in UN forums along a new pattern for world conferences: the official UN Conference and an NGO forum held simultaneously or sequentially in the same city (Sauvant 1981).

Within the antiglobalization networks, a loose coalition of NGOs began to focus specifically on the issue of third world debt in the 1980s. Their activities were informed by the notion that developing country debt places an immoral burden on the backs of the poor (Sauvant 1981). In 1997, the Jubilee 2000 coalition called for a cancellation of debt it portrayed as a new form of slavery. Many members of the coalition opposed the conditionally based lending programs of the IMF and World Bank. Callaghy (2001) argues that these NGOs have nonetheless come to play a role in the governance of debt, determining to a large "degree who is empowered and who is not, who is represented and who is not." Unlike the bloc system of developing states that operated within UN organs and sought to expand UN activities, NGOs operate across both UN and Bretton Woods organizations. They do not necessarily seek to move jurisdiction from one organization (e.g., the GATT) to another (e.g., UNCTAD), but rather seek to engage in a policy dialogue with states, TNCs, and IOs on behalf of a given constituency.

Following the 1997 Asian financial crisis, activists, academics, and policymakers from developing countries commenced discussions about proposals to reform the global financial architecture. Among these groups, the New Rules Coalition united around the goals of an equitable, and environmentally sustainable, future; nonetheless, they acknowledged that financial resources can and must be harnessed for their vision to become a reality. Founded and chaired by Jo Marie Griesgraber, the director of policy and external relations for Oxfam America, the coalition takes issue with the "Washington Consensus" policies, yet does not seek to overthrow the international financial system.[7] Rather, it seeks to reform the existing system to benefit a wider group of participants. As is the case with many economic development NGOs, the New Rules Coalition includes religious and nonreligious NGOs. Certain key participants, such as Oxfam and the Heinrich Boll Foundation, have provided funds to allow representatives from the South to attend conferences on topical issues, such as the Tobin tax. Foundations, such as the C.S. Mott Foundation and the Open Society Institute, have provided finance as well.

The new representative arrangement challenges some longstanding modes of international participation. NGO representatives are not necessarily from the countries whose peoples they represent. Moreover, NGOs break down issues in such a way that their activities do not necessarily concur with the former groupings of states. In fact, since NGOs and coalitions of activists seek to achieve their goals in such a variety of contexts, they have an ambivalent relationship with official state representatives who perform a fixed function at a specific IO. While this arrangement lacks the solidarity of the old bloc voting system in UNCTAD, it allows for a greater diversity of perspectives to emerge from debates on financial issues. Coalitions among state and non-state actors are far more fluid.

STATE, NGO, AND G24 REPRESENTATION AND THE SDRM

When the issue of an international insolvency mechanism for sovereign debt reentered these forums in the 1990s political groupings among states and non-state actors formed, based on developing states' access to development finance, yet they also reflected the new fluidity among actors. Anne Krueger, the first deputy managing director of the IMF, presented the most significant of these proposals for a sovereign debt workout mechanism in late 2001 and early 2002. In presenting them, Krueger was motivated by her concern that an international bailout was the only mechanism available to resolve emerging market financial crises since the current system lacks incentives for countries with unsustainable debts to resolve them promptly (Krueger).

Emulating the domestic example of a U.S. Chapter 11 bankruptcy court, Krueger's proposal would have given a debtor country legal protection from creditors that obstruct necessary restructuring. In return, the debtor country would have been obligated to negotiate with its creditors in good faith, and to enact policies aimed at preventing a similar problem from recurring. In theory, debtors and creditors would have been encouraged to negotiate debt restructuring privately with this system, as opposed to defaulting on their debt as Argentina, Ecuador, and Russia have in recent years. The existence of such a court would thus move the process of debt restructuring from public to private sphere, and keep it orderly. Krueger revised her proposal after its introduction by backing off on some of its more controversial elements. In the modified proposals, the IMF's role was reduced, and the creditors role enhanced (Blustein).[8] By 2003, the four primary elements of the proposal were: a standstill period in debt collection, responsible action by the debtor, inducement for financing the sovereign during the stay, and an agreement by creditors to be bound by the final agreement.

Because the Krueger proposal chiefly addressed the issue of private debt, it was directed at the financial crises in Latin America and other "emerging markets." It would not have had a significant effect on the stock of sovereign African debt, which was mostly addressed through the Heavily Indebted Poor Countries (HIPC) initiative (Claessens 1997).[9] Nonetheless, the proposed SDRM would potentially have affected African debt in the longer term. The HIPC program is not mandatory. Thus, an SDRM would have altered compliance with HIPC by making it compulsory, and eliminated the problem of any noncompliant creditors. Furthermore, as the HIPC program has progressed, a certain degree of African debt has been sold as distressed credit to vulture funds and would have been subject to the terms of the SDRM (IMF and World Bank 2002).

Despite these differences, and the lower degree of regional differentiation in the G24's work, certain commonalities in formal positions taken by states can be determined from the statements of the constituencies of the G24. For example, statements by the Africa Group I constituency (with the exception of South Africa) expressed support for Krueger's efforts to construct an SDRM, yet only to deal with the unsustainable sovereign debts due to private external creditors and foreign debt. An SDRM could possibly proceed to other classes of debt, but only at some later time. The underlying goal of the mechanism should be to adopt an approach that creates broad debtor and creditor ownership of the process. Nonetheless, the Group I constituency supported the establishment of a Sovereign Debt Dispute Resolution Forum (as part of the package), which could operate independently from the IMF's board and management with clearly defined and limited powers (Bessa 2002; Cobb 2002). The Group I was joined in this qualified support by the representative from India (Singh 2002).

The strongest support for the IMF proposal came from the European countries and the UK. The Governor of the National Bank of Belgium, Minister of Finance of the Netherlands, and the Finance Minister from Switzerland expressed the view that an SDRM would fill a gaping hole in the existing international financial architecture. The sense of the Europeans was that with a bankruptcy court, debtors and creditors could work out problems with each other, and avoid the type of bailouts that seemed to have become increasingly necessary.

Tepid support for the proposal also emerged within the NGO community. While NGOs agreed with the IMF on the need for a court, they expressed reservations over the role of the IMF and creditors in the sovereign insolvency process. For example, Jurgen Kaiser of the German Jubilee Committee noted that the Krueger proposal was a constructive contribution to the development of a fair resolution to the debt crisis of many developing countries; the Jubilee 2000 campaign openly called for tougher controls to prevent vulture funds from making millions out of the debt crisis. However, Kaiser objected to the placement of the IMF at the center of the SDRM, and argued for a need to exempt creditors from the process, should they be willing to step in to help a country through a crisis. Any proposal would need to avoid excluding middle-income countries from its benefits, as the HIPC program does(CIDSE 2002). The South Centre expressed limited support for proposals aimed at creating a system of international bankruptcy resolution (South Centre 1999). Oxfam voiced support for the concept of collective action clauses in international bond issues as soon as possible (Oxfam 1999).

The Austrian economist Kunibert Raffer, and Jubilee Research Director Ann Pettifor expressed stronger reservations than the other NGOs over the IMF proposal on the grounds that it would not return debtor countries to sustainability, and that it would enshrine an increased role for the IMF in international law.[10] Raffer in particular favored a bankruptcy court modeled after U.S. Chapter 9, the section of the U.S. Code that deals with bankruptcies of municipalities. This approach would include all debt (i.e., official, private, and multilateral) and would allow for citizen input during the initial debt verification state. Citizens could request the invalidation of debts classified as "odious," that is, debts that lenders could have reasonably been aware were incurred by unrecognized regimes to finance expenditures that were not for the benefit of the people. This provision would have addressed the problems of corruption and theft by giving lenders an incentive to lend only to honest regimes (Palley 2005).

The G24 did not support the SDRM for two reasons. First of all, countries with access to international capital markets (i.e., the "emerging markets") were apprehensive that any open expression of support for a bankruptcy mechanism would be interpreted by the private banking community as indicating their intention to default at some future time on their commitments. Thus, support would impede their access to these markets, or raise the cost of capital in them. The second objection of the broader group had to do with the role of the IMF in the process. The G24's concern was that the IMF should not exert influence in any adjudicatory process in which it is an interested party as a creditor (Ali Mohammed).[11] Reflecting this more critical position, Mr. Pedro Malan (the Brazilian finance minister) argued that the costs of an SDRM would far outweigh its benefits. He stated that the mechanism would not resolve difficulties with determining when debt becomes unsustainable and the high costs of restructuring. Moreover, Malan argued that an international dispute resolution forum would be plagued with conflict of interest problems (Malan 2002).

As a group, the private sector was more or less united in their opposition to the proposal on the grounds that the existence of a formal mechanism would create more uncertainty, and thus drive up countries' borrowing costs. Under the Brady Plan, private lenders take losses of up to 40 percent in country workouts. IFIs and the Paris Club of government lenders reduce their claims only for HIPC countries (Rhodes 2002).[12] They argued that a formal mechanism might encourage more restructurings, which would reduce private capital flows. Countries meeting their debt obligations, but facing temporary liquidity problems, might come under domestic political pressure to file for bankruptcy.

Some others argued that of the previous eight financial crises, including Mexico, Korea, Russia, and Brazil, only Argentina's involved the type of foreign debt that the schemes are supposed to solve. Moreover, international chaos associated with these crises may be inevitable, simply due to the magnitude of the debt (Colitt 2002).[13] The Emerging Markets Traders Association (a group comprising mostly large financial institutions) argued that the proposal would severely compromise creditors' rights. The Securities Industry Association took issue with the domestic bankruptcy analogy, and questioned whether or not a collective action problem even existed among creditors on terms for restructuring (CIDSE 2002). The Financial Restructuring Group of Bingham

Danna, LLP, in New York took a less adversarial position, and argues for the need for creditors to "bail in" to a fair and participatory process that balanced the interests of creditors (UN International Conference on Financing for Development 2002).

The position of the Bush administration and the U.S. Treasury was not completely unified. Anne Krueger had been a Bush administration appointee. Paul O'Neill, then secretary of the treasury, supported the SDRM proposal as well as voluntary agreements between debtor nations and bondholders. John Taylor, the undersecretary of the treasury for international affairs, advanced a proposal for the broader use of collective action clauses in bonds, which would eliminate the need for a restructuring mechanism. Generally found in international sovereign bonds issued under English law, such clauses would limit the ability of holdout creditors to disrupt a restructuring. Similar proposals for collective action clauses had been discussed in various G7 finance ministers' statements in the 1990s but investors and issuers had rejected them: investors arguing they would make restructurings more likely, and issuers arguing they would never default (Gelpern 2003). Moreover, much of the outstanding stock of bonds does not contain these provisions and will not mature for many years. The clauses only bind holders of the same bond issue. So they do not generally affect broad restructuring, covering a wide variety of debt instruments (Krueger).[14] Despite these objections, Taylor argued that the U.S. government should favor this approach because it is more market oriented (Hill 2002). When John Snow replaced Paul O'Neill as treasury secretary, he indicated that he shared Taylor's view, and the Treasury Department adopted it as well.[15]

Outcome of the IMF's Initiative

The International Monetary and Financial Committee of the Board of Governors of the IMF considered the proposal in April 2003 and determined that there was not enough support for an SDRM to proceed with it. In the future, the committee would work on individual issues connected to the orderly resolution of financial crises, yet most observers expected further discussions concerning an SDRM to cease with this meeting (IMF 2003). Unlike the earlier UNCTAD proposal in the G77, the chief opponents to the plan were the "emerging markets" Brazil and Mexico, and individuals within the Bush administration backed by private sector interests. Therefore, the plan shared many key aspects of the earlier UNCTAD plan, and broke down over the composition of debt, as the earlier one had. As was the case in the 1980s, powerful financial interests aligned with key borrowers but did not necessarily do so publicly.

In March 2003, while the SDRM debate progressed, the Mexican government issued a US$1 billion global bond with a collective action clause. Since the private sector absorbed the issue without raising borrowing costs, the action quietly mooted a significant portion of the SDRM debate immediately prior to the IMF meeting. The Mexican Central Bank's President Guillermo Ortiz was later quoted as saying that despite the government's initial reluctance to issue bonds with collective action clauses "We were worried because it would increase our financing costs. The truth is we did it because it was a way to get rid of the SDRM."[16]

Rather than seeking creditor coordination, the industry solution brought together buy-side investors, sellers, and the official sector to protect enforcement rights and guard against "debtor mischief"(Gelpern 2003). Between the release of industry model clauses in 2003 and February 2004, seventeen countries included collective action clauses in bonds issued under New York law (Finance 2003).

Thus, while public discussions of an SDRM may have widened beyond those actors participating in the early UNCTAD proposals, the outcome was nonetheless negotiated among public and private participants aligned on the issue of continuing access to private capital markets. Both the UNCTAD and the IMF proposals sought to change the institutional arrangements surrounding sovereign debt. In both cases the public deliberations refined thinking on the policy proposals at hand but neither resulted in the establishment of a formal bankruptcy mechanism. Both proposals were defeated for the same reason: sovereign borrowers sought to preserve access to future lending and lenders sought to maximize the likelihood they would be repaid.

CONCLUSION

This chapter has argued that participatory systems in IOs have moved from more constrained, state-centric blocs where citizens' interests were packaged within the polity and then within the bloc to systems where interest groups operate directly and citizens' interests have been broken down into their constituent units and industries (e.g., women, the environment, human rights, poverty, health care, etc.) (Porter 2003). Despite these changing patterns, predictable alliances occur among borrowers and lenders. Lenders retain an interest in repayment, and borrowers retain an interest in access to capital markets. The range of actors participating in the global process reflects the new reality of transnational lending. Moreover, the complexity of this process must be accounted for in notions of democratic decision making that involve public deliberations and not just voting mechanisms, particularly when they are private, such as on the IMF's board.

The initial UNCTAD proposal responded to a set of circumstances where private lending to middle-income states had only begun to develop. Lenders were relatively homogeneous, and the borrowers advanced the proposal within the negotiating system of the G77. Within this structure, each state was represented at the bloc meeting, and then the G77 meeting, preceding an UNCTAD conference. Although it was a system of indirect representation, the NEIO proposals were generated and promoted by leadership originating in the South, such as Raul Prebisch, Julius Nyerere, Gamani Corea, and Kenneth Dadzie. The regional groups relied on the policy analyses of the regional economic commissions, and the UNCTAD secretariat. The UNCTAD debt commission proposal was one of the last of a long line of NEIO policy initiatives. It emerged at a time when UNCTAD itself had past its heyday and the G77 had fractured and operated in several venues. The directly confrontational bloc system did not produce a significant policy success in this instance, albeit it did result in some cosmetic changes in procedures at the Paris Club. Notably, though, it advanced the normative propositions that wealthier countries exploited poorer ones and that market forces result in an unequal exchange between rich and poor in the global discussion on development.

As markets for the debt of developing countries grew deeper and more sophisticated, the IMF proposal sought to solve a more recent problem in sovereign debt finance: the problem of disorderly workouts caused by holdout creditors. The confrontation over the proposal between the IMF and G24 *within* the organization has been far less hostile than the North-South confrontations of the 1970s. There has been a general agreement between the IMF and its member states that something needs to be done to coordinate repayment in increasingly atomized lending arrangements, and to prevent creditor litigation with respect to vulture funds. Thus, much of the debate was not over the need for a solution, but between using a statutory solution (i.e., collective action clauses in bonds), or an institutional solution (i.e., a more extensive SDRM) to address it. Therefore, confrontation with respect to this issue moved out of the formal institutional confines of the IMF, and G24 and into non-state actors where it was broader, yet the actors accountable to a different set of constituents.

While the IMF and Anne Krueger supported the SDRM proposal, the alliances opposing it coalesced around middle-income countries with access to private capital markets (i.e., Brazil, Mexico, and South Africa), non-state actors (i.e., banks, fund managers, etc.), receptive individuals within the Bush administration, and NGOs (i.e., Jubilee 2000, Oxfam, etc.) that sought to influence specific features of the SDRM. The debate did not take place exclusively at arranged meetings, or in preparation for a meeting. It also progressed through formal position papers posted to Web sites for this purpose. Each of the major NGOs posts its position papers online, and even certain academics have Web pages dedicated to this topic.[17] The IMF disseminated regional positions by holding press conferences with finance ministers, and then posting the transcripts on its own Web site.[18] Representatives from the IMF's legal department met with business leaders across the United States to build support for the proposal.

As expected, the lines of conflict came down to an alliance of private banking interests in the United States (emerging market creditors) and middle-income states (emerging market debtors), against the IMF and G7 states that wanted to avoid costly bailouts of the former. African states' most likely financial ally in this issue area would be multilateral lending institutions, since these institutions are the most significant source of external capital. Indeed, African states (exclusive of South Africa) expressed a degree of support for the IMF's proposal. Thus, in this issue area, sovereigns forge alliances with lenders based on the sovereigns' interest in borrowing, and the lenders' interest in repayment. These alliances are based on the states' need for capital, and the institutions' interest in repayment.

In such a system, notions of democracy need to account for the fact that these actors are thus accountable to cross-cutting constituencies. The IMF is ultimately accountable to its board and its member states. NGOs likewise are accountable to their boards, members, and the global populations they serve. Banks and bondholders are accountable to their shareholders and investors. As participation among these groups has broadened, it has not necessarily grown more transparent.

NOTES

The author would like to thank Aldo Caliari from the Center for Concern, and Frank Schroeder from the Friedrich Ebert Foundation for their assistance with the research. She would also like to thank Carlos Fortin, Benu Schneider, and Shigehisa Kasahara at the UNCTAD secretariat, Ariel Buira and Aziz Ali Mohammed at the G24 secretariat, as well as Paul O'Neill and John Taylor of the U.S. Department of the Treasury for their insights. Grants from the W. P. Jones Presidential Faculty Development Fund at Case Western Reserve University supported research in Geneva, New York, and Washington, D.C.

1. Six Eastern European representatives, thirty-one developing country representatives (twenty-two African/Asian, nine Latin American), and eighteen Western country representatives.
2. A London Club is formed at the imitative of the debtor country. London Club "Advisory Committees" are chaired by a leading financial firm and include representatives from exposed firms and non-blank creditors, such as fund managers holding sovereign bonds.
3. See "Arusha Programme for Collective Self-Reliance and Framework for Negotiations," Arusha, Tanzania, 12–16 February 1979. As reprinted in Sauvant 1981.
4. The historic record shows the G77 coalition to have been deeply divided on both material *and* normative issues throughout its existence in UNCTAD and other international organizations. The commonly held meanings within the coalition were the products of the more industrial, advanced economies such as Brazil and India, and advanced the interests of elites within those societies. The G77 was forced to minimize differences on issues such as restitution for colonialism because the colonial period had ended in such different times, and different manners, for the African, Asian, and Latin American regions. The benefits of the NIEO, such as the Integrated Programme for Commodities, as well as the Common Fund, would have accrued disproportionately to Latin American states. Thus, Africans and Latin Americans divided over these plans. Language further divided the African Group internally (Rothstein 1988, 1979; Murphy 1984; Hart 1983).
5. The G24 was established in 1974 to coordinate the positions of developing countries on monetary and finance development issues in the IMF and World Bank; it is thus a smaller and more specialized body than the G77. See "Group of 77—A Voice for Putting the Issues on the Global Agenda," *Journal of the Group of 77, 1994*, Special Edition. The membership of the G24 is segmented into regions. Region I (Africa) has Algeria, Cote d'Ivoire, Egypt, Ethiopia, Gabon, Ghana, Nigeria, South Africa, and the Democratic Republic of Congo as members. Region II (Latin America and the Caribbean)

has Argentina, Brazil, Colombia, Guatemala, Mexico, Peru, Trinidad and Tobago, and Venezuela as members. The membership of Region III (Asia and developing countries of Europe) comprises India, Iran, Lebanon, Pakistan, Philippines, Sri Lanka, and Syrian Arab Republic.

6. The project receives financial support from the International Development Research Centre of Canada, the Governments of Denmark and the Netherlands, as well as the participating countries of the G24.

7. See http://www.new-rules.org.

8. Paul Blustein, "IMF Scales Down 'Bankruptcy' Plan," *Washington Post,* April 2, 2002.

9. With the HIPC program, a country could receive debt relief from the multilateral financial institutions within a total context of poverty reduction and economic growth.

10. See http://mailbox.univie.ac.at/~rafferk5/. See also http://www.jubileeplus.org/analysis/articles/vultures_raffer.htm and http://www.jubilee2000uk.org/latest/sdr220103.htm.

11. Personal communication, Aziz Ali Mohammed, G24 Secretariat, October 16, 2002.

12. William Rhodes, "Drawbacks of an Orderly Rescue: A Formal Procedure for Countries Facing Economic Crisis Would be Inefficient and Damaging," *Financial Times,* March 22, 2002.

13. Alan Colitt, "US Scorns IMF Plan for Bankrupt Governments," *Financial Times,* April 6, 2002.

14. "Bankrupt Veto," *Financial Times,* April 4, 2002. Paul Blustein, "IMF Reform Plan Makes Comeback," *Washington Post,* April 9, 2002.

15. Alan Beattie, "US Set to Block 'Sovereign Chapter 11' Proposals." *Financial Times,* March 31, 2003, 13.

16. Jennifer Galloway, "What CACs Lack," *LatinFinance,* December 2003.

17. See, for example, http://mailbox.univie.ac.at/~rafferk5/.

18. For example, the IMF posted the transcript of its recent SDRM conference on its Web site at http://www.imf.org/external/np/exr/siminars/2003/sdrm/.

REFERENCES

Aziz, A. M.. 2001. The future role of the International Monetary Fund. G-24 Discussion Paper Series, No. 11, April. New York and Geneva: United Nations Conference on Trade and Development and Center for International Development Harvard University.

Bessa, J. M. 2002. *Global economy and financial markets—Outlook, risks, and policy responses*. Washington, DC: International Monetary Fund.

Blustein, P. IMF scales down "bankruptcy" plan. *Washington Post*, April 2, 2002, E01.

Callaghy, T. M. 2001. Networks and governance in Africa: Innovation in the debt regime. In *Intervention and transnationalism in Africa: Global-local networks of power*, ed. Thomas M. Callaghy and Robert Latham, 115–48. New York: Cambridge University Press.

Carruthers, B. G. 1996. *City of capital: Politics and markets in the English financial revolution*. Princeton: Princeton University Press.

CIDSE. 2002. *Orderly debt workouts: Dialogue between private investors, the IMF, and NGOs*. Panel discussion.

Claessens, S., E. Detragiache, R. Kanbur, and P. Wickham. 1997. HIPCs' debt review of the issues. *Journal of African Economies* 6, no. 2: 231–54.

Cobb, C. Jr. 2002. Africa needs new debt approach say finance ministers. *allAfrica.com*, September 30, 2002.

Colitt, A. B. and R. 2002. US scorns IMF plan for bankrupt governments. *Financial Times*, April 6, 2002, 7.

Cordovez, D. 1968. *UNCTAD and development diplomacy*. Middlesex, England: Journal of World Trade Law.

Dodd, R. 2002. Sovereign debt restructuring. *The Financier*, accessed at http//www.the-financier.com 8 April 2005.

Gelpern, A. 2003. How collective action is changing sovereign debt. *International Financial Law Review* (May): 19–23.

Hardt, M., and A. Negri. 2000. *Empire*. Cambridge: Harvard University Press.

Hart, J. 1983. *The NIEO: Conflict and cooperation in North-South economic relations 1974–1977*. New York: St. Martin's Press.

Hill, T. 2002. UNCTAD and NGOs: A "loyal opposition." New York: United Nations Non-Governmental Liaison Service.

IMF and World Bank. 2002. Heavily indebted poor countries (HIPC) initiative: Status of implementation. Washington, DC: IMF and World Bank.

IMF, International Monetary and Financial Committee of the Board of Governors of the. 2003. Communique. Washington, DC: IMF.

Institute for International Finance. 2003. Annual report, 2003. Washington, DC: Institute for International Finance.

Joshi, N. 1980. *Power vs. poverty: A view of UNCTAD V*. Ahmedabad, India: New Order Book Company.

Krueger, A. 2002. The evolution of emerging market capital flows: Why we need to look again at sovereign debt restructuring. Paper read at Economics Society Dinner, January 21, at Melbourne, Australia.

———. 2001. International financial architecture for 2002: A new approach to sovereign debt restructuring. Paper read at National Economists' Club Annual Members' Dinner, November 26, at American Enterprise Institute, Washington, DC.

Lavelle, K. C. 1996. Invisible hand, invisible continent: Liberalization and African states in the United Nations Conference on Trade and Development. PhD Dissertation, Political Science, Northwestern University, Evanston, Illinois.

———. 2001. Ideas within a context of power: The Africa Group in an evolving UNCTAD. *Journal of Modern African Studies* 39, no. 1: 25–50.

Malan, P. 2002. Statement by Mr. Pedro Malan. Washington, DC: International Monetary Fund.

Mittelman, J. H. 2000. *The globalization syndrome: Transformation and resistance.* Princeton: Princeton University Press.

———. 2002. Globalization: An ascendant paradigm? *International Studies Perspectives* 3.

Murphy, C. N. 1984. *The emergence of the NIEO ideology.* Boulder: Westview.

O'Brien, R., A. M. Goetz, J. A. Scholte, and M. Williams. 2000. *Contesting global governance: Multilateral economic institutions and global social movements.* Cambridge: Cambridge University Press.

Oxfam. 1999. Outcome of the IMF/World Bank September 1999 annual meetings: Implications for poverty reduction and debt relief.

Palley, T. I. 2005. Sovereign debt and restructuring proposals: A comparative look. *Ethics and International Affairs* 17, no. 2: accessed at http://www.carnegiecouncil.org April 2, 2005.

Porter, T. 2003. Technical collaboration and political conflict in the emerging regime for international financial regulation. *Review of International Political Economy* 10, no. 3: 520–51.

Rhodes, W. 2002. Drawbacks of an orderly rescue: A formal procedure for countries facing economic crisis would be inefficient and damaging. *Financial Times,* March 22, 2002, 13.

Rieffel, A. 1985. The role of the Paris Club in managing debt problems. *Essays in International Finance* 161.

Rothstein, R. L. 1979. *UNCTAD and the quest for a new international economic order.* Princeton: Princeton University Press.

————. 1988. Epitaph for a monument to a failed protest? *International Organization* 42: 725–48.

Sauvant, K. P. 1981. *The collected documents of the Group of 77, the third world without superpowers.* New York: Oceana.

————. 1981. *G-77: Evolution, structure, organization.* New York: Oceana.

Singh, J. 2002. Statement. Paper read at Board of Governors Annual Meeting, IMF and World Bank, September 29, at Washington, DC.

South Centre. 1994. *Thirty years of the Group of Seventy-Seven.* Geneva: South Centre.

————. 1999. *Financing development: Issues for a South agenda.* Geneva: South Centre.

South Commission. 1990. *Challenge to the South: The report of the South Commission.* New York: Oxford University Press.

Thomas, C. 1997. Globalization and the South. In *Globalization and the South*, ed. Peter Wilkin and Caroline Thomas, 1–17. London: Macmillan.

UN International Conference on Financing for Development. 2002. Report on side event on international insolvency framework: Advantages for indebted Southern countries? UN DESA, March 19.

Zettelmeyer, K., Rogoff, and Jeromin. 2002. Bankruptcy procedures for sovereigns: A history of ideas, 1976–2001. *IMF Staff Papers* 49, no. 3: 470–507.

11

THE COMPLEXITIES OF GLOBAL BUSINESS AUTHORITY AND THE PROMISE OF DEMOCRACY

TONY PORTER AND KARSTEN RONIT

INTRODUCTION

What conclusions can we draw about global business and democracy? The previous chapters have illustrated the enormously rich varieties of ways that global business influences or intervenes in issues relevant to democracy and that other actors seek to support or counter this. We are definitely not in the land of traditional democratic practices anymore. At the same time we also are not lost in a thicket of unfathomable complexity, nor are we bound by abstract forces operating beyond our control. The previous chapters reveal identifiable patterns, practices, vectors of force, and organizational arrangements that allow us to begin to know this new world of interaction between global business and democracy, to better understand how these two defining features of our contemporary world, which often seem to be at odds with one another, can begin to be reconciled, and to anticipate the problems that will complicate this.

The previous chapters have also strongly confirmed the urgent need to reconcile global business authority and democracy. The expansion of businesses and business authority at the global level has far outpaced the expansion of democracy, and even where elements of transnational democracy have appeared the influence of citizens is

279

usually much weaker than the influence of business. Relative to the ideal of democracy at the national level that is so fundamental to the identity and legitimacy of an increasing number of states today, the shift in authority to a much less democratic global level definitely represents decay, and this gives this book's topic its urgency. However, as we discuss further below, change in particular global settings or particular industries is not unidirectional. This too is a crucial message of the book for democracy. If we ignore areas in which transnational democracy is subtly growing we will fail to seize opportunities to further renew democracy. Our disaggregation of the levels of business and the elements of democracy is important in avoiding using too broad a brush in assessing the renewal, stalemate, or decay of democracy, and thereby painting over the emergent democratic elements that might otherwise be nurtured.

The first of this chapter's two parts addresses the ways in which the multilevel organization of global business is relevant to democracy. Certain themes are reminiscent of discussions of democracy and business at the national level in an earlier historical period, including the way in which business organizes itself to leverage the state and to exercise other forms of power and influence. However, at the global level this is much more complex.

A great deal of attention has been devoted to the way in which globalization has been accompanied by the reconfiguration of public authority, using concepts such as multilevel governance. However, comparable attention has not been devoted to the political significance of the reorganization of business power. A first task of this chapter, then, is to address this shortcoming in our knowledge. The three level distinction introduced in the introductory chapter provides a useful starting point, and we begin our analysis of the organization of business power by reviewing the significance of each level across the various cases presented in the volume. However, the preceding chapters have revealed key aspects of business power that cut across and complicate these three levels. Most important is the role of structural power, which both cuts across and supports the expressions of business power operating at one or another of these three levels. Relatedly, an exercise of business power often draws upon elements of power associated with more than one level so simultaneously and inseparably that it is not possible to meaningfully categorize that exercise of power as belonging at one level. Sometimes this reflects the emerging or ongoing constitution of a new industry or policy field (such as intellectual property or the environment). Finally, business power interacts with multiple levels of public authority in ways that further complicate the three-level typology. In short, there is a great deal of complexity that works through and around the three levels. This complexity relates both to the fluidity associated with our late-modern globalizing world more generally and to particular cases of business strategically engaging in a politics of scale.

The second of the chapter's two parts addresses the way in which these multiple levels of business organization interact with democratic practices and principles. We start by assessing the presence and absence of participation, transparency, and accountability across the different levels of business organization and different policy fields that the preceding chapters present, highlighting the potential and limitations of aligning business interests with democracy that these reveal. Of course, the chapter authors are not engaged in a single joint dispassionate measurement of democracy. As noted in the introduction, this in itself would run counter to the idea of democracy, which is and should be inherently contested, and the preceding chapters are important for the variation they display in frameworks for making their assessments of democracy.

We then discuss how, just as with the organization of business, the practice of democracy overflows the threefold typology we set out in the introductory chapter. Participation, transparency, and accountability are interdependent. As well, although these properties of democracy are more generalizable to complex global contexts than more traditional ones such as competitive party elections, they cannot subsume all the interactions that are crucial for understanding the interaction of global business and democracy. Three additional factors are especially evident from the preceding chapters: (1) contestations over the structural power of business; (2) contestations over the boundaries of the public sphere, and therefore the ranges of activities that should properly be subject to democracy; and (3) how the public interest is determined.

In our use of participation, transparency, and accountability as generalizable properties of democracy it is important not to forget or obscure the importance of particular institutional forms. Governments that are elected and held accountable at the national level in traditional democratic practices continue to be important. Deliberative democracy, direct action, voluntary initiatives, and interstate politics, including ones that involve democracy and power asymmetries among states and regions, involve a variety of institutional forms that have differing implications for democracy, and drawing these out from the cases examined in the book is also important.

THE COMPLEX ORGANIZATION OF GLOBAL BUSINESS

Understanding how business organizes for political action is important for analyzing its relationship to democracy, not only because this helps us assess the power of business, and thus the degree to which this power improves, maintains, or undermines democracy, but also to assess the concrete institutional mechanisms that pertain to business adherence to democratic principles and practices. In other words, its organization can both enable and constrain business, and in either case it provides a key interface with which business interacts with other actors and modes of social organization.

Before examining the particular forms of business organization that are revealed by previous chapters it is useful to briefly reflect on a prior question of the ontology of business organization: Is the organization of business a fundamental social category itself or is it better understood as an expression of different social category, such as transactions, law, capitalism, etc.? Or, put differently, looking at business organization as a link in a chain of causation, should we start with the organizational business forms that can be identified and look at their significance for democracy, or should we push back farther in the chain to those other social categories?

One approach to this question can, for instance, be discerned in the literature on business associability, where forms and changes in the multi-tiered character of business associations can be considered. Accordingly, business responds in functional ways to business association factors such as the logic of membership (the effects on organization of the need to represent and service members) and the logic of influence (the impact on organization of the need to influence government and other actors), including features of industry (for instance, concentration) and of public authority (for instance, federalist versus unitary structures).

An alternative approach to these ontological issues would foreground both the process by which actors and agents are constituted and legitimized and the politics of scale involved in the appearance of activities at one or another level. From these perspectives there is a greater emphasis on contingent factors in the successes and failures of business to organize itself and to operate at the scale that best allows it to achieve its goals. In this context much may depend on the ability of business to discursively frame its goals in ways that resonate with broader principles or enroll other actors that in turn may be most evident at one scale or another. One can include also in this approach questions about the way that corporations can make use of outsourcing and subcontracting so that their core remains but there is an outer band, which is sometimes (and for some purposes) within the corporate organizational structure yet remains deniable and outside it for other purposes such as when the corporation faces criticisms. This can blur and unsettle the definition of any specific corporation, turning aspects of their organization into chimera-like ghostly edges that fade and disappear—i.e., the ontology of the corporation is soft at the edges.[1]

These different approaches to the ontological status of business organization have implications for democracy because they can affect assessments of the degree and manner in which the functional or structural imperatives of business can or should be molded to democratic imperatives. Our chapters display considerable variation in their approaches to these ontological issues. To some extent the organizational forms and practices adopted by business seem to respond to functional imperatives, such as the need to optimize organizational form to varying opportunity structures offered by the three international organizations that Kellow and Murphy examine; the functional requisites associated with constraining free riding and building reputation and credibility that Prakash and Potoski analyze; or the "profit-imperative" of corporations to which Smith refers. At the same time, there are numerous examples of initiatives by business and its critics that do not seem predetermined by functional imperatives, but instead reflect political clashes that are played out across different jurisdictions and scales, as with the conflicts associated with the World Health Organization (WHO) in Thailand analyzed by Sell or the undue influence of financial market actors in policy processes that Underhill and Zhang analyze. May explicitly challenges the functionality and legitimacy of the corporate form that has often been taken for granted in analyses of business organization. The various chapters suggest, then, that the forms of business organization that this section discusses involve variation in their mutability, but also that in analyzing these variations we need to be mindful of ontological differences that will not be fully resolvable empirically but will be and should be always open to debate.

THE MULTIPLE PATTERNS OF BUSINESS POLITICAL INVOLVEMENT

Corporate Actions and Arrangements

There are numerous examples of unilateral firm level initiatives in our chapters. These include Gilead's Viread Access Program for (glacially slow) delivery of anti-retroviral medication to developing countries,

Abbott's conflicts with Doctors without Borders over its HIV/AIDS med-
ication, and the similar conflict between Thai activists and Bristol-Myers
Squibb. Sell also discusses Novartis's targeting of leukemia patients in
South Korea, Abbott Laboratories' threatening legal action against ACT-
UP Paris, and Pfizer's aggressive lawsuits against two individuals in the
Philippines. Individual retailers and their brands are important in the
private food safety arrangements discussed by Fuchs and Kalfagianni.
As analyzed by Smith, the Global Compact (GC) really depends upon
the actions of individual firms to achieve its stated goals, and this is a
key part of its ineffectiveness. Lavelle provides the example of the "vulture" firms such as Elliott Associates, which in picking up distressed
sovereign debt and threatening legal action to recover the full value of
that debt from governments changed the structure of interactions
between states and financial markets. May notes the role of General
Motors in securing the dominance of leaded gasoline, of Microsoft in
securing the dominance of Windows, the roles of Ford and Fergusson
in agricultural tractor technologies, ICI's role in the conflict with paint
inventor Kane Kramer, and Electrolux's with inventor John North. In the
financial case analyzed by Underhill and Zhang individual firms play an
important role not just in influencing regulators but in implementing
regulatory standards. In the case of banking this includes the integration of proprietary internal risk management systems into regulatory
arrangements, and in the case of securities a great many stock
exchanges and their regulatory arrangements have been "demutual-
ized"—converted from clubs to firms. In the case of the clubs analyzed
by Prakash and Potoski many of the reputational effects that motivate
clubs are experienced at the individual firm level, and indeed it is this
interplay between the firm and club levels that is crucial for understanding club formation more generally. To some degree individual
firms play a role even in the public sector arrangements analyzed by
Kellow and Murphy, such as when a complaint by a firm leads to a
trade dispute at the World Trade Organization (WTO). However, in
these intergovernmental organizations this type of firm initiative must
be mediated through public sector actors and accordingly they are
weaker than in other cases.

In each of these cases these firms' initiatives would often be seen
as simply the pursuit of commercial opportunity in the marketplace and
therefore irrelevant to politics and democracy. However, the contexts
provided by the chapters in which these are presented make clear that
this view is far too narrow. In each case, sometimes using politics,
sometimes using market power, sometimes using the law, corporate initiatives are important. According to Levi-Faur an important shift in cor-

porate activity can be discerned in regulatory capitalism. Major efforts are invested in adapting to markets but more and more battles between corporations over the rules of competition take place on the political scene, and policy outcomes are here decisive in gaining the competitive edge. However, this does not necessarily suggest that individual corporations avoid collective action but then battles are fought over the industry's strategy in relation to regulation. Sometimes also through the dominance of a technology, these firms seek to influence rules and norms, alter distributions of wealth, or deter critics in ways that go beyond the commercial interests involved in the exchange of a product and concern the public interest or the underlying rules that shape or constitute commercial transactions—issues that should properly be the subject of democratic deliberation and discussion. This points us to a set of related issues, including structural power, the public interest, and the boundaries of the public sphere, which we address in the subsequent sections.

Industries and Regulation

Our chapters also provide examples of business organized at the industry level. Some bring a smaller number of firms together on a voluntary basis but do not seek to cover the whole industry, whereas some associations embrace more or less all corporations in a global context. The private food standards groups discussed by Fuchs and Kalfagianni, including the British Retail Consortium (BRC), the Global Food Safety Initiative (GFSI), GLOBALGAP, and FOODTRACE, are examples. Also Levi-Faur investigates one of these schemes, namely the GLOBALGAP, which is a voluntary scheme and a business-to-business standard that is very encompassing. Producers and retailers in a vast number of countries are involved and it spans various corporate entities along the production chain. It is, however, difficult to include civil society or public institutions, and it lacks strong coercive power.

As Lavelle notes, in the international financial debates about debt mechanisms the Emerging Markets Traders Association (EMTA) (with a membership of mostly large financial institutions) and the Securities Industry Association (SIA) played a role. As analyzed by Underhill and Zhang, in the work of the Basel Committee on Banking Supervision (BC) the Institute of International Finance (IIF), which was founded by transnational banks, played a crucial role, while in the case of the International Organization of Securities Commissions (IOSCO) the private sector World Federation of Exchanges (WFE) also worked to ensure that outcomes were favorable to business. In the pharmaceutical industry analyzed by Sell, the U.S.-based Pharmaceutical Research and Manufacturers of America (PhRMA) and the International Federation of Pharmaceutical Manufacturers Association (IFPMA) are involved. Kellow and Murphy comment on the formalized relationship between the OECD and the international organizations of agriculture, and they also note the role of single corporations such as Nestlé, Coca-Cola, Unilever, and Monsanto in influencing food standards at FAO's Codex Alimentarius Commission.

While the chapter by Prakash and Potoski talks about clubs in a generic fashion that could apply at both the transindustry and industry levels, probably the types of collective action problems they address are most often associated with a field of business activity that is sufficiently perceived as having a common identity and established boundaries that it would be seen as meriting an "industry" label. The chemical industry's Responsible Care club and the forestry industry's Sustainable Forestry Initiative are examples that they provide. However, ISO 14001 and the Environmental Protection Agency's Performance Track are examples of transindustry-related regulation to which clubs analysis is also applicable, but in these cases broader organizational support from private and public bodies are relevant. Indeed, this may reflect greater difficulties for business of independently organizing strong clubs where the boundaries and recognized identity that are associated with specific industries are absent.

At the industry level, more informal arrangements are also some of the basic features of the organization of business, and these can be sustained by particular practical problems or technologies. For instance, Lavelle notes the collaboration of banks in negotiating with developing countries in the 1980s debt crisis. The collective action clauses that were instituted in bonds following the crises of the 1990s involve in effect the legalized and contractual constitution of a temporary community of bondholders, including businesses and individual investors, a reflection of the more dispersed character of global financial flows in the later period. Fuchs and Kalfagianni discuss the supply chains that extend from the retailers through to small producers in developing countries, a set of entities that are constituted by a hybrid mix of contracts, reciprocity, trust, dependence, and electronic technologies. Mergers, acquisitions, and increasing concentration levels in industries such as food retailing and pharmaceuticals enhance the power of those industries.

Taken together, these examples show that industry-level forms of business organization can be effective either in promoting the interests of business at the expense of other interests, including the public interest, or in aligning the interests of business and democracy. Since the types of business challenges analyzed by Prakash and Potoski are often likely to be especially common to firms in an industry, they should also often therefore help strengthen collective action on the industry level. Part of the difficulty of holding accountable businesses active in promoting transindustry projects, such as the Global Compact analyzed by Smith or the intellectual property case analyzed by May, is the greater variety and fewer established institutional arrangements as compared to industry associations. Nevertheless, while the business level is especially important organizationally, cases such as those analyzed by Fuchs and Kalfagianni and Underhill and Zhang certainly remind us that effective business organization at the industry level will need effective public sector rules if it is to be compatible with democracy.

Encompassing Business Activities and Policies

Our chapters provide a number of examples of general or transindustry forms of business organization. As noted in chapter 1, the International Chamber of Commerce (ICC) bills itself as the only global business organization. Smith notes the importance of meetings with the ICC for UN Secretary General Kofi Annan in strengthening the links between business and the UN. The World Economic Forum (WEF), the annual meeting bringing together high-level figures from business and governments, played a similar role. Kellow and Murphy also note the prominence of the ICC as one of a few global transindustry associations, but point out that the very wide range of business interests it seeks to represent can paralyze it on certain issues, such as climate change.

There are also general or transindustry organizations that have been fostered by public sector initiatives. The Business and Industry Advisory Council (BIAC), discussed by Kellow and Murphy, created alongside the Trade Union Advisory Council (TUAC) by the OECD in 1962, is the oldest and most general of these. While the BIAC has limited participation in the OECD's subsidiary bodies, it does provide a gateway for more general access to the OECD for business. As the OECD has developed an increasing number of collaborations with other actors these have increased opportunities for business influence. Until recently the OECD's significant role in shaping national and transnational public sector institutions has been generally overlooked but as this role begins to be more recognized the significance of BIAC becomes more evident as well. However, Kellow and Murphy note that like the ICC sectoral divisions can hinder the ability of BIAC to represent business.

The Global Compact (GC) analyzed by Smith is a different example of an encompassing initiative brought to life by the public sector, which is a meeting place for a relatively fragmented global community rather than a business organization per se. Although its Web site lists the UN as "an authoritative convener and facilitator" of the GC, and actors other than business are involved, Smith highlights the degree to which the GC is strongly oriented toward the interests of business. Unlike the BIAC, its ostensible purpose is to alter the conduct of its business members rather than to influence public policy. However, this distinction should not be overstated. As the example of the OECD's Corporate Governance Guidelines shows, the OECD's business-related work can seek directly to influence business conduct, and as Smith argues, the Global Compact has had a more general impact on public policy by forestalling alternative and more effective mechanisms of accountability.

A more recent example of a transindustry association fostered by public sector initiatives, which Kellow and Murphy also note, is the regional European Services Forum (ESF), the origins of which date back to a search by governments for business interlocutors during the Uruguay Round. The U.S.-based counterpart to the ESF, the US Coalition of Service Industries (CSI), was also formed during the Uruguay Round, but both organizations have evolved to become very assertive voices for a range of business interests on service issues. The CSI is a founding member of the Global Services Network (GSN), which brings together leading business actors from around the world concerned about the liberalization of trade in services.

Intellectual property is an issue that is inherently transindustry but not equally relevant to the whole business world, and the chapters by Sell and May provide further examples of forms of transindustry business organization. As illustrated by May, the eighteenth-century Cornish mine owners who sought to resist James Watt's attempt to use patents to monopolize steam engine technology, while coming from a particular industry, were addressing an issue that cut across many industries. The Business Software Alliance's (BSA) recent opposition to the pharmaceutical industry's attempt to further strengthen patents is similar. However, business organizations devoted to strengthening intellectual property rules, such as the International Intellectual Property Alliance (IIPA), have been much more frequent.

As analyzed by Sell, the Intellectual Property Committee (IPC) represented the pharmaceutical, agricultural chemical, software, and entertainment sectors in its successful effort to put the issue on the agenda in the Uruguay Round trade negotiations. The Intellectual Property Owners Association (IPO), established in 1972 and now priding itself on "serving the intellectual property community in the US and worldwide," is an older and more general purpose business organization. Also the American BioIndustry Alliance (ABIA) can be regarded as a transindustry association, although biotechnology is in the process of becoming a distinct industry.

Although it has a longer history as being defined as an industry, finance displays some of the transindustry characteristics evident in intellectual property since it is so important for industry in general, both in terms of the financial resources it mobilizes and financial control mechanisms such as financial reporting and accounting. The sovereign debt controversies analyzed by Lavelle drew in a great many actors and took the form in part of interstate negotiations because the implications of the controversies extended far beyond the financial industry. The two international institutions analyzed by Underhill and Zhang—one focused on bank regulation and one on securities regulation—in addition to having implications for business in general, also are sufficiently autonomous that they could be treated as involving two distinct industries which share some transindustry features.

The various general and transindustry forms of business coordination are important but their different sources should not be forgotten. Levi-Faur reminds us that democratic policymaking at the global level very often builds upon a range of previous experiences at domestic levels and forms a new synthesis. Although the varieties of regulatory capitalism are not always tied exclusively to particular states, these models have strong links with states, and they feed into global patterns of policymaking. In particular, the Americanization of global order has been successful but it is in no way unchallenged, and national regulation is not simply replaced by a neoliberal order uprooting existing forms of regulation by means of deregulation. Instead, new forms of contestation over re-regulation characterize current processes of globalization. Many of the clubs that Prakash and Potoski analyze cut across industries, such as those involved with environmental issues, and this contributes to the complex transindustry re-regulation analyzed by Levi-Faur. Similarly, although Fuchs and Kalfagianni focus on the food industry, some large retailers like Wal-Mart that source from multiple industries with extended transborder supply chains may exercise a form of transindustry governance, although these are likely to exhibit the same shortcomings with respect to democracy that they identify with regard to food retailers.

ASPECTS OF BUSINESS POWER OPERATING
THROUGH AND AROUND THESE LEVELS

Our discussion of the above three levels of business organization begins to highlight the multiple ways in which business organizes itself to maintain or enhance its power to respond to demands for participation, transparency, and accountability. Many of the arrangements analyzed in this book are primarily designed to affect public policy, signifying a shift to a transnational level of political action that in other forms is quite familiar in traditional domestic democratic systems. In a number of cases these arrangements were fostered by public sector actors eager to get business input. In addition to mechanisms to maintain or enhance business power there were also ones whose stated intention is to increase the formal or informal participation of affected actors, to improve practices of transparency, and to improve the accountability of business, including, for instance, the Global Compact, many club arrangements, and the private food standards arrangements.

In chapter 1 we suggested that the range of social institutions considered in discussions of global business and democracy needed to be seen in the context of the structural power of business. Very often the literature on business and democracy has limited itself to such exercises, which is quite unsatisfactory. Instead, the study of the plethora of arrangements can be enriched by drawing on insights from analysis of business power. The theme of business power is itself enormous and without in any way pretending to deliver an exhaustive analysis we sketched three basic forms of structural power: the dependence of governments on business to generate growth, and the deference to business interests that accompanies this; the ability of transnational business to play one jurisdiction off against another; and the compatibility with business interests of powerful cultural and institutional tendencies such as individualism, consumerism, an orientation toward growth, markets, and the personal accumulation of wealth, and hostility to the public sector, a phenomenon that overlaps with what Fuchs and Kalfagianni referred to as "discursive power." The importance of these aspects of the structural power of business runs through our chapters, but the chapters also indicate limitations and challenges to that structural power. The chapters reveal that challenges to the structural power of business are very varied, and at times are themselves linked to structural features of the contemporary global political economy.

Examples of the ability of business to play one jurisdiction off against the other, along with the dependence of governments on business to generate economic growth, are highlighted especially by the

"TRIPS-plus" process scrutinized by Sell. Individual developing countries trade away policy options that are important to their citizens' well-being because they need access to the U.S. market, and U.S.-based pharmaceutical firms are able to mobilize their influence with the U.S. government to use this power associated with the dependence of developing countries on markets centered in the United States to get their preferred policies accepted. To treat this as simply a voluntary contractual decision made by the developing country government obscures the way in which the structures of the global economy limit those choices even before they are considered. A similar theme is evident in Lavelle's analysis of sovereign debt, in which developing countries were not prepared to limit the rights of creditors because they feared it would damage their future access to capital markets. The forum shifting noted by Sell "from WIPO to WTO and back again...as well as the vertical shifting between multilateral, bilateral, and regional negotiations" is another variant of this capacity of business to find the most appropriate scene of policymaking.

The structural power to grant or withhold access to markets is also evident in a more exclusively private sector–based form in Fuchs and Kalfagianni's analysis of the power of food retailers over not just small or local farmers but nongovernmental standard setters as well, whose standards can be punished or rewarded, an aspect also pointed to by Levi-Faur. Patents too involve the power to grant or withhold access to needed resources, as Sell and May demonstrate in their chapters. The boundary between structural power and behavioral power is not always defined well, and they often work in tandem, as seen when business simultaneously hires lobbyists and produces the technical knowledge and discursive frames that those lobbyists draw upon, as noted for instance by Smith and Sell.

Structural power in the form of the compatibility with business interests of prevailing cultural and institutional tendencies is also evident in the chapters. Smith emphasizes the role of the market ideology in globalization, and the profit imperative of corporations along with the reinforcing cultural effects of business-oriented institutions, which worked to discredit the traditional UN organizations and assist the UN Secretary General Kofi Annan in shifting the UN in a more business-friendly direction. May highlights the structural power that is conferred on business by the corporate legal form, which in turn is strengthened by the two myths that he criticizes: that the corporation is like a rights-holding individual and that the rights accorded to innovators are not commercial rights but rather are presented (mythically) as political rights. Similarly, Sell notes that intellectual property is a particular form

of private "real" property that underlines the role of private property
rights in the United States.

Despite the prominent presence of the structural power of business
in our chapters there are also numerous structural limitations and contingencies that offset this power. The "brand" can be a mechanism that
empowers business, or certain corporations, as evident in the food and
pharmaceutical industries, but it can also create and express vulnerabilities and thus accountabilities, as highlighted by Prakash and Potoski's
analysis of reputation and credibility, a theme that we will return to in
the next section. The information asymmetries enjoyed by firms' greater
knowledge of their products relative to the knowledge of regulators
and stakeholders in society is not just a source of power but also a liability, since it is difficult to construct the trust needed for their products
to be accepted by consumers and others.

Moreover, the ability of opportunistic firms to free ride on the good
conduct of other firms is a form of structural power that benefits some
businesses at the expense of others. The threat posed to brand name
pharmaceutical companies by generic companies and parallel importation is another example of the way in which contemporary economic
structures can complicate the power of business. Indeed, this emphasizes that it is often difficult to treat business as a unitary category.
Lavelle notes the vulnerabilities that can be created for creditors whose
assets are tied up in projects of debtors or who want to maintain
debtors as future customers, even if the shift to more disintermediated
markets increases the ability of suppliers of financing to sell their expo-
sures in markets and thereby mitigate this vulnerability. At least this
plays out on the level of each individual investment, with some of the
vulnerability being transferred to the collective level. Kellow and
Murphy note that where NGOs undertake governance functions within
developing states they, like business, can develop a form of structural
power, and they also note that international organizations, because they
are not directly dependent on business, are more indifferent than states
to business threats and promises to locate in one jurisdiction or
another, even if such threats remain important at the national level.

Overall, the structural power of business can complement and
strengthen the more manifest business organizational forms that appear
at the general transindustry level, within particular industries, and in the
context of single corporations. However, this discussion of structural
power also reminds us of the ontological issues discussed at the beginning of this section, which should caution against reifying such formal
organizational forms. Through its actions a corporation can simultaneously reproduce or perform the presence of the corporate form; directly

express its own interests; contribute to an industry association; and generate discursive constructions that are amplified by general or transindustry associations. Moreover, structural elements that can appear to be a source of organizational strength for business can simultaneously be a constraint, as with the reputational factors. The multiple levels of the public and private sector are also often inseparable, because public sector institutions are important in developing relevant platforms for business. These various structural factors that enhance and limit the power of business have significant implications for democracy, and how such important dimensions of democracy as participation, transparency, and accountability are considered. We further consider these issues in the next section on democracy.

DEMOCRATIC PRACTICES:
PARTICIPATION, TRANSPARENCY, AND ACCOUNTABILITY

The chapters in this book all take a careful look at some of the democratic practices in relation to particular areas of business activity and specific policy fields. These practices are not everywhere solid and stable, but even where they are immature and weak there are important lessons to be learned, and they shed light on the richness of institutional arrangements. Sometimes the picture is so varied that forms of renewal, stalemate, and decay are not just found across the different contributions, making a simple diagnosis of global business authority and democracy problematic, but in each case evidence may also point in different directions. Renewal, stalemate, and decay are not durable situations, stages that have been achieved and cannot be rolled back, and have once and for all secured a certain democratic quality. On closer inspection a case may be disaggregated into a number of small controversies and battles where changes of business authority can be detected in some areas but not in others, and where changes in practices are not consistent. Finally, this complexity is also attributable to the fact that business is not a uniform category and does not necessarily respond in a coordinated way to challenges but finds different answers according to interests, traditions, and perceptions. Let us in turn see what different properties of global democracy have developed and how business authority is challenged.

In the following sections we analyze our findings with regard to participation, transparency, and accountability, identified in chapter 1 as key elements of democracy. It should be noted, however, that these are intrinsically connected. There are important spillover effects because advances in one area may have implications for the other, and lack of initiative in one field may halt development in the other. This connectedness, however, does not denote any simple and predictable logic. Participation can be used to establish formal rules that will make business—in the form of either single firms or collective entities—accountable to those actors involved in or attributing importance to a given arrangement, apart from the accountability driven by moral obligations. Participation can also be used to access information and disseminate this to the public at large. Transparency is also coupled with ambitions in business to become accountable to broader groups in society, and, of course, widened transparency offers these groups much better opportunities to hold business accountable than if business operations are veiled in secrecy. Furthermore, transparency may lead to a greater willingness to let affected interests participate and, as a matter of fact, directly become included in a larger transparency strategy. Accountability, for its part, challenges business to exchange with different interested parties on a more formal basis and accept their participation in relevant private or public bodies. Accountability also puts pressure on business to recognize interested parties and even to see an advantage in entering into a serious dialogue and finding a suitable form of cooperation.

Participation

Much analysis of participation in international rule making has been restricted to states, and while our chapters have shown the inadequacy of this perspective it is nevertheless clear that intergovernmental organizations continue to play a prominent role. Major inputs from business and civil society are through states, and play out in the work of these organizations. In this context a variety of national bodies are relevant. National courts and legislatures provide channels for participation in rule making and implementation, as stressed by Kellow and Murphy in their discussion of NGO involvement at national levels, and in the role of the Indian and U.S. courts restricting the more expansive treatment of intellectual property favored by the pharmaceutical industry.

In numerous ways, however, intergovernmental organizations themselves can be vehicles for transmitting democratic impulses into global policy processes, but they also set agendas and design the rules that give different groups in business and civil society access to relevant forums, or in some cases deny participation. One issue is balancing business and civil society; another is to choose between different business actors.

Lavelle provides an account of this changing landscape in showing how the earlier elements of interstate democracy were expressed in state-centric blocs negotiating across the North-South and East-West divides, which was superseded by a much more varied and fluid set of individual state interactions together with more direct involvement of Wall Street. Sell's analysis of the role of the World Trade Organization and the series of "TRIPS-plus" agreements that have been signed also show that both have the effect of creating and reinforcing patterns of exclusion with regard to the availability of pharmaceuticals, and while this does not directly pertain to participation in policy processes it sets a problematic starting point that creates needs for participation to redress this exclusion that are extraordinarily challenging to address. The bilateral TRIPS-plus process structurally harms participation at an interstate level by requiring relatively weak developing country partners to negotiate on their own with more powerful states. Smith's study of the Global Compact emphasizes how the UN has designed a completely new mechanism involving individual corporations rather than associations to which in the past it had restricted its interactions. She shows how in doing this the UN favored business at the expense of civil society actors.

The chapter by Kellow and Murphy addresses this structuring role of intergovernmental organizations through their comparison of the OECD, IMF, World Bank, and the WTO. They show that rules governing participation among member states in the organizations themselves have impacts on patterns of participation of other actors in those organizations. The specific character of member state voting in the IMF and the World Bank has restricted the influence of associations at those organizations and led them to focus more on influencing powerful member states such as the United States, although the character of World Bank lending has provided more opportunities for the involvement of associations in program delivery and governance.

The more democratic and freewheeling interstate relations in the WTO have led some civil society groups to establish closer relations with some developing countries. The relatively smaller importance of funding at the WTO also reduces the influence of wealthy states. While the OECD's long history of involving business and labor through its BIAC and TUAC is formalized, its relatively fluid structure of interstate relations corresponds to the informal way in which it has engaged civil society and business more recently.

The organization of business can have an impact on its own participation and that of other actors. In some sectors of the economy the organization of business is coherent, whereas in other sectors it rather tends to fragment into a diversity of outlets. These forms of organizing interests pose different challenges to civil society but in general participation in policy processes is weaker and more fragile than business. Underhill and Zhang show that the financial industry is a very strong player in these contexts, and Kathryn Lavelle analyzes how the financial services industry has participated in policy debates about sovereign debt through the EMTA and the SIA. The clubs analyzed by Prakash and Potoski have the effect of enabling citizens in their roles as consumers to participate in forms of social regulation. Fuchs and Kalfagianni show that the role of retail associations in setting food standards has excluded small retailers and farmers, especially from developing countries. Smith emphasizes the way in which vast business resources and organizational capacities can eclipse the efforts of civil society actors to influence an institutional arrangement such as the Global Compact. At the same time, however, only a small proportion of businesses participate in the process, and the quality of their participation is not especially high, diminishing its effectiveness. May points to the ability of business to use the corporate form to promote its rights to participation by having businesses treated as comparable to individual citizens.

The chapters in the book have also scrutinized the character and pattern of civil society participation relative to business. Usually this is organized, as evident in the varied involvement of civil society in the intergovernmental organizations studied by Kellow and Murphy, the role of organizations and initiatives such as ACT UP or the People's Health Coalition for Equitable Society (PHCES) in pharmaceutical controversies examined by Sell, or the relatively ineffective involvement of civil society groups in the Global Compact in the study by Smith. In rare cases groups of individual citizens can also become directly involved, as with the efforts of Stanford students and alumni to oust the CEO of Pfizer from the Stanford Advisory Board over Pfizer's "bullying" of Philippine government drug regulators. Thus, a variety of channels are available to business as well as to civil society. In this context, participation hinges on which models of regulation are applied. In Levi-Faur's analysis, some forms of regulatory capitalism are better suited to enhance participatory elements of democracy than others. The battles over the content of re-regulation at global levels do not automatically include citizens. "Regulatory corporatism" usually aims at including affected interests in the policy process, but this is a form of corporatism that is different from the tripartite arrangements found in the labor market in industrial societies.

Transparency

It is also an important quality of democracy that those actors making decisions and those actors affected by decisions have proper high-quality information and that strong information asymmetries are eliminated or mitigated. As to the affected parties, they must have access to information, and this is an important aspect of their empowerment. Although exceptions can be found, it is generally assumed that the producer side in the economy has better information than the consumer side, and that this can be a key aspect of business power. Especially when multinational enterprises work in highly technical policy processes at the global level, there is often concern that it will be difficult for citizens to monitor or understand what is occurring, let alone engage in meaningful participation. These pertinent issues have also been dealt with in this book. Making information available beyond business is here coupled with the creation of new institutional mechanisms.

This is particularly urgent due to new patterns of regulation. Levi-Faur seeks to debunk one of the prevailing assumptions in the study of global politics, namely, that current developments lead to the free and uncontrolled unfolding of markets. Re-regulation is introduced rather than deregulation and it becomes an urgent matter to monitor developments in relation to the public and private regulation of markets. Nevertheless, as Underhill and Zhang show, these re-regulatory arrangements can be skewed toward business, and the lack of transparency that is characteristic of some very close relationships between regulators and business certainly contributes to this. Moreover, as May notes, certain business-friendly legal arrangements, such as the corporate personality, extend back centuries, and the myths associated with these arrangements can be problematic for democracy. Put differently, transparency is not just about the volume of a flow of information, but also about the quality of the content of that information. Lavelle's historical analysis suggests that global policy interactions have become more complex and have involved more actors, but that this doesn't necessarily mean that transparency has increased, since consolidating the information in a way that can be meaningful for developing states or citizens can be more difficult.

Several intergovernmental organizations are today undergoing various reforms, also in the field of transparency, and some spill over into business. Indeed, new consultation mechanisms may also propel business transparency, as illustrated in Kellow and Murphy's study of different international organizations. One thing is clear: there is variation across policy fields, and even within areas such as trade and finance, things turn out to be issue specific. However, the precise translation and relationship between different kinds of public and private transparency needs to be studied more carefully.

In the case of Thailand, discussed by Sell, the nontransparent free trade negotiations with the United States led to protests and to the ouster of the prime minister who had been conducting the negotiations. The apparent retaliation against the American WHO representative to Thailand raised the question of freedom of speech for WHO employees and the general lack of transparency. Commercial secrets, especially when reinforced by intellectual property rules, can be problematic for transparency when information about the product is relevant for policy decisions. Smith also finds weaknesses in business reporting under the Global Compact, which raises questions about the usefulness of such reporting for enhancing transparency.

As noted above, Prakash and Potoski point to the incentive for firms to work through clubs to enhance the transparency needed to attain the trust of stakeholders. They suggest that such clubs can help address social externalities that extend beyond the narrow interests of club members, especially when this is enhanced by a link to state regulation. Yet Fuchs and Kalfagianni point out that although transparency in the narrow sense of being able to trace the history of a product backward and forward through the production chain to eliminate food dangers has improved with private food standards, a broader category of "normative transparency," which includes knowledge about the sustainability of food production practices, for instance, has been quite limited. This points to the need to be careful in assessments of the significance of private sector rules for accountability to a broader public, especially a global one.

Our findings show that changes in the patterns of transparency are not always introduced in a very explicit fashion, and that initiatives do not always emanate from business. It is necessary to remember the structural aspects of business power, and the degree to which public authorities believe they must respect the premises on which market economies rest, but, as civil society increasingly is drawn into global policy processes and consumers expect more information about firms and products, demands for greater transparency will increase. Thus, seen from a civil society perspective, more transparency in business can be demanded indirectly from international agencies, from national authorities, from courts, and directly from business. Indeed, transparency is also practiced at different levels. Although single firms can pioneer solutions embracing a whole industry, they basically develop their own strategies of transparency and are focused on their own behavior, whereas industry associations develop more encompassing strategies but have to rally firms around common standards. The paradox is that especially the latter can be valuable in extending transparency, but it is often harder to achieve.

Accountability

Basically, business sees itself as accountable to its key stakeholders, but how broadly are these defined? The participation of interested parties gives us some preliminary clues as to how encompassingly stakeholders are perceived by those public agencies regulating business as well as by business itself. On the one hand significant variation exists in the patterns of stakeholder participation and their role in relevant policy processes, but on the other hand we cannot conclude that participation is the only and determining factor in making business accountable. Let us again see how business—and also which levels of business, more specifically—is geared toward meeting today's expectations of accountability and how this is embedded in the context of advancing democracy.

Through its participation in various international agencies, one might expect business to comply with public regulation and the spirit in which these bodies operate, and to align itself with the public interest. In this way business should be accountable to governments and international agencies. However, it can be difficult for governments to follow the global operations of firms, and for international agencies to follow their local operations. As well, public sector actors often appear to be promoting or encouraging business, and under these circumstances accountability mechanisms can be weak or nonexistent. Interesting examples are provided by Sell in her study on drugs, in May's analysis of intellectual property more generally, in Lavelle's investigation of the sovereign debt mechanisms, and in Smith's inquiry into the processes of the Global Compact. In the case of the latter, for instance, verification of claims is weak, as are the lines of accountability to the UN system, and there are concerns that these weak forms of accountability may make stronger alternatives less likely to be developed. A somewhat similar asymmetry in accountability is found in the analysis by Fuchs and Kalfagianni of the large retailers in the food industry where private regulation and accountability to consumers does not sufficiently take into account the impacts on small farmers and problems in developing countries. Problems of accountability are at the center of

the analysis of Underhill and Zhang—they especially stress the importance of accountability in linking input legitimacy (which relates to participation) and output legitimacy and find these links lacking in their
financial cases. Several of our contributors stress the importance of the
public sector in enhancing the accountability of business. Although
public sector institutions such as those analyzed by Kellow and Murphy
certainly can strengthen the role of states, and consequently of national
democratic practices, they too can display variation in the degree to
which they facilitate relations of accountability.

Prakash and Potoski highlight the complexity of establishing
accountability in business "clubs." They are clear that public regulation
provides a baseline, but then explore the degree to which private clubs
can complement and extend the accountability of business beyond that
baseline. In addition to whatever accountability of business clubs to
public authorities may exist, there are two other key forms of accountability. The first set of accountabilities is internal to the club, involving
the prevention of the shirking that occurs when a firm engages in
behavior that undermines the club's reputation or capacity but also the
exploitation that can occur by club members by demanding too much.
To counter shirking, they specify different mechanisms of accountability
involving varying uses of third party audits, disclosure, and sanctioning
and they identify mechanisms to counter exploitation. The second set
of accountabilities is to external actors, and here issues of transparency
and accountability are closely entwined: for example, the desire and
need of firms to overcome the information asymmetries that make it difficult for consumers and other stakeholders to know if they should trust
club members.

It is interesting to note that these developments take place against
the backdrop of more general trends in regulation. Public authority was
in the past typically associated with the welfare functions of the state
and the provision of a variety of services, but states have to varying
degrees moved beyond performing these tasks and have, accordingly,
boosted their regulatory capacities. The regulatory functions can more
easily be transferred to the global level and it is primarily in these areas
that public authorities—in the regulation of business—and industries
and corporations themselves must be accountable.

Often, the question of who or what constituency business should
be accountable to is contested. May, for instance, contests the notion
that intellectual property in a firm should be treated as involving
accountability to an individual inventor, and instead argues that the firm
should be accountable to the public interest. In corporate governance
more generally, the question of whether managers should be solely

responsible to shareholders or if instead they should be accountable to other stakeholders has been a very longstanding matter of debate. We return to this issue below.

Beyond Participation, Transparency, and Accountability

Participation, transparency, and accountability are key properties of any democracy, and so also of an extremely fledgling global democracy. Whereas it can be problematic to speak of a global democracy because of the many institutional weaknesses of the global political system, it is easier to identify some specific properties of democracy without making this wider, more ambitious and systemic claim.

However, just as the issue of structural power forces us to move analytically beyond the initiatives of firms and business associations, the complexity of the idea and practice of the relation of global democracy to business requires us to go beyond participation, transparency, and accountability as the sole markers of democracy. These three criteria are valuable in assessing the performance of any particular institutional arrangement, and in establishing goals for institutions in general, but it is useful as well to focus on issues of structures and boundaries that may limit or empower in advance the range of problems and alternatives that are seen as legitimately subject to democratic practices and these criteria.

Thus, we have noted the overwhelming complexity of challenges. To the extent that business adopts principles of participation, transparency, and accountability and those international agencies regulating business give access to relevant information, new avenues of influence open, but, as Levi-Faur holds, new regulation is constantly expanding and new micro regulatory regimes emerge across a vast field of business activity giving rise to new problems of transparency. It is extremely difficult for civil society organizations to keep track of these developments, coordinate activities and find appropriate responses to these challenges.

Several overlapping structural and boundary issues are also apparent in our chapters. The first is how the structural power of business can be addressed. The second is how and where the boundaries of public interventions can be set. The third is how it is possible to address the public interest.

Our first problem concerns the basic issues of structural power. All democracies have constitutions that set boundaries around democratic practices and have a further set of established rules to support and limit exchanges in the market. At the international level, however, the structural and boundary issues our chapters identify go beyond the analogy of the domestic constitution, since important rule making facilitates structural change, including economic globalization, without traditional constitutional processes that can accompany such changes at domestic levels.

In our previous section about the organization of business we highlighted both the structural power of business and the structure-related factors that complicated and weakened this power. The latter certainly provide opportunities for nonbusiness actors in challenging the ways in which the structural power of business can restrict democracy. The discursive dimension of the structural power of business can seem overwhelming, as evident in "the market ideology," as Smith puts it, or in "the consumer culture," as expressed by Sell.

Yet alternative ideas that potentially can have structural effects are also possible and promote alternative visions of the economy. May, in criticizing the myths supporting the conferring of property rights on corporations, challenges this feature of the discursive power of business and points to an alternative emphasis on the public interest. Lavelle shows that the fear of the power of finance that made developing states initially reluctant to use collective action clauses in sovereign bonds evaporated when Mexico used one and nothing happened. These points reinforce an emphasis on the remarkable ability of weak actors to launch alternative models that can gain surprisingly widespread acceptance.

Our second problem grapples with the boundaries of the private and public spheres. Traditionally, democracy has been restricted to the public sphere and has been seen as inappropriate for the private sphere. Critics have emphasized the way in which the treatment of economic matters as private leaves many crucial aspects of our societies outside democracy. Accordingly, business authority is by definition anathema to the public sphere and not embraced by public deliberation, an essential feature of democracy. So where and how should the boundary of the private and public sphere be set?

The case of intellectual property raises this issue in a particularly sharp way. Sell and May argue strongly that the boundary that firms have largely succeeded in setting leaves far too many decisions and processes on the private side of that boundary. Their cases reveal that this boundary setting is based on a mix of beliefs about the inherent value of private rights and private property, and functional arguments about the way in which privileging or protecting the private can enhance economic growth and innovation for everyone.

Other chapters, in scrutinizing relative to democracy factors that might otherwise be considered outside the political domain because of their economic, structural, or private character, such as Fuchs and Kalfagianni's study on food standards and Smith's treatment of market more generally, also challenge the location of the public/private boundary. In a different way, Prakash and Potoski, in stressing the way in which private interactions and arrangements can be saturated with social externalities, are also taking a turn with this boundary. The growing integration of nongovernmental actors into public institutions is also an example of the changing boundary between the private and the public and is dealt with by Kellow and Murphy. Indeed, there are numerous ways in which this boundary can be further explored. At the global level, the emergent and weak character of the public sphere can be seen as either positive for democracy because it is more open to new practices, or a problem because it allows the untrammelled expansion of the private sector. Regardless, our book strongly argues that it is problematic to take prevailing public/private boundaries for granted in determining which activities should be subjected to democratic scrutiny.

Our third issue of boundary setting concerns how the public interest is constituted, and is raised most directly in May's chapter. We here must move away from theories that assume that governments and their leaders automatically work in the public interest. Rational choice theories and studies on the failure of various public policies have helped destroy these comfortable assumptions. Indeed, some of these theories then deny the possibility of a genuine public interest or claim that it is constituted through a variety of battles over the content of the public interest. However, like the setting of the public/private boundary such arguments are themselves contestations that are both *about* democracy and the *substance* of democracy. The interest of organized business and civil society to participate in policy processes, as demonstrated across many contributions in the book, shows that these groups have their own visions about democracy and do not passively observe and accept policies formulated by governments in the context of intergovernmental organizations. As a matter of fact, conflicts over the rules and norms of consultation shows the strong value attributed to participation and that policies are never entirely the outcome of interactions between states. In other words, the public interest is contested. Likewise, the discussion over the appropriate locus of regulation—public or private—also is a discussion where the public interest can be defended, and whether this is possible within a private framework. Contributions by Fuchs and Kalfagianni and Prakash and Potoski suggest that the public interest can be woven into private regulation under some specific conditions, however.

In recent years a great number of close substitutes to the notion of a public interest have also circulated globally, including "global public goods" and "good governance" or even "security and prosperity." Explicit or implicit in the chapters is the view that the identification and pursuit of a public interest at the global level is crucial for democracy.

DEMOCRACY AND GLOBAL BUSINESS: PRACTICES AND PROSPECTS

In a period of economic globalization that questions existing forms of democracy, a general assumption is that business authority is strong. However, the chapters of this book point to both a strong resistance from business to developing new mechanisms of participation, transparency, and accountability and an openness to experiment with such elements of democracy—if not for other reasons, then in the enlightened self-interest of business. Indeed, the ability of business to adapt to new demands and expectations is an important performance criterion.

However, advancement in one field does not automatically lead to positive side effects elsewhere. One major reason is that business is not always consistent in implementing strategies. There may be disagreement in business itself because different firms or industries see different advantages or perils in adding new democratic practices. They have different experiences and fear that changes will affect their authority. At the same time there are also different perceptions among forces in civil society. Indeed, some will see possible smaller changes as not worth struggling for because they do not alter the basic features of the economic system in which corporations rule, whereas other groups strongly welcome them. For their part, however, it is still a matter of their capacity and ingenuity to extend democratic practices and see that advances have a cumulative effect. Agency is here required, and the implementation of democratic practices is very much an interactive game between business and broader groups in society rather than a unilateral concession from business or the result of activist pressures.

There is definitely a reform potential available in the business community, although it is not always exercised, and authority is sometimes interpreted very rigidly at the corporate level, as pointed to in several of the contributions. Business is neither a simple democratizing force, nor is it an overall impediment to democratic practices. Indeed, a research program investigating business authority and global politics must work with open questions and be open to different answers.

This sense of contingent, strategic, and interdependent initiatives involving public authorities, business, and civil society is an important theme that emerges from this book. To return to the ontological distinctions set out above, the functional imperatives make their appearance in our chapters in the form of opportunities and constraints, but even when they appear most strongly they are typically questioned and are not simply natural and unalterable features of business organization or globalization. Again, business is not a unitary actor and among corporations and industries interests are conceived differently and understandings of actions to be taken vary significantly. This is especially important in any discussion of democracy, because imperatives that are purported to be naturalistic can trump and severely limit democracy.

It has also been interesting to see the multiple levels and locations at which interactions relevant to global business and democracy can occur. Our starting point was the three levels of business organization: the general or transindustry; the industry level; and the firm level. In various ways these were embedded in a more general context of business power. The relevance of levels can be multiplied by adding the levels of public authority, including intergovernmental organizations, states, and domestic institutions such as courts. Civil society actors work at all these levels as well. The complexity of such a "dispersed multi-level democracy" is not just due to the connections that can occur between each of these levels, but also in the way in which an action or actor can simultaneously be at and help construct more than one level. In some cases hierarchy is important, in other cases horizontal forms of policymaking involving overlapping responsibilities, and crosscutting lines of authority is predominant. The conduits and spaces in which global business and democracy interact include elements of both hierarchical and horizontal forms of policymaking, with particular combinations fusing and then disaggregating in response to the contingent factors noted above. It is important not to simplify this complex topography, because to do so would close off conduits and spaces that might otherwise carry and amplify democratic impulses.

A further theme that emerges from this book grapples with the private and public divide and the promise and perils of different form of privately driven policy arrangements as instruments for aligning global business interests and democracy. Our contributors do not fully agree on the usefulness of such arrangements. The broad range of views mirrors broader debates about this issue. Overall, however, there is consensus in the analysis of these cases that voluntary self-regulation alone, especially without various forms of monitoring and incentives, is likely to be ineffective, and that the more such arrangements are expected to go beyond the area of overlap between self-interest and public interest the more they are likely to fail. Our analysis of participation, transparency, and accountability as generalizable elements of democracy enabled us to disaggregate the elements of democracy and to compare across very different cases and institutional arrangements.

However, our chapters also revealed that some issues that are critical to democracy cannot be subsumed within these three elements alone. As criteria, participation, transparency, and accountability tend to assume that an institutional site in which public policy-relevant decisions are made already exists. But the way in which such sites are created, and the determination of whether the decisions that are made there are relevant to public policy, are also contested issues that are important for democracy.

The picture of democracy and global business that emerges from this study is quite different than other alternatives. Sometimes competition among self-interested states and the power of global business are seen as creating such an inhospitable terrain for democracy at the global level that its prospects there are hopeless. Sometimes hopes are pinned on global civil society, or on the creation of new formal processes of governance in intergovernmental organizations such as the UN. Sometimes a return to national politics and a rejection of the global are envisioned as the only viable way to reinvigorate democracy in face of the challenges it meets from global business. Sometimes profound critiques are matched with profound visions of transformation that are hard to link to immediate practical developments. In contrast, the picture that emerges from this book is one of democratic advances and reversals occurring in multiple locations and involving multiple actors, some very traditional and some that are only beginning to emerge and be recognized. Taken together, our chapters criticize the structures, boundaries, and assumptions that limit democracy, while combining this with close attention to relevant practical developments.

In illuminating the relationship between global business authority and democracy the chapters in this book also point to important new research directions that deserve to be explored and developed further. Three are especially important.

First, more detailed research on the ongoing history of particular global democratic practices is needed. The unfolding of democratic practices is taking shape in an evolutionary process, and the institutional structures that today underpin democracies at the domestic level have taken a very long time to build up. The time frame is much shorter at the global level where these processes are of more recent origin. It goes without saying that unlike these democracies it is difficult to seek inspiration from and transfer practices from other polities of similar size, but experiences are transferred across different areas of business activity. The factors that invigorate democratic practices are, however, more numerous, more entangled, and more fragile than we know from domestic politics. Identifying the diversity of these practices, as this book has, is an important first step, but it is also important to chronicle the advances and reverses in any particular process and to draw lessons from those. The more specific those lessons are the more they can be drawn upon to influence the practices themselves and to make them more democratic.

Second, in addition to closer examination of particular practices over time, it is valuable to continue to draw more detailed comparisons across issue areas and policy fields. Comparative case studies can advance our understanding of emergent patterns in the relationship between global business authority and democracy, but they can also encourage the dissemination of best practices—when talking about democracy, comparison is not just about revealing existing relations but also systematically searching for new ideas that have not yet been put into widespread practice, but should be.

Third, the book has brought normative and political economy questions together in a unique way, and further interaction between normative international theory and global political economy will also be valuable. Normative international theory has been valuable in reflecting on alternative ways that the ethical dimension of the global community can be conceptualized, but the distinctive problems posed by the authority of global business have not yet been adequately addressed in this literature. Similarly, international political economy has very effectively criticized the power asymmetries that come with the expansion of global business authority, but this has not adequately engaged normative theorizing about the ethical potentials and challenges of thinking about democracy at the global level.

As this book has shown, bringing "global business" and "democracy" together is a demanding exercise because these are generally regarded as each belonging to its domain and having its own language. Studies of business tend to focus on firms and their authority in relation to the market, whereas studies of democracy seek to understand the behavior of citizens and political institutions, and these consequently pull in different directions. The chapters in this book have bridged this divide in many ways, but there is certainly an ongoing need for more research into the linkages between global business authority and democracy.

What then can we conclude about the question posed by the title of the book? Is democracy and global business exhibiting decay, stalemate, or renewal? Some would see the market economy as not only important in itself but also as a harbinger of democratic progress, and although it can be argued from a cultural perspective that there are such linkages it is also safe to say that markets do not automatically bring democracy forward.

Inevitably, our assessment of the progress of democracy is affected by the implicit benchmarks against which we measure such progress. For those who emphasize structural power and the negative effects of markets on democracy, the changes that have occurred are unimpressive at best. Stalemate, or even decay, can be observed because more and more areas of the world and more and more sectors of society are harnessed by market logics rather than democratic ones, often studied as a neoliberal order. Accordingly, the current state of democracy looks gloomy. From this perspective, however, it could be added that there is considerable variation across the globe, and the decay label is especially appropriately applied to the situation in the South, whereas elements of renewal may be brought about through alliances with some civil society groups and governments in the North. In much of the literature there is a tendency to offer a more general analysis of this decay, or merely stalemate, of democratic practices but as the contributions in this book demonstrate it is also possible to extend notions of decay or stalemate to concrete dimensions of democracy, such as participation, transparency, and accountability. In this critical perspective it is even possible to treat these three key dimensions and their importance for democracy separately and examine where advancements have been made more specifically, and although overall progress is slow, patterns of participation have been affected. These changes in participatory practices, however, are not so profound, and such elements of renewal take place within a broader context of stalemate or decay.

Another line of reasoning puts more emphasis on the prospects of renewal without linking these with a need for a radical change of the basic structures of the market economy. Claims are not made that the unfolding of markets will lead to democratic changes per se, but it is argued that different forms of institutionalization can promote democratic practices, not necessarily at a grand scale, but rather through piecemeal solutions in relation to specific sections of business. From a corporate viewpoint this scenario may seem more sympathetic because vital areas of business authority are modified but also kept more or less intact. Instead, forces are unleashed that do not question the core values of the market economy but rather challenge those forms of public or private regulation that do not sufficiently integrate a societal dimension. Various stakeholders contribute to this development, but also corporate compliance with various democratic practices is an important aspect of competition and one of the drivers in the process of renewal.

These analytical perspectives on the role of markets and global business authority are represented in this book. They are, however, also represented in the world of politics, and the chapters capture the many dilemmas in business, among civil society groups, and in intergovernmental organizations when trying to align business authority and democracy. At the same time as business authority seems to march forward, stronger demands for extended participation, more transparency, and better accountability mechanisms are voiced and experimented with. Many such demands are addressed with institutionalized changes in the relationship between global business and democracy, but battles will continue to be waged over the scope and content of these emerging practices.

NOTE

1. We owe this point to Christopher May.

CONTRIBUTORS

DORIS FUCHS is Professor of International Relations and Development at the University of Münster, Germany. She received her PhD in Politics and Economics in 1997 from the Claremont Graduate University and has since taught at the University of Michigan, Louisiana State University, the University of Munich, as well as the Leipzig Graduate School of Management. Her primary areas of research are private governance, sustainable development, food politics and policy, and corporate structural and discursive power. Among her publications are *Business Power in Global Governance* and *An Institutional Basis for Environmental Stewardship*, as well as articles in peer-reviewed journals such as *Millennium*, *Global Environmental Politics*, *International Interactions*, *the Journal on Consumer Policy*, *Agriculture and Human Values*, and *Energy Policy*.

AGNI KALFAGIANNI is Assistant Professor, Institute for Environmental Studies (IVM), Vrije University of Amsterdam. She has worked on the role of private and public actors in fostering sustainability and transparency in the food chain at the European and national (Dutch) levels. She has also published articles on corporate social responsibility strategies in European food and agricultural governance. Her main research interests include environmental policies and politics, sustainable development, environmental ethics, and democratic governance.

AYNSLEY KELLOW is Professor of Government, School of Government, University of Tasmania, Hobart, Australia. His research interests include environmental politics and policy, policymaking at the international level, and both business and environment groups at the national and international levels. He has published: *Transforming Power: The Politics of Electricity Planning* (Cambridge University Press, 1995), *International Toxic Risk Management* (Cambridge University Press, 1999) and (with Timothy Doyle) *Environmental Politics and Policy Making in Australia* (Macmillan, 1995). His most recent books are (with David Robertson): *Globalization and the Environment: Risk Assessment and the WTO* (Edward Elgar, 2001), and (with Sonja Boehmer-Christiansen) *International Environmental Policy: Interests and the Failure of the Kyoto Process* (Edward Elgar, 2003). He has also published in a number of international journals, such as *Political Studies, International Political Science Review, Policy Studies Journal, Politics, Natural Resources Journal,* and *Environmental Politics.*

KATHRYN C. LAVELLE is Ellen and Dixon Long Associate Professor of World Affairs, Case Western Reserve University. She received her PhD from Northwestern University and her MA from the University of Virginia. She has published *The Politics of Equity Finance in Emerging Markets* (Oxford University Press, 2005), as well as book chapters, articles, and book reviews appearing in *International Organization, The Journal of Modern African Studies, Third World Quarterly, Review of International Political Economy, International Studies Review,* and *The Columbia Journal of World Business.* Dr. Lavelle is spending the 2006–07 academic year serving as an American Political Science Association Congressional Fellow in Washington, DC. Her current book manuscript investigates financial politics in the United Nations system and Bretton Woods financial institutions by examining the activities of public and private sector interest groups active on policy issues related to global capital flows.

DAVID LEVI-FAUR is Associate Professor, Department of Political Science and The Federmann School of Public Policy and Government, The Hebrew University, Jerusalem, Israel, and the corresponding editor of *A New Blackwell Journal of Regulation and Governance.* He held research position in the University of Oxford, the Australian National University, and the University of Manchester and visiting positions in the London School of Economics, the University of Amsterdam, University of Utrecht, and University of California (Berkeley). He currently is working on a book manuscript, *Regulating Capitalism: Governance and the Global Spread of Regulatory Agencies,* to be published by Princeton University Press. His recent work includes special issues of the Annals of the American Academy of Political and Social Sciences (*The Global Diffusion of Regulatory Capitalism,* co-edited with Jacint Jordana) and Governance (*Varieties of Regulatory Capitalism*).

CHRISTOPHER MAY is Professor of Political Economy and an Associate Dean of the Faculty of Arts and Social Sciences, Lancaster University. He edited International Political Economy Yearbook 15: *Global Corporate Power* (Lynne Rienner, 2006). He is series co-editor (with Nicola Phillips) of the *International Political Economy Yearbook*, and recently edited volume 15, *Global Corporate Power* (Lynne Rienner, 2006). He has also published *Intellectual Property Rights: A critical history* (Lynne Rienner, 2005) (co-authored, with Susan Sell]; *Key Thinkers for the Information Age* (Routledge, 2003) (editor); *The Information Society: A Skeptical View* (Polity Press 2002) (Ukrainian edition: [Kiev: K.I.C., 2004]); *Authority and Markets: Susan Strange's Writings on International Political Economy* (Basingstoke: Palgrave Macmillan 2002) (edited with Roger Tooze); and *A Global Political Economy of Intellectual Property Rights. The New Enclosures?* (The Routledge/RIPE Studies in Global Political Economy series, now in its second revised edition (2010).

HANNAH MURPHY is an Associate Lecturer with the School of Government at the University of Tasmania, Australia. She recently completed her PhD dissertation on the agenda-setting roles of nongovernmental organizations (NGOs) at the World Trade Organization (WTO). Her book, *The Making of International Trade Policy: NGOs, Agenda Setting, and the WTO* is forthcoming with Edward Elgar.

TONY PORTER is Professor of Political Science at McMaster University in Hamilton, Canada. He is the author of *Globalization and Finance* (Polity Press, 2005), *Technology, Governance, and Political Conflict in International Industries* (Routledge, 2002), and *States, Markets, and Regimes in Global Finance* (Macmillan, 1993), and editor, with A. Claire Cutler and Virginia Haufler, of *Private Authority in International Affairs*, (State University of New York Press, 1999). His recent work has appeared in *Business and Politics, Policy Sciences, New Political Economy, Review of International Political Economy, Global Governance, Global Society,* and *Policy Studies Review.*

MATTHEW POTOSKI is Associate Professor in the Political Science Department at Iowa State University. He is the coauthor of *The Voluntary Environmentalists* (Cambridge University Press, 2006). His research on environmental policy and public sector contract management has appeared in the *American Journal of Political Science,* the *Journal of Policy Analysis and Management, Public Administration Review,* and the *Journal of Politics.* He is the co-editor of the *International Public Management Journal.*

ASEEM PRAKASH is Professor of Political Science at University of Washington-Seattle. He serves as the General Editor of Cambridge University Press Series on Business and Public Policy. He is the author of *Greening the Firm* (Cambridge University Press, 2006), the co-author of *The Voluntary Environmentalists: Green Clubs, ISO 14001, and Voluntary Environmental Regulations* (Cambridge University Press, 2006), and the co-editor of *Rethinking Advocacy Organizations: A Collective Action Perspective* (Cambridge University Press, 2010), *Voluntary Regulations of NGOs and Nonprofits: An Accountability Club Framework* (Cambridge University Press, 2010), *Voluntary Programs: A Club Theory Perspective* (The MIT Press, 2009), *Globalization and Governance* (Routledge, 1999), *Coping with Globalization* (Routledge, 2000), and *Responding to Globalization* (Routledge, 2000). He has published in *American Political Science Review, American Journal of Political Science, Journal of Politics, International Organization, World Politics,* and *International Studies Quarterly.*

KARSTEN RONIT is Associate Professor at the Department of Political Science, University of Copenhagen, Denmark. He has previously taught at the University of Constance, Germany, and been a visiting scholar at the Max Planck Institute for the Study of Societies, Cologne, Germany, and at the Institute on Globalization and the Human Condition, McMaster University, Hamilton, Ontario, Canada, and at the Elliott School of International Affairs, George Washington University, Washington, DC, USA. He has published widely on business and politics. He is editor (with Justin Greenwood and Jürgen R. Grote) of *Organized Interests and the European Community* (Sage, 1992); (with Volker Schneider) of *Private Organizations in Global Politics* (Routledge, 2000); and of *Global Public Policy: Business and the Countervailing Powers of Civil Society* (Routledge, 2006). His work has also appeared in: *Administration & Society, American Behavioral Scientist, European Journal of Political Research, Governance, Parliamentary Affairs, Policy Sciences, Science and Public Policy,* and *West European Politics.*

SUSAN K. SELL is Professor of Political Science and International Affairs, The George Washington University. Professor Sell has published three books on the politics of intellectual property: *Power and Ideas: North South Politics of Intellectual Property and Antitrust* (1998); *Private Power, Public Law: the Globalization of Intellectual Property Rights* (2003); and (with Christopher May) *Intellectual Property: a Critical History* (2006). She has published numerous articles in political science journals (e.g., *International Organization, International Studies Quar-*

terly, Global Governance) and law journals. She serves on the board of IP-Watch, a Geneva-based organization that reports on developments in intellectual property policymaking in international organizations. She teaches international political economy, international relations theory, and the politics of intellectual property rights.

JACKIE SMITH is Associate Professor of Sociology and Peace Studies at the Joan B. Kroc Institute for International Peace Studies at the University of Notre Dame, Indiana. Smith is known for her research on the transnational dimensions of social movements, exploring ways in which global economic and political integration have influenced how people engage in politics. She has co-edited three books on the subject: *Coalitions Across Borders: Transnational Protest in a Neoliberal Era* (with Joe Bandy); *Globalization and Resistance: Transnational Dimensions of Social Movements* (with Hank Johnston); and *Transnational Social Movements and Global Politics: Solidarity Beyond the State* (with Charles Chatfield and Ron Pagnucco). Her most recent books on contemporary activism for global economic justice include *Social Movements for Global Democracy* (Johns Hopkins University Press, 2008) and a collaborative book on the World Social Forums, *Global Democracy and the World Social Forums* (Paradigm, 2007). Smith has written or co-authored more than thirty-five articles and book chapters. She is completing a co-authored book (with Dawn Wiest) on the changing patterns of transnational organizing in the late twentieth and early twenty-first centuries.

GEOFFREY R. D. UNDERHILL is Professor of International Governance at the University of Amsterdam, Netherlands, specializing in international relations and international political economy. Underhill's current research concerns international cooperation for the regulation and supervision of cross-border financial markets, problems of legitimacy in global financial governance, understanding the origins of the current financial crisis in policy capture, including many journal articles and book chapters, and he is the author/editor of eleven books to date. His most recent books include *International Finance Governance Thirty Years On: From Reform to Crisis* (edited with J. Blom and D. Mügge) (Cambridge University Press, forthcoming 2010), *Political Economy and the Changing Global Order*, third edition (edited with Richard Stubbs) (Oxford University Press, 2006), and *International Financial Governance under Stress: Global Structures versus National Imperatives* (edited with X. Zhang) (Cambridge University Press, 2003).

XIAOKE ZHANG is Associate Professor in Political Economy and Asian Studies at the University of Nottingham, United Kingdom. He is the author of *The Changing Politics of Finance in Korea and Thailand* (Routledge, 2002) and the co-editor (with Geoffrey R. D. Underhill) of *International Financial Governance under Stress Global Structures versus National Imperatives* (Cambridge University Press, 2003). His research articles have appeared in *Review of International Political Economy, International Affairs, Journal of Public Policy, International Political Science Review*, and many other refereed international journals.

INDEX